THE ROUGH GUIDE TO

New York City Restaurants

2003 EDITION

www.roughguides.com

credits

Series editor Mark Ellingham
Text editor Samantha Cook
Production Michelle Draycott, Helen Prior
Cartography Maxine Repath
Photography Nelson Hancock

publishing information

This first edition published October 2002 by
Rough Guides Ltd, 80 Strand, London WC2R 0RL.
Penguin Putnam, Inc. 375 Hudson Street, NY 10014, USA.

distributed by the Penguin Group

Penguin Books Ltd, 80 Strand, London WC2R ORL
Penguin Putnam, Inc. 375 Hudson Street, NY 10014, USA
Penguin Books Australia Ltd, 487 Maroondah Highway,
PO Box 257, Ringwood, Victoria 3134, Australia
Penguin Books Canada Ltd, 10 Alcorn Avenue,
Toronto, Ontario, Canada M4V 1E4
Penguin Books (NZ) Ltd,182–190 Wairau Road, Auckland 10, New Zealand

Typeset in Bembo and Helvetica to an original design by Henry Iles.
Printed in Spain by Graphy Cems.

© Daniel Young 2002
464pp includes index

A catalogue record for this book is available from the British Library.
ISBN 1-85828-857-6

The publishers and authors have done their best to ensure the
accuracy and currency of all the information in *The Rough Guide to
New York City Restaurants*; however, they can accept no responsibility
for any loss, injury or inconvenience sustained as a result of
information or advice contained in the guide.

THE ROUGH GUIDE TO

New York City Restaurants

2003 EDITION

by
Daniel Young

with additional contributions by
Sean Brady, Andrea Strong, Laurie Woolever

ROUGH
GUIDES

about the author

Daniel Young splits most of his time and meals between his hometown New York, where he was the popular restaurant critic of the *Daily News* from 1996–2000, and Paris, where he authored the acclaimed *Paris Café Cookbook*. His most recent book, *Made in Marseille*, was published by HarperCollins. He has written extensively about food and restaurants for such publications as *Gourmet*, *Bon Appetit*, *Condé Nast Traveler*, the *New York Times*, the *Los Angeles Times*, and the *International Herald-Tribune*. As the original "Eats" columnist of the *Daily News*, he reviewed New York's inexpensive restaurants from 1985–1996.

acknowledgements

A heartfelt thanks to my good friend Arthur Schwartz for his invaluable advice and encouragement. I also benefited enormously from the insight and wit of Steven Forbis, Mark Giles, Irene Sax and Jeff Weinstein, as well as the contributing reviewers Sean Brady, Andrea Strong and Laurie Woolever. I wish to express my gratitude to the good pals and fearless dining companions who made each restaurant visit a memorable one: Mary Barone, Diana Biederman, Steven Biondolillo, Nina Blaine, Mitchell Brower, Ray Chen, James Chew, Alan Cohen, Anne de Ravel, Leslie Laurence, JoAnn Makovitsky, Marco Moreira, Neil Manson, Anahita Mekanik, Bob Nicolaides, Olivier Wittmann and Pamela Wittmann. Finally, I am especially indebted to my editor Samantha Cook for her professionalism and resolve; to Robert Shepard for introducing me to Rough Guides and making this undertaking possible; to Jonathan Buckley for applying the highest standards to the Rough Guides' restaurant series; to Maxine Repath for her meticulous work on the maps; and to those two great New Yorkers, Mimi and David Young, for their love and support.

help us update

We've tried to ensure that this edition of the *Rough Guide to New York City Restaurants* is as up-to-date and accurate as possible. However, New York's restaurant scene is in constant flux, and standards, of course, do go up and down. If you feel there are places we've underrated or overpraised, or others we've unjustly omitted, please let us know. Comments or corrections are much appreciated, and we'll send a copy of the next edition (or any other *Rough Guide* if you prefer) for the best letters. Please address letters to Daniel Young at: Rough Guides, 345 Hudson Street, New York, NY 10014, USA; Rough Guides Ltd, 80 Strand, London WC2R ORL; or send email to: mail@ roughguides.co.uk

contents

contents

Queens 359

The Bronx 399

Staten Island 405

index 411

introduction

The great quality, diversity and magnitude of the New York restaurant scene may go a long way towards explaining the notoriously neurotic behavior of the city's diners. Only in this worldly metropolis of 18,000 restaurants does the simple act of settling upon a place to eat provoke the despair that comes from passing up hundreds of outstanding options. This guide's 321 restaurant reviews, each a discerning outline filled in with local color, insight, attitude, specific recommendations and prices, will offer you invaluable assistance in making the best possible choices given your particular tastes, cravings, whereabouts and budget. From taqueria to trattoria, old hamburger joint to new American bistro, Thai hideaway to French hotspot, all the restaurants covered are enthusiastically recommended and none is exorbitantly priced.

The **Rough Guide to New York City Restaurants** is organized by **location**. If you know where you plan on being or in which part of the city you'd like to eat, you can consult the chapter in question and compare the dining options in that area. Detailed neighborhood maps help you pinpoint each restaurant. (If you prefer to choose by cuisine, check the indexes in the back of the guide.)

Whether you have a lifetime, a week or 22 minutes to devote to dining out in **Manhattan**, **Brooklyn**, **Queens**, **the Bronx** or **Staten Island**, it will be virtually impossible to flip through the pages of this guide and wish you were somewhere else. New York is not, thank goodness, the be-all and end-all. The city of immigrants depends heavily on culinary capitals and unspoiled hinterlands the world over for inspiration. Nevertheless, this guide makes a very solid case for it being the greatest dining destination on the planet. There are arguably better locations for a single meal or a particular specialty. But nowhere else can you do it all so well in so little time.

The restaurants

New York City's restaurant landscape is more enticing today than ever before. More ethnic cuisines are ably represented. Chefs are better trained and more cosmopolitan. Breads are infinitely superior. Wine lists and wine-and-food pairings are more adventurous. Service staffs are better informed. Farm-fresh, organic produce, much of it from the city's Greenmarkets, has become prevalent. Hudson Valley foie gras and Brooklyn brick-oven pizza rival their French and Italian counterparts.

This guide explores such **current trends** and developments as the French bistro and brasserie boom, the progression of Nuevo Latino and Asian fusion, the bourgeois-bohemian colonization of Brooklyn, the mainstreaming of Korean cuisine, and the rediscovery of open-fire cooking. Reviews elucidate the city's changing tastes and fashions, from uncooked fish (sashimi, ceviche, carpaccio, tartare, crudo) to fatty, nutritionally incorrect meats. Be it Italian (braised oxtail at Lupa), French (glazed pork belly at Pastis), Chinese (braised jellied pork shoulder sandwiches at New Green Bo), or American (fried suckling pigskins at Prune), this "bad-for-you" food fad reflects a widespread yearning for rustic, peasant-style cooking.

You will also read here about great **New York classics** ranging from the legendary—the Grand Central Oyster Bar, Katz's Delicatessen, Dominick's, Gage & Tollner, Nathan's Famous—to the peerless yet lesser known—Barney Greengrass, Totonno Pizzeria Napolitano, The Pub Room at Keens Chop House—to the comparatively obscure—Gino, the Prime Burger, Mei Lai Wah.

introduction

Pricing, costs, and tipping

Value was a decisive consideration in deciding which restaurants to include. Not every place that made the final cut is inexpensive. Often, a pricey meal can be more of a bargain than a cheap one. Still, although you can spend upwards of $100 for dinner and feel like you got more than your money's worth, the guide's emphasis on value made it necessary to exclude very expensive restaurants. At every featured restaurant it is possible, if not always likely, to eat a full dinner, beverage, tax and tip included, for less than $50.

Each review features a **dollar spread** that indicates the minimum and maximum amount you are likely to spend on a meal, tax and tip included. The first figure relates to what you could get away with, perhaps by sharing an appetizer, skipping dessert, or ordering the least expensive dishes. The second figure estimates what a meal would cost without any such economizing. Diners with an insatiable thirst for cocktails, fine wines, and bottled waters may leave the upper limit far behind. But in most instances, the cost of a meal will lie somewhere within the middle of the spread.

A **service charge**, though included in this guide's estimates, will not appear on the dinner check, except at restaurants that apply one for large groups. It is customary to tip between 15 and 20 percent of the check total, depending on how generous you are feeling and how good the service was. Many use the 8.25% **sales tax** that appears at the bottom of the check as a guide to calculate the proper tip. They double the tax to an amount totalling 16.5% of the check total and then round out that figure up or down as they feel appropriate.

Rough Guide favorites

The Rough Guide to New York City Restaurants does not rank or rate its 321 restaurants. Each of them is wholeheartedly recommended. Nevertheless, to guide you towards the five favorites in some essential categories, here are some "best ofs".

Best breakfast

Best brunch

Best sandwiches

Best steak frites

introduction

Best in theater district

Best local haunts

Best for kids

Best perennially hip

Most worth the wait

introduction

MANHATTAN

THE BRONX

HARLEM/HAMILTON HEIGHTS

Columbia University

Cathedral of St. John the Divine

NEW JERSEY

Hudson River

Central Park

American Museum of Natural History

UPPER WEST SIDE

Lincoln Center

UPPER EAST SIDE

Metropolitan Museum of Art

MIDTOWN WEST

Museum of Modern Art

THEATER DISTRICT

Rockefeller Center

GARMENT DISTRICT/ LITTLE KOREA

New York Public Library

Grand Central Station

MIDTOWN EAST

Empire State Building

Chrysler Building

Penn Station

United Nations

CHELSEA

MURRAY HILL/ KIPS BAY

FLATIRON DISTRICT/ GRAMERCY PARK/ UNION SQUARE

WEST VILLAGE

UNION SQUARE

QUEENS

GREENWICH VILLAGE /NOHO

EAST VILLAGE

SOHO

East River

TRIBECA

LITTLE ITALY/ NOLITA

LOWER EAST SIDE

Woolworth Building

City Hall

CHINA-TOWN

Former Site of World Trade Center

WALL ST./ LOWER MANHATTAN

MANHATTAN BRIDGE

WILLIAMSBURG BRIDGE

Battery Park

BROOKLYN BRIDGE

FRANKLIN D. ROOSEVELT DRIVE

N

BROOKLYN

0   1 mile

Downtown

Chelsea

Bottino

(🍽) Weighing the beautifuls (decor, garden, people) against the unremarkables (food, service, cordiality) should help determine your relationship with this glamorous trattoria. But then again you may ultimately be swayed by the X factor: Bottino's forgive-all bread pudding. At any rate, Daniel Emerman and Florentine chef Alessandro Prosperi have fulfilled their ambition to do for Chelsea's art gallery scene what Barocco, their other trattoria, did for TriBeCa's in the eighties. Situated opposite Manhattan's Getty—the gas station, not the museum—this spin-off is hip, noisy, breezy, and vaguely Tuscan. There's no pretension or artificiality on the forthright menu, in the simple dishes, or hanging from the white-painted brick walls.

Cost	Lunch $20–55
	Dinner $35–75

Address 246 10th Ave, between 24th & 25th Sts
☎212/206-6766
Transportation C,E to 23rd St
Open Sun & Mon 6–10 pm, Tues–Sat noon–3pm & 6–11pm
Accepts All major credit cards
Reservations Required

The art of Bottino is in how architect Thomas Lesser's mid-century modern decor preserves fixtures from an old hardware store. The antiquated wood shelving, in a bar furnished with Charles Eames bentwood chairs, still stocks liquid treatments—but today it's moderately priced Pinot Grigios and Chianti Classicos rather than lacquers and paints. The sparse dining room keeps its tin ceiling and worn hardwood floors. And then there are the gardens, two outdoor spaces so enchanting they provide Bottino's most unfortunate challenge: what to do about diners who don't want to leave, and what to do about diners kept waiting for their tables.

The single candle on each garden table takes the idea of romantic light a bit too far. After sundown, you can't see a thing. Bring along a flashlight to read about such appetizers as the nice grilled eggplant salad with arugula, shaved Tuscan Pecorino cheese, balsamic, and excellent olive oil ($9), or the tuna tartare topped with cubed beets, arugula, and red onion ($12). Main courses are generally decent. The cooks, unlike the reservations crew, know their limits. It's impossible to fault the grilled steak ($27), with its juicy, pristine slices of New York strip, sautéed broccoli rabe, and lumpy mashed potatoes, or the spaghetti with fresh shrimp, sea scallops, and clams in a peppery tomato garlic wine sauce ($17). Besides its famed vanilla bread pudding, Bottino has a second dessert savior in its smooth and genuine tiramisu ($7).

5

Chelsea

Cafeteria

🍴 Originally, the glass-paneled, garage-door facade and stark-white modernism of Cafeteria evoked a Richard Meier knockoff better suited to the West Coast than the West Side. The name itself didn't really fit, either, intimating a humble, counter-service institution rather than the Los Angeles-fashioned import of a self-consciously stylish, table-service commissary. But like a pair of leather pants, Cafeteria has

| Cost | Lunch $15–40 |
| | Dinner $20–55 |

Address 119 7th Ave at 17th St
☎212/414-1717
Transportation 1,2 to 18th St
Open Daily 24hr
Accepts All major credit cards

become softer and comfier with repeated wear and scuffing. The crowd is interesting: a fashion-aware, manifestly Chelsea mix of buff, protein-loading gym rats and their equally ravenous if less perfectly bodied neighbors. Members of the latter group should not, however, expect to join the former merely by eating as they do. A waffle with strawberry sour cream and a crème brûlée-styled topping of caramelized maple syrup is not, unfortunately, the fastest route to a fitter you.

Most happy habitués would agree on one thing: when our mothers stressed the importance of a *healthy* breakfast, they were referring to its size, as opposed to its nutritional facets. The dietary benefits of the summer berries or winter apples that garnish the tantalizing croissant French toast ($6.95) are an afterthought. And if an order of poached eggs with a buttermilk biscuit, sausage, gravy, spinach, and gloppy Hollandaise ($7.95) just happens to cover all the major food groups, that's just a side benefit.

While everyone can agree about breakfasts, Cafeteria's conception of the term "appetizer" is perhaps a little quirky. Are you really expected to eat something *after* the lyrical macaroni and (two-) cheese ($5.95), the steamed mussels in cilantro tomato broth ($9.95), or the almost legendary Caesar salads with a one-eyed Susan (poached egg; $7.95) or grilled chicken ($10.95)? Are you really supposed to nosh something *before* the awesome hickory-smoked chicken club with tomato confit, avocado, arugula, and basil mayo on sourdough ($9.95) or triple-decker grilled tuna club with roasted tomatoes, arugula, avocado, and red onion ($13.95)? Keep in mind, these sandwiches, which stretch from late afternoon to early morning, all come with large, spectacularly crisp steak fries. And then there's that incredible banana pudding thing ($5.95)—a coffee mug filled with thick cream, sweet bananas, and butterfingers—to confront.

Cuba Libre

Seeking to ride the Latin-fusion wave and the Buena Vista Social Club-sparked craze for anything with a Cuban beat, Robert Ianniello had to travel all the way from the dining room to the kitchen of his Little Italy restaurant, Umberto's Clam House. There he gave Rene Garcia the chance to say *adiós* to the linguine with white clam sauce, move to Chelsea, and prepare foods much closer in spirit, if not origin, to his native Mexico. Once the chef was installed behind an iced bank of raw oysters in an open kitchen, a large set of hanging copper pots within arm's reach, the rest was as easy as mixing a Cuba Libre (rum, Coke, lime juice, ice): mount palm branches, cigar memorabilia, and fluorescent tubes in green, orange, and yellow on the exposed brick walls. Then crank up the bass on that cha-cha version of Rudolph the Red-Nosed Reindeer.

| Cost | Lunch $18–40 |
| | Dinner $30–65 |

Address 200 8th Ave, between 20th & 21st Sts
☎212/206-0038
Transportation C,E to 23rd St
Open Sun–Thurs noon–3.30pm & 5–11pm, Fri & Sat noon–3.30pm & 5pm–midnight
Accepts All major credit cards

The most appealing thing about the effort is its small size and modest ambitions. There's neither the capacity to inebriate hundreds of cruising singles nor the need to make big statements about Nuevo Latino cookery. With an emphasis on seafood brought over from Umberto's, Garcia's pan-Latin ideas are generally quite good, and fussy in the most innocent sense. When he cleverly refits fried, blue-cornmeal-coated oysters into their shell with smoky collard greens and salsa ($9.95), it's as if to show you there's an experienced and creative chef in the kitchen. (Most people would gladly trade the shells for more oysters. The same is true of the fresh lobster empanada stylishly set in mango lentil salad ($9.95).

The lightly sweet and smoky, delectably crusty, ancho-chile-rubbed slices of pork tenderloin ($17.95) allay all fears about Mojave-dry pork. Served with sweet plantain mash and black bean sauce, it'll hold up to repeated replays (unlike the cha-cha Rudolph). Chicken stuffed with chorizo and garlic spinach ($16.95) is also juicy and tender. Seafood entrees, though properly cooked, tend to err on the sweet side. Best leave that job to the desserts ($5): fried plantains, tres leches cakes and domino (dark and white chocolate) cake are all perfectly acceptable.

Chelsea

F&B

(YI) In geographic terms, this franchise prototype is situated on the same landmark block as the Chelsea Hotel, the Clearview Chelsea Cineplex, and Manhattan's first Krispy Kreme donut shop. In emotional terms, the counter-service concept has occupied a warm spot in hungry New York hearts ever since its debut in summer 2001. The periwinkle walls and blond-wood counters on either side of this sleek and slender emporium may be seen as a fashion runway leading to several precious letters of the alphabet. While

Cost	$6–25

Address 269 West 23rd St, between 7th & 8th Aves
☏646/486-4441
Transportation 1,9,C,E to 23rd St
Open Mon–Fri 11am–11pm, Sat & Sun 9am–11pm
Accepts All major credit cards
Reservations Not accepted

the F and the B give star billing to the frites and the beignets, the title sadly overlooks many marquee attractions. You may know and love them as HDs; others adore them as Ws, Fs, or TSs. Translation: hot dogs, wieners, frankfurters, tube steaks.

This being Chelsea, the HDs are not neglected when it comes to their wardrobe. These European-accented street foods have more designer outfits and de rigueur accessories than a Barbie doll. In all there are fifteen ensembles, ranging from the Great Dane (a supermodel-skinny Danish dog with remoulade, mustard, apple tomato ketchup, and cucumber disks; $3.25) to the shorter, plumper Sheep Dog (rosemary-spiced lamb sausage with ratatouille and scant crumbled feta; $4.50). In terms of the meat itself, the firm garlic sausage is the pick of the hot dog litter. But veggie (tofu) dogs do subtract 90 percent of the guilt and, assuming there are plenty of spicy toppings draped over them, no more than a quarter of the pleasure. The perfectly tanned Belgian-style frites ($3.25) are lightly crisp and substantial. F for Fabulous! Defying the laws of physics, the sweet potato fries ($2.50) are uncommonly crisp. BTE for better-than-ever! And the fried onion loops ($2.50) are lip-smacking. None of these fried nibbles requires the special dips—aioli, pesto, or blue cheese—on offer.

As for the beignets (3 for $1.75), these warm, pillow-shaped donut puffs offer truly profound gratification. Though their sugar coating alone unleashes a definitive melt-in-your-mouth moment when sweet powder turns to liquid, a dessert dip addition—caramel, dark chocolate, mango, etc—is in this instance warmly encouraged.

Markt

(🍴) The factory clock that glows in the middle of this Belgian bistro is frozen at five minutes to midnight. So propitious a stoppage may be viewed as a stroke, or, rather, five non-strokes of luck by assorted Cinderellas fearful of 12am curfews. But it should not be taken to mean that Markt, Flemish for "market," is a fairy-tale destination run with quartz precision. The chance of a dinner without a service-related incident is still remote. That said, good, decent cooking nourishes this handsome haunt, which buzzes with more than enough possibilities for 150 diners stuck together in time. Many huddle at the 70ft marble bar, enjoying Belgian brews,

| Cost | Lunch $20–50 |
| | Dinner $30–75 |

Address 410 14th St at 9th Ave
(☎)212/727-3314
Transportation A,C,E to 14th St; L to 8th Ave
Open Mon–Thurs 11am–4.30pm & 5.30–11pm, Fri 11am–4.30pm & 5.30pm–midnight, Sat & Sun 10.30am–4.30pm & 5.30pm–midnight
Accepts All major credit cards
Reservations Suggested

raw oysters, gratis fried mussels and, in their own way, each other. Others sit at the mahogany tables spread over a hardwood floor set with inlays of vintage decorative tiles.

Not surprisingly, the workhorse specialties, acting as shared appetizers, main courses, beer accompaniments, or all three, are big pots of exceptionally meaty steamed mussels paired with good frites ($14). Mussels also stand in for snails in a variation of the French classic escargots à la Bourguignonne ($15). This gratin of mussels arrives at the table dripping in hot, garlicky butter sauce. Few main courses could be described as light. Among the traditional stews known as waterzooi, the "Mer du Nord" version ($24) gathers cod, shrimp, mussels, scallops, and salmon in a cream sauce touched with some fish stock as opposed to a fish stock touched with cream. Naturally, the whole ensemble is a knockout. Similarly, the sweet and fabulously juicy split grilled lobster ($29) swims in a buttery sauce with only a hint of white beer. Meat options ($15–26) are pretty dependable. The huge portions simply add to the diet-busting damage. At lunch, baguette sandwiches (ham and cheese, beef tartare, shrimp salad) are just $7–8.

To finish, pare down the so-so selection of nine desserts ($7-9) until you're left with the warm-centered chocolate cake with pistachio ice cream and the Dame Blanche, a Flemish ice cream sundae with Belgian chocolate sauce.

Chelsea

El Quijote

While Cervantes' El Quijote is a masterpiece of satire, its namesake tribute in the landmark Chelsea Hotel is a kitsch-congested classic without a single iota of irony. And if the Spanish restaurant is more popular and magical than ever, it's precisely because in 75-plus years it never turned into a parody of its sentimental self. The blue-glass back-lit bar patronized by hundreds of artists—both professional and con—who've stayed for a spell in the Chelsea is marvelously intact. The partition of fluted wood and glass that separates

| Cost | Lunch $15–60 |
| | Dinner $25–60 |

Address 226 West 23rd St, between 7th & 8th Aves

☎212/929-1855

Transportation 1,2,C,E to 23rd St

Open Sun–Thurs noon–midnight, Fri & Sat noon–1am

Accepts All major credit cards

Reservations Suggested

them from the Naugahyde-bracketed diners is unblemished. The Dulcinea Room remains an ideal party space to celebrate, if nothing else, Dulcinea. And when a waiter praises the virtues of the veal extrem na ($14.95), an enormous casserole loaded with veal, green peppers, chorizo, garlic, and garlic (there's so much of it we need to list it twice) in a Sherry sauce, he means it. Anyone familiar with the mediocrity of this dish will appreciate just how much training and dedication that testimonial requires.

The tearing sound made whenever someone opens a menu is the same *shtshtsht* you hear when you pry apart the plastic pages of a photo album. In perusing the laminated listings you might conclude that all dishes distinguished as extrem na or "El Quijote" are similar, regardless of whether they contain veal, chicken, or beef. This is not actually true. There are only two constants: garlic and garlic. In any event, ordering requires of the diner exactly what the cooking lacks: finesse. You'd do well to start by sharing the extremes varidos ($15.95), a mixed appetizer of fried calamari, grilled shrimp (very salty), grilled chorizo, chicken croquettes, stuffed mushrooms, and maybe six or seven other items. Three people would have a chance of finishing a single order before taking on a paella. That is, one paella for the three of them.

El Quijote has long been a leading player within the local langosta circuit, a small group of apparently unrelated Spanish places in the vicinity of 23rd and Seventh offering competing lobster deals. As of this writing, the 1lb steamed or broiled lobster was selling here for $17.95.

The Red Cat

NEW AMERICAN

Were its interior sided with Moroccan tiles rather than barn-red wainscoting, the large Moorish lanterns dropped from the wood-beamed ceiling would make perfect sense. But in a made-up farmhouse inn that recycles bent cutlery as coat hooks, those lighting fixtures reflect only the logic of a vacationing Vermonter. "I don't care if they don't go with anything we have," asserts the stubborn tourist. "I like them, and I'm getting them." Such provincialism amid the cutting-edge design and pretensions of the Chelsea art gallery scene suits a friendly, knowing restaurant where the chef cooks the way his guests eat: for pleasure over effect. "I don't care if the steak comes with potato chips," asserts the wilful diner. "I like chive mashed potatoes, and I'm getting them, too."

Cost	$35–80

Address 227 10th Ave, between 23rd & 24th Sts
☎212/242-1122
Transportation C,E to 23rd St
Open Mon–Thurs 5.30–11.30pm, Fri & Sat 5.30pm–midnight, Sun 5–10pm
Accepts All major credit cards
Reservations Required

In constructing his New American, Mediterranean-highlighted menu, chef/co-owner Jimmy Bradley gives every dish at least one hook. His food is catchy. Just one look reveals the fried shrimp appetizer ($12) to be a surefire hit. Four crisp, meaty, golden-brown jumbos hang on the rim of a martini glass like sun-bronzed legs surrounding a swimming pool. Other appetizers rely on supporting, often scene-stealing, ingredients for their sensuality. A pleasantly chewy risotto cake ($10) is upstaged by its lush Champagne cream sauce enriched with poached oysters. Wonderfully gritty, toasted orzo benefits from mussels, roasted tomatoes, chives, and chile flakes ($9). Main courses accentuate the fondness shared by Bradley and chef de cuisine William McDaniel for fresh herbs and garlic. There is so much chopped thyme on and around the garlic-sauced roast chicken ($18) you may wish to put on a green shirt before you order it. Sage and garlic are central to the outstanding sautéed calf's liver ($18), too, with smoky bacon and sweet onion confit clinging to every bite.

Pastry chef Colleen Grapes' desserts ($6–8) are, like The Red Cat, at once countrified and cosmopolitan. Instead of choosing between the banana bread ice cream sandwich, the steamed chocolate cake, and the Gorgonzola-stuffed pear, headstrong diners may persuade their companions to order all three. "We don't care...We like them, and we're getting all of them."

Chelsea

Rocking Horse Cafe

In choosing the name, design, and philosophy of their distinctive Mexican bistro Roe DiBona and Marvin Beck were inspired by architect Luis Barragan, the late Mexican modernist who loved horses and was partial to pure planes of sumptuous color as well as designs based on indigenous sources. With its walls of tomato red, lime green, and cafe-con-leche and its grasp of genuine regional flavors, the Rocking Horse is a terrifically modish, if modest, expression of these principles. Its idea of interacting with its natural environment produces different results than the master's, largely due to that environment itself. It reinterprets the boisterous street life outside its red garage-door storefront within a rollicking shoebox of tequila-marinated merriment.

Cost	Lunch $18–45
	Dinner $27–70

Address 182 8th Ave, between
19th & 20th Sts
☏212/463-9511
Transportation C,E to 23rd St;
1,2 to 18th St
Open Sun–Thurs 11am–11pm,
Fri & Sat 11am–midnight
Accepts All major credit cards
Reservations Suggested

The vibrant, savory, and amusing cooking has survived the departure of innovative chef Sue Torres to Hell's Kitchen (see p.218). Infrequent setbacks are probably due to the frenzied and cramped conditions in which the diligent kitchen and dining room staffs must cope. They need not worry. Once in the company of their companions, their Technicolor margaritas, and warm homemade tricolor tortilla chips (cilantro, black bean, ancho red) with rich guacamole ($8.95), diners are more likely to be grateful for than upset by delays. The relaxed attitude is just one good reason for limiting a dinner order to pass-around appetizers like fried calamari citrus salad ($8.95), chipotle-glazed, tangy organic pork ribs ($9.95), and triple-decker wild mushroom quesadilla with jicama green apple slaw ($8.95). The second reason is that each of these stands well on its own—and besides, who's to say the steamed mussels in chipotle broth ($7.95) cannot be a main course?

There are some good entrees if you make it that far. Enchiladas filled with pulled chicken leg roasted in pomegranate juice and ancho chile ($14.95) boast an appealing, sweet tartness. Pan-seared mahi mahi ($18.95) floats in shrimp chile broth enriched with cacahuazintle (hominy grains) and cockle clams. The dessert of distinction is the Valrhona chocolate tortilla ($5.95), a steamed, spongy, doubly dark-chocolately, ring-shaped cake with cinnamon ice cream.

The Tonic

🍴 Classic but not dated, stylish but not ostentatious, lively but not frenetic, composed but not muted, The Tonic is the kind of New York experience you're always looking for but never expecting to find. Set in a gaslight-era townhouse, The Tonic's main dining room possesses an amber glow emitted by Edison bulbs suspended from iron chandeliers. The overall effect spells romance with a small "r." It's a suitable place to pop any number of questions: will you marry me? Did you up your offer for the co-op? Should we have the torchon of foie gras or Maine crabcake? When do we dine here again?

Cost	Lunch $25–50
	Dinner $40–85

Address 108 West 18th St, between 6th & 7th Aves
☎212/929-9755
Transportation 1,2 to 18th St; F,V to 14th St; L to 6th Ave
Open Mon–Thurs noon–3pm & 5–10.30pm, Fri noon–3pm & 5–11pm, Sat 5–11pm
Accepts All major credit cards
Reservations Suggested

When it comes to The Tonic and its chef, Joseph Fortunato, it's hard to determine who is better for whom. The space frees Fortunato to be creative without the pressure to cause a stir. And his contemporary American cooking motivates a serving staff genuinely excited about the food. Appetizers can be as crisp and refreshing as an asparagus and baby beet salad ($11) or as unapologetically lush and brash as the braised oxtail tart with vanilla whipped potatoes and horseradish crème fraîche ($11), the trio of tartares ($13)—tuna, salmon, red snapper—abetted by avocado purée, or the braised rabbit ravioli ($11) rich with chanterelles, onion confit, and black truffles.

The selection of ten entrees is as balanced as the dishes themselves. Case in point: lamb three ways ($28). Grouper marinated in harissa ($26) is not as spicy as foods flavored with that North African hot sauce typically are. But there is just enough bite to make you thankful for the soft landing of its crabmeat brandade and saffron crème fraîche. The lemon-crusted cod ($21) is perhaps too subtle, its tartness lost amid the braised fennel and garlic broth.

To finish, pastry chef Dalia Jurgensen's designer desserts (all $8) and true-flavored ice creams are showstoppers. The warm banana tarte tatin with rum ice cream and macadamia nut brittle is perhaps better than it sounds, while the sour cream spice cake with slow-roasted apples and whipped cream is a stirring illustration of grounded sophistication typical of The Tonic.

Chinatown

CHINATOWN

Bowery Savings Bank

GRAND STREET

BROADWAY

HOWARD STREET

BAXTER STREET

MULBERRY STREET

MOTT STREET

ELIZABETH STREET

BOWERY

CHRYSTIE STREET

Sara D. Roosevelt Park

HESTER STREET

XO Kitchen

Harmony Palace

WALKER STREET

CANAL STREET

CONFUCIUS PLAZA

LAFAYETTE STREET

CENTRE STREET

WHITE STREET

Mei Lai Wah

Mandarin Court

New Green Bo

FRANKLIN STREET

BAYARD STREET

Yeah

Baba

New York Noodle Town

LEONARD ST.

Shanghai Cuisine

Shanghai Deluxe

MOTT STREET

PELL STREET

DIVISION ST.

Columbus Park

EAST BROADWAY

Ping's

WORTH STREET

HENRY STREET

N

Thomas Paine Park

ST. JAMES'S PLACE

MADISON STREET

DUANE STREET

PEARL STREET

READE STREET

PARK ROW

STREET

Police HQ

0   200 yds

Baba

(🍴) Anyone who cares to admire the lovely folkloric paintings and punched-metal wall menus installed under the copper ceiling should make haste. Those who want to emulate the ordering habits of the young, food-fanatical ABCs—American-born Chinese—at whom Chinatown's most stylish Malaysian eatery is targeted must do so in a hurry. Because once your table is beset with a front assault of intensely spicy, sour, sweet, and salty stimuli, everything

Cost	$10–40

Address 53 Bayard St at Elizabeth St
℡212/766-1318
Transportation J,M,N,Q,R,W,6 to Canal St
Open Daily noon–midnight
Accepts Cash only
Reservations For large groups

else becomes a blur. Opened by Suan Lee and June Khoo, Baba is a descendant of the popular Malaysian restaurants Penang and Nyonya (see p.136 and p.109). It's distinguished by its wide selection of meticulously garnished crab dishes, its rich, almost smoky "House Special" sauce made with dried chiles, dried shrimp, fresh cilantro, lemongrass and ginger, and its friendly young waitstaff.

The compulsory starter is the rice-flour crêpe called roti canai ($1.95) that you fold between your fingers and dip into a chicken curry sauce. Crisp yet delicate, Baba's rendition is a golden standout. Match it with a nicely charred beef and chicken satay ($4.95) or baba lobak ($6.95), a mixed fry of tightly wrapped pork rolls, tofu, and shrimp pancake. Large soups range from the aggressively sour asam laksa ($4.95), with rice noodles, fish flakes, and pineapple in a lemongrass broth, to the soothingly sweet herbal pork broth bah kut tey—"meat bone tea" ($5.95).

Among entrees, avoid the cloyingly sweet mango dishes. Opt instead for squid with House Special sauce ($8.95) or the "stingray" (more accurately, skate) which is wrapped, and kept moist, in a banana leaf before it hits the grill. The shrimp paste tucked under the fish bone melts into the peppery coconut broth to complete a trio of salty, spicy, and sweet sensations ($11.95). The very idea of Baba curry fish head ($10) may repel some, but as the most strongly flavored part of the fish, the head is exactly what a stew like this needs. Think of it as a scintillating fish gumbo, enriched with tomato and okra. For the squeamish, there's a beef equivalent ($9.95). To close, the warm chunky peanut roti pancake ($3.50) is unmissable.

Chinatown

Harmony Palace

Because its English name was not displayed for years, fans came to know this 500-seat dim sum palace only by its address, 98 Mott. And while its dim sum service has drawn packed houses for nearly a decade, the name Harmony Palace still means nothing to many who pine for its peerless parade of steamed, baked, fried, stuffed, wrapped, or rolled Chinese morsels. The cavernous dining room is set up as if for a banquet, with tables crowded together on the main floor and a dais for honored guests, while the gaudy decorations—glass chandeliers, gilded mythical creatures, framed displays of shark fins and Cognac bottles, illuminated photos of waterfalls—are beginning to look as worn-out as the waitresses after pushing the dim sum carts around for seven hours.

Cost	$10–25

Address 98 Mott St, between Canal & Hester Sts
☎212/226-6603
Transportation 6,J,M,N,Q,R,W to Canal St
Open Daily 8am–3pm
Accepts MasterCard & Visa
Reservations Not accepted

The widest and freshest assortment of dim sum is available for weekend brunch. You should come no later than 10.30am, get settled in, and, to show the staff you know what you're doing, request a pot of bo nay tea. (They serve that full-bodied black tea to Chinese and weak jasmine tea to Westerners.) Never feel pressurized into taking something you don't want or aren't sure you want. You aren't going to miss anything by passing on the first go-rounds. That said, rarely is the cost of experimentation—chicken feet anyone?—so little. Most items are $1.95 and nothing from the carts exceeds $3.95.

Begin with har gow, the shrimp dumplings (three to a bamboo steamer) that are elemental to dim sum. The casing here is starchy and desirably flimsy; the filling, fresh and compact. Other standards to watch for are siu mai (pork dumplings wrapped in egg noodles), pan-fried chive dumplings, steamed beef balls with watercress, and shrimp rice noodles. You could compare the last to the Buddhist roll, which is chubbier and chewier and not nearly as slippery, its lasagna-thick rice noodle enveloping a dozen chopped vegetables. Lastly, the faintly sweet home dumpling is a bulging, translucent crescent packed with peanuts, mushrooms, celery, sesame seeds, water chestnuts, and taro. They call it the Harmony Dumpling; you can call it 98 Mott.

Mandarin Court

(🍴) The Chinese residents and habitués of Chinatown tend to be more loyal to chefs than restaurants. If they read in the Chinese press that a favorite chef is moving to another restaurant, they're likely to follow him. But while this game of musical woks plays out, Mandarin Court defies the rules. Its fine reputation for Hong Kong-style cuisine and, in particular, creative dim sum has outlasted the periodic turnover in kitchen personnel. As a rule, change is anathema to owner Carol Baluyut, who has main-

Cost	Lunch $9–30 Dinner $15–75

Address 61 Mott St, between Canal & Bayard Sts

☏212/608-3838

Transportation 6,J,M,N,Q,R,W to Canal St

Open Daily 8am–11pm

Accepts All major credit cards

Reservations Not accepted

tained the same prices for years and not fixed up the (once attractive) decor since 1988.

Such steadfastness makes recent developments all the more dramatic. An assortment of chef Po Lui's masterful dim sum is now offered *in the evening*. Although you still need to go earlier in the day for a freshly made and comprehensive selection, the dinner menu nevertheless encompasses his signature steamed scallop dumplings, steamed lotus seed buns, chicken turnovers, and bean curd rolls with oyster sauce. Prices are slightly higher at night: dumplings and rolls jump from $1.95 during breakfast and lunch to $2.95 at dinner, while the garlicky and spicy clams in black bean sauce increase from $4.95 to $5.95.

The balance of the dinner menu, including 22 different soups, is supervised by chef Sam Chan, who follows his predecessors' practice of preparing Cantonese food with an occasional spicy spin. His repertoire is so comprehensive we doubt even Carol has sampled every dish. Diners who love moo shu, spring rolls, and other savory wraps will not want to miss the minced oysters in lettuce ($11.95)—a hash of dried oysters, vermicelli, Chinese sausage, and vegetables wrapped tableside with fresh cilantro in an iceberg leaf, and then dunked in thick hoisin sauce. Delicious. Sautéed prawns, as sweet and snappy as can be, are teamed with crunchy mustard greens and equally al dente green beans ($14.95). And Peking duck ($32) is divided into two courses. The crackling skins are first served with steamed buns and shaved scallion, while the duck meat is shredded and served with various accompaniments. Duck dow miu, for example, gets young pea shoots.

Chinatown

Mei Lai Wah

Before the 1980s Hong Kong invasion filled Chinatown with glitzy dining palaces, dim sum was largely the province of modest tea rooms and coffee houses run by immigrants from China's Taishan County. A case in point is the antediluvian Mei Lai Wah, which, with a six-stool counter on the left, tiny and tattered booths on the right, and creepy fluorescent panels above, resembles a sinister Chinatown hideout in some 1960s thriller. The prices hand-printed on the wall menu, from 50¢ to $1.40, only reinforce this impression. Fortunately, the coffee house has yet to be discovered by downtown hipsters or slumming suburbanites. It endures as a proletarian haunt filled with Chinese working men who peruse newspapers in the morning, discuss what they've read in the evening, and sip strong coffee or tea no matter the hour.

Cost	$5–15

Address 64 Bayard St, between Mott & Elizabeth Sts
℡212/925-5435
Transportation 6,J,M,N,Q,R,W to Canal St
Open Daily 7am–11.30pm
Accepts Cash only
Reservations Not accepted

As tempting as the booths are, their worn Naugahyde faded to the color of a regular coffee, the round table in the back is the prime seating location. It affords a mesmerizing view into a red-painted kitchen from another world. Giant woks and steam pots are set over old stoves fed by prehistoric gas pipes. Buns and pastries are loaded into an antiquated oven. A cook hacks up everything—whole chickens, blubbery pork skin, bamboo shoots—on a round, concave chopping block. And trays of steaming-hot dim sum keep coming. Sample the puffy, bready buns fresh from the oven or steamer and you'll never accept them again any other way. The roast pork bun (60¢) is filled with salty (saltiness at Mei Lai Wah is a given) diced pork marinated in oyster sauce. The larger "Special Big Bun" ($1.10) contains pork, chicken, sausage, egg, and mushroom. Technically, it's a meal. The oval-shaped sausage bun (60¢) is a Cantonese hot dog.

Siu mai dumplings ($1.40 for three) are so big they resemble pork meatballs. The beef rice noodles ($1.40) are overstuffed with unctuous braised meat. And the plump shrimp dumplings ($1.40), though mealy, have plenty of minced bamboo shoots. Among desserts (50¢), the custard tart is pleasantly flaky, while the apple turnover and almond cookie are, respectively, the wrong and right kind of dry.

New Green Bo

(🍴) The demise in 1998 of Say Eng Look was seen as a painful irony by devotees of that venerable Chinatown institution. The last of the city's old-line Shanghai dining palaces was closing just as a new generation of more modest eateries was making Shanghai-style dumplings, cold delicacies, and red cooking the talk of Mott Street. Sadly, the now retired owner of Say Eng Look never looked back. But his wife Helen Hsu did. She helped open New Green Bo, whose utilitarian ways first came as a shock to

Cost	Lunch $10–30 Dinner $15–45

Address 66 Bayard St,
between Mott & Elizabeth Sts
☎212/625-2359
Transportation 6,J,M,N,Q,R,W
to Canal St
Open Daily noon–11pm
Accepts Cash only
Reservations Not accepted

old-timers familiar with its grand, flamboyant forerunner. But those Chinatown regulars who, through reverse snobbery, actually prefer the no-frills style, instantly loved the place and its fluorescent lighting, bent-metal chairs, and, even, its frightening subterranean restroom. For their reading pleasure, copies of rave newspaper reviews in English and Chinese are framed between the tabletops and the glass that covers them.

It's vital that you order in stages so that all the food does not come at once. From the winning selection of nineteen cold appetizers you'll enjoy thinly sliced braised beef in a sweet soy ginger sauce ($4.95), vegetarian mock duck (irresistible strips of cilantro-garnished bean curd inserted with mushrooms; $4.50), and ultra-crisp shards of fried eel ($5.95), which, coated in honeyed ginger and scallion sauce, become pure candy. The two varieties of Shanghai-style dumplings ought not be taken as an either/or proposition. Go ahead and get them both: the elongated pan-fried pork beauties ($4.25) *and* the dangerously explosive shao lung bao ($6.25), better known among non-Chinese as "soup dumplings." Besides their crab and pork filling, the shao lung bao also contain jellied meat juices that turn to hot liquid upon steaming.

Main-course standouts include seaweed-battered yellow fish fillets ($12.95); stewed pork bundled in bean curd skin ($8.75); and whole red snapper ($11.95) with the rich, sweet-and-sour brown sauce typical of Shanghai's braised—or "red-cooked"—dishes. Ready for a long-term love affair? Then introduce yourself to tong po pork ($8.75)—truly luscious barbecue-like sandwiches that you assemble yourself with hot steamed buns, baby bok choy, and sweet, wondrously fatty red-cooked pork.

Chinatown

New York Noodle Town

It's got less ambiance than a Midwestern strip mall, with a sketchy bathroom and a silly name, but New York Noodle Town is one heck of a Chinese restaurant, with an unusual menu, friendly, if abrupt, service, and reasonable prices. At the day's various rush hours, you may be asked to share a table. Have a cold Tsing Tao, or a cup of complimentary tea, and relax—the minor inconvenience is well worth it, and you may even end up bonding over the food, which will arrive when it's ready, in no particular order.

Cost	$12–35

Address 28 Bowery at Bayard St
☎212/349-0923
Transportation J,M,N,Q,R,W,6 to Canal St
Open Daily 9am–4am
Accepts Cash only
Reservations For large groups

Despite its name, New York Noodle Town specializes in barbecued meats. Decide for yourself which is best among crisp-skinned, tender baby pig ($6.95 with rice), sweet and succulent duck ($3.50 with rice), or roast pork loin ($4.25, with duck, inexplicably). Adventurous eaters will want to sample the more exotic varieties of thick congee (rice porridge), notably the one with pork stomach ($3), which has a pleasing, fried-tofu texture and mildly liver-like taste; meatball and pork liver ($3); or frog ($6.75). Dumplings in soup are a more conservative but no less pleasing choice; the simple shrimp variety ($3.75) is a marvel. The dumplings, soup, and just about everything else on the menu is enlivened with a dab of scallion, ginger, and garlic sauce, so make sure to request a bowl for the table.

New York Noodle Town also specializes in dishes served with flowering chives, which are a mature, slightly woody-stemmed version of the herb and are delicious on their own. Sea bass with flowering chives ($9.95) is inconsistent; at its best the dish is overloaded with snowy-white chunks of gently sautéed and lightly sauced fish, but on an off night the chunks are more like flakes, and tend toward saltiness. Moist shredded roast duck with chives ($10.95) is more reliable. A variety of seafood is available baked in salt, including crispy squid ($8.95), huge scallops ($10.95), and, when they're in season (mid-spring to early summer), soft-shell crabs ($14 for two). If you've only tasted crabs pan-seared, you should try the salt-baked variety, which are marvellously flavorful.

Ping's

🍽 Since Chuen Hui Ping won't tell people where he's cooking at any particular time, it would be nice if the darling food press volunteered to wear an electronic tracking device. After leaving Triple Eight Palace, his first New York platform for contemporary Cantonese cuisine infused with Hong Kong-style theatrics and regional Chinese, Thai, and Japanese influences, in 1996, Ping pinballed between four restaurants. Even now that he's cut back his movements to two newish Ping's restaurants—one in Queens (83–02 Queens Blvd; ☎718/396-1238) the other, this handsome, modern, cherrywood-paneled Chinatown duplex—Ping generally avoids his kitchens during service hours, an aversion increasingly common among entrepreneurial star chefs.

Cost	Lunch $8–45
	Dinner $20–45

Address 22 Mott St, between Mosco & Worth Sts; ☎212/602-9988
Transportation 6,J,M,N,Q,R,W to Canal St
Open Mon–Fri 10am–midnight, Sat & Sun 9am–midnight
Accepts MasterCard & Visa
Reservations For large groups

CHINESE

With or without the executive chef's hands-on participation, the fussy food presentation alone merits a look-see. Mini-woks, mini-casseroles, and ceramic soup bowls are brought directly to the table and set atop steel stands, releasing their rigorously aromatic vapors right under your nose. Brilliantly colored and choreographed dishes are elegantly arranged on round, rectangular, triangular, or shell-shaped plates. Beyond the visuals, Ping's mastery of situational spicing is usually apparent. Deceptively basic seafood dishes— snails with black bean sauce ($9.95); marvelously crunchy, juicy, salty, sautéed shell-on jumbo shrimp with black pepper sauce ($16.95)—are customized so that Ping's beloved ginger, garlic, scallion, and cilantro can take on a variety of supporting roles. Since dim sum-style appetizers are not truly a specialty, it's best to start by sharing seafood such as these or maybe the Thai-styled mussels with peppers and spicy basil sauce ($12.95).

More elaborate fusion entrees such as the steamed whole chicken ingeniously inlaid with ham and mushrooms ($24.95), Ping's hand is clearly missed. Though his lieutenants can handle Dungeness crab steamed with ginger and scallion or fried with a minced-garlic crust, they don't get the steamed version with lemon butter broth. That's hardly a slight. Their enigmatic boss is probably the only Chinese chef in New York who does.

23

Chinatown

Shanghai Cuisine

(🍴) Shanghai, the "Paris of the Orient", has been portrayed as a harbor of intrigue ever since it was opened to foreign trade in 1842. Its reputation as a hotbed of shady fortunes achieved a notoriety even the Communists couldn't chill when, in the 1932 film *Shanghai Express*, Marlene Dietrich's prostitute remarked: "It took more than one man to change my name to Shanghai Lily." Today, however, it's the city's braised and not its brazen temptations that attract attention. And Shanghai Cuisine is an

| Cost | Lunch $10–30 |
| | Dinner $20–45 |

Address 89 Bayard St at Mulberry St
☎212/732-8988
Transportation 6,J,M,N,Q,R,Z to Canal St
Open Daily 11am–10.45pm
Accepts Cash only
Reservations Not accepted

enticingly genuine platform for the city's specialty, red-cooking, whereby meats and fish are blanketed in the honeyed flavor of sweetened soy sauce. A second treat from China's Jiangsu province consists of wine-marinated meats often consumed with beer. Their sweet and sour offer a bold alternative to the spicy sameness of Szechuan and the subtlety of Canton. Appropriately, the restaurant's casual corner space stands out in the Chinatown crowd. Attractive French doors are backed by bamboo shades, while a brick wall is adorned with old posters that owner Josephine Feng picked up at a Shanghai flea market.

Pot-roast-like slices of braised beef scented with star anise ($5.25) provide the easiest introduction to the cold appetizers. Consider also the vegetarian mock duck ($5.95), with mushrooms and bamboo shoots tucked into glistening strips of bean curd skin, and spicy cabbage in vinegar ($3.95) sharpened with mustard and fresh cilantro. The mania for shao lung bao (soup dumplings; $5.50) overshadows the delight of another specialty, pan-fried pork dumplings ($3.75). The potstickers served here, with golden-crisp bottoms, delicate seams, and juicy contents, are sensational. Nothing quite prepares you, for the drama of the crispy duck entree ($12.95).

You can taste the red-cooking sauce in a variety of braised dishes: atop a whole yellow fish ($12.95), over crisp strips of fried chicken with chopped garlic, scallions, and ginger ($11.95), or around fatty pork shoulder ($11.95). But the finest option of all are the tender, juicy ground-pork balls ($12.95)—sometimes called "lion's head"—in an elegant laurel of crunchy baby bok choy.

XO Kitchen

Had a French-trained, media-savvy chef introduced XO's custardy gratin of razor clams, he would have been hailed as a genius. And had this genius served a squab as outrageously lacquered, roasted, and underpriced as XO's $7.95 rendition, he would have been reclassified just as quickly as a lunatic. Maybe there are no mad geniuses toiling towards immortality behind the XO counter. But in spinning out more than 150 of the pop-Chinese foods captivating young diners in Hong Kong, Taipei, and New York, these cooks assemble some remarkably imaginative, amusing, and cheap chow. Ordering is, however, a difficult business. Because some dishes are repeated in different menu categories, the eager servers rarely get your order exactly right. Moreover everything comes out at once.

Cost	Lunch $8–25
	Dinner $8–35

Address **148 Hester St,**
between Elizabeth St & The
Bowery
☎212/965-8645
Transportation **6,M,N,Q,R,W**
to Canal St
Open Daily 8am–11pm
Accepts Cash only
Reservations Not accepted

The repertoire is largely devoid of the fusion fiascos (French toast peanut butter sandwiches, anyone?) featured at other westernized Chinese cafes. The lone clunker is the French-style escargot ($5.95) paired with American coleslaw. The baked razor clams cheese ($4.95) are nifty, while the beef curry stew ($4.95) with coils of pre-twirled broad noodles is scrumptious. The part of the menu called "Appetizers" is confusing. It covers a few entrees, including the essential salt-baked shrimp ($7.95), while excluding such starters as the seafood and ham dumplings (a clever but leaky adaptation of Shanghai soup dumplings; $4.95) and dim-sum-style steamed rice noodles ($2.50). Watch out for little bones in the otherwise commendable sliced fish version.

Congees and noodle soups ($2.75–6.50) presented in small cast-iron cauldrons are the theatrical warm-up acts to the high drama of sirloin steaks ($13.95) delivered on sizzling iron platters. Tableside, the waiter douses each enormous steak with a good half-cup of black peppercorn sauce, mushroom sauce or, best of all, chopped garlic sauce—thus splattering every unprotected garment within a 4ft radius. Don't leave before sampling the fresh papaya chunks with honeydew soup and ice cream ($3.75), the warm egg custard pudding with ice cream ($3.50), or any other dessert you've likely never had before.

Chinatown

Yeah Shanghai Deluxe

When they opened Yeah Shanghai across the street from the very popular New Green Bo (see p.21), the owners weren't thinking they could make it on overflow business alone. They were going to offer something different. This, no doubt, partly explains the ersatz tropical garden with fountain and footbridge in the middle of an otherwise generic Chinatown eatery. But while the appeal of the plastic palms is fleeting at best, it's the figurative flowerbed the cooks carve out of fish that draws most attention.

| Cost | Lunch $7–40 |
| | Dinner $15–40 |

Address 65 Bayard St, between Mott & Elizabeth Sts
℡212/566-6111
Transportation 6,J,M,N,Q,R,W to Canal St
Open Daily 11am–10pm
Accepts Cash only
Reservations Not accepted

Chrysanthemum fish ($12.50), for example, which consists of fried fish clusters shaped like flower heads that, with the aid of a sweet-and-sour sauce undergo a miraculous color change from golden to reddish orange.

Why elaborate on the cold Shanghai appetizers, you may well ask, if the mere mention of the ingredients—hairy beans, mock ham, ox tongue, beef stomach—turns Westerners off? Because a combination plate of the cold starters ($13.95 for four delicacies) is Yeah Shanghai's best point of departure—far more interesting than the usual steamed buns and pan-fried dumplings. Either way, you want to get into the entrees as quickly as possible. There's lots to cover in the seafood category alone. A lovely, pale-pink mound of sautéed shrimp surrounded by a glistening green laurel of pea shoots ($12.95). Yellow fish fried two ways, seaweed battered (that's the norm) and wrapped in bean curd skin ($12.95). Sliced, sautéed, and sizzling eel draped with Shanghai brown sauce (reduced soy sauce; $19.95). Or even, for the adventurous, fleshy sea cucumber bejeweled with caviar-like shrimp eggs and the same brown sauce ($21.95).

As for the meats, few chef's specialties anywhere can beat the drama of mau tai (paper-wrapped) chicken ($17.95), a stuffed whole bird marinated for three hours, wrapped in lotus leaf, foil, and cellophane, and steamed. When a waiter cuts open the mummified bird, the perfumed vapors of ginger, mushroom, and garlic drift overhead. You could also go for the pork meatball casserole known as "lion's head" ($10.95), which carries cellophane noodles as well as the customary greens (in this case crunchy baby bok choy).

East Village

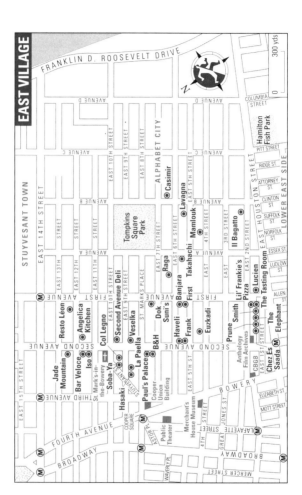

EAST VILLAGE

FRANKLIN D. ROOSEVELT DRIVE

STUYVESANT TOWN

Tompkins Square Park

ALPHABET CITY

LOWER EAST SIDE

Hamilton Fish Park

EAST 15TH STREET
EAST 14TH STREET
EAST 13TH STREET
EAST 12TH STREET
EAST 11TH STREET
EAST 10TH STREET
EAST 9TH STREET
EAST 8TH STREET
EAST 7TH STREET
EAST 6TH STREET
EAST 5TH STREET
EAST 4TH STREET
EAST 3RD STREET
EAST 2ND STREET
EAST HOUSTON STREET

AVENUE D
AVENUE C
AVENUE B
AVENUE A
FIRST AVENUE
SECOND AVENUE
THIRD AVENUE
FOURTH AVENUE
BOWERY
LAFAYETTE STREET
BROADWAY
MERCER STREET

ST. MARK'S PLACE

COOPER SQUARE
ASTOR PL
WAVERLY PL

COLUMBIA STREET
PITT STREET
RIDGE ST
ATTORNEY ST
CLINTON ST
SUFFOLK ST
NORFOLK ST
ESSEX ST
LUDLOW ST
ALLEN ST
ELIZABETH ST
MOTT STREET
GREAT JONES ST
4TH STREET

Jade Mountain
Bar Veloce
Iso
Resto Léon
Angelica Kitchen
Hasaki
Soba-Ya
St. Mark's-in-the-Bowery
Col Legno
Second Avenue Deli
Veselka
La Paella
Paul's Palace
B&H
Cooper Union Building
Dok Suni's
Banjara
Raga
Lavagna
Casimir
Takahachi
Mamlouk
Haveli
First
Frank
Euzkadi
Prune
Smith
Lil' Frankie's Pizza
Lucien
Il Bagatto
The Tasting Room
Anthology Film Archives
CBGB
Chez Es Saada
The Elephant
Public Theater
Merchant's House Museum

N

0   300 yds

Angelica Kitchen

To appreciate Angelica Kitchen you don't need to believe that eating something that once swam, flew, or roamed the earth is the moral equivalent of throwing an old lady in front of a bus. The oak, picnic-style tables of this warm, bright, organic vegetarian are perpetually packed with nose-ringed, heavily tattooed vegans, stylish, yoga-mat-carrying model-types, fresh-faced young professionals, and mature hippies. The eclectic crowd is proof that vegetarian cuisine, when prepared with wit and imagination,

Cost	$7–35

Address 300 East 12th St, between 1st & 2nd Aves
☎212/228-2909
Transportation L to 1st Ave; 4,5,6,N,R to 14th St–Union Square
Open Daily 11.30am–10.30pm
Accepts Cash only
Reservations Not accepted

VEGETARIAN

can appeal to a diverse and happy audience. Regulars are wont to call the hotline to hear about specials like tofu squares roasted in a thyme mustard vinaigrette with porcini and walnut sauce even on days when they have no plans to come in for dinner.

Salads are fresh, enormous, and stunning. Even the simple house salad gets dressed up with a colorful tangle of shredded carrots, beets, daikon, red and green cabbage, and crisp pea shoots ($3.75/$5.75/$8.50). Soups change daily ($3.25/cup, $3.95/bowl) and are invariably hearty and tasty. Thankfully, the three bean chili ($7.50/$9.95) never comes off the menu: it's a thick stew packed with lentils, kidney and pinto beans, homemade seitan, sundried tomatoes, and a heavy hit of spicy chiles, all topped off with tofu sour cream. The dragon bowls ($5.95–9.95), one-pot macrobiotic meals brimming with rice, beans, tofu, and steamed vegetables, are very healthy, and alas very bland. You'll need to add lots of soy sauce.

Large sandwiches are loaded with flavor. In one favorite, thick slices of lemon-herb tofu are joined by roasted vegetables and almond parsley pesto between chunky slices of mixed grain or wheat-free sourdough spelt bread ($7.50). The warm tempeh Reuben ($7.50) is a clever twist on the classic, with cumin-marinated tempeh, sauerkraut, and tofu Russian dressing (not at all bad) assembled between slices of caraway bread with lots of oomph. Home-baked desserts vary: working your way through the apple banana crumb pie with maple tofu whip ($4.95) is a dream, but the plodding effort required to enjoy the wheat-free, upside-down pear ginger cake with raspberry sauce ($4.95) is just too much to ask.

B&H

Today they classify the place as "vegetarian." But the eight globe lights that hang down from the ceiling like black-stemmed lollipops illuminate a living Formica memory: the Jewish dairy restaurant. That once prevalent East Village/Lower East Side institution has been reduced to the obscenely narrow dimensions of a hallway, with room for six tables-for-two (a pair are pushed together to seat four) and a dozen counter stools. The action behind the counter is itself a piece of Second Avenue theater

Cost	$5–15

Address 127 2nd Ave, between St Mark's Place & 7th St
☎212/505-8065
Transportation 6 to Astor Place; N,R to 8th St
Open Daily 6.30am–10pm
Accepts Cash only
Reservations Not accepted

played in several languages and accents. The Hispanic grillman is backstaged by Ukrainian and Polish women stirring up soups from another century. The counter contingent is a nutritionally correct community of hip and haggard, wholesome and sickly, scholarly and street-educated. The prevailing melancholy could transform Reese Witherspoon into a sallow-skinned loner.

Happily, the superlative soups restore color to all complexions: double-thick lima bean, hot rich borscht, salty split pea, and a matzoh ball variety that challenges the Second Avenue Deli's (see p.55) pricier rendition for downtown dominance. So good are these soups that regulars enter the days of the week when their favorite is featured (for curative cabbage soup, it's Mondays and Thursdays) as recurring appointments in their Palm Pilots. You need not be an NYU mathematician to figure out that at a $3 bowl of soup is a better value than a $2.75 cup. But you would need a behavioral psychologist to explain the motivation behind the small price differential. Both sizes come with two slices of sweet, crusty, tan-colored, unbraided challah bread freshly baked in loaf pans. This foundation for the solid and mercifully unfussy French toast ($4.25) will replace any previous notions of challah you might have.

Plenty of other used-to-be standards are perfectly okay: blintzes ($4.75), year-round matzoh brie ($4.25), vegetarian chopped liver sandwich ($4.20), and so on and so forth. Wheatgrass juice and carrot juice are freshly squeezed antidotes for a number of ills and woes, not least of them a fear of B&H's vulnerability. One day it will close and a small New York food light—actually eight hanging food lights—will go out.

Il Bagatto

Il Bagatto's 1995 arrival in Alphabet City augured a turnaround for that then squalid, crack-ridden, last-to-be gentrified section of the East Village. It's been packed nearly every night since, first with appreciative locals and soon after with slumming uptowners pleasantly shocked to find such knowing, rustic cooking in so unlikely a location. At the time, the prevailing idea of Italian sophistication at busy pasta joints around nearby Second Avenue was adding strawberries to

Cost	$20–50

Address 192 East 2nd St, between Aves A & B
☎212/228-0977
Transportation F,V to 2nd Ave
Open Mon–Thurs 6.15–11.45pm, Fri & Sat 6.15pm–12.45am, Sun 6–10.45pm
Accepts Cash only
Reservations Suggested

mixed salads. Il Bagatto limits such quirks to red Christmas lights and spooky grape vines strewn on the brick walls of its dark, noisy, cramped dining room. The downstairs bar/lounge is a merry purgatory for tolerant diners waiting on their table.

All start with a basket of lightly oiled, sometimes-warm focaccia flecked with sea salt. The wondrous antipasto Il Bagatto ($6.50), billed as a sampler plate from an antipasti table which remains mysteriously out of view, can include a slice of spinach frittata, caramelized pearl onions, grilled zucchini and eggplant, a chickpea salad, and gently stewed lentils and tomatoes. It's not going to change your life, but, true to Italian style, each vegetable, free of excessive seasoning, can express its true flavor. Although New York's tomato season is torturously brief, the kitchen manages to procure sweet love apples all year round. Even the January tomatoes spooned atop the grilled, garlic-rubbed, must-have bruschetta ($4) are lively.

Chef-owner Beatrice Tosti's homemade pastas are demonstrably superior to versions in the same low end of town and price range. Gnocchetti verdi e blu ($10) are tiny, feathery spinach gnocchi inseparable from their pungent Gorgonzola. Tortellini con ragu ($9.50) are delectable pasta twists smothered in a toothsome veal ragu. Beyond stuffed and unstuffed pasta (even simple penne and spaghetti soar), the saltimbocca alla Romana ($14.50) is a generous veal scallop nattily cloaked in prosciutto and fried sage leaves, sided with potatoes roasted to their amber-hued peak. For dessert, the winner is the tartufo ($5), a ball of chocolate ice cream and lusciously eggy, frozen zabaglione rolled in cocoa.

Banjara

In the New York restaurant universe, everything is relative. Had Banjara opened elsewhere with the same menu, decor, and staff, it could well be admired for its affordable menu, cozy informality, and cute, delivery-friendly reformatting of traditional Indian dishes. But because it's spread out in two adjacent storefronts at the bottom of a block packed with dirt-cheap Bangladeshi joints, Banjara is instead tolerated as the

Cost	$15–45

Address 97 1st Ave at 6th St
℗212/477-5956
Transportation 6 to Astor
Place; F,V to 2nd Ave
Open Mon–Thurs 3.30pm–
midnight, Fri–Sun noon–1am
Accepts All major credit cards

expensive and quasi-fancy place on East Sixth, with refined service and cuisine that's too precious by half. This is only to be expected when the $17.95 that you're fairly charging for a fistful of charcoal-broiled prawns buys a complete dinner at your next-door neighbor's.

Location should not matter in a place named after a colorful gypsy tribe from Rajasthan who've roamed the 22 states of India. And it certainly becomes irrelevant once you appreciate that Tuhin Dutta is, to our knowledge, the only chef in Manhattan preparing Indian-style dumpakht. The subcontinent's counterpart to British meat pies, American pot pies, and French *en croûte*, dumpakht (the name and origin are Persian) is a centuries-old concoction. A mildly spiced stew is encased in a pastry and then baked, effectively sealing in its juices until the diner's fork breaks the lid. Banjara prepares four dumpakht varieties in a lightly salted shell that supposedly contains only water, salt, and flour: lamb ($12.95), chicken ($12.95), shrimp ($17.95), and vegetable ($11.95). Even without the benefit of a pastry, Dutta does a splendid job keeping his tandoori dishes moist. The adraki chop ($17.95) consists of ginger-spiced grilled lamb chops that exit the clay oven in superbly succulent shape. There are few better chops at this price anywhere.

The "cutesy" label does fit several of the appetizers, including the dhakshin se shuru ($6.95), a Southern Indian mixed dish of bite-sized idli (steamed rice and lentil cakes) and mini-dosa (potato-filled pancakes) that are nothing more than teasers. The condiments (mango chutney, raita, lemon pickles) and breads, however, are outstanding. When ordering a plain, garlic, or potato-stuffed nan, be sure to ask for it "dry." Otherwise it comes needlessly slathered in ghee (clarified butter).

Bar Veloce

The Italian films that play silently on the plasma flat screen TV at Bar Veloce are not meant to be a distraction. Concerned that people might clog the front of his narrow wine bar, owner Frederick Twomey wanted only to intro- duce some movement in the rear of a confined space. And there's a practical benefit, too. If your companion, existing or prospective, has his or her back to a screening of Fellini's *La Dolce Vita*, the English subtitles are there to be used like some cinematic Cyrano, feeding you clever dialogue. Need an icebreaker? "It may seem strange but I know you well" flashes across the bottom of the screen. Is the conversation getting too heavy? Then repeat as follows: "If you're going to be serious I shan't listen to you." Is he or she resisting your charms? Then pass on the immortal message: "Let yourself be dominated body and soul."

Cost	$20–40

Address 175 2nd Ave, between 11th & 12th Sts; plus other locations
☎212/260-3200
Transportation L to 1st Ave; 4,5,6,N,Q,R,W to 14th St–Union Square
Open Daily 5pm–3am
Accepts All major credit cards
Reservations Not accepted

ITALIAN

Choosing just the right Italian wines, panini, and various bread-top- ping tidbits requires no prompting from Marcello Mastroianni. You need only consult the stain-resistant menu, which has a list of bruschetta (toasted bread with toppings), panini (grill-pressed sandwiches), tramezzini (small sandwiches on untoasted bread), and easy-to-share platters on one side and a list of thirty young wines, each with a mod- estly helpful description, on the reverse. The harmless 1998 Aglianico from Cantina del Taburno in Sicily ($7/glass) and the fruity 1997 Nebbiolo d'Alba from Luca Abrate in Piedmont ($14/glass) are among the bottles suspended behind the bar in a back-lit, zigzag wine rack. The bar itself, all polyurethane plywood, further displays architect Anthony Caradonna's modern and very cool blueprint.

The design of the slender sandwiches merits favourable and repeated notice; the proscuitto di Parma panino ($8) with its melted mesh of mushrooms, truffle oil, and Fontina, or the dainty, triple-decker tramezzino of black olive paste, arugula, and pristine mozzarella on white bread ($4). And anyone with a sweet tooth will love the dreamy dessert panino of Nutella and gelato ($5) that is a crunchy cross between a wafer and a Felliniesque ice cream sandwich.

Casimir

(🍴) The lazy ceiling fans and dim globe lights suggest a low-voltage locale beside a Mediterranean port. The ochre-painted walls are hung, as we imagine all authentic Parisian bistros to be, with mirrors distorted by age and rusty placards advertising brands of classic French drinks. But just as the magic of the movie *Casablanca* is a reflection of Hollywood's making, not Europe's or Morocco's, the enchantment of Casimir reflects a blend of ingenuity and budget sophistication more at home on Avenue B than on the boulevard Saint-Germain. Its owners and origins, though Parisian, have found their special place, like so many emigrés before them, near the Lower East Side. The great ambition of Casimir is not only to make possible a pretty good order of steak frites for $14, but also to keep their eye on what the pricey, trendy eateries are up to uptown. Signs of trickle-down gastronomics include salads covered with Jackson Pollock-like splatters of balsamic vinegar and vertically assembled entrees poked with a mad flourish of fresh herb stems. Somewhere in the kitchen is a pent-up painter or, at the very least, a frustrated florist.

Cost	$30–50

Address 103–105 Ave B, between 6th & 7th Sts
☎212/358-9683
Transportation 6 to Astor Place
Open Daily 6pm–midnight
Accepts AmEx
Reservations Required

Best among the appetizer arrangements (mostly $7.50) are the toss of sautéed chicken livers, sweet balsamic, greens, and fried onions; the sliced grilled garlic sausage with a roast potato salad; and the "Velodrome" salad with enough arugula, shaved parmesan, and garlic croutons for two adults to share.

The main course menu offers lots of appealing places to go. For simplicity, take the superbly crisp-skinned duck confit ($14). For rusticity, go in the direction of the pig's feet ($14), palatably served off the bone in a chopped mound of soft, gelatinous meat cushioned by celery root mashed potatoes. For domesticity, hop on to the hamburger New Orleans ($10)—a fat, juicy, two-fisted, five-napkin job topped with bacon and grilled onions and slipped into a ciabatta roll. Desserts ($5-6) are uneven, but you could do worse than go for the molten chocolate cake, an abstract work of art that might better be titled as "black and red composition with chocolate orb."

Chez Es Saada

(icon) When Charles Boyer melted the defenses of Hedy Lamarr with his immortal line, "Come wiz me to the casbah," he surely had a place like Chez Es Saada in mind. But it's worth betting that *she* wouldn't have expected to find the "house of happiness" and its labyrinth of dark rooms, narrow archways, and rose-petal-strewn passages in an old red schoolhouse on the Lower East Side. Photographer Michael James O'Brien and agent Robert McElroy conspired with

Cost	$35–75

Address 42 East 1st St, between 1st & 2nd Aves
℡212/777-5617
Transportation F, V to 2nd Ave
Open Sun–Thurs 6pm–1am, Fri & Sat 6pm–3.30am
Accepts All major credit cards
Reservations Suggested

FRENCH/NORTH AFRICAN

restaurateurs Nicola Kotsoni and Steve Tzolis to bring the intrigue, decadence, and French colonial flavor of old North Africa to an unmarked building way east on First Street. Passers-by enticed by the first-floor cafe and its mosaic tables salvaged from Matisse's favorite hotel in Tangier respond to the subterranean cocktail lounge, bar, and noisy dining room in different ways. Some perceive a discreet hideaway for exotic drinks; others, a place to see and be seen. But most behold a cozy, pricey bistro beautifully outfitted with Moroccan antiques and fabrics.

Consulting chef Frank Crispo composed the simple menu and its takes on French and Moroccan standards. The assorted Salades Marrakesh ($13), among them crisp endive leaves cradling cumin-scented fava-bean dip and roasted red beets with basil, lemon juice, and olive oil, are superb. Consider also the quartet of braewats ($10)—flaky, ungreasy phyllo triangles filled with either spinach and cheese or a seafood mixture (sole, shrimp, squid) spiced with the ubiquitous cumin and cilantro. From the French column, splendid chicken liver pâté gets a Mediterranean makeover of tomato concassée, olives, fine herbs, and croutons ($11).

The steak au poivre ($26) and the succulent roast chicken, with its roast garlic-thyme sauce and potato-fennel purée ($21), stand up to any you'll find at your favorite French bistro. And the Moroccan entrees won't offend purists, though both varieties of bisteeya (the traditional phyllo pie; $24) are not as sweet as usual. The folded pouch filled with chicken, saffron, veggies, and toasted almonds has the edge over its seafood counterpart. A decent dessert like the chocolate pot de crème is an afterthought ($5): mint tea is the surest way out of the casbah.

Col Legno

(icon) On a block brimming with Japanese food outlets of every shape and color, Col Legno stands out for its Tuscan plainness. A single room in the requisite shade of golden yellowish sienna (can you even buy white paint in Tuscany?) has a conical wood-burning pizza oven tucked in the corner. Col Legno means "with wood" and is probably a pun referring to the pizza oven and apple-wood grill, but it can also describe the technique whereby a violinist strikes the strings with the wooden part of the bow. Inside the spa-

Cost	$25–55

Address 231 East 9th St, between 2nd & 3rd Aves
☎212/777-4650
Transportation 6 to Astor Place; N,R to 8th St; E9 between 2nd and 3rd Aves
Open Tues–Sun 6–11.30pm
Accepts AmEx
Reservations Suggested

cious, semi-open back kitchen, a rustic table (does this Italian region permit any other kind?) can be reserved for up to ten people. The resolutely unassuming restaurant attracts neighborhood regulars, NYU grad students and faculty, those attending the Public Theater or more avant-garde performances at P.S. 122, and anyone with persistent yearnings for honest Florentine food.

Except for seasonal shifts in ingredients and upward ticks in the low-to-moderate prices, the trattoria menu has changed very little over the years. It's a welcome break from trendy eateries where everything has to be new and the recitation of specials requires a superhuman attention span. Consistency and hospitality of this high standard are plusses in themselves. Chef-owner Chris Trilivas is always on hand to ensure the integrity of his recipes, starting with soup ($6.95)—a brothy white bean and sage soup in the winter, and a summer purée soup of cold tomato, red bell pepper and basil—or perhaps fried baby artichokes flattened and splayed in the Roman "Jewish" style ($6.95). Country bread imported from Hoboken and several wine finds under $20 keep all appetizers in the very best company.

Among pastas, only the spinach lasagna doesn't inspire lasting loyalty. Try the pappardelle with rosemary-scented wild boar ragu ($13.95) or the spaghetti with mint-flavored paste ($12.95) and you'll have a hard time coming back for anything else. That would be a shame, though. The wood-grilled, fennel-infused pork chops ($14.95) are dandy. And the rosemary-rubbed bistecca ($15.95) is one of the best grilled steak bargains in the city. Right up to the hazelnut gelato, Trilivas hits all the right notes.

Dok Suni's

(🍴) Though several chefs, restaurateurs, and journalists can claim
some credit for guiding Korean food into
the Manhattan mainstream, Jenny Kwak
and her mother Myung Ja are indisputably
the city's original pioneers of kimchee
chic. Back in 1993, the idea of a hip
Korean place that didn't limit itself to
tabletop barbecue was outrageous, and
might have stayed that way too if Kwak,
then 19, wasn't so naïve. "I didn't know
better," she recalls. "Just coming out of
school, I was so excited to be eating the

Cost	$25-50
Address 119 1st Ave, between St Mark's Place & 7th St	
☎212/477-9506	
Transportation 6 to Astor Place	
Open Sun & Mon 4.30–11pm, Tues–Sat 4.30pm–midnight	
Accepts Cash only	
Reservations Not accepted	

food I loved again." A year later, the small, dark, cramped space was filling
up early and staying full late with quasi-trendy clubbers, NYU students, and
in-the-know audiences from the catty-cornered P.S. 122. Nowadays, Dok
Suni's cachet even extends to the burbs. Pierced and savvy waitresses
have grown accustomed to serving saketinis to Benetton-clad couples
who've hooked up through Internet dating services.

The menu is country Korean mom's food with a couple of ethno
twists, best exemplified by the jalapeno chicken ($12.95), battered, pan-
fried chicken nuggets with jalapenos, soy sauce, and garlic sauce. It's supposed to be a main course, but it certainly doesn't have to be. You'd be
wise not to choose it over two stellar appetizers, though: the fritter-like
kimchee pancakes with soy and vinegar dipping sauce ($5) and the o-
bok salad of green perilla leaves and barley noodles in a tangy-spicy
mustard and vinegar dressing ($9). Traditional broths and stews, like the
feel-good miso stew with tofu, zucchini, and mushrooms, or the vegetable dumpling soup in an egg-drop beef broth are, at $9.95, delight-
fully affordable. In each there's a meal for one or an appetizer for three.

No main course can beat the tender, slow-broiled pork ribs in a spicy
chile pepper and garlic sauce ($14.95). But you should still try the
broiled squid with mixed veggies in a spicy red pepper sauce ($14.95),
assuming you haven't already had the cornmeal fried squid starter, and
bibimbop ($13.95), the catch-all rice dish tossed hot or cold with that
deadly red pepper sauce. Before leaving, say "an-nyong-hi" with a shot
of the sweetened cinnamon drink.

The Elephant

🍴 An anchor tenant smack in the middle of East Village's restaurant row, the mouse-sized Elephant shows no signs of slowing down despite having enjoyed several years happily spilling out onto the sidewalk. With its softly glowing zinc bar, sprays of red Christmas lights, dangling banana bunches, beaded curtains, and zebra-striped banquettes, this diminutive Thai bistro generates a seductive, psychic warmth that helps you put up with, and even enjoy, the jostled wait for a tiny table. It helps to set yourself up with a glass of sangria ($7) ladled from the bowl behind the bar and watch the loud, thirsty, and beautiful crowd shout at themselves over the bass-rumbling music.

Cost	$15–45

Address 58 East 1st St,
between 1st & 2nd Aves
☎212/505-7739
Transportation F,V to 2nd Ave
Open Mon–Thurs 11.30 am–
3.30pm & 5.30pm–midnight,
Fri & Sat 11.30am–3.30 pm &
5.30pm–1am, Sun 5.30pm–
midnight
Accepts AmEx

It's prudent not to get distracted by the French-inflected options (and staff), but to order as you would at a favorite Thai takeout. Hot and sour soup with lime leaves and prawns ($5.75) and summer rolls with shrimp ($6.75) are light, well-balanced expressions of standards. The plentiful and eminently biteable grilled calamari ($7.75) is set off by a vibrant salad of spinach, frisée, mango, and a stealthy leaf or two of cilantro dressed with tamarind and lime. Moist if unremarkable chicken satay ($8.75) begets a thick, sweet peanut dip. As a main course, good old pad Thai ($16.75) earns its place on a grownup white dinner plate. The peanuts taste freshly ground, the bean sprouts stand to attention, and the large and tender tiger shrimp abound in a piping hot jungle of spice-tinged rice noodles.

The beef in an eponymous salad ($16.75) is discernibly seared to order, and is served with a puff of steaming jasmine rice, shredded mint leaves, and harmlessly silly swirls of mango purée and spicy red pepper that one associates with mid-90s decadence and dime-store squirt bottles. Order dessert ($6.50) if you must, but prepare for a letdown after the decisive, clear flavors of your savories. The lemongrass and lime tart with passionfruit sorbet alone comes close to approximating the cool and sexy heat of earlier courses.

Euzkadi

🍴 Euzkadi is a political name meaning either "Basque Fatherland," or, here on East Fourth Street, "budget bistro opportunistically highlighting a hitherto overlooked regional cuisine we the owners don't really know all that well." The design, though not patently Basque, does have the feel of a hideaway for romantic bohemians if not radical separatists. Outside, brickwork paved into the tiny sidewalk terrace is inlayed with a broken-tile mosaic spelling "Euzkadi." Inside, small wood tables, bentwood chairs, red

Cost	$28–55

Address 108 East 4th St, between 1st & 2nd Aves
☎212/982-9788
Transportation F,V to 2nd Ave
Open Sun 4–10pm, Mon–Thurs 6–11pm, Fri & Sat 6pm–midnight
Accepts Cash only
Reservations Required

banquettes, and stark ceiling fans are crammed into a dark, noisy, smoky room in which round-cornered, wood-framed antique mirrors are hung on the exposed-brick walls. As getting up and down from tables is a strain both on you and your neighbors, it's a good idea to visit the restroom before settling down to eat.

Chef Serge Buzkowski isn't Basque, but he apparently owns a fine Basque cookbook or two which he's put to good use. You'll have no trouble digesting your meal, or your dinner check, and you will get a diverting, three-course immersion in the key components of Basque table: garlic, peppers, olives, shellfish, salt cod, fennel, beans, potatoes, but, oddly, not rice (unless ordered as a side dish). Top starters include perfectly grilled sardines with herb oil ($7), sautéed calamari piperade with stewed onions, peppers, and tomatoes ($7), crab and fennel remoulade accompanied by a golden eggplant beignet ($8), and a salt-cod pairing of an okay crabcake and decent stuffed piquillo pepper ($8).

About half the entree choices are served "a la plancha," meaning they're sizzling on a cast-iron skillet. All are $14. Best of these is an enormous, whole, stunningly pink duck breast with olives in a sticky-thick red wine reduction (great for sweeping into garlic mashed potatoes) and sweet, juicy head-on shrimp with lemon and garlic. But the skate with brown butter sauce gets cooked out in this format. Better to go outside the category to the flaky, roasted cod encrusted in black olives ($15). Among desserts (all $5), the sensation is the fig brochette speared with rosemary. But the prune clafoutis, quince tarte tatin, and chestnut rice pudding all use their flavors well.

East Village

First

There was a time, not so long ago, when the East Village was a culinary ghetto nourished by curry-in-a-hurry, pierogi-in-a-pinch, and fettuccine-on-the-cheap. Nothing high-rent or high-minded. This did not deter Sam DeMarco, an energetic and talented chef, from attempting in 1994 a first on First with First, a self-consciously slick, steel-accented spot that soon became *the* after-work chefs' haunt for globally aware contemporary American cuisine. DeMarco clearly had vision. It wasn't the neighborhood that gave life to the chef and his groundbreaking restaurant. It was the other way around. Consequently, he's the pioneer who deserves much of the credit—or blame—for the ensuing influx of trendy, pretentious, and pricey bistros.

Cost	$25–75

Address 87 1st Ave, between 5th & 6th Sts
℡212/674-3823
Transportation 6 to Astor Place; N,R to 8th St
Open Mon–Thurs 6pm–2am, Fri & Sat 6pm–3am, Sun 6pm–1am
Accepts All major credit cards
Reservations Recommended

It is easy to see now why First was so quickly accepted: DeMarco's food is fun, tasty, and reasonable. Start off with lots of his signature appetizers: fiery Buffalo lollipop wings with warm blue cheese fondue ($14); Mexican seafood tacos packed with rock shrimp, cheese, and black beans ($11); a quartet of mini-cheeseburgers with a vat of thin, crisp, 22-carat fries ($14). Fried oysters paired with wasabe mayo ($11)—once, if you can imagine, an original idea—are golden and greaseless.

If you're still hungry after those must-haves, entrees won't let you down. Moist, buttery, sage-roasted chicken is teamed with a rustic butternut squash gratin ($19), while soy-honey marinated duck comes with a pile of fluffy kasha and a blackberry Burgundy sauce ($24). And for the ultimate in beef indulgence for two: a 42oz porterhouse with fries ($75). Share it with someone "special" (ie, they're paying), or just with a good friend who likes to eat lots of tender, juicy, flavorful steak. The full menu is available at the bar, but this is not really a bar for dining. It's usually three-deep with martini-swigging hipsters drawn to the infamous Tiny Tinis: a dozen creative concoctions available in three sizes—medium ($8), large ($14), and gigunda (read: pass out fast for $22). These 'tails are guaranteed to quench your thirst and make you forget your worries or your name, whichever comes first.

Frank

(🍴) The good fortunes of Frank Prisinzano and his Neapolitan-Sicilian-Pugliese-American baby have ushered in a new era for cheap, cheerful, and physically challenged Italian joints. Whereas its predecessors wowed the hungry masses by fitting such uptown fashions as tricolore salads, flavored pastas, and anything remotely Tuscan into a low-rent, no-frills mold, Frank's formula is based on indulging nostalgic yearnings for yummy tummy food. The flea market jumble of mix-and-match tables, baroque mirrors, sepia-toned family photos, and bric-a-brac assembled in this tiny trattoria create an irresistible setting for old-fashioned, red-sauced satisfaction.

| Cost | Lunch $11–50 |
| | Dinner $18–50 |

Address 88 2nd Ave, between 5th & 6th Sts
☏212/420-0202
Transportation F,V to 2nd Ave; 6 to Astor Place
Open Mon–Thurs 10.30am–12.45am, Fri & Sat 10.30am–1.45am, Sun 10.30am–midnight
Accepts Cash only
Reservations For large groups

Curiously, Frank's feel-good foods don't belong to any single place or era. Like the decoration, they comprise a contrived hodgepodge reflecting both the owner's Italian roots and New Yorkese ingenuity. A golden oldie like garlic bread ($4.25; $7.25 topped with Sicilian salted anchovies), for instance, looks nothing like the article of red-checkered tablecloth pasts. But its mere suggestion hits the right note and its thick layer of chopped roasted garlic suggests grandmotherly excess. Similarly, the Tuscan crostino nero ($6.95), smeared with mashed chicken livers, may be new to many of us, yet it has the qualities of something comfortingly familiar. And the use of the word "gravy" to identify a tomato ragu is itself a shrewd example of menu manipulation, inviting as it does all sorts of warm associations with a happy American childhood. That gravy coats both the rigatoni al ragu ($9.95) and the polpettone ($11.95), the mammoth meatball that leads otherwise sensible people to endure long waits and cramped conditions. The main course well worth knocking elbows with strangers for is fava e cicoria ($13.95), a soothing purée of fava beans with chicory and roasted vegetables. Desserts succeed mostly in bumping up the check.

With 400 Italian wines stocked in three, 520-bottle wine cabinets, Frank likely offers more wines per square foot than any restaurant in America, and makes it possible to pair a $200 Barolo with a $12 meatball.

East Village

Hasaki

Despite the huge number of sleekly designed sushi bars in NYC, nightly waits endure at the overcrowded and deceptively uninviting Hasaki. Many spend so much time huddled in the doorway and on the steps outside it that that they ought to pay rent for the space. First-timers told of Madonna sightings and celebrity regulars are baffled to behold a place so thoroughly devoid of glamor. The only features that might possibly be called decorative—at a stretch—are the empty wooden wall frames that could, after a few glasses of sake, be mistaken for surreal windows. There are just two viable reasons to be here: for exceptional sushi artistry at a moderate price or to flirt with one of the singles waiting in the vestibule.

Cost	$25–65

Address 210 East 9th St, between 2nd & 3rd Aves
☎212/473-3327
Transportation 6 to Astor Place; N,R to 8th St
Open Mon–Fri 5.30–11.30pm, Sat & Sun 1–4pm & 5.30–11.30pm
Accepts All major credit cards
Reservations Not accepted

When sitting at the bar you quickly become aware that the graceful sushi chefs are not a trio of equals. The even-tempered Kawano, stationed left, appears to do most of the heavy lifting. When an order comes in for a house specialty, say the naruto zukuri ($14)—sea urchin rolled in a meticulously fluted tube of squid and then thinly sliced—the assignment is his. A request for the comparatively routine, yet exquisitely perfumed, roll of ume (plum) paste and shiso leaf ($3.50) on the other hand, may go to any one of the chefs.

While the best bet is to order what you like, know that there are some winners in some unlikely places. The precise cut of the carrots in the futomaki ($6) is itself worth the price. And the yellowtail special ($6) is indeed that: an inside-out roll of lush yellowtail pieces, carrot, and scallion all coated in flying fish caviar. Individual pieces of Portuguese octopus ($2.50), Japanese red snapper ($4), and the mackerel-like shima-aji ($5) shine, as literally does anything with eel, warmed in a Bagel Best toaster oven before being draped over rice. Finally, notice the details: the impossibly fine strands of nori (purple seaweed), the faintly coarse wasabi, the lingering fragrance of the pickled ginger. With jewels as precious as these, who cares how lacklustre the box they come in?

Haveli

🍴 This bold attempt to upgrade East Village Indian dining can no longer be regarded as an experiment. The frosted-glass storefront of the stylish, design-conscious Haveli is now a Second Avenue fixture, as is its host Mohammed Hazim. And once you've been exposed to the rich, complex cooking of chef Siradul Islam (who, like most of the chefs in the area's Indian restaurants, hails from Bangladesh), a return to one-note curries

Cost	$20–55

Address 100 2nd Ave, between 5th & 6th Sts
☎212/982-0533
Transportation 6 to Astor Place; F to 2nd Ave
Open Daily noon–midnight
Accepts All major credit cards

and generic spice blends is problematic. Indeed, the downside of your trying the $8.95 mushroom shaag will be your subsequent distaste for the mushy, $5.95 versions that used to make you happy. As it happens, the cost of being so spoiled is rarely this reasonable. Only near East Sixth could Haveli's moderate prices be described as exorbitant. Move this place uptown and it would be the pride of the neighborhood.

The pleasures may be as subtle and soothing as rasam ($3.95), a Southern Indian soup with lentils, sesame, and the gentle tang of curry leaf, or as jazzy and jaunty as do-piaz curry (lamb cooked with plenty of onions and an orchestra of spices; $8.75). The distinct, wholewheatness of the flaky paratha ($2.50) is not lost when that bread is filled with onions or potatoes. To go with it, spinach raita ($2.95) is a lovely alternative to the cucumber version. Poori bhajee ($3.50), an appetizer of fried chickpeas and fluffy poori bread, is nicely salted and almost lemony. The sautéed chicken livers ($3.95) are pleasantly spiced. And vegetable pakora ($3.95) are superbly fresh and far-from-greasy fritters.

Yogurt-marinated tandoori entrees—mixed grill ($15.95), mugha tikka (boneless chicken breast chunks; $12.25)—are unexpectedly succulent. But the best grilled dish must be the reshmi kabab ($15.50), a skewer of chicken chunks buzzed with ginger and garlic. Another house specialty that's practically a New York exclusive is the chicken, lamb, and vegetable balti ($14.95). A British cooking craze that originated in Northern Pakistan, balti refers to the sizzling, cast-iron bucket in which the meats, tomatoes, cilantro, and spices are cooked and served. Come dessert, homemade mango ice cream ($2.50) leaves you thinking, "Isn't mango the best fruit in the world?"

East Village

Iso

🍴 That Iso is closed on Sundays would seem to support the maxim that you shouldn't eat seafood in a restaurant on the day when there are no fresh fish deliveries. But this never-on-Sunday rule mistakenly assumes restaurants are serving all their fish the day they get it. In fact, you would feel more secure eating sashimi on a Sunday at Iso than on other days at many other places. Iso, the older gentleman behind the sushi bar, has proven himself to be one of Manhattan's shrewdest fish buyers. The view from the sidewalk is telling: the

Cost	$25–60

Address 175 2nd Ave at 11th St

☎212/777-0361

Transportation 6,N,Q,R,W to 14th St-Union Square; L to 1st Ave

Open Mon–Sat 5.30pm–midnight

Accepts All major credit cards

Reservations Not accepted

menu posted in the window relies heavily on specials, reflecting a selection determined by what fresh fish Iso chooses to buy from purveyors and not the other way around, while the line of loyalists waiting to get in assures rapid and regular turnover.

The ceiling's network of black piping and spotlights may suit an off-off-Broadway theater, but their purpose in a cramped eatery is not immediately clear. The three fixtures of note are the stainless-steel sake pitchers, the logo of circling dolphins and human figures designed by the late artist and former regular Keith Haring, and Iso herself, the sweet, mop-topped hostess who answers to the same name as her husband. The amiable waiters go into performance mode when reciting such specials as marinated mackerel with garlic and marinated grated onion ($7.50); sea urchin on the half-shell ($9.50); extremely tender orange clam sashimi with a sharp ponzu sauce ($10.50); and rolled and steamed monkish liver ($9.50)—the Japanese foie gras—that manages to be both unctuous and light. The bonito sashimi appetizer ($9.50) is a pleasure.

The benefit of the stage lighting becomes clearer when the sashimi combo ($22) makes its entrance. It consists of six large, lush, and astoundingly fresh fish chosen by Mr Iso. The sushi special combo ($21) with nine pieces and a tuna roll is similarly stunning. The green tea (hot water and a tea bag) and desserts are disappointments. After consuming all this great fish, every day is wrong for apricot Grand Marnier cake ($5.75) or triple chocolate mousse cake ($6.75).

Jade Mountain

(🍴) "Chow Mein" billboards like the red-neon original hung here between the windows of apartments 2A and 3A would once have functioned as lighthouses for the hungry and the dislocated. Nighttime navigators returning from long absences at war, at work, or at the corner saloon recognized them as the first sure sign home was near. Others saw them as beacons when home—or, more precisely, the kitchen—was the last place they wanted to be. This relic designates the last of the Manhattan Chinese chop

Cost	$7–30
Address 197 2nd Ave, between 12th & 13th Sts	
☎212/533-3770	
Transportation L to 1st Ave; N,R,Q,W to 14th St-Union Square	
Open Daily 11.30am–11pm	
Accepts Cash only	
Reservations Not accepted	

suey houses as we, our grandparents, and Ralph Kramden understood them to be. Who had as much as a clue about Szechuan and Hunan, Hong Kong and Shanghai, Fukien and Canton, Shantung and Taiwan at a time when all neighborhood Chinese restaurant menus were broken down into two groups, column A and column B?

Forlorn Jade Mountain faithfully preserves the genuine chop-suey-parlor experience. Its menu upholds such forgotten classics as pork chop suey ($4.50), chicken egg foo young ($4.50), moo goo gai pan ($6.25), lobster Cantonese-style ($15.95), and nine varieties of chow mein ($4.50-7.95). These may be ordered from columns A and B in value-oriented family meals—as if the prices were not low enough.

None of this is to suggest that Jade Mountain is a very good "good restaurant." It is, however, a very good "bad restaurant." The kitchen does do "bad"—greasy, starchy, gloppy, salty, phony, or merely bad-for-you—food extremely well. And though we may congratulate ourselves for faithfully reading the food pages and learning how to eat better, our new-found sophistication should not deny us the pleasures of an occasional cheap chowdown. Besides, there is culinary merit at Jade Mountain, if you look hard enough: witness the butterfly shrimp ($8.75), which predates the current fashion for bacon-wrapped seafood by decades, and the war sho op, which requires a whole duck to be fried, boiled, skinned, and boned before the meat can be ground, stuffed back into the skin, cut into cubes, sautéed, and topped with toasted almonds and brown sauce. That's a lot of labor for $7.50. A labor of love.

ITALIAN

Lavagna

At first glance, Lavagna appears too perfect to be the rustic East Village *trattoria del giorno*. The exposed-brick and burgundy walls come across as overly polished, the untarnished pressed-tin ceiling gives the impression of bronze plastic, and the yellow-glass shades of the wrought-iron, 1950s-Gothic chande-liers seem to have been salvaged from a New Jersey roadhouse rather than a Tuscan osteria. Inside the kitchen, the double-stone-arched, copper-encased,

Cost	$25–60

Address 545 East 5th St, between Aves A & B
☎212/979-1005
Transportation F,V to 2nd Ave
Open Mon–Thurs 6–11pm, Fri & Sat 6pm–midnight, Sun 5–11pm
Accepts AmEx

wood-burning oven is surely a rich kid's toy. And the knowledge that Sami Kader also owns Le Tableau, the French *bistro du jour* on the same block, fuels speculation that Lavagna is the skilled forgery of an opportunist.

Nothing is as palpably calculated, however, as executive chef Amanda Frietag's Italian adaptations. Her cooking is way too good for what they're charging. Something suspicious is going on and we're deter-mined to get to the bottom of it—if it takes dozens of visits to do so. What's this business with the soft polenta matched to a lush, sautéed sweetbread ragu with wild mushrooms and white truffle oil ($9)? That's no appetizer. That's a great main dish. And what's this fritto misto (mixed fry; $9) doing in the top appetizer position normally reserved for cala-mari? The freshly fried and speedily delivered tiger shrimp (so *that's* what shrimp taste like!), sea scallops, fennel, and zucchini are incredible.

Pastas too are suspiciously first-rate. The fresh pappardelle with braised, mega-shredded rabbit, thyme, and olives ($14) is phenomenal. Specials like fresh tagliatelle with shredded duck confit, chopped leeks, and crem-ini mushrooms ($16) display unusual delicacy for so harried a kitchen. Of the meats and fish, the grilled pork chop ($14) reveals itself to be a juicy sensation—once you can tear yourself away from the accompany-ing velvety chestnut flan. And wood-roasted whole red snapper ($17 per person) is solid. The flat crust of the intriguing pizzettes ($9) is cracker crisp and biscuit-like, but there's no life to it. For dessert ($6), consider the superb pistachio biscotti plate served with a sweet Sicilian wine for dunking. *Then* try to figure out what is really going on with this amaz-ing restaurant.

Lil' Frankie's Pizza

🍴 This spin-off of the madly popular Frank (see p.41) begins with the same set of sentimental, mismatched curios—dinette tables, cutlery, and dishware; old family photos; gilded mirrors—which give that Italian eatery such charm. The low prices, and the lines outside the door during peak times, are also reminiscent of its forerunner. The great departure here starts with the wood-burning brick pizza oven, supposedly built with real Neapolitan lava from Mount Vesuvius, and concludes with a lofty rear dining room that features beautiful dark-wood wine racks, a lacquered floor adorned with happy flowers, and, painted on the wall above a round communal table, a cherub-faced sun. The only thing that could make this sky-lit space feel airier would be to remove its ceiling entirely—which is hardly necessary since there is already a backyard garden for warm-weather dining.

Cost	$10–40

Address 19 1st Ave, between 1st & 2nd Sts
☎212/420-4900
Transportation F,V to 2nd Ave
Open Sun–Wed 9am–2am, Thurs 9am–3pm, Fri & Sat 9am–4am
Accepts Cash only
Reservations For large groups

Though the cracker-thin pizzas ($4.95–9.95) lack the pleasing chewiness and puffed rims of a classic New York pie, the 12-inch disks are nevertheless crisp and unexpectedly light, allowing you to dig more deeply into the menu. First-rate toppings range from the Napoletana, with tomatoes, garlic, oregano, capers, black olives, Sicilian salted anchovies, and—as is proper with authentic anchovy pizzas—no cheese, to the Polpettini, with tomato, mozzarella, fresh sage, and baby meatballs the size of blueberries.

The most welcome surprise is the quality of the other foods cooked in the intense heat of that brick oven. The stemless wood-roasted Portobello ($6.95), plated with sweet roasted tomato and peppery arugula, is clearly the best appetizer. Only the house-cured tuna ($6.95), served with white beans, red onions, parsley, and olive oil comes close. The whole roasted eggplant ($3.95) is sliced open at the table and thus still steaming as you scoop out its softened, smoky pulp. Talk about a pure pleasure! And the oven-roasted chicken, with sage, capers, lemon juice, and a side of mashed potatoes ($10.95) is a joy from first bite to last. Decent tiramisu ($6.75) and panna cotta ($5.95) appear overpriced in comparison to the budget-priced pizzas and savories.

East Village

Lucien

🍴 Lucien Bahaj has worked in two places where $80 can amount to pocket change: the French Riviera and Manhattan. But at this magical little rendezvous of Gallic charm and New York verve, that measly amount buys a bottle of fruity red, garlicky escargots, steak frites, a warm chocolate cake, and a short espresso. Lucien's notion of New York glamor, though admittedly more

Cost	$30–75

Address 14 1st Ave at 1st St
☎212/260-6481
Transportation F,V to 2nd Ave
Open Daily 10am–2am
Accepts Cash only
Reservations Suggested

black turtleneck than blue collar, is a world apart from a manic restaurant scene fueled by helium dinner checks and status-bestowing tables so in demand they could be sold as time shares. When sufficiently settled down into one of the makeshift bistro's old chairs and young wines, you can even see the rationale, if not the sanity, of Bahaj's most outrageous claim: the Lower East Side is more beautiful, he says from experience, than France's Mediterranean coast. The narrow space, with ochre walls, dark-wood, and somber globes emitting Left Bank melancholy, is shaped like a telephone headset. Small dining areas in the front and back are connected by the four-seat bar that faces a kitchenette.

The top appetizer offered by the Serbian chef known as Vule is mussels marinières ($9), coming as it does with enough meaty mollusks to occupy three diners and enough buttery white wine broth to drench three sliced baguettes. Grilled fresh sardines ($8) benefit from timid seasoning, whereas the chunky salmon tartare on a black-peppered plate ($10) does not. Thankfully, no such restraint afflicts the Provençal fish soup ($6).

Among three steak frites variations ($20), all of them served with bronzed shoestring fries, the grill-striped flank steak is the one you want. The squab "Christopher" ($26), on the other hand, is a tougher call. Considering the rough-and-ready setting, it's a rather preposterous idea. Inspired by a specialty of the acclaimed Parisian restaurant Taillevent, it uses all of Lucien's vertical space to stack tender roast squab with good-quality foie gras and sautéed Portobellos. The dessert menu lists three outstanding options: the chocolate cake, the crème brûlée, and the chunky, beautifully caramelized tarte tatin. Any one of these makes $6 go a long way.

Mamlouk

On a block of grimy, weather-beaten tenements, Mamlouk's dated distressed-wood facade is no more convincing than a pair of antiqued blue jeans from J Crew. But word of the seductive inducements within the dark and diminutive dining space—namely gracious service; pure, vibrant, flavors; and a six-course, $30 prix fixe (and choice-fixed) dinner—lures amenable eaters from far and wide. With no menu and only the entree option of meat or fish for expressing personal choice, Mamlouk is not for control freaks. But anyone willing to trust the owners and staff who've honed their skills at the fresh and lovely Moustache restaurants (see p.170) can relax among stacks of silk and velvet cushions and prepare to be well fed.

Cost	$37–60

Address 221 East 4th St,
between Aves A & B
℡212/529-3477
Transportation F,V to 2nd Ave
Open Tues–Sun 7–10pm
Accepts MasterCard & Visa
Reservations For large groups

Dinner typically begins with a plate of crunchy, picked vegetables—carrots, radishes, cucumbers, sweet peppers, and so on. Next, a modest bread salad, or fatoush, is eclipsed by a mezze of babaganoush, vinegary grape leaves stuffed with rice and olives, rich, herb-inflected labnee (strained yogurt), and artichoke salad all accompanied by warm pita bread. The single, crusty felafel to follow is paired with a deep-fried phyllo triangle with an oozing feta cheese center and, for dipping, a sweet tahini dressing. At the midway point you want to sit back, sip a glass of white or red from the short list, or maybe take a mid-prandial puff on some fruit-enhanced tobacco from a hookah ($15 for the table)—although most people wait until after dining to do that.

Representative of main courses is the astounding stew of chickpeas, yogurt, garlic, nutmeg, and the most incredibly tender chicken you'll ever meet. The stew is flecked with squares of sautéed phyllo, whose nutty, caramelized flavor pervades every bite. There is fragrant jasmine rice alongside, as well as a tangy mixture of chickpeas, eggplant, tomato, and cilantro that cuts the richness of the stew. Course five may be lamb kebabs with an acidic tomato and parsley compote, and with it, an unremarkable okra stew that you can safely skip to make room for the finale, a sweet cheese baklava topped with chopped pistachios and drizzled with rosewater syrup.

La Paella

(🍴) Folding your legs in this tiny Spanish kitchen/tapas bar, an anomaly on a block chock-full of Japanese eateries, is as tricky as bending your fingers in the hip pocket of a pair of tight-fitting Levis. That's not to say that getting comfortable is impossible, however, especially with the aid of a limb-loosening sangria or Sherry with a plate of ceviche ($9) and a couple of pleasing tapas ($4–14; try the potato-omelet-like tortilla Espanola and the Basque cheese

Cost	$25–55

Address 214 East 9th St, between 2nd & 3rd Aves
☎212/598-4321
Transportation 6 to Astor Place; N,R to 8th St
Open Sun–Thurs 5–11pm, Fri & Sat 5pm–midnight
Accepts MasterCard & Visa

sampler). At that point, it should take about forty minutes to fall in love with one of the paellas. That wait is no fault of the sometimes apathetic service. Rather, it is a matter of not measuring beautiful paellas by first impressions. Such responses are clouded by the dizzying vapors released from a steaming-hot paella as the two-handled pan of saffron-scented rice, shellfish, and sausage is delivered to an expectant table. As a consequence, judgment does not become unclouded until the fifteenth forkful, when the excitement and temperature are diminished, the choice seafood and meats are depleted, and the now tepid rice is at its most vulnerable. Remember, a paella is above all a rice dish. The rest is clothing, make-up, and accessories.

At their best, the short, plump grains of rice in two mildly flavored La Paella paellas—the Catalana (chorizo and chile peppers) and the Marinera (langoustines, clams, shrimp, mussels, squid)—possess a moist, almost sticky coating. In the Negro, the rice absorbs the flavor of squid and squid ink, while in the Verdura, the grains are strictly vegetarian. In the Basque, meanwhile, the rice does battle with nearly all the ingredients contained in its sibling paellas. Each one costs between $22 and $34 and is enough for two.

Desserts ($6) have never been a strong suit at La Paella, but you have to admire the management's fortitude for sticking with them since 1995 through thick (tedious chocolate mousse) and thin (flan-like crema Catalan that should be as creamy as crème brûlée). Such loyalty, so unencumbered by taste considerations, is truly rare. The cheesecake is an inoffensive lightweight.

Paul's Palace

(icon) This greasy spoon may be a hole but it sure isn't Jackson Hole, the local chain known for its soft, fatty, face-stuffing variation on the crusty New York burger. The one-and-only Paul's Palace does a superior, indie version of Jackson Hole's notorious hardhat burger. The hardhats in question are stainless steel cups which are fitted over the half-pound mounds of loosely packed chopped beef as they sizzle on the griddle. This effectively steams them in their own grease. As you sink your teeth into a Paul's burg-

Cost	$6–20

Address 131 2nd Ave, between St Mark's Place & 7th St

☎212/529-3033

Transportation 6 to Astor Place; N,R to 8th St

Open Daily 11am–midnight

Accepts Cash only

Reservations Not accepted

er, the meat crumbles and spills out from the sides of the bun. You can swallow this squashy, five-napkin job without even chewing.

There's a real Paul, who obviously woke up one day and said, "I'd like to make a great burger for my friends." The pals in question seem to be skinny rockers smoking up a storm in leather jackets and leopard-patterned tights, along with every off-duty cop and firefighter in lower Manhattan. The occasional drag queen, too. Most of the neon-streaked scenery is in black and white, from the checkered contact paper sloppily pasted under the counter and over the tabletops to the framed posters of movie legends. Whimsical placards herald such specialties as the "Lo Calorie Burger," so called because the cheeseburger comes with no bun. We'd hate to shake the hand of anyone who'd just handled one of those.

You can get a burger with anything you want (fried egg, chili con carne, *da woiks*). A plain burger is $3.70. A bacon cheeseburger draped with ham, mushrooms, tomatoes, and onions is $8.75; $10.60 with frozen steak fries (you don't want these, especially considering the proximity of Pomme Frites, an excellent takeout just a few doors away—it's tempting to smuggle in a bag of Pomme Frites' frites under your coat). Nothing on the menu beyond the burger and the chocolate egg cream ($1.50) should be taken seriously. The hot dog ($1.25) is sorrier than the fries. But were we to perish from unsanitary food-service choices, we'd want it to be from the garlic pickles supplied gratis in bowls passed from table to table.

Prune

Partly in an attempt to prevent Prune from becoming trendy, chef-owner Gabrielle Hamilton loaded her menu with the nutritionally incorrect indulgences we might relish more often were there no judgmental friends and mirrors to stare back at us. Her attempts were futile, however: this is a trendy elbow-to-trendy elbow downtowner whose cachet reflects the current rage for rustic, soulful, peasant cooking. Distressed mirrors mounted over the long wooden banquette and the zinc bar look

Cost	$35–75

Address 54 East 1st St, between 1st & 2nd Aves
☎212/677-6221
Transportation F,V to 2nd Ave
Open Mon–Thurs 6–11pm, Fri & Sat 6pm–midnight, Sun 5–10pm
Accepts All major credit cards
Reservations Required

just the part. But the absence of bread on the small, butcher-paper-covered tables seems odd. Perhaps it is Hamilton's ruse to unburden diners of that great dilemma: to butter or not to butter. Instead, she performs the business on our behalf, floating rafts of bread into a variety of dishes in many guises: buttered, deep-fried, drenched with garlicky meat drippings or, in one pajama party dessert dream, as butter-and-sugar sandwiches dunked in half-and-half.

The caloric pattern is established by the sweetbreads appetizer with bacon, fried olives, and fried chicken livers ($14). A trio of marinated white anchovies, celery hearts, and toasted almonds pleases with a lighter touch ($9), but who really wants to chew on almonds when there are fried oysters and thick homemade tartar sauce for the taking?

Roast suckling pig ($21) accompanied by two mayos (garlic and chipotle) competes with braised short ribs piled over Yorkshire pudding for the distinction of most decadent main course. Roofing the assortment of succulent piglet meat with not one but three layers of cracking skins attests to a chef who truly loves to eat. Using a soufflé baked in meat drippings to absorb the sweet, fatty juices of the short ribs is downright inspiring. To be fair, not everything is quite so sinful. Seared sea bass rubbed with dry, Berber spices sits in a saffron broth ($23) that is as light as it is lovely. Desserts ($7–9) are less auspicious. The dulce de leche brûlée, though its double richness suits the surroundings, is a bit intense, while the ice cream flavored with sour cream and buttermilk barely elevates the warm chocolate cake and pistachio pastry beyond the ordinary.

Raga

(🍴) If people go gaga for Raga, it's due to their finding so inventive a bistro in a neighborhood where cheap knock-offs are the norm. Whereas new currents in music, theater, and fashion typically originate around the East Village and Lower East Side before drifting uptown, culinary tides have tended to flow in the opposite direction. Geetika Khanna's Indian fusion menu, on the other hand, debuted a year before such cooking become trendy north of Fourteenth

Cost	$25–65

Address 433 East 6th St, between 1st Ave & Ave A
☎212/388-0957
Transportation F,V to 2nd Ave; N,R to 8th St
Open Tues–Sun 6–11pm
Accepts All major credit cards
Reservations For large groups

Street. Initial resistance was on economic rather than creative grounds. Raga stands just east of a block packed with lovably cheap Bangladeshi joints. Locals accustomed to paying less for an Indian meal than others typically spend for checking in their coat were taken aback by Raga's comparatively high prices and high-minded food. But they soon gained a measure of tranquility from the decor. Brick and plaster walls painted paprika red are dimly lit by bare, saffron-yellow bulbs. High, straight-backed banquettes that Gumby alone might find comfortable divide the snug room into cozy subsections.

Khanna's use of Indian curries and garnishes brings new life to the New American repertoire. Toasted cumin added to a lime dressing trans-forms a salad with perimeter points of garlicky and roasted Portobellos ($5). Seared sea scallops benefit from a tomato and black cardamom chutney ($9). The must-have starter consists of mussels steamed in coconut and beer ($8). For a more traditional slant, a terrific trio of samosas comes with mint and tamarind chutneys ($6).

Noting the similarity between the saffron-and-anise-like flavors found in bouillabaisse and those that imbue Indian cooking, Khanna has come up with a Marseille seafood stew with a twist—chile and cumin in the rouille-like spread ($17). Other good entrees include filet mignon, a beau-tiful hunk of meat rubbed with homemade garam masala and topped off with a velvety cashew paste ($22), and the roast chicken ($14) treated with yogurt, mustard seeds, and red chiles—juicier than any Tandoori chicken in memory. The technicolor vegetable platter ($12) is gloriously unmushy. Among desserts, basmati rice pudding with saffron and pistachios ($7) and chocolate soufflé with raspberry sauce ($7) merit your devotion.

53

Resto Léon

The diamond-shaped red cylinder mounted above the French-doored storefront hangs as a welcome sign to a convivial refuge. The so-called "carotte," the traditional signpost for a French cafe/tobacconist, marks a delightfully curious addition to the East Village streetscape. Inside, the faded billboards for Lu biscuits and martini-brand vermouth painted on the bare brick walls look like they've weathered a half-century of summers in the French countryside. The tilted-down mirrors and old bistro chairs and tables transport us back to a time and place when and where those well-aged objects were new. Enthusiasm for this cozy, amusing, and inexpensive place is tempered only by the occasional blandness of the food. But even that can be forgiven in the sort of easy-going haunt where you order second and third coffees just to postpone your departure.

Cost	Lunch $10–35
	Dinner $25–50

Address 351 East 12th St, between 1st & 2nd Aves
☏212/375-8483
Transportation L to 1st Ave
Open Mon–Thurs 11.30am– 11.30pm, Fri & Sat 11.30am– 1am, Sun 11.30am–11pm
Accepts Cash only

Resto, of course, is a French shortening of the word restaurant, just as Léon's cooking, with its pretty plates and modern touches, represents an abbreviation of contemporary French cuisine. The hand-scripted menu may initially confuse English-only speakers. Starters are listed under the heading "entrée," the French word for appetizer. Whatever you call them, these starters are cute and satisfying. The tiered tuna tartare ($7.50) with tabouleh is appealing, while the napoleon of tomato and brandade ($6), with its mildly garlicky salt cod-and-potato purée, gets better as it sits at the table and the flavor of the fresh herbs sets in. The asparagus vinaigrette ($5) and the dense country pâté with green bean salad ($5) are pleasers from first to last bite.

Main courses can be superb: herb-roasted chicken with good mashed potatoes ($14); hanger steak with red wine sauce ($17.50); rabbit confit in a black-olive ragout with wide noodles, its leg meat dripping off the bone ($16). And we would keep going back for the copious Niçoise salad, packed with fresh tuna, alone. The dessert to commit to is the round financier ($6), an almond sponge cake given a zing by the timeless rendezvous of orange (sauce) and chocolate (ice cream).

Second Avenue Deli

Those who think the Jewish delicatessen experience is limited to corned beef and pastrami need to refine their expectations when coming to this full-service, family-friendly deli. Smoked meat sandwiches ($9.95) are not the forte of the sole surviving kosher delicatessen on this stretch of Second Avenue— once dotted with such establishments and the Yiddish theaters they fed off. Regrettably, skilled purveyors of kosher pastrami and corned beef have all but disappeared. Even Abe Lebewohl,

Cost	$15–55

Address 156 2nd Ave at 10th St

☎212/677-0606

Transportation 6 to Astor Place; N,R to 8th St

Open Sun–Thurs 7am–midnight, Fri & Sat 7am–3am

Accepts All major credit cards

Reservations Not accepted

the late, great, and dearly missed owner of the Second Avenue Deli, lamented the so-so quality of his pickled meats. Frankly, the popularity of the pastrami here only goes to prove: you can't be with the pastrami you love, love the pastrami you're with.

Other than sandwiches, the standard of the Jewish/Eastern European cooking is unchallenged. You'd need to be invited into the home of a Jewish mother or grandmother to find a comparable matzoh ball soup ($4.75) or chopped liver ($7.95). The only viable complaint about them would ordinarily be considered a virtue: they embody compromise. The matzoh balls are neither floaters (light and fluffy) nor sinkers (dense and heavy) but something between the two. The chopped chicken livers are neither pasty nor chunky. No such culinary diplomacy influences the gefilte fish (poached fish quenelles; $8.50), however. Their sweet freshness elicits only praise.

Foregoing an appetizer would reflect poor judgement, if not outright heresy, were it not for the all-inclusive pleasures of the legendary chicken-in-the-pot ($17.95). It contains world-class chicken soup, noodles, matzoh balls, and enough chicken for dinner tonight and lunch tomorrow (chicken salad anyone?). Twosomes could also split the classic Roumanian tenderloin steak ($22.95). No other restaurant in America serves cholent ($7.95) every day. The Lebewohl family bills this slow-cooked and typically leaden Sabbath stew of fatty meats, beans, and potatoes as the Jewish cassoulet. As a side dish, outstanding fries ($4.50) possess the color of a Jerusalem sunset. For dessert, the rugelach ($3.50) and chocolate babka (more chocolate than cake; $3.95) do the trick.

East Village

Smith

🍽 Apparently, giving his restaurant a name that already occupied five pages in the Manhattan white pages wasn't anonymous enough for Brian McNally. The British expat who had taken to dubbing his trendy eateries after streets or addresses (Canal Bar, 150 Wooster, 44) kept "Smith" off the entrance and the menus of his first incursion into the East Village. The rear dining room, though appealing in its maple-paneled and block-wood-floored minimalism, is devoid of identifying features. Even the lampshades that hang from the high, barreled ceiling lack a designer's signature (Christian Liegre? Philippe Starck?). Sitting at roomy booths beside a row of illuminated yet blank wall recesses like figures in a Magritte painting, you could almost believe that McNally is saying, "Ce n'est pas un restaurant."

Cost	$35–80

Address 64 East 1st St, between 1st & 2nd Aves
☎212/260-3189
Transportation F,V to 2nd Ave
Open Daily 6pm–1.30am
Accepts All major credit cards
Reservations Suggested

The no-label posture is a droll irony for a hip haunt packed with more designer duds than last month's *Vogue*. Still, that alone is probably not enough to keep the chic brats from decamping to the next restaurant of the moment when the time comes. Neither is the bar, despite back-lit shelves that set blue vodka bottles aglow and a nice variety of edible amusements, including chopped liver from Russ & Daughters ($9) and sardines from a can ($8). No, what's likely to turn this place into a fashionable fixture is Kenny Addington's contemporary bistro fare, which is arty in composition but pure in delivery.

Salmon tartare with mini-quenelles of avocado purée and cornmeal pita chips ($10) would be an all-star appetizer if it weren't so comically stunted. Breaded rougets (mullets) are small too, as the best ones are, but fresh parsley, cold split peas, and pickled mango stretch them into a satisfying starter ($11). Among splendid entrees, silky, slow-cooked salmon with a gritty green olive and pistachio topping is rare—but not raw—throughout ($21). The aged rib-eye with roasted potatoes ($28) is one great hunk of beef. And a first-rate risotto contains sweet, juicy chunks of lobster, crayfish, grilled baby asparagus, and peas ($25). No finish is sweeter than the chocolate-encased peanut butter mousse with caramelized banana slices and chocolate-peanut biscuits buried like hidden treasures ($6).

Soba-Ya

(🍴) This is as close to modern Tokyo as you can get in NYC for under $30 per person. Small, sleek, serene, and immaculate, the blond-wood noodle house gets a recurring ring—or at least a ring tone—of authenticity from the home-sick, cell-phone-holding Japanese students, many from nearby NYU dorms, who form the core clientele. Much to everyone's relief, Soba-Ya is a sushi-free zone. There's already too much darn sushi in this neighborhood.

Cost	$12–40

Address 229 East 9th St, between 2nd & 3rd Aves
☎212/533-6966
Transportation 6 to Astor Place; N,R to 8th St
Open Daily noon–3.45pm & 5.30–10.30pm
Accepts All major credit cards

Most begin by choosing from an adventurous assortment of elegant small-plate "delicacies" to go with a beer or a fine sake, among them daily items like homemade shrimp shumai (dumplings; $6), squid stuffed with sticky rice ($5.50), boiled spinach ($3.50), assorted seaweeds ($6), Japanese mountain yam ($4), sliced duck breast ($7.50), and chilled sesame tofu ($3.50). Regulars know to keep an eye out for such specials as sesame-flavored (or sometimes chile-detonated) tuna tartare with quail egg and scallion ($6), grilled sea and bay scallops with miso sauce ($6.50), and warm herring with seasoned rice ($3.50). And every table seems to get at least one order of edamame (green soybeans; $3). Next up, the glorious homemade soba (brownish buckwheat noodles) are served in bowls of chilled or hot broth. Among the eight cold soba selections, you'd do best to go for either the salted salmon roe option ($12.50) or the alternative with whipped yam, an enduring fascination that could easily be mistaken for egg drop soup ($11.50). It's also available in a hot version. From the nine hot sobas choose the variety with gently battered tempura shrimp (not to worry, it doesn't get the least bit greasy; $12.50) or another topped with a high pile of shredded herbs and vegetables ($9.50).

Udon—the thick, white, chewy, spaghetti-like Japanese wheat noo-dle—may be substituted for the soba in all its hot and cold varieties. Good tempura, seasoned rice bowls, adorable bento-styled lunch boxes, and the best wasabi honey ice cream in the area round out the list. All told, you'll get a near flawless meal and, considering what other Japanese noodle houses of this caliber charge, a phenomenal bargain.

Takahachi

Anytime the words "sushi" and "cheap" appear in the same sentence, as they do throughout the East Village, it's a risky proposition—though that doesn't dissuade fearless young sashimi fans from packing themselves in at even the most dubiously dingy joints. Takahachi's decor is hardly high-style Japanese and not likely to inspire confidence straight off. But look closer and you'll find that the terribly crammed quarters are adorned with some nice wall hangings, light-wood fixtures, and horizontal lines—the most noticeable of which leads out the door and vestibule. As for the sushi—it won't win any design awards, but it is simple, fresh, bountiful and absurdly cheap. And it's a friendly place, the affable hosts and overworked servers eager to establish good relations with their repeat customers. As if superbly inexpensive sushi were not enough of an enticement, gifts are occasionally handed out (a nibble of this, a bottle of that) to loyal habitués.

Cost	$17–45

Address 85 Ave A, between
5th & 6th Sts
☎212/505-6524
Transportation F,V to 2nd Ave;
6 to Astor Place
Open Daily 5.30pm–12.45am
Accepts All major credit cards
Reservations Not accepted

A deluxe sushi for two, including an extra hand roll of choice, is just $25. And the two maki trios are winners: "Avenue A" ($11) features tekka (raw tuna), California, and yellowtail rolls; rolls in the superior "Avenue B" ($12) hold eel, buttery yellowtail, and nicely broiled salmon skin. Not bad as far as pre-selected sushi combos go. From the a la carte menu, nasu hasami (a sandwich of eggplant tempura stuffed with whitefish; $4.50) and kinuta maki (cucumber-wrapped eel, avocado, and seaweed; $6.50) are chopstick-stopping sensations.

Cooked food selections are pretty good too. The shumai (crab potstickers; $5) are infinitely more delicate than anyone has a right to expect. And the sake aspara make ($5), consisting of five fried asparagus rolls wrapped in salmon and seaweed, makes a terrific appetizer. The blackened tuna ($7), however, is one of only a few bad ideas listed on this menu. Noodle soups, broiled fish platters, and tempura all offer good value, while kushiyaki (Japanese barbecue) make for great beer snacks: grilled skewers of marinated squid, shrimp, shiitake, and bacon-okra varieties are just $2 apiece; the bean curd and asparagus, $1.50.

The Tasting Room

Even in the East Village, an area saturated with cute eateries, there's something instantly appealing about this closet-sized, exposed brick room, enticingly framed by its large picture window. Peering in, you'll spy about a dozen tables, each about an inch apart, crowded with open bottles of wine and small square plates filled with the inspired market-driven creations of chef Colin Alevras. At the door to this cozy shoebox of a place, you'll find Colin's wife Renée, who invariably greets you with a grin. And if you are lucky enough to score a table at their restaurant, you'll be reminded that an exceptional dinner comes from a combination of many things—food, wine, space, service, and, perhaps most of all, the people that make you feel at home.

Cost	$35–75

Address 72 East 1st St, between 1st & 2nd Aves
☎212/358-7831
Transportation F,V to 2nd Ave
Open Tues–Sat 5.30–11pm
Accepts All major credit cards
Reservations Required

The menu lists about a dozen seasonal, Greenmarket-inspired dishes, each in two sizes—"Tastes" ($6–15, the size of a large appetizer) or "Shares" ($11–29, similar to a large entree). The best way to go, given the lure of Alevras' creative cuisine, is to order lots of tastes. Warm roasted baby eggplant sprinkled with fresh feta is perfect—the slightly salty cheese a clever foil for sweet chucks of rosemary-scented eggplant ($6/$11). Luscious scallops, the size of giant marshmallows, are marinated in soy sauce tinged with chiles, mint, and lime ($13/$25). Use the soft ciabatta bread on the table to mop up every last drop. Sheep's milk cheese, cured olives, and caramelized wild onions mingle in a tangle of fresh homemade fettuccine soaked in a meaty lamb jus ($13/$25), while braised and roasted duck leg ($11/$21) rests on a bed of hominy, with collard greens. The gumbo sauce gives it a sneaky kick.

Like the impressive 300-bottle wine list, the cheese plate is all-American, and you should leave room to indulge ($15/$29). Desserts rotate, but if Renée's Grandmother's cheesecake ($6) is on, order the whole thing and see if you can sweet-talk Renée into giving you the recipe. Truth be told, it just won't taste as good. Home is nice, sure, but it's not The Tasting Room.

East Village

Veselka

(icon) Many New Yorkers are convinced that Veselka's alternately irritable, inattentive, and sloppy service was a much better. fit before the recent makeover. The negligence suited a place as worn, constricted, and difficult to discard as an old pair of jeans. Now that the Ukrainian coffee shop has transformed itself into a bright, airy, unsoiled, and— whisper it—attractive place to eat, the Eastern-bloc hardships have lost much of their old country color. Veselka nevertheless endures, like a cup of strong java or a bowl of hearty soup, to stimulate or soothe the hopes and dreams of East Villagers. Its frank informality still attracts that extraordinary mix of characters—artists, students, middle-income bohemians, elder Eastern Europeans—that gives the neighborhood its abundant creative energy. Sometimes it seems as though every customer should either be writing a screenplay or having one written about them.

Cost	$8–25

Address 144 2nd Ave at 9th St
(phone)212/228-9682
Transportation 6 to Astor Place; N,R to 8th St
Open Daily 24hr
Accepts All major credit cards
Reservations Not accepted

A homemade soup ($2.75/$3.50)—cabbage, vegetable, mushroom barley, split pea, lentil—is compulsory, as are pierogi (Polish dumplings; $6.25) filled with potato, cheese, mushroom, sauerkraut, ground meat, spinach, or even sweet potato. Those pockets of goodness may be ordered boiled or, defying good judgement, fried. Both soup and pierogi accompany four combination dinner plates. The vegetarian deluxe plate ($9.25) assembles a salad, a meatless stuffed cabbage, and mushroom-sauced kasha to go with a pierogi trio. The deluxe meat combo ($9.50) includes a pork- and beef-stubbed cabbage, a grilled kielbasa, and a beet salad. Though the American standards—burgers, sandwiches, specials of the day—are generally less satisfying, you can't complain about the stalwart BLT ($3.45) or the milk shakes ($2.50) and ice cream sodas ($2.50) made with Ben & Jerry's.

The no. 4 breakfast special ($7), served until noon on weekdays and 4pm on weekends, includes an order of fluffy banana buckwheat pancakes, eggs, juice, coffee, and a choice of bacon, ham, kielbasa, sausage or corned beef hash. Or you could take another kind of late breakfast, just as satisfying in its way: a simple chunk of coffee cake (maybe a $2.50 slice of homemade poppyseed bread) with a cup of high-octane black java.

Flatiron District,
Gramercy Park & Union Square

FLATIRON DISTRICT, GRAMERCY PARK & UNION SQUARE

W. 30TH ST.

Church of the
Transfiguration

BROADWAY

FIFTH AVENUE

MADISON AVENUE

PARK AVENUE SOUTH

LEXINGTON AVENUE

THIRD AVENUE

SECOND AVENUE

W. 24TH ST.

W. 23RD ST.

W. 22ND ST.

Justin's

NY Life
Building

Dosa
Hut

L'Annan

E. 28TH ST.

Enoteca i Trulli

Blue
Smoke

East

E. 27TH ST.

E. 26TH ST.

Appellate Court

Eleven
Madison
Park

E. 25TH ST.

Madison
Square
Park

Metropolitan Life
Building

E. 24TH ST.

E. 23RD ST.

GRAMERCY
PARK

Beppe

E. 22ND ST.

Flatiron
Building

E. 21ST ST.

FLATIRON DISTRICT

La Pizza Fresca

National
Arts Club

Gramercy
Park

Plate 347

E. 20TH ST.

The Players

Tavern at Gramercy Tavern

Sushi Samba

W. 19TH ST.

Pipa

Craft
Bar

Angelo & Maxie's

E. 19TH ST.

City Bakery

Chicama

Los Dos Molinos

E. 18TH ST.

W. 18TH ST.

UNION
SQUARE

E. 17TH ST.

Republic

St. George's
Church

Stuyvesant
Square

W. 17TH ST.

Union Square
Café

Union
Square

IRVING PLACE

W. 16TH ST.

W. 15TH ST.

Farmer's
Market

Con Edison
Building

Bambou

W. 14TH ST.

E. 14TH ST.

0   200 yds

N

Angelo & Maxie's

This steakhouse/cigar bar takes its name from the song "Lullaby of Broadway," in which lyricist Al Dubin identified Angelo's and Maxie's as the hot spots where daffodils entertain. Given a choice between seeing smug carnivores chomping fat stogies and watching daffodils sing and dance, we'd take the daffodils. Still, the place that slightly misquotes its namesakes does showcase a few very good, very large steaks at extraordinarily affordable prices—a successful formula that has spawned a second Manhattan location (1285 6th Ave, Midtown West; ☎212/459-1222) and four others around the US. The theme-park-like entrance opens into a cigar store and a long bar mobbed with carousing hunks and slender cuts who create their own kind of meat market. Behind it, a clubby dining room with semicircular Hollywood booths, rich-wooded walls, and tall round pillars is encased in fluted, tobacco-colored mahogany.

| Cost | Lunch $25–70 |
| | Dinner $35–85 |

Address 233 Park Ave South at 19th St
☎212/220-9200
Transportation 6 to 23rd St
Open Mon–Thurs 11.30am–3pm & 5–11pm, Fri 11.30am–3pm, Sat 5pm–midnight, Sun 5–11pm
Accepts All major credit cards
Reservations Suggested

STEAKHOUSE

Appetizers, salads, and sides are big enough for family-style sharing. Two favorites: chopped shrimp salad in a subtle mustard vinaigrette ($13.95) and angel-hair onion rings ($6.95/$9.95). Bluepoint oysters ($9), hash browns ($6.95) and creamed spinach ($6.95) are satisfactory, but the shrimp in the Busby Berkeley-style shrimp cocktail ($11.75) too often possesses zero flavor. From the raw bar, a two-person sampler ($28) will keep a couple busy and happy for thirty minutes.

The kitchen merits most kudos for turning out distinctly flavored, precision-cooked steaks. The 26oz on-the-bone rib-eye ($25.95) protrudes from both ends of a plate as wide as Park Avenue. For value, it is challenged only by the firm, velvety, grilled filet mignon ($24.75) and the tender, 16oz charbroiled sirloin ($23.95). The porterhouse for two ($50), with T-bone and filet mignon portions, requires its own zip code; at the other end of the scale, the 10oz burger on a husky onion bun ($12.50) slashes your bill but not your enjoyment. A good alternative to beef: whole roasted chicken ($18.50) with an intense garlic-lemon-pepper crust. Desserts designed for couples—chocolate bread pudding ($6), deep-dish apple pie ($8)—can feed foursomes.

Flatiron, Gramercy Park & Union Square

L'Annan

The true test of an ethnic restaurant's New York neighborhood status is the junk quotient: are there enough quick, affordable, caloric, stuff-your-face impulse foods to ease the pain of bad video rentals, surprise visits from the in-laws, or Knicks' fourth-quarter collapses? A cheery spin-off of Sam's, a popular Chinese noodle shop one block north, L'Annan certainly comes up with the goods, without sacrificing the lighter, healthier side of Vietnamese cooking. The waitstaff and owners are Chinese, and the rushed service is familiar from local Chinese stand-bys. But this corner spot is distinguished by dark wood tables, Hollywood booths and a striking aluminum lighting fixture suspended over the bar.

| Cost | Lunch $7–25 |
| | Dinner $15–40 |

Address 393 3rd Ave at 28th St
℡212/686-5168
Transportation 6 to 28th St
Open Sun–Thurs 11.30am–11.30pm, Fri & Sat 11.30am–12.30am
Accepts All major credit cards
Reservations Not accepted

Though the manager insists that the chefs are Vietnamese, you shouldn't bet on it. There are, however, enough carefully prepared dishes to wager there's someone back there who knows how to cook. Routine appetizers—spring roll ($3.95), summer roll ($4.25)—are humdrum. But the delicately encased shrimp sui mai (pot-shaped dumplings; $3.95) and the steamed slippery rice crêpes banh cuon ($4.95) are splendid. Goi muc ($5.25), a refreshing salad of shredded baby greens and big loops of tender calamari, is enormously refreshing. And canh chua ($2.50–5.95), a mildly hot and sour soup with pineapple chunks, straw mushrooms, and bean sprouts is practically curative.

Heading the long entree list is curry tom ($9.25), a mild red curry with prawns, green beans, okra, eggplant, bell peppers, onions, and bamboo shoots. You can't, however, order better than fresh whole fish ($12.95) in an oniony lemongrass sauce. And then there are the junk dishes: no. 39 ($8.50), a Vietnamese take on the Chinese takeout addiction, General Tsao's chicken, consists of fried chunks of chicken in a cloyingly sweet, bright orange, honey soy sauce. Number 49 ($8.95) contains unnaturally tender chunks of beef in a thick, chunky peanut sauce. As unimpressed as you may initially be with either, you will not be able to stop eating them. For dessert, red bean and green tea ice creams ($2.50) cleanse the palate—especially useful for anyone who has ordered nos. 39 or 49.

Bambou

Bambou is a dreamscape that extends Manhattan's longest crosstown street even further, taking you to a guesthouse on a Caribbean plantation. Up front, the sensuously lit bar/lounge decked out with tropical plants, flowers, and fruits is separated from an intimate dining room by French windows and ivory drapes. The green-and-white color scheme looks very Ralph Lauren, at least until you notice the big picture of Bob Marley smoking something other than a cigar. The beautiful people huddled at candlelit tables also appear to be permanent fixtures. But they are here on their own volition to experience Bambou's upscale, nouvelle, West Indian-fusion cooking.

Cost	$35–75

Address 243 East 14th St, between 2nd & 3rd Aves
℡212/358-0012
Transportation L to 3rd Ave; 4,5,6,N,Q,R,W to 14th St-Union Square
Open Sun noon–3pm & 6–11pm, Mon–Sat 6–11pm
Accepts All major credit cards

Looking forward to the "soup du jour" can be agony when the odds of it actually being the scintillating eggplant soup with a chorus of sweet, spicy and smoky notes ($8) are pretty long. Lucky thing there are the steamed mussels ($11) and their piquant, coconut-enhanced broth—great for sourdough sopping—to fall back on. Demonstrating coconut's versatility, the broth has none of the sweetness of "A Shrimp Called Bambou" ($9)—crunchy, coconut-battered shrimp certain to invite poaching from fellow diners. You could also go for the crisp crabcake ($13), which has avocado butter, chive oil, and balsamic molasses syrup to counteract its fiery kick.

Despite their upscale presentation and aspirations, main courses rarely stray too far from their roots. Rather than mess too much with familiar dishes like grilled jerk chicken with avocado and rice-and-peas ($20) or braised oxtail with lima beans ($19), Bambou gives its Caribbean menu a French accent—or vice versa—by introducing new dishes like a two-alarm bouillabaisse Caraïbe ($26) and a succulent shell steak ($25) marinated with an Arawak spice mix made mostly of peppers indigenous to the Caribbean. The grilled vegetable roti ($18) used to be rolled like a burrito wrap and cut into angled cylinders. More recently it's been assembled as a Napoleon. The fine dessert assortment (all around $7) features an elegant, sorbet-topped fruit cocktail, a nice rum spongecake and the requisite warm chocolate soufflé cake.

Beppe

(🍴) Italian trade groups, travel editors, and foodies vying to promote some undiscovered region or other as "The Next Tuscany" share a common obstacle: if their wholehearted response to Beppe is any indication, New York Italophiles are perfectly content with the original one. Chef-owner Cesare Casella's mid-block farmhouse is a fabulous fiction of oak-planked antique flooring, dark-wooded ceiling beams, and walls brushed in ochre and burnt sienna. The rustic dining room is warmed by a stone fireplace.

Cost	$40–85

Address 45 East 22nd St, between Broadway & Park Ave South

☏212/982-8422

Transportation 6,N,R to 23rd St

Open Mon–Fri noon–2.30pm & 5.30–11.30pm, Sat 5.30–11.30pm

Accepts All major credit cards

Reservations Suggested

The Lucca-born chef had previously wooed the same audience from the kitchens of Il Cantinori, Coco Pazzo, and Il Toscanaccio. At Beppe he expands a notion of Tuscan cooking that he himself helped shape. His cuisine is simple, robust and earthy. But from countrified roots stem a menu of means: Casella has the resources to explore, procure, and thoroughly amuse; his clientele, the wherewithal to finance pastas priced in the high-teens and secondi pushing $30.

Antibaci—"no kissing"—is a $10 tasting of garlic (roast garlic soup, garlic-rubbed bruschetta) and onion (marinated rings, leek quiche, pickled scallions), while the grilled handmade sausage ($10) is spiced with a secret renaissance blend (cinnamon, nutmeg, cardamom—you figure out the rest) from an old apothecary in Lucca. Among recommended pastas, "the butcher's spaghetti" ($16) combines crumbled pork sausage and the Lucca blend with a New World influence, tomato. Potato gnocchi hold up beautifully to the weight of a wild boar ragu enriched with red wine and powdered bitter chocolate ($18). There are more fabulous flavors endowing the spicy, Scotch-soaked shrimp sweetened with chestnut honey ($29). Beppe's fried chicken ($26) owes much of its critical acclaim to the surprise of finding it and three other specialities of the American south—collard greens, black-eyed peas, fried green tomatoes—on a Tuscan plate. Couples who have succumbed to the romance-killing, anti-kiss appetizer will find some compensation in pastry chef Vera Tong's extreme chocolate tasting—chocolate panna cotta, chocolate semifreddo, and a tiramisu layered with chocolate sponge cake ($11).

Blue Smoke

(icon) Ever walk into a restaurant and know that you won't want to leave? It's a rarity to be expected every time you step into this down-home barbecue joint from Danny Meyer and partners—the same team that brought us Union Square Cafe (see p.83) and Gramercy Tavern (p.82). Here's why: the messy, sticky, spicy, juicy grub is just plain fun. At the long steel bar, smiling crowds stand three-deep, frosty, perspiring mugs of handcrafted Blue Smoke Ale in hand. And in the lively, rustic dining room, tables are packed with after-work suits, yuppie families, sexy waifs and the men who chase them (newsflash: waifs eat ribs) all wiping sticky barbecue sauce from their cheeks with one hand while reaching for more 'cue with the other.

Cost	$22–70

Address 116 East 27th St, between Park & Lexington Aves
☎212/447-7733
Transportation 6,N,R to 28th St
Open Mon–Fri 11.30am–2.30pm & 5.30–11.30pm, Sat & Sun 5.30–11.30pm
Accepts All major credit cards
Reservations Suggested

Executive chef Kenny Callaghan spent eight years at Union Square Cafe before moving over to man Blue Smoke's custom-made, apple-wood-filled smoke pits, each one the size of a VW van. Smoked beef brisket ($16.50) and sliced smoked pork butt ($14.50) are tender and intensely flavored, but the real showstoppers are the fall-off-the-bone ribs. Choose from baby back ($14.95/$22.95), St Louis ($12.95/$19.95), or salt and pepper beef ($14.75/$22.50), all dry-rubbed with a secret spice mix before getting thrown in the pit where they melt in their own fat, rotating for twelve to sixteen hours on the pit's rotisserie. Glazed in a molasses, brown sugar, cayenne, and tomato sauce, these racks demand lots of finger licking.

To pair up with your rack-o-ribs, don't miss the black pepper links and pickles—fiery hot pork sausages balanced out with cool, crisp, vinegar-brined pickle chips. Other stars include onion rings ($4.95/$7.50), each one perfectly wrapped in a golden, crispy crust, and collard greens braised to spinach tenderness in bacon fat ($3.95/$5.95). Pit beans ($3.50/$6.50) are ingenious. Callaghan lets them roll around on the rotisserie just to ensure they have enough fat and flavor. Pastry chef Jenny Giblin's best work is banana cream pie ($5.95) the sort you could actually imagine enjoying being thrown in your face.

Flatiron, Gramercy Park & Union Square

Chicama

First, ABC Carpet & Home reconstructed an old Brazilian farmhouse inside its Broadway store as the setting for an authentic Tuscan trattoria. When that didn't work, they changed the drapes, brought in chef Douglas Rodriguez, New York's founding godfather of contemporary, Pan-Latin-American cooking, and—voilà—rechristened the restaurant Chicama. Rodriquez and part of his staff were lured away from the seminal Nuevo Latino restaurant Patria by the promise of a larger space, a front section built entirely around a ceviche bar, and a kitchen equipped with a eucalyptus-burning rotisserie. More than anything, the change of venue has afforded Rodriquez the freedom and luxury to exercise greater control. Though he is still tempted to make a sensation with every dish and thus prone to excesses, he now succumbs less than before.

| Cost | Lunch $35–75 |
| | Dinner $40–85 |

Address 35 East 18th St, between Broadway & Park Ave South
℡212/505-2233
Transportation 6,L,N,Q,R,W to 14th St-Union Square
Open Mon–Thurs noon–2.45pm & 6–11pm, Fri & Sat noon–2.45pm & 5.30pm–midnight, Sun 5.30–10pm
Accepts All major credit cards
Reservations Suggested

Combination ceviches ($13–15) adorably served over ice in little glass fish bowls teach you to appreciate these piquant assortments of citrus-marinated raw fish as bracing cold soups. The hot chills of the Thai ceviche, with squid and tuna, are sent up and down your spine by the pungency of the lemongrass, ginger, lime, basil, and fish paste juices. In addition, all parties should pass around at least one order of the mixed and multicolored (parsley green, squid-ink black) empanadas ($13). You will also want one anticucho (Peruvian barbecue; $14) platter featuring spicy shrimp, chimichurri-bedecked chorizo, and tender little chunks of beef tenderloin in place of the more traditional beef hearts.

Frequent menu changes make it difficult to single out entrees. Still, to give you an idea of what's possible, it's worth mentioning the succulent, Peruvian-Chinese "chifa" rotisserie duck marinated in soy sauce, ginger, and chiles ($26). The eucalyptus-cooked black paella, with its generous assortment of shellfish dripping garlicky juices over smoky, squid-ink-dyed rice is another winner ($29). Desserts ($8) are not even remotely skippable. There's warm churros with both dulce de leche sauce and hot chocolate for double dunking, and a memorable coconut tapioca pudding.

City Bakery

Before there was a City Bakery, the great tart universe was split into two factions: those who preferred a triangular wedge cut from a large round pie and those who favored a crustier, individually sized tartlet. Around the Flatiron District and Union Square there is no longer this divisive dessert debate. The community has rallied around the tartlet format, its greatest New York champion, baker Maury Rubin, and as of April 2001, his new digs for a greatly expanded and spectacularly tantalizing City Bakery.

Cost	$6–25

Address 3 West 18th St, between 5th & 6th Aves

☎212/366-1414

Transportation F,V to 14th St; L,N,Q,R,W to 14th St–Union Square; 1,2 to 18th St

Open Mon–Sat 7.30am–7pm, Sun 9am–6pm

Accepts All major credit cards

Reservations Not accepted

According to Rubin's sleek, industrial design for this lofty space, the term "self-serving" refers not to egocentric behavior so much as the freedom to explore a number of immaculate food stations and load your tray with whatever you find most appealing. Every inch of the long, ovular counter up front is covered with Rubin's signature baked goods. Besides the signature tartlets (all $4.50), among them tapioca cherry, crème brûlée, cranberry carrot, and Milky Way, you'll find some of the best croissants, chocolate chip cookies, homemade marshmallows, lemonades, and hot chocolates in town. Seating is at high-backed banquettes against both walls and on the cozy mezzanine. Many creative professionals do their work here in the mornings and afternoons and lunch, as it were, at the office.

To the rear, a hot-foods station features a soup bar (tomato-vegetable, $4.75, is the house specialty), congee (Chinese rice porridge), mamaligah (Jewish grits), and macaroni-and-cheese all prepared by chef Ilene Rosen. And to the back is a salad bar unlike other salad bars, with all items priced at $10.95 per pound—certainly not too high a price to pay for the likes of Rosen's poached salmon with almond dressing. Side-course options from the same bar have included roasted fennel with dill, green beans with garlic and ginger, and black rice with snow peas, pea greens, and kaffir lime. The wonderful Caesar salad, the famous tuna salad sandwich ($6.75 outside the salad bar) and the three yogurt varieties are happily permanent fixtures.

Flatiron, Gramercy Park & Union Square

Craft Bar

Craft Bar does for the wine bar menu what Craft the highbrow restaurant does for contemporary American cuisine: pares it down to the bare and beautiful essentials. Chef-owner Tom Colicchio's first-come, first-serve spin-off trims its daily entree selection to one fish, one meat, and one pasta. It's possible the limited choice will deter some from returning, but that may just be wishful thinking. During prime-time hours there is not only a wait for a table. There's also a wait for the wait, meaning a place to sit or stand at the bar opposite its 500-capacity grid of chain-netted bottle hammocks. Although the high design is typical of the area's trendy gathering spots, the sound-absorbing ceiling and well-informed, solicitous service scale down the usual noise and nonsense.

Cost	$25–60

Address 43 East 19th St, between Broadway & Park Ave South
☎212/780-0880
Transportation 6,N,R to 23rd St
Open Daily noon–midnight
Accepts All major credit cards
Reservations Not accepted

A gleaming stainless-steel kitchen stretches across the rear of the dining area, making it absolutely clear who the stars of this show are. Anyone distracted by the kitchen view is not necessarily bored by their dinner date. They could well be trying to figure out how to prepare the fried stuffed sage leaves ($6)—five golden mini-logs tightly packed with ground sausage. Other bar snacks that do double duty as appetizers include salumi (Italian cured meats; $9 each, $16 for an assortment) and a dreamy bruschetta topped with tomato and poached egg ($7).

Main courses are programmed in the manner of a cable network that airs the same shows throughout the day but only on that day. Lasagna ($15) is on Sundays, braised pork belly ($17) on Tuesdays, and never the twain shall meet. Thursdays are something special, due to the roasted (and grill-marked) sardines with grapefruit and fennel ($16) and the creamy risotto with shrimp, saffron, olive oil, and great individual grain integrity ($15). Pastry chef Karen De Masco's dark gingerbread with quince butter ($8) and apple fritters with caramel ice cream ($8) run continuously, like the bulletins on CNN—and here the news is all good.

Los Dos Molinos

Were you cruising Route 66 on a Nabokovian quest for seedy motels, kitschy tourist traps, and elusive truths, Los Dos Molinos could very well be your Shangri-la. The ceiling and brick walls of an eatery dimly lit as if for illicit encounters (the drinking age in New York State is 21) are covered with holsters, sombreros, kachina dolls, synthetic chile peppers, and Mexican folk art. The snag is that this is not even the southwest side of Manhattan, much less the country, and even the cranked-up country-western tunes and the prodigious 3oz in a frozen Margarita goblet ($9) can't make big city

Cost	$12–45

Address 119 East 18th St, between Park Ave South & Irving Place

☎212/505 1574

Transportation 4,5,6,N,L,Q,R, W to 14th St-Union Square

Open Tues–Thurs 11am–3pm & 5–9.30pm, Fri 5–11pm, Sat noon–11pm

Accepts MasterCard, Visa

Reservations Not accepted

folk buy into the fiction. Only with the arrival of the two salsa pots—tangy, reasonably spicy green and smoky, throat-stinging red—do things begin to heat up a little.

Los Dos Molinos—"the two (chile) grinders"—is an outpost of the well-liked New Mexican-style cantinas of the same name in Arizona. As a warning to East Coast gringos, the menu carries a disclaimer about the liberal use of hot chiles. As it turns out, the sauces are no more unbearable that any Lexington Avenue vindaloo. Still, the biting, paste-like chile sauces, the homemade tortillas, and the oval dinner plates that extend from here to next Thursday represent a welcome north-of-the-border break from "real" Mexican. You're no more likely to complain about the cheerfully inauthentic Mexican pizza ($9.75) than the absurdity of listing this giant thing as an appetizer. Likewise, you'll be too busy sinking your chips into the pleasurably goopy guacamole ($5.50) to worry much that the genuine stuff is supposed to be chunky.

Everything is made to order, from the tostada covered with beans and succulent shredded beef ($5.50) to the cheese-stuffed, batter-fried chile relleno ($9.50). Shrimp Veracruz comes as six snappy shrimp alongside fiery red rice, chile beans, and a blistered, nan-like tortilla ($18.95). The best entree by a mile, however, is the Adovada ribs ($17.95): fatty, tender, just-this-side-of-mushy, off-the-bone pork ribs marinated in that red chile stuff. The thought of a dessert may not come easily, but the sopapillas ($4.50), fried pillows of dough drizzled with honey, are not to be missed.

Flatiron, Gramercy Park & Union Square

Dosa Hut

Expectant Dosa Hut devotees struggle to control their emotions as they take their places in this modest, pink-walled eatery. Just as the last minutes of a long journey can seem to drag on for hours, the whole business of menus, ordering, and waiting is grueling for the disciples of Veerappan Gownder. Having followed that dosa-master from Pongal, another Southern Indian vegetarian place in Manhattan's Little India, to here, they're all too familiar with the thrill when one of his enormous, paper-thin cones made from a fermented rice-and-lentil batter is set before them.

Cost	$10–30

Address 102 Lexington Ave, between 27th & 28th Sts
☎212/725-7466
Transportation 6 to 28th St
Open Tues–Sun noon–3pm & 5–10pm
Accepts MasterCard & Visa
Reservations Not accepted

A select minority exhibit sufficient patience to share appetizers. Such fresh, cleanly fried fritters as onion pakoda, spinach bhajjia and chickpea-coated eggplant bhajjia (all $3.95), served with two chutneys—sweet date and lethally hot, small-podded hari mirch (green chile)—may be ordered in a mixed $5.95 platter that also includes a fried minced-vegetable cutlet. The wholewheat breads, both poori puffed to a full sphere ($3.95 plain, $4.95 with mashed potatoes) and thin, flaky paratha ($3.95 stuffed with peas, potatoes, radishes, or fenugreek leaves), are outstanding.

The spectacular, golden-brown, paper sada masala ($6.95)—one of 16 dosas—are marked with the signature swirls made when Gownder slowly pours the batter onto the griddle. Too delicate and unwieldy to be easily attacked with a knife and fork, the dosa are best dealt with by breaking off a piece, topping it with some of the accompanying spicy mashed potatoes, adding a drizzle of tamarind-sweetened sambar (lentil sauce) and/or a hit of coconut chutney, rolling it all up, and popping it in the mouth. It is crisp and yielding, tart and sweet, fiery and earthy. Dosas also come in the form of a folded, wheat-rice flour pancakes, as in the onion rava ($7.95) filled with chopped onions and fresh cilantro. With the ends of the half-moon dosa hanging out on both sides of the plate, this too seems impossible to manage. It comes as some relief that payasam ($2.95), a sweet pudding of coconut milk and mung bean, is easily consumed with only a spoon and enthusiasm.

East

Kaiten—"revolving"—sushi is a craze in Tokyo that, for some reason, has never truly taken off in New York. Individual servings of sushi, along with Japanese appetizers, desserts, and various tidbits are covered with clear plastic hoods and placed on a conveyer belt that rotates past diners who can then pick what they like. Prices are calculated according to the color or pattern on each plate. At cheery, modish East, the floodlit sushi bar is shaped like a elongated tuning fork with seating around the outside and, between the prongs, an assembly station where sushi chefs do their wrapping, rolling, and pressing. Once they've transferred each preparation to the appropriate plate, quick as a flash they load it onto the conveyer belt that choo-choos clockwise.

Cost	$16–55

Address 366 3rd Ave, between 26th & 27th Sts
☎212/889-2326
Transportation 6 to 28th St
Open Mon–Fri noon–10.30pm, Sat & Sun 1–10.30pm
Accepts All major credit cards
Reservations Not accepted

In truth, the fresh sushi at East is distinguished neither by size nor artistry. But the prices are reasonable and the whole kaiten thing is fun. It's like the supermarket-style perfume shops that let you try everything. You may well regret the loss of personal service, but you can't resist the temptation. East regulars take pride in stacking up their finished plates into multicolored towers eight, twelve, or even fifteen layers high, while sneering at neighbors whose stack climbs no higher than four or five stories. Plate prices are as follows: $1 for white (California roll, salmon skin); $1.50 for pink (striped bass, spicy tuna roll); $2 for green (sardine, scallop-eel-cucumber), $2.50 for red (orange clam, tuna), $3 for blue (spicy yellowtail, toro-scallion roll); $4 for checker (sea urchin, dragon roll); $5 for gold (jumbo clam, toro).

Fishy, esoteric selections like scallop and herring roe tend to be best. Elaborate concoctions like the green Green River, an inside-out roll of eel, cucumber and avocado speckled with nori, go too heavy on the rice. Standard pieces—salmon, yellowtail, mackerel—are fine. The pink, green, and white little balls that revolve past you a hundred times are fortunately not priced as a sum of their colors. These sweet, yummy, red-bean-filled rice cakes are a red-plated dessert.

Flatiron, Gramercy Park & Union Square

Eleven Madison Park

The planter boxes behind Eleven Madison's tufted, black-leather banquettes must be bugged. How else to explain the fact the servers know exactly what diners want before they have a chance to ask? Such responsiveness, whether achieved through eavesdropping or something as prosaic as professionalism, is the hallmark of restaurateur Danny Meyer. His informal, unpretentious idea of multi-starred sophistication pervades this soaring rhapsody to Manhattan's Gilded Age. Through the vaulted entrance that corners a bulky Art Deco skyscraper, a towering ground-level space has been

| Cost | Lunch $30–75 |
| | Dinner $40–95 |

Address 11 Madison Ave at 24th St
☎212/889-0905
Transportation 6,N,R to 23rd St
Open Mon–Thurs 11.30am–2pm & 5.30–10.30pm, Fri 11.30am–2pm & 5.30–11pm, Sat 5.30–11pm
Accepts All major credit cards
Reservations Required

updated, like chef Kerry Heffernan's classically inspired cuisine, with sensitivity and good taste. Though rings of halogen lights hang down from period ceiling lamps, it's the terrazzo floors, Deco detailing in marble, wood and bronze, and giant arched windows that dazzle most.

That is until you experience the telepathic service, exquisite food, and expertly chosen wines. The drama of Heffernan's elegant dishes is experienced through incidental dashes of secondary flavors, not through radical combinations that steal attention from the star ingredients. A raw tuna appetizer ($13) has many things going on around it: caperberries, croutons, marinated cucumbers, outstanding Provençal olive oil. Still, the six narrow bars of pristine tuna are front and center. Tarte flambée ($12) lets smoked bacon, sautéed onions, and fromage blanc find their place, while blue hubbard squash flan with Brussels sprouts, black trumpet mushrooms, and marjoram butter ($11) is just one of the chef's many flan-tasies.

Main courses show off premium ingredients cooked to near perfection: a roasted loin and crisp braised shoulder of lamb is joined by orzo risotto, and goat cheese ($29). Succulent roast chicken, its crackling, St Tropez-tanned skin up, rests in with porcini broth ($25). The smoked bacon in roasted Maine lobster ($31) and Portuguese sausage in a monk-fish fricassée ($25) both understand their supporting roles. The $30.01 prix fixe New York market menu always features two of pastry chef Nicole Kaplan's fanciful desserts. Sadly, you only get to choose one.

Enoteca i Trulli

"There are 53 Barolos alone!" gushed the young man from Atlanta, scribbling notes into a spiral pad. "And all of them ready to drink!" Anyone as passionate about wines as this grande amatore will adore the wine bar that shares a wall, wine director, owner, Apulian ancestry, and pasta-making-mamma with the Southern Italian restaurant I Trulli. And even those unmoved by the list of some 400 bottles (how many can you drink in one sitting anyway?) will still find reasons to slot Enoteca into their dining itineraries. The shapely chairs of plywood and tubular steel, the twelve-seat, white-marble bar, and the large, gold-leaf-framed mirror add up to a cozy setting for sampling Italian wines, cheeses, and cured meats. And the three-course prix fixe ($20 at lunch, $25 at dinner) prepared by the close relation who lives next door is a steal.

| Cost | Lunch $20–60 |
| | Dinner $32–80 |

Address 122 East 27th St, between Park and Lexington Aves
☎212/481-7372
Transportation 6,N,R to 28th St
Open Mon–Fri noon–3pm & 5.30–10.30pm, Sat 5–11pm
Accepts All major credit cards
Reservations Not accepted

Fourteen wine-sampling "flights" ($8.25–24), grouped by region (Tuscany, Piedmont, etc), each consist of three wines poured into tasting glasses up to their 2oz lines. These let you assess the nuances of wines with comparable origins, varietals, and blends. You can then buy the one you like best, should you so desire, at Vino, the across-the-street shop co-owned by proprietor Nicola Marzovilla and wine director Charles Scicolone. On quantity alone, whole bottles (25oz) like the exceptional-value 1997 Brindisi Rosso Riserva from Vallone in Puglia ($24 in the eatery, $10 in the shop) do offer better value than the flights. Cheeses, cured meats, and olives may also be ordered as three-way samplers priced respectively at $10, $10, and $4. With the puffy, tomato-and-mozzarella-filled panzerotti (baked half-moon pastries; $10), one will do.

The prix fixe might start with lightly golden panelle (fried chickpea cakes) filled with goat cheese or a chunky caponata (a Sicilian relish of eggplant, tomato, olives, red peppers, and pine nuts). Next up, homemade pastas prepared by Dora Marzovilla, the owner's mother, are usually outstanding (chewy cavatelli with chopped broccoli rabe) and only occasionally disappointing (orecchiette with a overly sweet veal ragu). To close, the gelati are superior to the cookie plate.

Justin's

Velvet ropes and dumbbell-shaped door handles frame the red-carpeted entrance. Just inside, great-lookers with striking duds tracing the curves of their spectacular bodies huddle five-deep at the curvilinear bar. At the reception desk, it's difficult to tell if the usual refrain, "Can't seat you 'til your entire party has arrived," is passing through the lips of the diva hostess or coming from the sound system of the superstar record producer whose house this is. Sounds

Cost	$35–70

Address 31 West 21st St, between 5th & 6th Aves
☎212/352-0599
Transportation N,R,F,V to 23rd St
Open Daily 5pm–midnight
Accepts All major credit cards
Reservations Required

intimidating? You would be amazed how threatening Justin's is not. By snubbing neither fan nor foodie, the swank restaurant Sean Puffy Combs named after his son raises the bar or, more literally, the dining platform, for stylish, upscale, celebrity-owned eateries. Mere nobodies led up to the candlelit tables or the all-embracing corduroy booths are treated as privileged guests. And no one here is trying to modernize or glamorize Southern and Caribbean cuisine. Rather, the creative flourishes applied to familiar dishes seem inspired only by a desire to make things better.

Up first: dreamy smothered chicken livers set over fresh grits and garnished with fried and sautéed onions ($7). Great idea, great execution. Chicken wings in a sweet and sticky barbecue glaze ($7) are enticingly presented in a tiny, cast-iron skillet with blue-cheese dip. Spicy catfish fingers ($7) are so wonderfully delicate you wonder they don't fall apart when lifted out of the deep fryer. Among entrees there's plenty to choose from and plenty to eat. Nothing tops the Louisiana seafood gumbo ($21), though the Creole-style tomato-reddened gumbo also boasts an outstanding assortment of shellfish. Barbecued salmon ($22) has just enough of that sweet glaze that embellishes the chicken, while braised short ribs ($21) benefit from their heavy sweet-and-sour sauce. Only the smothered pork chops are heavy-handed, and eminently skippable.

To close, you're unlikely to find a better sweet potato pie ($7). There are two other desserts, though, that may intrigue you: the ethereal peach cobbler pastry, and the red-velvet pound cake with cream cheese frosting—fabulous, providing you don't try to figure out what makes it so virulent a red.

Pipa

The deliberately frayed and purposefully eccentric elegance of the in-store restaurant Pipa could well be defined as "Miss Havisham chic." Others may view its concoction of Venetian glass chandeliers, threadbare brocade, and decayed keepsakes as the result of a clever pruning of its inventory by home furnishings store ABC Carpet. Regardless, this estimation of what a Victorian attic might look like if submerged in the ocean for a century has certainly caught on with the young and restless. So few diners are over thirty years old that you might even assume there is someone at the door checking IDs.

| Cost | Lunch $15–50 |
| | Dinner $30–65 |

Address 38 East 19th St, between Broadway & Park Ave South

☎212/677-2233

Transportation 6,N,R to 23rd St

Open Mon–Thurs noon–3pm & 6pm–midnight, Fri noon–3pm & 5.30pm–midnight, Sat 11am–3pm & 5.30pm–1am, Sun 11am–3pm & 5.30–10pm

Accepts All major credit cards

Reservations Suggested

If any chef could upstage this elaborate staging it is the Nuevo Latino star Douglas Rodriguez (see Chicama, p.68), who has devised a thrilling concept of nuevos tapas untroubled by notions of authenticity. This goes unnoticed by the revelers who crowd the noisy dining room, communal table, and bar. Despite the impressive list of Spanish wines and sherries, most tables opt instead for a pitcher of superb sangria ($29). Moreover, no one sharing one of the enticing "cocoas" much cares if the makeup of these flatbreads has come entirely from the chef's imagination. The Moroccan lamb flatbread combo ($15) consists of ground lamb *and* rosemary-seared lamb tenderloin, with raisins, pine nuts, and goat cheese. The mushroom alternative ($14) carries a herb-seasoned mushroom purée and is topped with Manchego cheese, truffle oil, and grilled Portobellos.

Two of the better tapas are the trio of fried oysters ($12)—refitted into their shells with banana lentil salad, horseradish aioli, and slab bacon—and the almond-stuffed, bacon-wrapped dates ($8), poised at the tip of endive leaves. The lamb meatballs ($9) need an accompaniment to soak up their rich salsa. Although the small plates seem best suited to Rodriguez's big excesses, his "new paella" ($24) possesses an awesome array of shellfish. It takes a good fifteen minutes to get down to the rice. Among desserts ($8), the three-chocolate terrine is a pretty confection.

Flatiron, Gramercy Park & Union Square

La Pizza Fresca

When you fold a slice cut from a great New York pizza, its oozy overlay of molten mozzarella streams down a puddle of piping-hot tomato sauce towards the tip of the triangle. The expectation of that sensual first bite makes it difficult for natives to appreciate pies of another origin and style, including those from Naples, the birthplace of pizza Margherita. That's why chauvinistic locals may at first be cool to the authentic, soft, and dainty Neapolitan pies baked in a wood-fired brick "igloo" at La Pizza Fresca. But those who stop comparing and start relishing soon learn to cherish the city's only pizzeria to be awarded the "Attesta" certificate of authenticity by the Associazione Vera Pizza Napoletana in Naples. Though the decor merits no such accolades, wall murals do add whimsy and warmth to a narrow dining room imparted, like the pizza crusts, with the smoky aroma of the wood-fired oven.

| Cost | Lunch $20–40 |
| | Dinner $25–60 |

Address 31 East 20th St, between Broadway & Park Ave South

☎212/598-0141

Transportation N,R,6 to 23rd St

Open Mon–Fri noon–3.30pm & 5.30–11pm, Sat & Sun 5.45–11pm

Accepts All major credit cards

Reservations For large groups

The exacting standards of the Associazione require the use of fresh mozzarella di bufala (Buffalo), San Marzano tomatoes, Italian olive oil, a special flour, and a wood-burning oven. The upshot is a thin, lightly charred, appealingly bubbly crust that provides gentle resistance and compression. Small individual pizzas ($8.95-16.95) come in fifteen varieties. The house pie, "La Pizza Fresca," adds the drama of explosive cherry tomatoes and black olives to the pure Margherita (tomato, mozzarella, basil). The Quattro Stagioni, with prosciutto, mushrooms, and artichokes, is also recommended.

Pizza Fresca also serves up some pretty good starters. Best of the lot is the teepee of grilled zucchini, eggplant, carrot, and peppers drizzled with balsamic, propped over salad greens, and served, as all appetizers are, with wonderfully thin, focaccia-style bread baked in the brick oven ($7.95). The cleanly fried squid and sautéed spinach are decent alternatives. Though pastas are in general no better than anything offered at other nearby Italian restaurants, the simplicity of the rigatoni alla Siciliana (sautéed eggplant woven with mozzarella, basil, and marinara; $13.75) does complement the elemental pizza approach.

Plate 347

(icon) Chefs and jazzmen follow comparable paths to notoriety. They gain notice by gigging with the greats, but rarely achieve stardom until they go out on their own. At Plate 347, Francisco Diaz has made the successful transition from "roundsman," as utility cooks are known, to front man. He mastered his riffs playing backup. Now he's composed his own worldly but unfussy menu. His cooking distinguishes a bistro with the soft glow of a classic, untrendy New York haunt. The tin ceiling, exposed brick wall, light-wooded floorboards, and copper-

Cost	$25–65

Address 347 2nd Ave, between 20th & 21st Sts
(phone) 212/388-0526
Transportation 6 to 23rd St; L to 3rd Ave
Open Mon–Thurs 5–11pm, Fri 5pm–midnight, Sat 11.30am–3pm & 5pm–midnight, Sun 11.30am–3pm & 5–11pm
Accepts All major credit cards

FRENCH/NEW AMERICAN

plated bar make you want to become a fixture yourself. The white-clothed tables constitute a tight if cozy squeeze for a crowd of up to 35 that gets younger and less dressy as the evening progresses. More space surrounds the Moorish mosaic tables in the 35-seat courtyard garden.

You can taste a hint of Le Bernardin's signature shellfish fricassée in the faintly creamed tomato-garlic-shallot broth of the steamed mussels ($7.50). Served with garlic croutons and crusty Sullivan Bakery bread, this is a stupendous sopping opportunity. Other fine starters include sautéed calamari curls detonated with spicy piquillo peppers and garlic ($9). The pears, walnuts, and Roquefort in the classic frisée salad are collected inside crisp triangles made with ultra-thin sheets of strudel dough ($8). Inspired! The braised Moroccan lamb shank ($21) is an entree of great magnitude. Last-minute heating creates a crusty coating that seals in the unctuousness of the meat. Another standout entree is the solid—though not terribly tender—grilled sirloin topped with the fat-fueled pungency of horseradish marrow butter ($21). The accompanying fries are frighteningly close to perfect. You'll like too the potato-crusted salmon with sautéed spinach and piquillo peppers ($17) and the seared, black-sesame-seed-dotted yellowfin tuna with soba noodles ($22).

Desserts are limited, with only two selections you'll want to get intimate with: the delicately crisp apple tart ($6) and the mini-chocolate "bundt" cake with fresh whipped cream and raspberries.

Republic

🍽 The Asian noodle shop conforms to a new political order at this soaring, whimsically designed, and frighteningly efficient Republic. Communal seating on blond-wood benches provides monastic austerity without zen-like quietude. And if the thunderous clamor and lighting-fast service still fall short of giving you and yours the jitters, the ludicrously arty, black-and-white blowups of women with noodles wrapped around their bare bodies can always be counted on to irritate more females than they do titillate males. Be that as it may, Republic is a winner. The eating is good, the people-watching (and that includes the black-clad servers) is even better, and the cost of doing both is extremely low for so enduringly stylish a concept eatery.

Cost	$15–40

Address 37 Union Square West, between 16th & 17th Sts
☎212/627-7168
Transportation 4,5,6,L,N,Q, R,W to 14th St–Union Square
Open Sun–Wed 11.30am–11pm, Thurs–Sat 11.30am–midnight
Accepts All major credit cards
Reservations Not accepted

After ordering at most restaurants, there's usually time to wash your hands, tell a knock-knock joke or, at the very least, lay an unfolded napkin over your lap before the appetizers arrive. At Republic you must be ready to eat seconds after your server punches in your request on a hand-held keypad and instantaneously transmits it to the behind-the-counter kitchen. Luckily, dishes don't suffer from the advance prepping. The vaguely Thai, Vietnamese, and/or Japanese food is fresh, flavorsome, and never oversalted. And the occasional citrusy excesses do perk up the salads and broths. Top picks among the so-called "small dishes" include an acutely spicy cold seafood salad with shrimp, calamari, teeny bay scallops, crunchy jicama, and Thai basil ($5), grilled calamari in a scrumptious but not cloying soy glaze ($5), and a seaweed salad with cucumber, mint, ginger, and a tofu-sesame vinaigrette ($4).

The best of the noodle soup entrees is the steamed salmon with vermicelli and bean sprouts in a coconut broth ($8), but for the tastiest options you should head for the soup-less noodle dishes. Here you'll find galangal-marinated, lettuce-wrapped grilled beef slices paired with angel-hair rice noodles ($9) and flat, leathery strips of BBQ garlic pork with julienned daikon, cucumber, and carrot propped over cold vermicelli ($9). Coconut sorbet ($3) is worth staying for, if you're not in too much of a hurry to get your sore butt off the hard bench.

Sushi Samba

Due to Japanese immigration to Brazil, sushi and samba have long shared the same turf and surf. But at Sushi Samba the Brazil/Japan pairing isn't quite on the mark. Eiji Takase ("Taka"), the mastermind behind this creative restaurant, is actually inspired by the food of Peru, not Brazil. It was Lima he visited to learn about ceviche and devise a fusion cuisine, not Rio. That said, the Brazilian gimmick does work beautifully. With bossa nova pouring from its speakers, and cachaca, the Brazilian liquor, poured into its cocktails, this smash success now has a second locale in the West Village (87 7th Ave South; ☎212/691-7885) and a third in South Miami Beach.

Cost	$30–60

Address 245 Park Ave South, between 19th & 20th Sts
☎212/475-9377
Transportation 6 to 23rd St
Open Mon–Wed 11.45am–1am, Thurs–Sat 11.45am–2am, Sun 1pm–midnight
Accepts All major credit cards
Reservations Required

The stunning, glass-paneled storefront of the original resembles a Mondrian pieced together with a tropical palette. The interior is wrapped in mango-orange walls and guava-red banquettes, all dotted with a touch of 1960s futurism. Overhead, a galaxy of Plexiglass domes illuminates the central sushi bar. Servers are rightly programmed to ensure that no diner overlooks the sashimi-like ceviches, best sampled in tasting platters of four ($27) or eight. To accompany the ceviche Taka plays with an assortment of Japanese garnishes, setting them off with Peruvian chiles. From the apples, soy sauce, and sake dressing to the shaved coconut, coconut milk, and mango paste that anoints the sea urchin, each seems to pack more refreshing thrills than the next.

Elsewhere on the menu, chile peppers take over, sometimes to detrimental effect. Korean chile paste overpowers a good yellowtail tartare ($7.50), a mistake repeated by firing the yellowtail sushi roll with minced jalapenos ($7). The sweet standout among sushi is the Rainbow Dragon ($13), a beautifully crafted roll of eel, daikon sprouts, and red and yellow pepper meticulously wrapped in thin, smooth slices of mango and avocado. The same artistry inspires the hako ($7.50), a spicy salmon roll with a thick spread of marshmallow-like mozzarella, a pile of fried onions, and a few squiggles of mayo. Cooked foods hold less interest. For dessert, it's difficult to resist the silky coconut panna cotta ($7) or the chocolate tamale ($7), essentially a warm dark chocolate cake.

Tavern at Gramercy Tavern

Many of New York's best-value bistros profit from trickle-down gastronomics. They adapt, simplify, and slash the price of food fashions introduced by star chefs like Tom Colicchio and award-winning pastry chefs like Claudia Fleming at elite, trend-setting restaurants like Danny Meyer's Gramercy Tavern. Colicchio and Fleming might have a slightly less flattering characterization of these imitations, some of them produced by ex-employees. Fortunately for him and us, the Tavern's fifty-seat tavern gives Colicchio the chance to design his own knock-offs (he does the same for Craft, his second restaurant, at Craft Bar; see p.70). You get access to the true flavors, easy elegance, and outstanding wines-by-the-glass and cheeseboard selections of a great New York restaurant without having to make reservations or loan applications.

Cost	$25–65

Address 42 East 20th St, between Broadway & Park Ave South
℡212/477-0777
Transportation 6,N,R to 23rd St
Open Sun–Thurs noon–11pm, Fri & Sat noon–midnight
Accepts All major credit cards
Reservations Not accepted

Sure, the Tavern's tavern requires sacrifice. You'll wait for one of the smallish, cafe-style tables and you won't be seeing any foie gras after you get there. But appetizers like marinated quail with polenta and grilled radicchio ($12) and grilled baby octopus with shaved fennel, lemon confit, and sweet pepper caponata ($12) suggest zero compromise. Colicchio's inventive associations of Greenmarket-driven, razor-sharp flavors are as salient here as they are in the dining room. The kitchen isn't cutting back. It is devising simpler dishes better suited to the comparatively compressed and informal circumstances.

If there's envy in the air, it could just as easily be felt for as by diners restricted to the Tavern menu. The marinated vegetable and buttery Taleggio cheese sandwich on ciabatta ($14) is an unfettered, hands-on delight that wouldn't fly in the dining room. Who in so formal a setting would dare lick the caper aioli that's prone to leak from that sandwich? In addition, no part of the filet mignon with mashed potatoes and balsamic-onion relish ($19.50) can be improved upon. Not even by Colicchio himself. The only complaint with Fleming's desserts is that she tires of (and consequently replaces) her oft-copied successes much sooner than her fans do.

Union Square Cafe

As new and original as it was—and still is—for its time, the beloved Union Square Cafe was already a classic on the day it opened in October 1995. It's hard for anyone to recall this block without the distinctive USC awning and, seen through the picture windows, the colorful modern art hung on its dining room walls. Someday this address will bear a plaque marking the site where restaurateur Danny Meyer pioneered and perfected the Meyer Touch, a service style that was at once friendly, helpful, casual, and omnipresent. Every time you looked up there was a waiter to assist, if not necessary yours. The ensuing acclaim, first local and then national, was unprece-

Cost	Lunch $25–65 Dinner $45–85

Address 21 West 16th St, between Union Square West & 5th Ave

℡212/243-4020

Transportation 4,5,6,N,Q,R,W to 14th St-Union Square

Open Mon–Thurs noon–2.30pm & 6–10.30pm, Fri & Sat noon–2.30pm & 6–11.30pm, Sun 5.30–10pm

Accepts All major credit cards

Reservations Required

dented for so informal a restaurant and distinguishes Meyer's achievement as a patently American success story. Given its lofty reputation, some first-timers are shocked and, in an odd way, dismayed to discover the famous Union Square Cafe to be so devoid of opulence and stiffness. Their disappointment rarely lasts through dinner, however, as the four-week wait for its 125 seats will attest.

Chef Michael Romano's eclectic but accessible cuisine was always a great match for the service and every bit as influential. Signature dishes that were innovative then are now commonplace at contemporary American and Italian-nuanced restaurants around the country: most of the 1001 lobster (or seafood) shepherd's pies, mascarpone-creamed polentas, rare tuna steaks, and caramelized banana tarts of our dining lives can all be traced back to Sixteenth Street.

The noteworthy pricing policy is reflected in the $12.50 tag on the USC hamburger. Sure, that seems a high for a burger. But once you get your hands on that marvel, its juices sealed in a delicately packed patty with no cracks or crevices, the lunch-only sensation is instantly appreciated as an unparalleled bargain on a poppyseed bun. Likewise, the dinner entrees, though up in the twenties ($26 for grilled salmon, $25.50 for lemon-pepper duck, $26.50 for seared wild stripe bass), constitute a price leap down from other elite New York restaurants.

83

Greenwich Village & NoHo

Arturo's

🍴 NYU students, Greenwich Village musicians, Italian expats, movie buffs from the nearby Film Forum and Angelica Film Center, and pizza lovers everywhere should raise a glass of inexpensive red to local kid Arturo Giunta and the friendly haunt he opened in 1957. Romantic attachments to this dowdy looking cheap-date favorite are unrelated to the presence of a bathtub in the restroom. They've more to do with the cool breeze of live jazz that blows the steam off sizzling, coal-oven-baked pizzas esteemed for their crisp and resilient crusts, pristine mozzarella, zesty (to the point of fruity) tomato sauce, and matchmaking attributes. Suitors who discard crust ends like fish bones may be hopelessly neurotic, but they do get along quite well with the shameless scavengers who scoop them up.

Cost	$15–55

Address 106 West Houston St at Thompson St

☎212/677-3820

Transportation A,C,E,F,V to West 4th St; 1,2 to Houston St; 6 to Bleecker St

Open Mon–Thurs 4pm–1am, Fri & Sat 4pm–2am, Sun 3pm–midnight

Accepts All major credit cards

Reservations Weekdays only

ITALIAN/PIZZA

A large pie, which could conceivably be shared by four people, costs between $12 and $17, depending on your choice of extra toppings: anchovies, bacon, eggplant, meatballs, mushrooms, pepperoni, peppers, onions, sausage. The Arturo's Fiesta is a tempting and fortunately not top-heavy compilation of sausage, mushrooms, peppers, and onions. A little fresh chopped garlic doesn't hurt either. A full menu of Italian food is also available and, were you to judge from the eating habits of the people who ostensibly know Arturo's best, worth investigating. Just before dinnertime, the kitchen and service staffs can be seen gleefully gorging on unidentifiable pasta concoctions of one sort or another. Oddly, while you'll never see them eating pizza, you yourself will regret any foray beyond the pizza list. The best advice is to stray no further than the inoffensive cold antipasto ($4.75).

Choice front-room booths close to the bar and the music prove to be worth a short wait, while the sidewalk tables on Houston and Thompson are ideal for moonlit summer evenings. There are also two rear rooms, which double as galleries. The paintings, though signed by an artist who, like Leonardo and Michelangelo, is widely recognized by his first name, are unremarkable. Pizza is Arturo's shtick, and we raise a glass of Chianti in praise of his art.

Greenwich Village & NoHo

Babbo

No road atlas will help you pinpoint the origins of Mario Batali's cooking. But understanding the appeal of Batalian cuisine, with its Italian regional influences and New World inventions, is simple: its founding father crowds his plates with crisp flavors and properly cooked, piping hot food. Babbo, which is Italian for daddy, is the two-papa partnership of restaurateur Joe Bastianich (Esca, see p.216) and Batali, whose charisma as a TV Food Network personality helped make Po one of the hottest meal tickets in Manhattan. Babbo is quartered on two

Cost	$45–95

Address 110 Waverly Place, between 6th Ave & MacDougal St

☎212/777-0303

Transportation A,C,E,F,Q,V to West 4th St

Open Mon–Sat 5.30–11.30pm, Sun 5–11pm

Accepts All major credit cards

Reservations Required

floors of a one-time coach house off Washington Square. On the lower level, beyond the bar and its oak library of liquid diversions, is a softly lit room that, like the menu, splits the difference between dressy and casual, upscale and rustic. From leather banquettes, couples sitting side-by-side face out towards a beautiful round service table displaying fruit, cheeses, wines, olive oils, wines, and a floral arrangement.

Appetizers establish Batali as the daddy of 100 vinaigrettes. He accents that mother sauce with spicy quince for grilled octopus ($14), or with thyme for thinly sliced testa (headcheese) coated with a mustard-seed crunch ($10). These notes never drown—or drown out—a dish. It's the tricolored beets and not the rhubarb dressing you notice most on the sopressata starter ($13).

It's fine to order a pasta in lieu of a main course, but never the reverse. Star turns include the mint love letters ($18), elongated parcels of mint purée accompanied by a spicy lamb sausage ragu, and chopped beef cheek ravioli ($19) with a squab liver purée and sliced truffles. The seven-course, pasta-heavy tasting menu, including matching wines, offers great value at $59. If you're not choosing pasta, you'll enjoy the excess of the grilled lamb chops, a teepee of meat with caponata and cumin yogurt ($29), or the elegance of whole roasted branzino fish ($27) with lemon oregano jam. For dessert, pastry chef Gina De Palma wows with her chocolate-sauced pistachio semifreddo ($9), her orange-sauced chocolate hazelnut cake ($9), and her enchanting sorbetti-gelati tasting presented in six mini-glasses ($8).

Bar Pitti

🍴 No ostensibly rational individual can leave Bar Pitti without a strong opinion about Giovanni Tognozzi, its bald-headed host/co-owner, and his service brigade. To cope with the nightly overflow at this bargain Florentine annex to the forever trendy Da Silvano, tables both inside and on a hip terrace prized for its people-watching are hastily filled and hurriedly emptied in an arbitrary manner. Detractors maintain they've been seated behind others who've arrived after them

Cost	$20–55

Address 268 6th Ave, between Bleecker & Houston Sts
☎212/982-3300
Transportation 1,2 to Houston St; A,C,E,F,V to West 4th St
Open Daily noon–midnight
Accepts Cash only
Reservations For large groups

and then felt bullied to eat fast and get out. Devotees insist the seating policy is fair and regard the service as prompt and professional with a flavorsome give-and-take between knowing server and diner. Though many subscribe to the second position, it may be because they're simply desperate to stay in Giovanni's good graces. The best advice is either to take pleasure in this fascinating blend of Italian brio, gusto, and impertinenza, or to come during off-hours.

When, sooner or later, you do sit down, a laminated menu is immediately tossed your way while the specials blackboard is leaned against the nearest wall, empty chair, or diner's shoulder. It's the oft-running specials that interest most, with such appetizers as the heartiest of ribollitas (Florentine vegetable and bread soup; $5.50), insalata pitti (peppery arugula topped with sautéed artichokes and sheets of Parmesan; $7.50), grilled cuttlefish ($10.50), and a herb-perfumed melanzane alla parmigiana (thinly sliced eggplant casserole; $8.50) that two could easily share—as an entree!

The most requested pasta is pappardelle alla fiesolana ($10.50), its ribbons sensuously entwined with smoked bacon in a creamy tomato sauce with Parmesan. It and the similarly sauced rigatoni Pitti (with turkey sausage and peas; $10.50) can only lead to a re-evaluation of all self-imposed bans on cream sauces. Oven-roasted whole fish (market price about $15) is dependably fresh. Ask which desserts are homemade—the waiters like this question—and you get a choice between chocolate mousse, tiramisu, and panna cotta. The tiramisu ($5.50) isn't bad, but the dark chocolate-sauced panna cotta ($6) is brilliant.

Blue Hill

🍴 Located in a townhouse just south of Washington Square, Blue Hill does cutting-edge, market-driven (as in the Union Square Greenmarket, not Nasdaq) contemporary American cuisine with bistro-styled informality. What it does not do, however, is offer bistro-styled pricing. Cheap it is not. Tremendous value and a wonderful dining experience it is. Indirect lighting hidden beneath both the high-backed banquettes and the low ceiling's recessed perforations gives a welcome impression of space in this confined room. This

Cost	$45–75

Address 75 Washington Place, between MacDougal St & 6th Ave
☎212/539-1776
Transportation A,C,E,F,V to West 4th St
Open Mon-Sat 5.30–11pm, Sun 5.30–10pm
Accepts All major credit cards
Reservations Required

artful enhancement of volume reflects the cooking approach of co-owner Dan Barber, who, with kitchen partner Michael Anthony, brings intensity, texture, but not heaviness to his contemporary, seasonal cooking. Few chefs can do more things in more ways to a sauce, a purée, a broth, or a foamy emulsion than Dan and Michael.

A crabmeat lasagna appetizer ($14), assembled between two thin homemade pasta sheets, benefits both from the amplification of grain mustard and the intensity of spinach purée. Gently steamed foie gras ($14) is served with red wine to absorb the broth left from its garbure (Southwest French stew) of summer vegetables. Every evening, a different ceviche ($10) is featured under the "simply raw" heading: sea bass with pomegranate vinaigrette, perhaps. Rotated seasonal main courses might include poached cod with a delectable starchy vichyssoise broth ($22) and, if you're very lucky, the exceptional hanger steak ($25) with crusty, caramelized chunks of deep-pink meat joined by pancetta-laced potatoes and an astonishing loose spinach purée that's practically an ink. The poached duck ($25) is a revelation. Rounds of tender breast meat as perfectly pink as prime rib contrasts with the crispness of the confit.

Be warned: since the menu changes regularly, some great relationships between dish and diner can be painfully brief. Happily, the outrageously fine chocolate brioche pudding ($10) is available every night of the year. A very good argument can be made for skipping dessert elsewhere and stopping at the bar here for an order.

BondSt

BondSt's instant allure was no shocker. Its owners had already licked the trick of flicking a switch and having hordes of beautiful people turn up before the lights go on. That the quartet behind the eternally hip Indochine (see p.95) was able to repeat its gravity-defying feat is, however, remarkable. Since opening in 1998, the Japanese triplex refuses to come down from its fashionable high. Inside a bleached brownstone and directly above a dark and sexy cocktail lounge/sushi bar is a deafening dining room whose stark modernity is softened by elegant lighting and gossamer fabrics. Diners may lean their backs against curvilinear booths or throw pillows, both of which are preferable to the cramped seating in the brighter, more stylized rear sushi room.

Cost	$40–80

Address 6 Bond St, between Broadway & Lafayette St
℡212/777-2500
Transportation 6 to Bleecker St
Open Mon–Sat 6pm–midnight, Sun 6–11pm
Accepts All major credit cards
Reservations Required

The appeal of Hiroshi Nakahara's sushi is less about fish quality than innovative presentation. His adorable hini zuchi, with mini-pieces of tuna, yellowtail, clam, shrimp, fluke, egg, and salmon, delights his customers *and* his bosses. The former get novel, manageable, bite-size pieces; the latter, an $18 charge for half the usual quantity of fish. The hot eel dice ($10) is beautiful propped atop an inside-out avocado roll. Arugula crispy potato roll ($6), with the crunch of finely julienned potato sticks, is a revelation.

If BondSt aspires to be the Nobu of NoHo, it helps to have one of that acclaimed restaurant's former chefs at the helm. Two of Linda Rodriguez's soups, both made with a base of dashi (seaweed and dried bonita broth), proffer Zen-like goodness: truffle and mushroom ($8), and spicy, cirtrusy crab ($8). Other good starters: sliced duck breast in a rich, fruity glaze ($12); fried monkfish in a crystalline spicy and sour salsa ($12); juicy, grilled blue water shrimp with a purée of Japanese eggplant ($14). Entrees best for sharing include broiled, miso-marinated Chilean sea bass ($25); dry-aged rib-eye steak tossed in a thrilling stir-fry ($25); and succulent rack of lamb in an Asian pear sauce ($25). Despite the leanness of the servers and the regulars, the chocolate fondue ($14 for two) is not a gravity-defying dessert. It descends directly to the hips. The fruit alternatives ($8) are nicer anyhow.

Il Buco

You might initially be drawn into Il Buco, nestled among the galleries and shops at the east end of cobbled Bond Street, out of curiosity (how much is that creepy marionette in the window?), but it's the sophisticated wine selection, effortlessly artful food, and informed, gracious service that will keep you in your big wooden chair until the last drop of Barolo is gone. Unlike other Manhattan restaurants, whose attempts to transform their interiors feel expensive yet ephemeral, Il Buco, heaped with gorgeous antiques (all of them for sale) and discreetly oozing Italian charm, succeeds in convincing you that this space has always been a warm, fire-lit Tuscan farmhouse. Co-owner Alberto Avalle hails from Umbria and is passionate about the exquisite olive oils from that region. A novel way to launch your meal is with a tasting of oils ($3–5 per 2oz decanter, plus a basket of bread for dipping), whose qualities are explained, upon request, by sommelier Roberto Peras.

| Cost | Lunch $20-80 |
| | Dinner $40-80 |

Address 47 Bond St, between Bowery & Lafayette St
☎212/533-1932
Transportation F,V to Broadway-Lafayette; 6 to Bleecker St
Open Sun & Mon 6pm–midnight, Tues–Sat noon–4pm & 6pm–midnight
Accepts AmEx
Reservations Suggested

Starter ingredients are wholly governed by the seasons. In autumn and winter, you'll be wooed by radishes cooked in bagna cauda ($8), a heady bath of anchovies, garlic, and one of the featured Umbrian oils. Spring temptations encompass a salad of fava beans and pea greens ($8), or sardines a la plancha ($11)—rich, fresh fish split and seared. Thinly sliced cooked beets stand in for pasta year round in a goat-cheese-filled "ravioli" ($10).

There is risotto ($20) on the menu at Il Buco every night. During strawberry season (and a few weeks past), the chef prepares an odd-sounding but exquisite version with Parmigiano-Reggiano and the red fruits that makes a great case for sweet-savory taste combinations. On other nights, octopus and mussels, their flavors highlighted with a bit of saffron, hide among the creamy kernels of Arborio rice. Other choices include calf's liver with mashed potatoes and seasonal greens ($27)—fresh, tender, perfectly cooked—while the roasted baby chicken with baby carrots and smashed fingerling potatoes ($27) reinforces the sense that you're just a few steps away from the garden, the barn, and the hills of Italy.

Five Points

To break bread here on Great Jones Street is to emulate Al Capone, Lucky Luciano, and other members of the notorious Five Points Gang. But the gang's namesake eatery is not a recreation of their headquarters, the New Brighton Dance Hall. It's actually more of a woodsy, stylish, New Age dining car. Beneath the vaulted ceiling, and bisecting two rows of faux train windows, is a hallowed, 25-foot oak log that carries a southward flow of water. (Surprisingly, they don't seem to use it to cart dirty

Cost	$30–75

Address 31 Great Jones St, between Bowery & Lafayette St
☎212/253-5700
Transportation 6 to Bleecker St; F,V to Broadway-Lafayette
Open Mon–Sat 5pm–midnight; Sun 11.30am–3pm & 6–10pm
Accepts All major credit cards
Reservations Suggested

cups and glasses back to the dishwasher.) This is a stunning, if clamorous, showcase for the Mediterranean-accented, pleasure-principled cooking of co-owner Marc Meyer, a disciple of star chef Larry Forgione. Considering the value at Five Points, the day has come when Larry might want to put Marc's name on *his* resumé.

Opening acts from the rotated menu could be the star attractions in a lesser venue. Tough deal for any entree to follow the fritto misto ($8.50), a dizzyingly delicious "mixed fry" of golden artichokes, fennel, and lemon. A second destination appetizer is the sauerkraut with grilled quail and a thick slab of smoky bacon ($9.50). Yet a third starter standout is the brandade ($9), a garlicky purée of potato and salt cod bronzed like hash browns and inventively presented in a square iron skillet with crusty sourdough country bread. Alternatively, there are a couple of good seafood salads: one with lobster, asparagus, pea shoots, and fava beans ($11), and a larger dish with rare tuna, romaine lettuce, white runner beans, onions, and celery ($10). The wood-burning oven imparts character to such entrees as the baked lamb casserole ($21) and the buttermilk chicken ($18). Try also the house-cured, double-cut pork chop ($21) and the chargrilled bacon cheeseburger ($12.50).

The smart wine list features fruity reds and whites from France's Loire Valley as well as Alsatian whites ideally suited to the fresh, aggressively (sometimes excessively) flavored cooking. If there's two of you, try this dessert deal: one take the chocolate brioche pudding, one take the rustic apple tart, and then go halvsies.

Impala Café

(icon) Jean-Claude Iacovelli, the garçon-turned-restaurateur who built the model for bistros-on-a-shoestring, has become a victim of his own success. He must now contend with competitors in precincts throughout Manhattan, Brooklyn, and, any day now, Queens. These days you can't throw a rock through a restaurant window without hitting a waiter who dreams of opening a bistro. In light of this, the lines of expectant diners that used to greet the opening of a Iacovelli bistro have been missing

Cost	$15–50

Address 132 West Houston St, between Thompson & Sullivan Sts
☎646/602-1147
Transportation 1,2 to Houston St; A,C,E,F,V to West 4th St
Open Daily 8am–midnight
Accepts Cash only
Reservations For large groups

from Impala Café. Though we care about Jean-Claude's success, and drink often to his good fortune, the instant access to a choice table on even a Friday night bothers us very little. A $6.50 bowl of mussels tastes every bit as good without the anticipatory build-up of a ninety-minute wait.

Iacovelli can put together an endearing bistro like Impala in his sleep. Old floorboards topped with lipstick-red banquettes. Chrome-trimmed yellow Formica tables beside a red Formica bar. Stamped-tin ceiling. Superb bread from Sullivan Bakery. The new wrinkle here is a rear lounge with low-slung seating and a $14 prix fixe from 5pm to 8pm. Even without that early bird special, the value is still extraordinary. You'll pay $8 for a large salad of chickpeas, grilled corn, tomatoes, peppery arugula, and a balsamic drizzle, or $6 for a pile of good fried calamari with a bland remoulade. And how does $7 for buttery escargot with garlic, lemon, and parsley sound?

Entrees, too, are bargains. Although the cooking is perhaps too straightforward to write home about, at least you won't need to phone mom and dad for a loan. Perfectly acceptable cod with black olive mashed potatoes is a steal ($13); so too would be the steak au poivre ($15), were it not for the dreadful frozen fries. Shame on you, Iacovelli. All is forgiven, however, when it comes to the pressed pork sandwich on ciabatta with melted Gruyère and chive garlic ($8). It's a sort of a Cubano-Provençal panini, and it's delicious. Lastly, the crème caramel is divine. An exact copy should be coming any day to a bistro near you.

Indochine

🍽 It was a little past eight on a Thursday evening and only three tables were occupied. The conclusion was clear. Indochine, the perennially trendy haunt with higher interest rates than a loan shark had finally hit rock bottom. Not so fast. One hour later, the French colonial bistro, with its palm-leaf wallpaper and seductive lighting, was filling up. By 9.30pm it was obvious that the only feature about the place that had dropped to new lows were the waistbands. Bare belly buttons and the flat-tummied gazelles attached to them were everywhere. The green banquettes were mostly obscured by the black garb of shoulder-to-shoulder diners. And the heady glamor throughout made every other place in town seem as hopelessly unhip as, well, Indochine at 8pm.

Cost	$35–70

Address 430 Lafayette St, between 4th St & Astor Place
☎212/228-5555
Transportation 6 to Astor Place; N,R to 8th St
Open Sun–Thurs 5.30pm–midnight, Fri & Sat 5.30pm–12.30am
Accepts All major credit cards
Reservations Suggested

So how's the Frenchified Vietnamese food? Certainly no worse and probably better than ever. Huy Chi Le, the Saigon native who started here in 1984 as an off-the-boat bus boy, is now the executive chef and co-owner. (He and partners Michael Callahan and Jean-Marc Houmard also own BondSt and Republic; see p.91 and p.80). His remarkable rise might suggest that this was just the man to finally bring the entrees up to the level of the appetizers. But no. Loading up on appetizers and going light on—or ignoring altogether—the mains is still the best approach.

Crunchy spring rolls plucked from the hot oil come with two fillings: seafood ($7) or chicken ($8), with vegetables and vermicelli. Get them both. Pristine slices of deep-pink beef make up a good two thirds of the spicy beef salad ($11.50), and crisp breaded shrimp stuffed with artichoke and shiitakes ($9.50) are fitted so that their tails protrude like handles—ideal for dipping into the pimento-plum sauce. Don't miss the outstanding spare ribs ($8.50), which are marinated and grilled yet neither glazed nor sauced. The notes of lemongrass and anise turn "chewy" and "dry" into positives. If you must have an entree, try fat-rimmed roast duck with ginger sauce ($18.50); steamed sea bass fillet with fresh ginger, scallions, and asparagus ($20); or roasted five-spice Cornish hen ($18.50).

Knickerbocker Bar & Grill

Just as the waitress served the young couple crispy duck breast with duck confit, a fig-and-caramelized onion tart, and balsamic vinaigrette ($18.75), her colleague brought to the next table a T-bone steak-for-three ($84) large enough to stagger a hockey team. The guys taking on the beef checked out the young lovers' order and they theirs. Then they each turned back to their companions and sneered: "Do you believe those guys, ordering something like *that* at a place like *this*!" Such encounters are commonplace at a neighborhood main-

Cost	Lunch $20–55
	Dinner $35–75

Address 33 University Place at 9th St

☎212/228-8490

Transportation N,R to 8th St

Open Sun & Mon 11.45am–midnight, Tues–Thurs 11.45am–1am, Fri & Sat 11.30am–2am

Accepts All major credit cards

stay equally comfortable with po' boys and porcini flan, conversational lunches and live-jazz suppers, $25 Montepulciano and $350 Bordeaux, discreet celebrities and flashy nobodies, undergraduate cliques and solitary seniors. There's something undeniably reassuring about this place, with its dark-wood fixtures and comfy crescent-shaped booths, Abe Hirshfeld prints and old New York posters on the burgundy walls.

The Knickerbocker is a deceptively nostalgic showcase for contemporary cooking. The kitchen embraces innovation as well as it preserves tradition. Perhaps too well. While such appetizers as salmon carpaccio ($8.75) or crisp flatbread with grilled lamb, sausage, and goat cheese ($10.75) are generally good, it's archaic specialties like the eccentric caviar pie ($9.25)—a cake-like wedge of egg salad, sour cream, and cream cheese "iced" with black caviar and toast points—that you won't get anywhere else. And who could resist late-night (after 10pm) snacks like the mini-meatballs and the Cuban sandwich ($13.75) made with suckling pig and mango mustard?

Among pastas, the fettucine with short ribs Bolognese ($15.75) effectively skirts the divide between timeless and timely satisfactions. The famous T-bone endures ($29) as the house favorite, but the grilled filet mignon ($25.50) is also a power hitter. You'll go back in a flash for the seared tuna ($19.95) or, from the lunch and late-night menus, the solid Knickerbocker bacon cheeseburger ($11). Choosing between the chocolate soufflé-for-two ($8.75) and the hot fudge sundae deluxe ($6.50) is a decision that no one can make for you.

Lupa

🍴 Alas the world is not perfect. Yes, at Lupa there exist adorable bowls of superlatively simple pasta for as little as $9. True, entrees on the cutting edge of rustic chic do max out at $15. Sure, some dozen Italian wines are poured by the carafina, perfect for sip-sampling the moonlit Manhattan night away. Yet this 70-seat paradiso shatters its utopian scenario with one omission. A choice table has not been kept open at all times in anticipation of the possibility of your coming in. Named after the she-wolf of Roman mythology and inspired by Rome's neighborhood trattorias, Lupa is the second of three smash-hits from co-owners Mario Batali and Joe Bastianich (Babbo and Esca are the others; see p.88 and p.216). Managing partner Jason Denton ('ino; see p.157) unsnarls traffic jams in the countrified space and assists an informed service staff. Chef Mark Landner plays with the Italian regional influences and New World constructions that together define Mario's "Batalian" cooking. If the performance at Babbo is electric, Lupa's act is more of an acoustic set.

| Cost | Lunch $25–50 |
| | Dinner $35–65 |

Address 170 Thompson St, between Houston & Bleecker Sts

☎212/982-5089

Transportation A,C,E,F,V to West 4th St; 6 to Bleecker St

Open Daily noon–2.30pm & 5–11.30pm

Accepts All major credit cards

Reservations Restricted

ITALIAN

Antipasti are stripped down to the basics. Citrus-curing blunts the fishiness but not the character of iridescent sardines dangling over a pilaf-like pillow of cracked wheat ($10). That addictive nibble known as cacciatorini sausage is sided with artichokes and anchovy vinaigrette ($10). Foregoing pasta? At $9–14, you shouldn't. At lunch, bucatini, the thick-gauge spaghetti unrivaled for slurping but disastrous for dating, acquires a black-olive pesto. At dinner, pappardelle gets tossed with a super-rich, bittersweet duck ragu. On Thursday—gnocchi night in Rome—semolina gnocchi dissolve under a melted stracchino blanket.

Talking main courses, dry-rubbed hanger steak ($17) acquires a delectable crust, while quail ($17) is lacquered in honey and balsamic. Lush braised oxtail is great either as a dinner entree ($14) or as a lunch sandwich. For closers, the rich honey panna cotta ($7) lures few away from the tartufo ($8), an ice cream treat from Rome served here with a halzelnut-chocolate sauce. When in Lupa you do as the Romans do.

Time Cafe

Since storming the scene in 1990, Time Cafe has joined the ranks of faded beauties whose white-hot phase has come and long gone. Nowadays it's a relaxed fallback for impromptu meals, casual first dates, and friendly gatherings. The high ceilings, quiet trance music, and desert photo-mural all contribute to a happily hungover, drinking-in-LA kind of feel—even as the number 6 train rattles underneath the bleached-wood chair you'll recognize as a grownup cousin of the one you suffered in grade school.

Cost	$15–40

Address 380 Lafayette St, between Great Jones & East 4th Sts
☎212/533-7000
Transportation 6 to Bleecker St; F,V to Broadway-Lafayette
Open Mon–Fri 8am–11.30am & noon–midnight, Sat & Sun 10.30am–1am
Accepts All major credit cards

While too eclectic to be categorized as comfort food, the extensive menu of salads, pastas, pizzas, sandwiches, and entrees holds minimum shock value and maximum name-recognition. The homemade hummus ($7), served with a basket of warm pita bread, is light and perfectly smooth, with the barest bite of garlic. Crispy calamari ($7.75) is just that, served with a tangy, moderately spicy tomato sauce. Cobb Salad ($13.75), heaving with chunks of well-seasoned grilled chicken, crumbled bacon, quartered hard-boiled egg, avocado wedges, romaine and iceberg lettuces, and a bland mustard-based vinaigrette, is an homage to the legendary Brown Derby, the Hollywood restaurant where the salad was invented. Black-sesame-crusted salmon ($17.50) is served smartly and simply with a pungent wasabe vinaigrette and sautéed spinach.

Most pizzas ($11.50) are joyously overloaded, with chicken, black beans, Jack cheese, grilled apples, and all manner of kooky ingredients sure to infuriate purists. They feel like something fabulously forgettable you'd eat while watching a game or B-movie on TV. The Time Burger ($9.75 plus $1 for cheese, bacon, or avocado) gets you a respectably hefty 10oz of beef on a Parker House roll, consistently cooked as requested, and accompanied by perfectly good fries. Among the homemade desserts, the winner is the spiced apple crisp ($6.50), although there is too much of the firm, buttery crumb topping and fresh, juicy apple chunks for the relatively skimpy scoop of vanilla-bean-flecked ice cream.

There's another Time Cafe at 2330 Broadway, Upper West Side (☎212/579-5100).

Tomoe Sushi

(🍴) "Nobody goes there anymore," Yogi Berra once remarked about a particular restaurant. "It's too crowded." His skewed logic could just as well be applied to this, Manhattan's most wildly popular, thoroughly uncelebrated sushi place. The skinny-downtown-intellectual-arty-NYU types who wait in line for the chance to knock elbows at drab tables in a nondescript environment do so for one reason only: oversize sushi at low-to-moderate prices. Other words that come to mind when sampling the fresh raw fish are "silky," "velvety," "buttery," and just

Cost	$20-55

Address 172 Thompson St, between Bleecker & Houston Sts
☎212/777-9346
Transportation A,C,E,F,V to West 4th St
Open Mon & Wed–Sat 1–3pm & 5–11pm
Accepts AmEx
Reservations Not accepted

JAPANESE

plain "big." Although sushi is ordinarily measured in terms of artistry and not dimension, there is decadent pleasure to be had when taking on a nigiri with long, Rubenesque pieces of glistening tuna and salmon sensually draped over cushions of rice or, within rolls, buttery chunks of tuna that dissolve in the mouth. Besides, you get a little bit of artistry, too— Tomoe's trio of sushi chefs are skilled craftsmen.

The sushi deluxe ($25) features tuna, salmon, fluke, Spanish mackerel, orange clam, shrimp, salmon roe, flying fish roe, egg, a tuna roll, and a yellowtail scallion roll. It's serious business and clearly the exception to the rule about not ordering sushi deluxes. If there are two of you, the best strategy might be to share that platter and then do a round—or two, or three—of a la carte selections, being careful not to overlook the inside-out salmon skin roll ($5) and the piece of indomitable sea urchin ($5) that presents the ultimate challenge to chopstick dexterity. Then again, you cannot do much better than the straight sashimi deluxe ($28.50) or, for lighter appetites, the "battera" quartet—nuggets of Osaka-style pressed rice with eel, shrimp, mackerel, and salmon ($12.50).

If you're not going for sushi, at least three appetizers merit attention: the ethereal shumai (crab dumplings; $5), a deep bowl of marinated squid in spicy chile sauce ($6.75), and the yellowtail in a teriyaki-like marinade ($6). And as for the either/or of miso soup and salad with your deluxe ($2.50 a la carte)—there's no competition. While the soup is delicate and lovely, the salad is, frankly, pathetic.

FRENCH/AMERICAN

Village

You could have walked in a second after Village's 2000 opening and asked yourself: why didn't I know about this place before? The clandestine grandeur suggests a well-used, well-loved restaurant. Relaxed first-time diners effortlessly adopt the comportment of longstanding regulars. Whether bistro or brasserie, retro or contemporary, American or French, Village has something New Yorkers know how to use. Past the crush of cosmopolitans—liquid and human—in the bar/cafe is an oval-domed, curved-glass skylight rising some 30ft over the handsome, balconied, Depression-era dining hall. Down below, slim bodies tightly folded into the red-and-black banquettes along the wainscotted perimeter lean close to hear each other speak. Chef-owner Stephen Lyle is quietly making noise with the beautiful-people-and-homely-food formula he mastered at Odeon (see p.144) and Independent.

Cost	$25–65

Address 62 West 9th St, between 5th & 6th Aves
☎212/505-3355
Transportation A,C,E,F,V to West 4th St
Open Mon–Fri 6pm–midnight, Sat & Sun 11.30am–3pm & 5pm–midnight
Accepts All major credit cards
Reservations Required

Lyle's dishes are devoid of frou-frou. Good food on a plate is what matters. His appetizers encompass ingredients—pork cheeks, smoked calf's tongue, herring—that would seem to lack widespread appeal. Yet grilled "crepinettes" made with that cheek meat are lovably crusty ground-pork patties ($7.50). And the tender slices of smoked calf's tongue are indispensable to a terrific antipasto ($9.50). Though no starter can match the pan-roasted oysters in a chipotle-heated crème fraîche bisque ($11) for pure excitement, the wild mushroom bruschetta ($9) topped with a creamy layer of truffled caciotta (sheep's milk cheese) comes close.

Entrees, too, revel in the rich and the unctious. Homemade folds of ravioli, their veal stuffing braised to the brink of collapse, waft in rosemary cream and enriched veal stock ($16). Crushed pepper melts into the fatty juices of a New York strip steak au poivre. Even tuna opts for steak's clothing, stepping out in a buttery and loosely fitting Béarnaise ($24). With dessert, Lyle again proves he knows what we want. No amount of praise for the doubly tangy lemon tartlet ($7.50) and the ultra-rich tapioca pudding ($7.50) is likely to talk you out of the ice cream sundae with chewy, pistachio-nutted brownie cubes ($8).

Little Italy & Nolita

LITTLE ITALY & NOLITA

EAST HOUSTON STREET

Café Colonial

Puck Building

Rialto

JERSEY ST

Old St. Patrick's Cathedral

Café Habana

LAFAYETTE ST

PRINCE STREET

NOLITA

Rice

MULBERRY STREET

MOTT STREET

ELIZABETH STREET

BOWERY

CHRYSTIE STREET

Sara D. Roosevelt Park

SPRING STREET

Peasant

CLEVELAND PLACE

Lombardi's

Clay

BROADWAY

CROSBY STREET

KENMARE STREET

Funky Broome

BROOME STREET

LITTLE ITALY

Wyanoka

Old Police Headquarters

La Mela

Nyonya

Bowery Savings Bank

LAFAYETTE STREET

CENTRE STREET

GRAND STREET

BAXTER STREET

MULBERRY STREET

MOTT STREET

ELIZABETH STREET

BOWERY

HOWARD STREET

HESTER STREET

Ⓜ

Ⓜ

Ⓜ

Ⓜ

WALKER STREET

CANAL STREET

CHINATOWN

WHITE STREET

0   300 yds

Café Colonial

🍴 The late-afternoon sun angles through the storefront picture windows on the northern fringe of Nolita. A politely worded sign offers the gentlest reminder to turn off all cell phones and beepers. Young, über-fashion plates sip cappuccinos and wait their turn to recount their day's shopping conquests. A few hours later, the recorded ballads of a soft-voiced Brazilian crooner serenade the couples compelled to sit close at small, candelit tables. These are the easy-going, unhurried Latin rhythms that differentiate Café Colonial from any other formulaic bistro with a tile floor, marble-topped bar, and requisitely mismatched antiques. Nothing is as over these days as co-ordinated fashion, be it in threads, furniture or food.

Cost	Lunch $6–9
	Dinner $9–16

Address 276 Elizabeth St at Houston St

☎212/274-0044

Transportation F,V to Broadway-Lafayette; 6 to Bleecker St

Open Sun–Thurs 8am–11pm, Fri & Sat 8am–midnight

Accepts All major credit cards

BRAZILIAN/AMERICAN

The menu is every bit as relaxed. Steamed mussels with spicy tomato sauce ($8 for a large bowl, $5.50 half order) is as far as you can get from exotic in a neighborhood that is still, after all, part of Little Italy, but it's a great starter. The spinach salad with moist slices of grilled chicken breast and a velvety avocado dressing ($8.50) and the weighty hamburger Americano ($7.50) served with regulation-sized fries are the sort of post-adolescent fixations you expect from an off-campus coffeehouse.

As for entrees, the grilled organic chicken breast ($13.95) served with mashed sweet potatoes and daily vegetables could only possibly displease diners with cilantro issues. In truth, if you don't like cilantro you'll need to order very carefully here. The camarao a bahaiana ($12.95) is another cilantro-fest: shrimp cooked in coconut sauce dotted with green peppers, tomatoes, and, naturally, lots and lots of that zingy herb. Carnivores will flip for the flavorful seared and sliced sirloin ($16) pushed against arugula and cherry tomatoes, dressed with a rich balsamic vinaigrette and then topped with crispy, salty (what more could you want?) shoestring fries. When it's time for dessert, skip the pedestrian Brazilian flan (what makes it Brazilian is anyone's guess; $5), and order instead the exceptional chocolate croissant bread pudding ($5).

Café Habana

(🍴) Despite its name, its Cuban sandwich, and its roast pork, Café Habana is not Cuban. Inspired by a legendary Mexico City luncheonette of the same name, it dishes up inexpensive, mostly Mexican grub from co-owner Richard Ampudia's hometown. In moving into a corner formerly occupied by Bella's, itself a beloved luncheonette, Ampudia desired only a likeable and unpretentious place that wouldn't anger locals sorry to see him move in. His noble plan backfired when Nolita's shopping scene exploded in the late 1990s. Fashionistas who were

Cost	Lunch $12–40 Dinner $20–45

Address 17 Prince St at Elizabeth St

☎212/625-2001

Transportation 6 to Spring St; F,V to Broadway-Lafayette; J,M to Bowery

Open Daily 9am–midnight

Accepts All major credit cards

Reservations Not accepted

dropping $200 on high-heeled mules at nearby Siegerson Morrison were also flooding into this adorable dive for $7.75 chicken quesadillas slathered with smoked Cheddar and accompanied by a mound of rice and beans. Soon it was a challenge just to fit in, either because the 35 seats were full or simply because you didn't have the right haircut.

That isn't to suggest you'll get attitude from the young servers, most of them chatty imports from the Lower East Side and Williamsburg who, if they have any restaurant experience, do a magnificent job of hiding it. They are, however, friendly and do overcome madhouse conditions to deliver the spicy slop while it's steaming hot. Tlacoyo tres marías ($8.50), a popular street food in Mexico City rarely seen in the US is presented here as a blue cornmeal cake stuffed with sundried tomatoes and goat cheese. The chilaquiles ($7.25), a soufflé-like casserole of corn tortillas, shredded chicken, and tomatilla salsa, is somewhat more familiar, as are the wonderfully sloppy huevos rancheros ($5.75), which make a splendid breakfast, lunch, or brunch, but the grilled chicken and corn salad ($7.95) is a Café Habana invention. Here they take the cafe's best single item—Mexican-style grilled corn with chile powder, Cotija cheese, and lime ($3.50)—and expand it into a lunch plate.

At dinner, the chicken enchiladas ($10.95) have a marvellously rich, chocolate-free mole poblano. For dessert, the flan with ricotta and cream cheese ($3.25) is something you can get nowhere else but in the kitchen of Ampudia's mother, a native New Yorker, who concocted it in Mexico City while pining for her beloved cheesecake.

Clay

Clay's chef/owner Edward Lee is a Korean-American who studied French cuisine, cooked at the Moroccan hotspot Chez Es Saada (see p.35), and, once the travel bug was out of his system, cut a new culinary path inspired by ancestral food. His ever-evolving and steadily improving menu, which consists of twelve tasting plates and six entrees, is not hardcore authentic, but its flavors do convey with stylish simplicity the spicy, pungent, and sweet extremes found at more traditional Korean restaurants in Midtown and Flushing. The playfully modern interior—

KOREAN

Cost	Lunch $20–35 Dinner $30–60

Address 202 Mott St, near Spring St
☎212/625-1105
Transportation 6 to Spring St
Open Mon–Fri noon–4pm & 5.30pm–midnight, Sat & Sun 5.30pm–midnight
Accepts All major credit cards
Reservations Suggested

trellised, cigar-shaped lamps, lacquered tables and school chairs—shares the kitchen's invention, while fitting in perfectly with the offbeat stylishness of the nearby Nolita stores.

Only in inexpensive Japanese joints is low-priced, casually served food prepared so meticulously. The kaennip roll ($6) is composed of finely julienned and evenly crunchy carrots, peppers, radishes, and zucchini, all neatly wrapped in a sesame leaf. Stuffed rice cakes ($6) are works of art: tubular rice gnocchi striped with carrot matchsticks, filled with soy-marinated beef, tied with knotted baby scallion, and served with a thick and spicy sesame sauce. Ojinga soon-dae ($6) consist of eight thin loops of steamed, beef-filled cuttlefish accompanied by onions, baby scallions, and the ubiquitous (happily so) kimchee-style pickled radish. Other fine appetizers, or tapas, include the wonderful yaki dumplings ($4) which have a slightly crisp, almost toasted texture, and the kimchee sampler of pickled radishes, cabbage, and cucumbers spiced with chile peppers and salt shrimp ($12).

Of the entrees, highlights include the perfectly cooked salmon ($15) or red snapper ($14) marinated in a sweet ginger soy marinade similar to teriyaki. The spicy backbeat of barbecued pork ribs ($14) comes from their chile pepper and sesame seed rub. Bi Bum Bap ($12) is a jazzy crock of sticky rice topped with vegetables and a thick, pungent red pepper sauce. And as for dessert, you can't beat the poached pears with the double buzz of preserved ginger and ginger gelato ($5).

Funky Broome

Nearly every Manhattan neighborhood has at least one whimsically named and fancifully designed corner spot like Funky Broome. Gray walls and lightboxes highlighted in lollipop pink, lime, and fuchsia. Elliptical indirect lighting from a pink ceiling fixture shining over glossy tabletops. Synthetic lilies and white roses glistening with imitation dew drops. The only difference is that those other neon-lit, storefront businesses are nail salons, while Funky Broome is a Chinese restaurant, and a serious one at that. Don't be fooled by the address that, three blocks north of Canal Street, is in the heart of Little Italy. Funky Broome's all-encompassing selection of 278 Chinese dishes is of the quality, breadth, and value you'd expect from neighboring Chinatown.

Cost	$8–50

Address 176 Mott St at
Broome St
☎212/941-8628
Transportation 6 to Spring St;
J,M to Bowery
Open Sun–Thurs
11.30am–11pm, Fri & Sat
11am–11.30pm
Accepts All major credit cards

The appetizers you find all over town—pan-fried pork dumplings ($4.95), BBQ spare ribs ($4.95), cold sesame noodles ($4.25)—are generally superior at Funky Broome. But you'd do better to take advantage of such specialties as lemongrass chicken wings ($5.95), crispy beef strips ($5.95), and the wondrous, crisp, deep-fried, pinky-sized asparagus tip bacon rolls ($6.95 for six). The same intricacy is found in fabulous entree no. 59 (it's easiest to order by number)—shrimp-stuffed tofu with baby eggplant, bell peppers, and black bean sauce on a sizzling platter ($11.95). Among other hot numbers are the 75 (stir-fried and nicely oily sliced fish with minced pork; $13.95) and the 45 (a mini-wok of pork-stuffed lotus roots; $10.95). Even the simplest vegetable dishes are delightful—for sautéed pea shoots with garlic ($10.95) or crunchy water spinach cooked in chicken broth with a little sugar and garlic ($9.95) ask for numbers 164 and 165.

A meal without rice or noodles is unthinkable. The rice dishes under the heading "Rice in Bamboo" (nos. 183–191) are cooked and served in six-inch lidded bamboo logs (essentially casseroles). They contain rice and various stewed meats, vegetables, seafood, or poultry. Top combinations (all $6.50) include pork, duck liver, and ginger; and duck, peas, and preserved veggies. Among great noodle options, the no. 202 consists of knotted vermicelli with shredded beef and black pepper ($6.95).

Lombardi's

Opened in 1994, the third incarnation of America's oldest pizzeria is a virtuoso tribute to the Neapolitan immigrant Gennaro Lombardi's milestone achievement. Composed of two adjacent shops down the block from the long-closed, circa-1905, Little Italy original, the third-generation Lombardi's is outfitted with old photos, brick walls, a pressed-tin ceiling, a vintage beehive-patterned mosaic, and, more importantly, a coal-fired brick oven. And although that old oven was salvaged from a bakery and not a pizzeria, it is of the type undoubtedly used by Gennaro to turn out crisp, bubbling, coal-charred master-pizzas. During your first of hopefully several visits, be sure to get a peek at it.

Cost	$8–35

Address 32 Spring St, between Mott & Mulberry Sts
☏212/941-7994
Transportation 6 to Spring St; N,R to Prince St
Open Mon–Thurs 11.30am–11pm, Fri & Sat 11.30am–midnight, Sun 11.30am–10pm
Accepts Cash only
Reservations Not accepted

The first pies baked under the restored name and brickwork were promising, but their charred crusts sacrificed the flour-dusted surface of a New York classic in favor of an olive-oil sheen. Fortunately, more recent renditions baked by Ricardo and Victor Minthali have offered that almost powdery surface as a desirably dry counterpart to the combined ooziness of melted cheese and tomato. Now the only warranted crust criticism is that its firmness doesn't quite support the copious toppings. There is never a need to order extra sliced mozzarella, tomato sauce, or grated Pecorino Romano atop a six-slice small pie ($11.50 and up) or eight-slice large pie ($13.50). Additional toppings, like the San Marzano tomatoes used for the sauce, are top quality: ricotta impastata, sausage from Esposito's, Citterio pancetta, Hormel Rosa Grande pepperoni.

The white clam pizza ($13.50/$15.50), a variety more commonly associated with New Haven than New York, is distinguished by the density of fresh clams atop a pie also dressed with chopped garlic, oregano, grated Romano, and olive oil. Perhaps it might benefit from slightly fewer clams and, in their place, the flavor and color of chopped parsley. At any rate, the diminishing pleasure of a clam pizza as it cools and dries reinforces the ideal strategy for a Lombardi's outing. To assure you're always eating something hot, go with a group and take on one pie at a time.

La Mela

The stereotype of the Little Italy Italian restaurant as a sappy, tacky, tourist trap may be unfair to Mulberry Street's prouder dining establishments. But if that description does not quite fit La Mela, it's only because it understates its trashy excesses. For anyone thinking about coming here specifically for the cooking there's just one word: fuhgeddaboudit! But groups intent on a rowdy, singing, wisecracking, chugalugging pigout will discover these three adjacent storefronts and courtyard garden to be a blast. Fittingly, the setting, with its plastic-covered tables and fluorescent-lit walls papered with low-resolution blowups of diners caught in Polaroid moments, is not appealing in even the homey, humble, straw-Chianti-bottle sense. It's the apple of no one's eye. And the young barker who sings out "La Mela, La Mela" to restaurant-trolling passers-by in his best Neapolitan inflection is not even remotely convincing. He freely admits to being Dominican, his idea being, like La Mela's, to let everyone in on the joke.

| Cost | Lunch $20–40 |
| | Dinner $30–60 |

Address 167–171 Mulberry St, between Broome & Grand Sts
☎212/431-9493
Transportation 6,J,M,N,Q,R,W to Canal St
Open Sun–Thurs noon–11pm, Fri & Sat noon–midnight
Accepts All major credit cards
Reservations For large groups

There is a thing called a menu here, with real food and prices ($8-12 for pasta, $12 for chicken, $14 for veal, $15 for seafood). But this illustrated document has little to do with how things work. Basically, they keep bringing the food and you do your darnedest to put it away (the waiters will admonish you for unfinished portions). Dinner starts with a hot antipasto that might contain decent stuffed mushrooms and roasted peppers and pretty good baked asparagus with Parmesan as well as a cold salad of tofu-textured mozzarella, tomato, and basil. Next up is linguine, gnocchi, and tricolored tortellini served together on a single platter, their sauces running together into a creamy, ricotta-tomato mess.

The waiter may at this moment give diners a chance to call it quits. Most move courageously on to the satisfying "meat" course of chicken scarpariello (fried, on-the-bone chicken chunks with lemon-wine sauce), shrimp marinara, and tender veal scaloppine al limone. Dessert, like the pasta, is a gratifying if unsightly muddle of tartufo, cannoli, cheesecake, and fruit. The check total depends mostly on how much wine you drink and the mood of the waiter.

Nyonya

Nyonya novices seem preoccupied by a mysterious specialty commonly referred to as "that." Those who don't know what "that" is simply point to some dish before asking, "What is that?" Others make a similar gesture while asserting, "I want that." Since the menu offers inadequate translations of its 144 selections, "that" is what many rely on to experience this scintillating place in Little Italy's Chinatown suburb. Targeted towards Chinese, Malaysians and Nyonya (half-Chinese, half-Malay), the

| Cost | Lunch $10–25 |
| | Dinner $15–45 |

Address 194 Grand St, between Mott & Mulberry Sts
☎212/334-3669
Open Daily 11am–midnight
Transportation 6,J,M,N,Q,R,W to Canal St
Accepts Cash only
Reservations Not accepted

experience is fast and frantic. Diners are not so much served as they are bombarded by dazzling flavors—chile, cilantro, peanut, ginger, garlic, coconut, lemongrass, dried shrimp.

In an open kitchen, a cook flattens rice-flour dough into paper-thin sheets for roti canal—an Indian-style crêpe served with a spicy curry dip. Everyone orders it as an hors d'oeuvre ($3). In a second kitchen, a team of cooks furiously fry, steam, braise, and sauté as diners surrounded by blond wood and bamboo ogle each other's orders. Eager waitresses race between kitchens and tables to reduce the interminable seconds that separate diners from their appetizers: Nyonya lojak ($6.95), say, a mixed fry of shrimp pancakes, tofu cubes, and bean curd skin dumplings; or white turnip rolls ($6.95), logs of diced white turnip, scallion, dried shrimp, and mushroom in a peanut-thickened seafood chile sauce.

One favorite "that" is steamed sea bass Teow Chow style (seasonal price about $15–20) served in a bubbling broth over an aluminum pan heated by two oil burners. When first tasted, it seems like the salty broth has robbed the fish of flavor. Minutes later, with much of the liquid evaporated, the flavor returns to the fish. What a transformation! Entrees to order by name: sweet-and-tangy braised duck ($13.95); house special jumbo shrimp ($16.95) in a spicy sauce redolent of cilantro; fried whole red snapper "Thailand style" (seasonal price $15–20) in a sweet, red sauce spiced with chile, lemongrass, and tamarind. These spicy extremes may be extinguished by various sweet iced drinks or chendor ($3), a refreshing dessert of shaved ice, red beans, chendor (green pea flour), and coconut.

Little Italy & Nolita

Peasant

The best Italian restaurant in Little Italy is not what anyone would consider to be a Little Italy Italian restaurant. Peasant belongs to the historic neighborhood's hip enclave of Nolita, and could thus disappoint sightseers drawn to the area for a more of a touristy, frolicsome dining experience (see La Mela, p.108). Even so, don't be fooled by such style signatures as the iron-and-glass storefront lounge, the sleek concrete bar, and, behind it, the capellini-thin barmaid in a tagliatelle-strapped tank top. Frank DeCarlo's region-roaming Italian cuisine constitutes a dramatic throwback to rustic simplicity. When it comes to the food, it's peasant chic that makes Peasant chic.

Cost	$35–75

Address 94 Elizabeth St, between Spring & Prince Sts
☎212/965-9511
Transportation 6 to Spring St
Open Tues–Sat 6–11.30pm, Sun 6–10pm
Accepts All major credit cards
Reservations Required

The smoky aroma and fiery glow of open-fire cooking from the open kitchen warms the hard surfaces of the deafening dining room. In fact, the only fixture that absorbs sound is the polenta. You have to applaud the brevity of the menu, with its superb thin-crusted pizzas (go for the Margherita; $10) and wood-roasted sardines ($10), while questioning its reliance on Italian terms. Translation requests abound: "What is acciuga?" "What is fico?" "What is razza?" (Answers: anchovy, fig, skate.) This might prove tiresome were the waitresses not so well informed and the extensive list of good-value Italian wines not so easy to swallow.

You need not utter a word, Italian or English, to get crusty Sullivan Bakery bread with ricotta cheese for spreading and olive oil for dunking. From there it is a painless transition to the hot appetizer of choice: a mini-casserole of seppiolini (cuttlefish), white wine broth, and sweet cherry tomatoes ($12). Pastas depend on their sauces. Bucatini langostine is rich in crawfish flavor ($22), while a shellfish stock suffuses each individual grain of rice in the lobster risotto ($24). Meats, meanwhile, are cooked under intense heat with astounding precision, from the unimaginably tender rotisserie lamb ($22) to the wood-grilled T-bone ($24), topped with parsley butter. There is one classic to please Little Italy old-timers: zuppa di pesce ($24). Its lightly peppery tomato broth accommodates more seafood then ever before: razor clams, baby octopus, mussels, skate, orata, langoustines, seppiolini. The rough-hewn ricotta cheesecake proves similarly reassuring ($8).

Rialto

Chef-proprietor Sam Martinez feared the meltdown that afflicts eateries that get too hot too fast. While up-and-coming arbiters of downtown taste first called Rialto "the baby Balthazar," after the madly chic brasserie on Spring Street (see p.130), he preferred to think of it instead as "USC Jr"—in deference not to the University of Southern California but to the Union Square Cafe (see p.83). He even enlisted an USC alum to help execute a menu of reasonably priced American bistro standards interpreted with a Greenmarket shopper's vocabulary and the prerequisite Mediterranean, Tuscan, and Asian accents. Tin walls and semicircular booths in red Naugahyde give the dim, candlelit bistro a relaxed, retro flair, while beyond the smoking lounge a magical courtyard garden features a flowerbed set into its brick walls.

| Cost | Lunch $15–35 |
| | Dinner $25–65 |

Address 265 Elizabeth St,
between Houston & Prince Sts
☏212/334-7900
Transportation F,V to
Broadway-Lafayette; N,R to
Prince St; 6 to Spring St
Open Sun–Wed 11am–midnight, Thurs–Sat 11am–1am
Accepts All major credit cards
Reservations Suggested

The appetizer roster features several hot picks that could easily stand in for entrees: grilled homemade wild mushroom sausage counterbalanced by roasted shallot vinaigrette ($9.95); trenne (three-sided fettuccine) with asparagus, goat cheese cream sauce, and slow-roasted plum tomatoes ($12.95); crisp fried calamari with lemon aioli ($8.95), and Maryland crabcakes set against crunchy celery-root slaw. Main courses are somewhat less reliable. Granted, the succulent roast chicken with sautéed spinach and fabulous cornmeal (polenta) fries would be difficult to improve upon ($15.95); the same goes for the portobello Napoleon layered with grilled asparagus and roasted tomatoes on a bed of white beans, brown rice, and shaved Parmesan ($14.95). But the marinated yellowfin tuna with pickled ginger and wasabe cannot be rescued by neat, Asian-spiced fries ($20.95).

The New York strip steak with baked potato and garlic ($19.95) recalls the solid food that pre-radicchio families grew up on, while grilled salmon with a balsamic reduction, corn, tomato, and asparagus ($17.95) satisfies the post-portobello generation. Creamy cheesecake and strawberry shortcake with a homemade sugar biscuit ($5.95) highlight a winning dessert card.

Rice

This Nolita hotspot is an Atkins dieter's worst nightmare. Every single dish involves rice in some fashion or another. As you approach, you'll spot a tribe of tragically hip neighborhood folk nibbling on rice-centric concoctions hidden in brown paper bags and using tossaway chopsticks provided at Rice's takeout. Walk through the scene and into the restaurant. Inside, you'll find many of the same crowd who've decided to splurge, spend the extra fifty cents, and eat at a

Cost	$5.50–13

Address 227 Mott St, between Prince & Spring Sts
☎212/226-5775
Transportation 6 to Spring St; J,M to Bowery
Open Daily noon–midnight
Accepts Cash only
Reservations Not accepted

table. The decor is sparse; seductively dark, even on the sunniest afternoon. Black, slate-like tables sit close in a narrow space. Don't be fooled by the chopsticks trapped in the brown paper napkin—the menu at Rice features dishes cooked all over the world, including Mexico, India, and the United States.

Once you're seated, an overworked but capable waitress will make you feel at ease. As an appetizer, the Thai shrimp rice balls ($4.50) are an excellent choice. You'll wonder what holds these unusual alternatives to meatballs together. Spritz the half-dozen balls with the provided lime wedge for an even more intense flavor. You'll also do well with the tamales ($3). Peeling back the cornhusk of the chicken and mole tamale reveals a scrumptiously moist layer of sticky rice. Digging further (with the provided fork) reveals a mixture of plump, flavorful chicken, corn, and a superbly complex mole.

For a main course try the Thai beef salad ($5.50 small, $9.50 large). Thinly sliced beef, marinated in mint and vinegar, is grilled and placed atop shredded iceberg lettuce, carrots, and celery. Oddly, it's served with your choice of rice. Another excellent choice is the Thai chicken coconut curry ($5.50 small, $9.50 large). A creamy spicy-sweet curry of chicken, broccoli, and sweet red peppers, this dish screams for a rice accompaniment, unlike the beef salad, and, bizarrely, doesn't come with one. Even the desserts, such as the delicious Thai banana-leaf wrap ($2 small, $3 large) feature rice. This unique dessert, a sweet plantain wrapped in sweet sticky rice dotted with red beans, is completely encased in a large tropical leaf.

Wyanoka

At a time when designers are forever "exposing" elements, be they brickwork, windows, or views into a kitchen, it seems odd for Wyanoka to be seating diners under dropped panels that veil the pressed-tin ceiling. Why obscure such beauty? Why affix Venetian blinds around the posts that rise behind banquettes? Why are there live fish installed in the bathroom walls, and four remote video monitors above the tiny marble bar? Speculate among yourselves. These

Cost	$25–70

Address 173 Mott St, between Broome & Grand Sts

☎212/941-8757

Transportation J,M to Bowery; 6 to Spring St

Open Mon–Wed 6pm–1am, Thurs–Sat 6pm–2am

Accepts MasterCard, Visa

GLOBAL

design elements, while certainly provoking discussion, somehow combine to give Wyanoka a warm, sexy, and slightly decadent feel.

The food too has an easily seductive quality that obscures what careful thought and skill is required to produce such grownup dishes as a superbly balanced Asian lobster stew ($9 appetizer/$19 entree). The coconut milk base, shot with lemongrass, ginger, and hot pepper essences, is just rich enough to offset the earthy charm of the snap peas, carrots, and shiitakes as they sidle up to generous chunks of lobster tail and claw meat. Chipotle-grilled shrimp ($11) are served with a moist corncake and laden with a chunky, pungent tomatillo, feta, and cilantro salsa. If you love to share, you could do no better than the grilled pizza ($11), an oval of flatbread in which bacon, figs, red onion, Roquefort, and truffle honey all have their say.

Some people love fusion cuisine; others loathe it. Think of tagliatelle with rabbit-sausage ($16) as the neutral ground where the two parties can meet. The Asian inflections contributed by the moist, gingery sausage, cilantro, and Thai basil are intelligently applied, and the perfectly toothsome pasta and its presentation will be loved by Italian traditionalists. When considering the dry-aged hanger steak frites ($19), keep in mind that the classics grow up quickly at Wyanoka, and your old bistro fave will be robed in a rich, smoky sauce of reduced balsamic vinegar bulked up with double-smoked bacon, sliced, and lounging against crispy herbed frites. If you're up for something sweet to end the meal, stick with the intense chocolate fondue ($12) served with fresh fruit and marshmallows.

Lower East Side

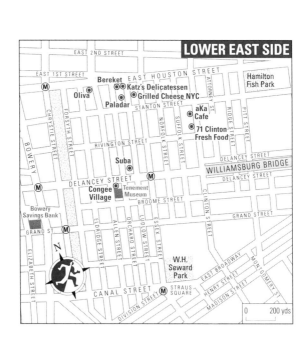

LOWER EAST SIDE

EAST 2ND STREET

EAST 1ST STREET

EAST HOUSTON STREET

ATTORNEY ST

Hamilton
Fish Park

Bereket
Oliva
Katz's Delicatessen
Grilled Cheese NYC
Paladar

STANTON STREET

aKa
Cafe

71 Clinton
Fresh Food

RIDGE STREET

PITT STREET

NORFOLK STREET

SUFFOLK STREET

CHRYSTIE STREET

FORSYTH STREET

BOWERY

RIVINGTON STREET

Suba

DELANCEY STREET

WILLIAMSBURG BRIDGE

DELANCEY STREET

DELANCEY STREET

Congee
Village

Tenement
Museum

BROOME STREET

CLINTON STREET

GRAND STREET

Bowery
Savings Bank

GRAND ST

ELDRIDGE STREET

ALLEN STREET

ORCHARD STREET

LUDLOW STREET

ESSEX STREET

ELIZABETH STREET

N

W.H.
Seward
Park

EAST BROADWAY

WON MONTGOMERY STREET

HENRY STREET

CANAL STREET

STRAUS
SQUARE

DIVISION STREET

MADISON STREET

0   200 yds

71 Clinton Fresh Food

No matter where they live, the connoisseurs' preoccupation is the same: getting in early on the next big thing. When 30-seat 71 Clinton opened behind a garage-door grid of metal and glass in 1999, the waft of greatness drew social climbers down from the high grounds of Manhattan to the darkest, deepest, depths of the Lower East Side. The first dinners of chef Wylie Dufresne, a protégé of Jean-Georges Vongerichten (Mercer Kitchen and Jo Jo, see p.135 and p.263), were attended with the excite-

Cost	$30–75

Address 71 Clinton St, near Rivington St
℡212/614-6960
Transportation F,J,M,Z to Delancey-Essex Sts
Open Sun–Thurs 6–10.30pm, Fri & Sat 6–11.30pm
Accepts All major credit cards
Reservations Required

ment of Bob Dylan's early sets at the fabled Folklore Center or Eddie Murphy's stand-up acts at the Comic Strip. The cramped confines closed the distance between the open-windowed kitchen and open-minded diner, while ensuring a waiter as slender and agile as Gumby was never more than a few feet away. From this immediacy came a sense of possibility that, beyond the heady discovery phase, still qualifies 71 Clinton as a distinctly New York restaurant find.

Dufresne maneuvers his New American menu in ingenious ways. It's as if he were operating his dishes by remote control, ensuring you experience their interplay of flavors and textures in the right sequence: the bitter tickle of parsley root before the sweet kick of faintly peppery crab in a velvety soup ($8); green apples and cider-cooked lentils bringing tartness before and after a lush foie gras terrine; pickled radish, chives, Tabasco, and horseradish throughout the avocado-encased chopped Scottish salmon ($11).

Precise cooking and controlled spicing distinguish the entrees. Comfy side attractions bring out their homier side. The gritty, crunchy mix of soybeans and rye breadcrumbs that tops but does not encrust black sea bass ($22) lets diners transfer the garnish to the accompanying chive mashed potatoes. Droplets of red chorizo oil and green basil oil run into each other, but not, until you desire it, the beautifully seared sea scallops and gooey risotto cake they encircle ($22). A puddle of thick sauce under lusciously sweet, beer-braised short ribs somehow does not spill over to the chewy hanger steak that is the plate's co-star ($24). The desserts and wine selection are, by comparison, a letdown.

117

Lower East Side

aKa Café

Baby bistros spawned by multi-starred chefs are no longer a novelty. What culinary luminary hasn't launched a *prêt-à-porter* alternative? Nevertheless, aKa Café embodies a novel concept in restaurant reproduction: a casual, cramped, and cheap spin-off of something already casual, cramped, and, if not cheap, moderately priced. It is found down the block from its acclaimed parent, 71 Clinton (see p.117), in a former clothing store that, according to the cursive etched on the vintage terrazzo, was called Kupersmith's. Peculiar fashions are still displayed in the shop windows, only now the models can move their lips,

| Cost | Lunch $10–25 |
| | Dinner $20–45 |

Address 49 Clinton St, between Rivington & Stanton Sts
☏212/979-6096
Transportation F,J,M,Z to Delancey-Essex Sts
Open Mon–Fri noon–4.30pm & 6pm–midnight, Sat 6pm–midnight
Accepts All major credit cards
Reservations Suggested

if not their limbs. The undersized tables barely accommodate twos and fours. Forcing threes and fives to share them is an egregious act of discrimination against odd-numbered groups. White sangria (with vodka-macerated fruit!) and fresh pear martinis only help so much.

Chef Scott Ehrlich cooks with the passion of a freshly liberated student, applying a global reach to close-to-home hankerings. One of the $7 pressed sandwiches, a gushy "slider" of chopped hanger steak, is assembled with a Gus' pickle and a Kossar's bialy (for the uninitiated, a flat round roll sprinkled with chopped onion). And while those classic accoutrements salute the Lower East Side's Jewish origins, the egg-washed empanada filled with roast turkey, smoked paprika, and Parmesan tomato marmalade ($7) honors the neighborhood's Latino and increasingly bobo present. The Smithfield ham, Swiss, and pickled-pepper panini ($7)—a glorified Cubano with Reuben leanings—perhaps encapsulates this multiculturalism best of all. Be sure it finds its way into your dinner program, which should be structured around small plates.

If you prefer a conventionally configured meal, a couple of soups and entrees allow for that. Choose the silky squash soup with popcorn crumbs ($6) over the thinner oyster soup ($6). At an astonishing $12, braised pork practically dissolves into its celery-root purée. You'll melt too for the chocolate empanada with vanilla ice cream ($4) and the near-liquid dolce de leche pudding ($4).

Bereket

Where there is art in transition there is gyro on the cutting edge. The scope of the gyro, or kebab, extends from Paris' Latin Quarter through Amsterdam's Jordaan to New York's Greenwich Village. The oft-feared and sometimes legitimately scary mystery meat has journeyed from the great cultural centers of the Middle East, Greece, and Turkey to inspire and feed shoestring travelers, famished students, and starving artists. A window rotisserie spinning with a large mass of dripping lamb meat is a symbol of creative-creature comfort—cheap eats for the nonconformist. And at garish, friendly, 24/7 joints like this Turkish kebab house, it is no less than a fluorescent-lit beacon for late-night revelers with pre-, post-, or between-club attacks of the munchies.

Cost	$4–20
Address 187 Houston St at Orchard St	
☎212/475-7700	
Transportation F,V to 2nd Ave	
Open Daily 24hr	
Accepts Cash only	
Reservations Not accepted	

That Bereket, positioned on the bohemian frontier between the East Village and the Lower East Side, also draws couples, families, and working men from Turkey and other areas of the Middle East and Southeast Europe tells you there is more to this fast-food place than wee-hours chowdowns. Moreover, the superior quality of the prepared salads and appetizers demonstrates this is no ordinary kebab house. The doner kebab, as Turkish gyro is known, is clearly the big draw and the big feed. Never have you seen so much thinly sliced meat (supposedly lamb *and* beef) packed into a single pita pocket with yogurt sauce, lettuce, and tomato (a sandwich is $5). Still, the tasty shards of doner are not crisp-edged and they're no more succulent than the chicken kebab or baby lamb kebab (also $5 in a pita). Could the meat be too lean?

Nobody could dispute the appeal and freshness of the cold vegetarian dishes, which are served in sandwiches ($2.50–3), platters ($3.50–5), or large combination plates ($8). These last are composed of four items: perhaps crunchy white bean salad with red onion, parsley, and bell pepper; fried eggplant with stewed tomatoes; marinated leeks; and turmeric-tinted kisir (bulgur wheat) with pepper and parsley. To close there is decent baklava ($2.50), which, unlike the custardy, cinnamon-dusted rice pudding ($2.50), generally requires some chewing.

Congee Village

The very existence of Congee Village is enough to make you kiss the sidewalk and thank providence you're in New York. Only here, within earshot of police sirens closing in on the Williamsburg Bridge, could you find a tropical oasis and rice shop showcasing 29 varieties of the Chinese breakfast porridge, congee. With commendable optimism, they've placed a few faux tree stumps outside to serve as stools and tables. They're the seating option of choice for

| Cost | Lunch $6–25 |
| | Dinner $10–35 |

Address 100 Allen St at
Delancey St
☏212/941-1818
Transportation F,J,M,Z to
Delancey-Essex Sts
Open Daily 10.30am–midnight
Accepts Cash only
Reservations Not accepted

those who want to keep an eye on their parked cars. Most people, however, prefer the artificial vegetation inside the amusing, jungle-themed dining areas.

No one skips the congee ($2.50–4.75), of course, enclosed in a bamboo casserole brimming with enough bubbling, silky rice porridge to fill five tiny soup bowls. The rising steam carries the scent of scallions and the promise of inner peace. Though shellfish varieties (fresh scallops, shrimp, squid) are generally best, the pristine chicken-abalone combo is a nice alternative. Each may be consumed with a long cruller-like pastry for dunking. But the fried bun, which comes with a sweet, condensed-milk dip, makes a better treat.

Despite the namesake specialty, the real treasure here is rice in cylindrical bamboo pots. These exotic cooking vessels are laid horizontally on serving plates. Flip open the hinged lid, scoop out some rice, and close the lid again. The rice then stays hot, absorbing the flavor of its garnishes. For bold, smoky flavor, the top bamboo pots hold rice baked either with Chinese sausage or with salty, fatty preserved duck (both $6.25). For a cleaner, less nutty taste, the mixed seafood ($6.75) buzzes with ginger and scallion. Only bony frog ($7.75) is a letdown. Other house specialties reflect the spicier ways of modern Cantonese cooking. Sautéed crab ($9.95) carries a hot, peppery kick, while succulent chicken ($8.95) and tender sautéed short rib ($8.95) maintain a silent sizzle of dazzling flavor long after the hissing has subsided. The reddish sprocket wheels that the Chinese kids at the next table are invariably digging into are crunchy slices of lotus root in a gently bitter fermented red bean sauce ($5.50).

Grilled Cheese NYC

Blink and you'd miss this petite twelve-seater, which is making quite a name for itself as *the* place to come for the ultimate comfort food—a perfect grilled cheese sandwich. The heady aroma of Swiss cheese wafts out of the tiny storefront onto happening Ludlow Street, while inside the restaurant exudes the unique flavor of the Lower East Side. Patrons casually sit at small cafe tables, bobbing their heads from side to side in time to ambient background music, and then not so casually devour the creative concoctions plonked down in front of them by the extremely friendly staff. All food is served on plastic or paper plates and diners use picnic forks. From the tin ceiling hangs a sign exclaiming the joint's mantra: "We Grill, You Chill."

Cost	$3.50–7

Address 168 Ludlow St, between Houston & Stanton Sts
☎212/982-6600
Transportation F,V to 2nd Ave
Open Mon–Sat 11am–midnight, Sun 11am–7pm
Accepts All major credit cards
Reservations Not accepted

Start off with a large cup of the homemade lime lemonade ($2) or try their definitive peppermint iced tea ($2). With its clean, unmuddled flavor, the tea will infuse the grayest and dreariest of afternoons with springtime freshness. To start your meal try the "I (heart) NY" cup of tomato soup ($2). Definitely not out of a can, this mild soup is brought to life with fresh cilantro. Or try the colossal side salad ($3)—a huge plate of spinach, tomato, onion, carrot, sprouts, roasted red pepper, cucumbers, and kalamata olives with a tangy, slightly emulsified balsamic vinaigrette.

Sandwiches can be custom-made from a list of almost unlimited ingredients or chosen from an equally long list of pre-determined combinations. The affordable prices vary depending on the toppings and sort of bread used. The Hamlet sandwich ($5.50) is a gooey mélange of Swiss and Cheddar cheeses, Black Forest ham, onion, and tomato. Another great choice is the Greensleeves ($3.50), an amusingly sloppy concoction of spinach, basil, roasted red peppers, and French yogurt cheese. Some may feel a pang of disappointment that Grilled Cheese doesn't serve grilled cheese the way mom used to make—with yellow-orange American cheese singles on buttery white bread. But after a bite of any of these sandwiches, you'll realize that even moms make mistakes.

Lower East Side

Katz's Delicatessen

Regulars of this landmark Lower East Side deli know you get a nicer, bigger pastrami sandwich (plus a sample taste!) by ordering it from—and slipping a buck or two to—a counterman than you would if you ordered it from a waiter at the tables along the wall. (Experiments have shown that a sandwich ordered from the counter is roughly 5oz heavier than one ordered from a waitress.) The tipping tradition is as essential to Katz's as the old terrazzo floor, the chestnut-colored wood paneling, the stainless-steel water fountain, and the hanging salamis. Another time-honored custom is the archaic system of distributing tickets to customers as they enter and having the servers mark off prices on them as items are ordered. Those who misplace their tickets may be required to pay the maximum amount or, heaven forbid, clean the premises.

Cost	$5–25

Address 205 East Houston St at Ludlow St
℡212/254-2246
Transportation F,V to 2nd Ave
Open Sun–Tues 8am–10pm, Wed & Thurs 8am–11pm, Fri & Sat 11am–3am
Accepts Cash only
Reservations Not accepted

The utter superiority of the pastrami sandwich ($9.95), assembled with hand-carved, black-edged, gloriously deep-pink meat freshly plucked from the steamer, is a comparatively recent development; Katz's pastrami did not supplant Carnegie Deli's (see p.209) as New York's best until the early to mid-1990s. Tender, peppery meat glistening with fatty moisture melts into the mouth. No crumbs or shreds on a sandwich, as is often the case at the Carnegie; just full slices. Don't order the pastrami lean. If you want lean, have turkey. Know too that Katz's corned beef ($9.95) tends to be a tad tough and dry and is not up to the standards of the pastrami. The frozen steak fries ($2.95) are nothing to get excited about either, though they're admittedly quite good for what they are. They're said to be the highest grade of frozen steak fries on the market (some distinction!) and a number of people love them.

Two budget items merit consideration. The knoblewurst sandwich ($7.65) gets a decent crunch from the crisp skins of its thinly sliced, garlicky, knockwurst-like meat. And the plump, naturally encased frankfurter—just $2.40—is consistently one of the best tube steaks ever.

Oliva

Madrileno restorer-turned-restaurateur Eduardo Fontan and Belgian actor Steve Benisty have reproduced the noise level of Pamplona's Fiesta de Saint Fermín as thoroughly as Hemingway captured its furor. The vaulted concrete ceiling installed by the co-aficionados can make the voices of 40 people sound like 400. The noise, however, is just about the only good reason not to go. Though too contemporary-American to feel authentic, Oliva is an adorably cool, cozy, colorful, and affordable expression of Basque flavor. Even diners not jovial by nature become that way after a single superbly mixed mojito—the sweet minty rum drink that was another Hemingway passion, from another land and another book.

Cost	$30–65

Address 161 East Houston St at Allen St
☎212/228-4143
Transportation F,V to 2nd Ave
Open Sun–Thurs 5.30pm–midnight, Fri & Sat 5.30pm–1am
Accepts All major credit cards
Reservations Required

Chef Joe Elorriaga is Basque by descent and cooking experience, American by nationality, and New Yorker by sensibility. Standards like gambas a la plancha, here an appetizer of garlicky prawns blast-sautéed on a hot griddle, are dependable and true ($11). Those fabulously snappy and juicy shrimp do double duty in the donostia, a chef's salad that also incorporates roasted red peppers, anchovies, Serrano ham, asparagus, and tuna ($9). Bacalao rellenos—roasted red peppers stuffed with a creamy salt-cod purée—is a nice rendition of a Spanish classic ($9). The recurring components of Basque cooking—tomatoes, sweet peppers, garlic—return as the foundation for clams piperrada, a rousing terracotta casserole of clams, fava beans, white beans, and chorizo ($8). Sensational cornmeal-crusted fried calamari ($8) need only the garlic mayo for embellishment.

Main courses, served on a variety of geometrically shaped plates, are somewhat less conventional and often less reliable than the starters. But roast monkfish ($16) is a rousing fiesta dish, taking on cep mushrooms, fava beans, dried tomatoes, Yukon Gold potatoes, and Spanish olives to best advantage. And tender filet mignon au poivre ($21), sauced with a reduction of Spanish brandy (sitting in for red wine) and sided with great paprika fries, is painless enough. And the decent desserts ($5–6) offer a little something extra: mint color and flavor for the poached pear, walnut cream for the apple tart, black cherries for flan.

Paladar

To dress properly for the backyard of Paladar you need to wear one cotton T-shirt and three pairs of woollen socks. While hot air from the heating elements swirls around the ersatz palms that act as the tent's support columns and then shoots up your back, a frigid breeze creeps under the picket fence and stings your toes and ankles. These fevers and chills certainly suit a hip, pan-Latin playground that runs very hot and cold: spicy cooking improvisations which borrow freely from Mexico, the Caribbean, and

Cost	$20–55

Address 161 Ludlow St, between Houston & Stanton Sts
☎212/473-3535
Transportation F,V to 2nd Ave
Open Sun–Wed 5–11.30pm, Thurs–Sat 5pm–2am
Accepts Cash only
Reservations Not accepted

South America are intermittently extinguished by refreshing, lime-infused cocktails—mojito, pisco sour, caipirinha—and bottled beers from the same sources. Enjoyment depends only on your ability to regulate these spine-tingling temperature controls.

The menu was composed by hotshot heartthrob Aaron Martinez, whole Latin knowhow is both inherited (his Mexican mom is *the* Zarela; see p.202) and learned (as well as Cuban at Isla, see p.165, he's cooked Nuevo Latino at Patria and Gulf coast fusion at L-Ray). For Paladar he's assembled a roster of appetizers so good you may want to construct your entire meal around them. A plump, crisp-edged arepa (yellow corncake) is set to advantage against stewed chorizo, onions, and crema fresca ($5.95). Chorizo and potato bring a robust satisfaction to the quesadilla with a thick roasted-tomato sauce and chipotle salsa ($6.95). And the mango and aji chile dip that accompanies lightly coated fried calamari ($6.95) is splendid.

There's little harm in main courses that top out at $14.95, even if they do lack some of the panache displayed by the starters. The prevalent shortcoming is one of muddiness. Braised short ribs with Mexican pozole and ancho chile broth ($12.95) disintegrate into a muddled stew. Pan-roasted fish gets lost within the coconut rice and orange chile vinaigrette ($14.95). But the hanger steak ($13.95) rubbed with a rather mild adobo (Mexican chile marinade) is one succulent slab of beef. Less ambitious items like the Cubano sandwich ($8.50) proffer greater rewards. Salvation from the dessert duds—bread pudding and flan—comes via the bar in many liquid forms.

Suba

Lower East Side chic, a concept inconceivable barely five years ago, hits new lows at this sleek and alluring tapas bar/restaurant. To get to the main dining area you must descend a steep, suspended staircase from the cocktail lounge to a basement space that, in another era, could have stood in for a Paris sewer in an off-off-off-Broadway production of *Les Miserables*. For Suba this cavern has been wondrously transformed into a sparkling subterranean fantasy. Beneath a brick ceiling supported by steel beams, poseurs sit atop an iron-railed cement barge that appears to float over a pool, their polished Pradas lit by the shimmering reflection of the water flowing around—but not actually under—the dining platform. Very cool.

Cost	$30–75

Address 109 Ludlow St, between Delancey & Rivington Sts

℡212/982-5714

Transportation F,J,M to Delancey-Essex Sts

Open Sun–Wed 6–10.30pm, Thurs–Sat 6–11.30pm

Accepts All major credit cards

Reservations Required

Outdoing the decor would have been a losing proposition for Stephane Buccholzer, formerly chef at the pretentious East Side brasserie L'Actuel. Fortunately, he does not take the bait from the dining room moat. Rather, he's put together a neo-Spanish menu crowded with interesting colors and whimsical flourishes. Defining ingredients sometimes get upstaged. Among starters, grilled sardines ($10) look flat and forlorn beside the intricate, chorizo wine-marinated goat cheese pizzette meant to serve in their cause. The puffed pastry business overshadows the focal element. Behold too the elegantly layered rafts of sobrasada, cremacabra cheese, and quince paste ($10).

The entree column is topped by a pan-roasted sea bass ensemble ($20) that might seem convoluted in more conventional surroundings. Here it is merely two shades too cute. Crusty fillets topped with poached quail eggs are arranged geometrically with a line of Manila clams, baby asparagus, and a sweet pea foam. Pollo Suba ($18) is not so contrived. The crackling skin of the roasted Cornish hen is set against a vegetable emulsion, a Basque-style piperrade, and mussel-chorizo croquettes. The crujientes de chocolate ($7), an artichoke-like knot of crunchy cocoa leaves, is the sort of dessert that begs to be seen and maybe tasted but not finished. Get your companion to order it, while you go for for the pastel vasco ($7), a warm, gooey, Basque counterpart to Christmas pudding.

125

SoHo

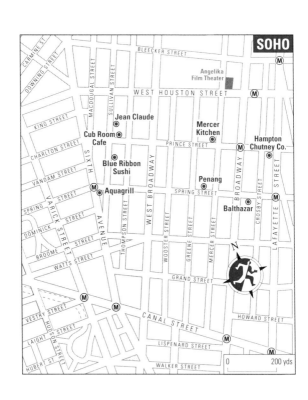

SOHO

CARMINE ST.
DOWNING STREET
BLEECKER STREET
MACDOUGAL STREET
SULLIVAN STREET
Angelika
Film Theater
WEST HOUSTON STREET
KING STREET
Jean Claude
Cub Room
Cafe
Mercer
Kitchen
Hampton
Chutney Co.
CHARLTON STREET
SIXTH
PRINCE STREET
BROADWAY
LAFAYETTE STREET
VANDAM STREET
Blue Ribbon
Sushi
CROSBY STREET
SPRING
Penang
STREET
VARICK STREET
AVENUE
Aquagrill
WEST BROADWAY
SPRING STREET
Balthazar
DOMINICK
THOMPSON STREET
BROADWAY
STREET
BROOME
WOOSTER STREET
GREENE STREET
MERCER STREET
N
WATTS STREET
GRAND STREET
VESTRY STREET
HUDSON STREET
CANAL STREET
HOWARD STREET
LAIGHT STREET
LISPENARD STREET
0   200 yds
HUBERT ST.
WALKER STREET

Aquagrill

Observing the bodies folded over thinly padded benches with only velvet throw pillows to cushion their backs, you are reminded that Manhattan invites two distinctly different dining postures: liquid and solid. Liquid people easily assume the shape of any container. Solids never really get comfy in loosey-goosey settings and sittings. Aquagrill, like a white-wine glass, best suits "liquids" with a nose for fish. By fitting clever seafood, proficient service, and a judicious wine list into a snug corner of SoHo, chef Jeremy Marshall and his wife/sommelier Jennifer provide a bohemian alternative to the best expense-account fish houses and oyster bars.

| Cost | Lunch $25–70 |
| | Dinner $30–85 |

Address 210 Spring St at 6th Ave
℡212/274-0505
Transportation C,E to Spring St
Open Sun noon–3.30pm & 6–10.30pm, Tues–Thurs noon–3pm & 6–10.45pm, Fri & Sat noon–3pm & 6–11pm
Accepts All major credit cards
Reservations Suggested

Great chefs tend to tire of their specialties much more quickly than their customers do, and thus update their menus prematurely. Happily, Marshall has kept on many of the hit dishes that first made a splash here in 1996. Choosing an appetizer is now, as then, a can't-miss conundrum between the pepper-crusted tuna carpaccio with avocado, lemon, and roasted Bermuda onions ($9.25); the elemental Manhattan clam chowder ($6.75); the Billi Bi mussel soup ($6.75); the roasted Dungeness crabcake Napoleon with cantilevered potato chips ($12); and the Maine lobster tossed with grapefruit, avocado, and ruby grapefruit in a Champagne vinaigrette ($18.50 with enough lobster to merit the price).

The signature main course, felafel-crusted salmon over hummus with cucumbers, tomatoes, and lemon cilantro vinaigrette ($20), is intact and as enthralling as ever. Elsewhere, the changes are minor. The seared diver sea scallops ($24) now take on Peekytoe crabmeat risotto rather than crabmeat polenta—hardly a cause for protest. And the beautiful set-up for the grilled Florida swordfish ($24) now consists of smoked shrimp pepper polenta, string beans, crispy onion rings, and a chipotle pepper sauce. Desserts ($7–8) like the roasted caramelized grapefruit with grapefruit sorbet, the warm apple tart with cinnamon ice cream, and the chocolate-crusted deep dish walnut pie with chocolate ganache topping and vanilla ice cream confirm Marshall's mastery of casual chic.

SoHo

Balthazar

Now several trendy-restaurant life spans removed from its 1997 debut, Keith McNally's Balthazar still incites more bubbly pleasure among its 160 diners than a caseload of *balthazars*—giant Champagne bottles sixteen times the standard volume. Recreating the and relentless élan of the great Parisian brasseries of the 1920s, arched aged windows soar over red banquettes strategically positioned on an old mosaic floor to maximize sight lines. Exquisite woodwork rambles through the vestibule, around the windows, up the pillars, and under the 27ft bars. Spectacular cold seafood platters like "Le Grand", a multitiered, $58 extravaganza of oysters, scallops, crab, periwinkles, mussels, and gigantic shrimp, affirm the utter impossibility of not having a great time.

Cost	Lunch $22–65
	Dinner $30–80

Address 80 Spring St at Crosby St

☎212/965-1414

Transportation 6 to Spring St; N,R to Prince St

Open Mon–Thurs 7.30am–3pm & 5.45pm– 1.30am, Fri 7.30am–5pm & 5.45pm–2.30am, Sat 7.30am– 3pm & 5.45pm–2.30am, Sun 7.30am–3pm & 5.45pm–12.30am

Accepts All major credit cards

Reservations Required

Co-chefs Lee Hanson and Riad Nasr excel at such French brasserie favorites as escargot with garlic butter sauce ($12.50), very good bistro steaks ($23 with awesome frites), and, as the Sunday plat du jour, rich, rustic cassoulet ($22). The serious hamburger ($11.25 lunch/$12.75 dinner) is an American imposition that's impossible to ignore. But perhaps wanting to impress *tout* SoHo, presentation is often too SoHo. Plates tend to emphasize cute over hearty. Even triumphant appetizers like the goat cheese and caramelized onion tart ($9) and the Balthazar salad ($11) of asparagus, haricots verts, fennel, ricotta salata, and truffle vinaigrette seem precious. And seafood entrees like crisp-skinned grilled brook trout ($19.50) and roasted bacon-wrapped monkfish ($22) are a tad demure.

Breads from the adjoining bakery—peasant rye, country sourdough, country baguette, white boule—provide the two-part pleasure of crusty resistance followed by agreeably chewy surrender as the air pockets within collapse. The dessert approach follows the same lines as the savory one: they're either true classics—profiteroles ($6.50), chocolate pot du crème ($7)—or stylized departures—banana tarte tatin with banana zabaglione ($7). Fruit tartlets and clafoutis ($8) are delightfully sweet exclamation points to a heady experience.

Blue Ribbon Sushi

The facade of Blue Ribbon Sushi is mysteriously unmarked. Were it not for the hand-lettered sign asking patrons not to sit on the steps of the adjacent building while they wait, you might completely miss this slim, handsomely low-lit place altogether. And once you find it, there's a process to gain access: give the harried-yet-congenial host your cell phone number, take a ticket, and prepare to wait for up to ninety minutes for a call-back. (There's a small lounge with wooden benches for those without cell phones.)

Cost	$25–65

Address 119 Sullivan St, between Prince & Spring Sts
☎212/343-0404
Transportation C,E to Spring St
Open Daily noon–2am
Accepts All major credit cards
Reservations Not accepted

When the call comes and you've been seated, either at a narrow wooden table or one of eight spots at the dramatically lit sushi bar, you'll be handed a piping hot towel and a menu. Those who forego the menu in favor of omakase (chef's choice; $75 for two) may be disappointed, as the selections include surprisingly conservative, Americanized rolls and sashimi. More adventurous diners will prefer specials like ankimo ($9.50), a smooth, sweet monkfish liver pâté, served cold with a mild paste of chile radish and a light, soy-based vinaigrette, and chutoro tataki ($15), a watermelon-pink lump of bluefin belly tartare, topped with a raw quail egg and meant to be mixed with the super-fine shreds of spring onion and dash of sesame oil that accompany it. The appetizers from the daily menu also hold appeal, especially the various sunomono dishes ($6.75–14) in which oysters, clams, octopus, and jellyfish come bathed in a smooth, piquant vinegar bath.

Daily sushi and sashimi selections are divided into oceans, "Pacific" and "Atlantic"; there is also a short list of prime meats available sushi-style, including gyu, or filet mignon ($3.50), which manages to be both pristinely fresh and obscenely flavorful. Blue Ribbon's maki (from $4 for standard California roll to $16.75 for lobster and black caviar roll) are uniformly excellent. Dessert seems absurdly beside the point, but the generously sized, timidly flavored green tea crème brûlée ($7.50), can be just the sweet, creamy, crackly thing to send you happily out the anonymous front door.

Cub Room Cafe

In the 1960s many people were guided by the maxim, "you are what you eat." In the 2000s, that's progressed to "you are what, where, and when you eat." And so, if your anything-but-average Joe SoHo does eat a 4.30pm order of fish and chips at an informal, kid-friendly, continuous-service eatery like the Cub Room Cafe, he doesn't dare tell anyone. The modest companion cafe to the more stylish Cub Room is an ideal spot for dine-down Fridays, ad-lib lunches, and other

| Cost | Lunch $10–30 |
| | Dinner $25–40 |

Address 183 Prince St, near Sullivan St
℡212/777-0030
Transportation C,E to Spring St
Open Mon–Fri noon–11pm, Sat & Sun 11am–9pm
Accepts All major credit cards

impromptu escapes from the restaurant rat race. It's a countrified space, with a French-windowed storefront, wainscoted banquettes, and parquet tables set with paper napkins. The menu is a comforting blend of traditional and contemporary American cooking, the difference between which Arthur Schwartz, the host of radio show *Food Talk*, explained thus: in "traditional", the meat, fish, or chicken are served to the side of the mashed potatoes; in "contemporary" they're stacked over them. Cub Room Cafe showcases its incredibly rich mashed Yukon Golds both ways.

Copious starters like the Tuscan pizza with three cheeses, caramelized onions, and truffle oil ($10), or the quesadilla del dia ($9) with guacamole and black bean salad would easily qualify as main courses. The terrific snapper rolls ($10) are cut from a tight wrap of grilled red snapper, shiitake mushrooms, fresh cilantro, and macadamia nuts. Outstanding fried calamari ($7) benefit from a chunky, peppery marinara dip, and slices of garlic-Parmesan toast.

Certain entrees are simplified versions of dishes chef/owner Henry Meer prepares at City Hall (see p.141): witness the cherrywood-smoked rib-eye steak ($14), and the tuna udon ($16), a big bowl of udon noodles, baby bok choy, shiitakes, and seared rare tuna. Weekend brunch includes decent brioche French toast ($8.75) and crisp potato latke with bacon and eggs ($8.25). Desserts are unchanged throughout the day and thus it is easy to keep up, as you should, with the nutty warm nectarine raspberry crisp and the arborio rice pudding (both $4).

Hampton Chutney Co.

Gary and Isabel MacGurn met at an ashram in Bombay, where they immersed themselves in yoga and meditation. While clearing their minds of the material world, they did their *seva*—selfless service—in the ashram's kitchen, where they learned a thing or two about Southern Indian cooking. Back home, partnered with chef Patty Gentry, the MacGurns have brought their know-how to less spiritual surroundings beside the chichi retailers in SoHo (**So**uth of **Ho**uston Street). On-site seating at this

Cost	$9–25
Address 68 Prince St, between Crosby & Lafayette Sts	
☎212/226-9996	
Transportation N,R to Prince St; 6 to Spring St	
Open Daily 11am–8pm	
Accepts All major credit cards	
Reservations Not accepted	

Indian-themed take on a wrap joint is limited to a dozen or so counter stools and a pair of high-top tables. Soft, melodic chants fill the air, and snapshots of the ashram's teachers adorn the walls. Grab a stool in front of the open kitchen, and you may even discover your own personal nirvana.

All thirteen options come in two formats made with a slightly sour fermented rice and lentil batter: dosa (a sheer, crisp, lacy crêpe filled like a fat burrito) or uttapa (pancake-style). Both are big enough to share with a friend, but you won't want to. Don't forget to choose your chutney (tomato, cilantro, mango, pumpkin, or peanut). You get one free per order, but the extra 50¢ you pay for a second will be two of the best quarters you ever spend in NYC.

Despite the veracity of the dosa batter, most fillings are no more Indian than the solid, hearty breakfast variety ($6.95), overflowing with fluffy scrambled eggs, spinach, roasted tomatoes, and Jack cheese. Likewise, the uttapa topped with smoked turkey, Jack cheese, and balsamic roasted onions ($9.95) is the cultural equivalent of barbecue chicken pizza. Bogus, but delicious. Just add ripe avocado for an extra buck and the transformation is complete. There are several vegetarian options, including a substantial dosa filled with grilled portobellos, roasted butternut squash, arugula, and Jack cheese ($8.95). The masala dosa ($6.50), stuffed with the traditional garam masala-spiced potato and onion filling, is one of the few choices at Hampton Chutney Co. which, though made in SoHo, could have come straight off the streets of SoIn.

SoHo

Jean Claude

Resembling for all the world a workaday Paris bistro with a few Mediterranean accents, Jean Claude is a diminutive restaurant with an inviting red-painted exterior that can be difficult to see, crowded as the sidewalk is outside. The no-reservations policy means you'll have to cool your heels on this civilized block of Sullivan Street or, if you're that type, stare in at the lucky diners already seated at one of the twelve tables and hope they get your "hurry up" vibe. But they probably won't, not while enjoying

Cost	$28–55

Address 137 Sullivan St, between Houston & Prince Sts
℡212/475-9232
Transportation C,E to Spring St
Open Sun–Thurs 6–11pm, Fri & Sat 6–11.30pm
Accepts Cash only
Reservations Not accepted

the warm, yellow-toned dining room, simple, elegant bistro fare and efficient service whose occasional lapses into bitchiness only add to the authenticity. The much copied formula was pioneered here by onetime waiter and now budget-bistro godfather Jean-Claude Iacovelli, who is also behind Impala Café in Greenwich Village (see p.94).

Early diners (6–7.30pm) are rewarded with a remarkably reasonable $18 prix fixe menu. Whether you choose from this or a la carte, bear in mind that the daily soups tend to be a bit slapdash. A better option is the shrimp ravioli ($6), surprisingly light, full of ocean-fresh shrimp, and bathed in a buttery tomato sauce. The quail appetizer ($6), roasted medium-rare so that it's still pink and juicy, is served with warm, sweet glazed pear slices and a bright salad of shaved fennel and frisée. A modest medallion of New York State foie gras ($8) has its smooth and mild flavor set off nicely by a Sauternes reduction.

When it comes to entrees, the kitchen has a way with fish, including a fine sautéed skate wing whose briny caper garnish is countered by a meaty roasted portobello cap ($16). Equally good, if short on sex appeal, is seared Atlantic salmon accompanied by a tender wedge of roasted fennel, delicate sweet peas, and crisp, earthy carrots ($15). Superbly roasted Cornish hen, smartly paired with an al dente, herb-flecked risotto and super-garlicky sautéed spinach ($16) is fine, but the pork loin with paprika sauce ($17) can be a little dry. Desserts, either crème brûlée ($6) or tiramisu, are true to form.

Mercer Kitchen

You enter superstar chef Jean-Georges Vongerichten's SoHo digs in the Mercer Hotel as you would a glam nightclub, descending a glass-walled stairway to a dark-wooded cellar partitioned like a Japanese bento box. Three long communal tables extending from the open kitchen to the salad assembly line blur the distinction between front and back of house. Candlelit tables surrounded by distressed-brick walls afford a measure of seclusion and—now that the notoriously chilly service has warmed some—romantic charm. The cuisine is self-defined as "Provençal," a description

| Cost | Lunch $35–75 |
| | Dinner $40–90 |

Address 99 Prince St at Mercer St
℡212/966-5454
Transportation N,R to Prince St
Open Mon–Sat 7–11am, noon–2.45pm & 6pm–midnight, Sun 7–11am, noon–2.45pm & 6–10.30pm
Accepts All major credit cards
Reservations Required

both limiting and, considering the sun-starved premises and black-on-black fashions, somehow preposterous. The hotspot is too worldly, too unconventional, and too full of full-of-themselves New Yorkers to be positioned north of 14th Street, much less in the South of France. The food is instead distinguished by the bare-naked flavors highlighted on every plate.

Crystal-clear flavors mark a number of appetizers: the elemental ensemble of fresh figs, prosciutto, aged balsamic, and rosemary pizza bread ($11); the salad of baby fennel, Parmesan, carpaccio-thin mushrooms, arugula, and lemon dressing ($10); the sliced and reconstructed tomato fitted with fresh basil ($11). Toppings on superbly thin, almost weightless pizzas range from artichokes, prosciutto, and Taleggio cheese ($13) to the raw tuna, shiso leaf, and wasabi ricotta pie ($17) named after Barry Wine, who introduced the concept at the defunct Quilted Giraffe.

To get the maximum pleasure from your entree you'll need to adore all its components. There is, for example, no ignoring the yogurt–dill garnish and olive-vanilla-cumin sauce adorning the rotisserie chicken ($19). Perfectly grilled dorade (sea bream; $25) requires you to delight in the drama of fennel, shiitakes, and cherry tomatoes. Other joys are effortless, such as the dripping braised short ribs with sliced steak ($26) and, from the pastry oven, a wood-grilled bruschetta of buttered toast topped with peaches and plums($7). And there's rarely any resistance to Jean-Georges' signature molten chocolate cake with vanilla ice cream ($9). For the best value, go for the $25 prix fixe lunch.

135

SoHo

Penang

🍴 With log-pitched huts, exposed ventilation ducts, and a tropical waterfall, Penang gives an industrial SoHo spin to the Paradise Island restaurant tradition. Among the best dining values in SoHo, it's a great, albeit small, place to introduce yourself to scintillating Malaysian cooking. And though you may be kept waiting at the sheet-metal bar for your table, the service, once you're seated, is friendly, patient, and well orchestrated, with shared appetizers arriving one at a time.

| Cost | Lunch $10–65 |
| | Dinner $22–65 |

Address 109 Spring St,
between Greene & Mercer Sts;
plus other locations
☎212/274-8883
Transportation N,R to Prince
St; 6 to Spring St
Open Mon–Thurs
11.30am–midnight, Fri & Sat
11.30am–1am, Sun 1–11pm
Accepts All major credit cards
Reservations Suggested

Servers rightly insist you begin with roti canai ($4.25), a thin, neither-crisp-nor-soft, Indian-style crêpe served with a neither-thick-nor-thin curry dip containing potato and chicken. Another appetizer to share is penang lobak ($6.25), a mixed fry of tofu, pork roll, and shrimp pancake with hoisin plum and chile sauces for dipping. Penang clay pot noodles and Penang chow kueh teow noodles (both $9.95) are full of flavors. The former packs all manner of five-star ingredients in its vegetable-laden broth: home-cut noodles, scallops, shrimp, squid, and an eggy gravy. The latter boasts seven co-stars: flat rice noodles, shrimp, squid, eggs, chives, bean sprouts, and a black soy chile sauce.

The pièce de résistance when it comes to ensemble dishes is sarang burang (known also as "monk's head"; $14.95), a cashew-sprinkled coronet of fried taro filled with baby corn, carrots, black mushrooms, baby mushrooms, shrimp, squid, and scallops. Other royal dishes are beef rendang (slow-cooked, almost shredded beef with a paste of ground onions, lemongrass, and chile in a thick coconut curry sauce; $12.95); kari ayam (chicken and potatoes in a red coconut curry; $11.95); and any one of three whole fish options (all $19.95): steamed striped bass with tamarind sauce, deep-fried red snapper with a spicy-pungent-fruit orange sauce, or grilled striped bass wrapped in banana leaf. The shaved ice desserts, like chendol ($5.50), with green pea flour noodles, coconut milk, and red beans, are for the adventurous only; there is no fitter finale than the warm peanut pancake a la mode ($7.50).

TriBeCa

Bubby's Pie Co

Cost	Lunch $8–25
	Dinner $20–60

Address 120 Hudson St at
North Moore St
℡212/219-0666
Transportation 1,2 to Franklin St
Open Mon–Thurs 8am–11pm,
Fri 8am–midnight, Sat
9am–4.30pm & 6pm–midnight,
Sun 9am–4.30pm & 6–10pm
Accepts All major credit cards

Though accepted from the outset as a wholesome, honest, unaffected neighborhood cafe and bakery, Bubby has something of a con going with its name. It was intended to suggest the Yiddish word for grandma. And you could well believe it was a genuine bubby who baked the old-world-hominess into the fruit pies, notably the mile-high apple and the sour cherry (both $5 for a generous wedge). But in truth, the co-founder (now sole proprietor) was no *bubeleh*, but a young guy named Ron Crismon. And the kitchen has *never* been headed by a woman old enough to have kids with kids.

Still, you could say the place has grown into its name. Many of the single downtowners who first came in 1990 today push strollers through the front door of an eatery cherished for its picture windows, child-friendly outlook, and small-town vibe. Movie stars like Julia Roberts, Ed Burns, and Spike Lee slip in quietly from time to time for the same reason anyone else does: compelling breakfasts, brunches, and lunches. Sit down and a freshly baked, scone-like biscuit materializes on your distressed-wood table. As if by magic, the strawberry jam is already coating the end of your knife. Soon you are surrounded by fluffy sourdough pancakes ($9.95), spinach-fluffed "green" eggs ($9.95), and peasant bread French toast ($9.95), with barely a spare inch for grilled ham as thick as a steak and well-done, terrifically oniony home fries. As for lunch, the twin pulled pork sandwiches ($10.95)introduce a new emphasis on barbecue with their faintly spicy tang.

At night the side room, with its dim light, copper-topped bar, and floral wallpaper, is cozy and romantic. Crismon has kept his signature rosemary roast chicken ($14.95) while also pushing meaty, tender-and-tart BBQ ribs ($13.95 with chicken). And if entrees are sometimes delivered before appetizers are cleared, it's for the best possible reason: starters like homemade potato chips swimming in melted blue cheese ($6.95) and equally messy corn nachos with the works ($8.95) are unending. You will, however, experience no difficulty getting to the bottom of the chocolate peanut butter pie ($5).

TriBeCa

Capsouto Frères

Welcome to the wonder of Washington and Watts Streets. Since 1980, the three Capsouto *frères*—Jacques, Sammy, and Albert—have occupied the ground floor of a gloriously eccentric TriBeCa landmark. Built in 1892, the Fleming Smith warehouse stands near the Hudson waterfront as a golden marvel of fanciful Flemish brickwork, gables, and arched windows. Inside, the bricks and tall windows enclose a spacious loft distinguished by the pine ceiling beams that lie 14ft overhead. The grandeur is counterbalanced by the sibling hosts' personal warmth. Romantic and unpretentious, the bistro is just as suited to young hopefuls on first dates as to old-timers celebrating silver-wedding anniversaries.

Cost	Lunch $16–55
	Dinner $25–65

Address 451 Washington St at Watts St
☎212/966-4900
Transportation 1,2 to Canal St
Open Sun & Tues–Thurs noon–3.30pm & 6–11pm, Mon 6–11pm, Fri & Sat noon–3.30pm & 6pm–midnight
Accepts All major credit cards
Reservations Suggested

The classic French kitchen is neither oblivious to, nor preoccupied with, modern food fashions, which, like skirt lengths, constitute fads and revivals more often than they do outright inventions. The consommé of desirably chewy duck and cepe ravioli ($7.50) will satisfy any fashion-conscious diner, while those who favor a more traditional plate can contend with the blasts of garlic and nose-burning grainy mustard in the Lyonnaise pairing of sausage and warm potatoes ($6.50). And diners of all persuasions would make a territorial claim on the potato-chip-tiered lobster Napoleon ($10) were it placed at the center of the table.

Main courses are solid and substantial and rarely any more than that. The arugula, wild rice, and sweet raspberry butter crowding a plate of grilled quail ($17.50) could not be less photogenic, but offers plenty of good nibbling and shoveling. Likewise, the sautéed sweetbreads with wild mushrooms and baby vegetables in an unrepentantly rich brown butter sauce ($19) will never make it to a glossy magazine spread, however tasty they are. The pot au feu of vegetables in a truffled broth ($16) is a noble, if short-lived gesture toward caloric correctness. Forget calories when it comes to dessert, and take note: no one can truly be happy with the hazelnut crème brûlée or warm tarte tatin—though these are perfectly okay—when everyone around them is dipping into the hot recesses of chocolate, raspberry, hazelnut, or lemon soufflés (each $6.50).

City Hall

🍴 Times have never been tougher for the bratty tycoons of Wall Street and Foley Square. No to interoffice flirting. No to topless live theater. No to red meat, raw oysters, buttered anything, morning martinis, and afternoon caffeine. City Hall, however, indulges a generation that will no longer be denied. With a Delmonico steak and a baked Alaska gracing its menu and back-lit vintage photographs of old downtown markets lining its handsome dining room, this restaurant conjures up the chophouses, oyster bars, and cafeterias of Tammany Hall days. Yet since the city's dining scene is much better now than at any time in its history, the nostalgic appeal is ultimately not for the old foods. It's for the old rules. Arched windows, cast-iron Corinthian columns, travertine marble floors, courtly circular booths, colossal steaks, and tiered shellfish extravaganzas recall a more permissive age when fatty meat and fat politicians could be had for the money and in plain view.

Cost	Lunch $20–40 Dinner $40–85

Address 131 Duane St, between Church St & West Broadway
☎212/227-7777
Transportation 1,2,A,C to Chambers St; N,R to City Hall
Open Mon–Fri noon–2.30pm & 6–11pm, Sat 6–11pm
Accepts All major credit cards
Reservations Suggested

The French-Jewish trio of herrings (pickled, brined, and creamed) paired with potatoes ($10) may not seem like a guilty pleasure, unless you think of your breath. If that's a consideration, the brothy she crab soup ($9), chicken consommé with matzoh dumplings ($7.50), and a half-salmon/half-tuna tartare ($11) are safer appetizer bets. Lightly fried oysters ($9) are served for the same price at lunch as a po' boy (sandwich). The signature main course is the Delmonico ($24)—a thin, 16-oz slab of charbroiled rib-eye with a layer of melted Maytag blue cheese. A tuna steak encrusted with tri-colored peppercorns ($22) works beautifully, as do the sensational, goose-fat-fried hash browns (like all side dishes, $6 extra) and the split chicken ($19) cooked in an infrared broiler with rosemary and shallots to crackling perfection.

Desserts (mostly $8) may at first seem fussy. But if you're compensating for years of denial, the baked Alaska made with devil's food cake, espresso ice cream, a two-inch meringue topping and kumquats might be just the thing. Likewise, the brioche apple pudding and the cheesecake.

TriBeCa

The Harrison

When looking back at the ill-fated date and location they chose for their downtown follow-up to the well-liked Red Cat (see p.11) executive chef Jimmy Bradley and partner Danny Abrams can only shake their heads and ask themselves, "what if?" Harrison opened nine blocks north of—and one month after—the World Trade Center disaster. It's probably safe to bet that under less trying circumstances, the ensuing reservations backlog of two to three weeks might have stretched closer to two to three months. The success of The Harrison confirms Bradley's mastery of the up-to-date, feel-good food that Manhattan feels like eating. And the white-washed barnwood, antique leather banquettes, oiled walnut, and French doors give his new digs the ambiance of TriBeCa clubhouse—just the ticket for nightly and noisy get-togethers.

| Cost | Lunch $25–60 |
| | Dinner $35–75 |

Address 355 Greenwich St at Harrison St
℡212/274-9310
Transportation 1,2 to Franklin St
Open Mon 5.30–11.30pm, Tues noon–2.30pm & 5.30–11.30pm, Fri noon–2.30pm & 5.30pm–midnight, Sat 5.30pm–midnight
Accepts All major credit cards
Reservations Required

The menu, as supervised by Joey Campanaro, applies Mediterranean highlights to contemporary American comforts. (Maybe it's better to instead specify "New York" comforts, as it's uncertain that the rest of the nation is as enamored of veal cheeks and sweetbreads as New Yorkers are.) There's no getting your feet wet at Harrison. Only the fried clams with lemon cilantro aioli ($7) allow an easy pace. Braised veal cheeks make an early entrance in an appetizer of ricotta cavatelli (the cheese is added to the dough) dressed with oven-dried tomatoes, escarole, and Pecorino Romano ($10). The prosciutto-wrapped sweetbreads saltimbocca suggests a rustic entree miniaturized for appetizer duty ($10).

Logic might dictate that entrees resemble expanded appetizers. Don't count on it. The grilled pork chop with toasted orzo, stewed tomatoes, and calamata olives ($21) and 14-oz shell steak ($21) are heavy-hitters. And the pan-crisped skate ($18) and signature pan-crisped chicken ($23) are heftier than you expect. (Pan-crisped is a euphemism for pan-fried.) To close, the buttermilk panna cotta ($7), chocolate beignets ($6) and warm quince and apple crisp with ginger ice cream ($14 for two) tack on a good three days to the table backlog.

Nam

In a high-windowed, ground-floor loft on Reade Street, Nam hits on a balanced mix of style, sophistication, warmth, and informality. Evocative family photos silk-screened onto the sides of hatbox-shaped lampshades illuminate the carved-wood walls with wistful memories of Saigon and Hanoi, while the chartreuse opalescence that back-lights both the dark-wooded bar and the wall display of bamboo branches casts a glowing promise of nocturnal pleasures. The fantasy is brought to life by the elemental Vietnamese cooking of co-chefs Tien Phan, Hoang Do, and Quy Tran. The lucidity of familiar flavors is so great as to make them seem mysterious and complex.

| Cost | Lunch $20–50 |
| | Dinner $25–60 |

Address 110 Reade St,
between West Broadway &
Church St
℡212/267-1777
Transportation A,C,1,2 to
Chambers St
Open Mon–Fri 11.30am–3pm
& 5.30–11pm, Sat 5.30–11pm,
Sun 5.30–10.30pm
Accepts All major credit cards
Reservations Suggested

VIETNAMESE

The irresistible bo bia ($5)—soft, rice-paper rolls of jicama, shrimp, and sausage with a chile bean dip—are a compulsory starting point. But the banh cuon—loose and slippery ravioli filled with chopped shiitakes and topped with fried shallots, basil, cilantro, bean sprouts, and lime vinaigrette ($5)—are also non-negotiable. The chao tom lets you wrap rice paper, vermicelli, crushed peanuts, lettuce, cilantro, and mint around a sugar-cane-speared brochette of ground, pressed shrimp ($8). And the goi muc—a vertical grilled calamari salad ($7)—is a thing of rare beauty.

The wonder of main courses is the way in which you can isolate and appreciate each ingredient. The drama supplied by the tomato, soft tofu, and crisp strands of ginger to steamed sea bass with noodles, shiitakes, ginger, and scallions ($15) is entirely unexpected. In mi xao, the stir-fried egg noodles, shrimp, chicken, pork, carrots, and peanuts ($8) are all distinct. Bun cha ($10) poses grilled chunks of desirably chewy, succulent, sweet-and-spicy barbecued pork alongside a nest of rice vermicelli and roasted peanut. The one criticism of entrees is that they rely too often on the same chile lime sauce. Lime makes a final appearance as a marinade for the mango chunks accompanying the ginger flan (a bit high at $7). Like the banana bread topped with flakes of toasted coconut ($7), it applies a stylish, tropical spin to an everyday dessert.

TriBeCa

Odeon

The arduous burden of staying fashionable, of anticipating trends and eluding obsolescence, of securing the right tables in the right places at the right times, is lifted for an hour or two of giddy, conversational pleasure at the former site of the Tower Cafeteria. In Left Bank Paris, the Odeon is a theater and a Metro station. In Manhattan, it identifies a brasserie and a guarantee to feel with-it, relevant, and relieved to be nowhere else. Co-founded in 1980 by Brian McNally (Smith), Keith McNally (Balthazar, Pastis; see p.130 and p.172), and Lynn Wagenknecht (Cafe Luxembourg, p.278),

| Cost | Lunch $22–60 |
| | Dinner $30–80 |

Address 145 West Broadway at Thomas St
℡212/233-0507
Transportation 1,2 to Chambers St
Open Mon–Fri noon–midnight, Sat & Sun 11.30am–5pm & 5.30pm–midnight
Accepts All major credit cards
Reservations Suggested

Odeon set the template for the retro bistro craze, not only with its 1930s look (salvaged terrazzo floor, hanging globe lights, wood-paneling, chrome details), but also in its newly minted brand of downtown cool that was practiced to look unpracticed.

The food has proved crucial to Odeon's staying power. As far as anyone knows—and hopes—there's no fashionable Odeon cookbook on the horizon. It's the absence of flashes in the pan that's so enduring; there's nothing to tire of. As on a cafeteria line, the aim is to crowd likeable food on a plate and let the diner figure out how to manage it. Disorderly salads have typically been the most challenging in this regard, especially the very satisfying frisée with crumbled Roquefort, bacon lardons, and Dijon vinaigrette ($10.50). With decent fried calamari ($10.50) or shrimp cocktail ($12) you have a better shot at keeping contents confined to plate and fork.

No matter who's manning the kitchen, steak frites (among which the superb, $13 steakburger must be included) continue to be the best choices, either as a splurge (the grilled sirloin; $28, $29 au poivre) or on the relative cheap (a fully functional grilled hanger with a wild mushroom garnish; $17.50). Tuna too is a great bet, either as a grilled steak ($24) or seared and then slid into a sandwich with arugula and wasabe mayo. The roast chicken ($17.50) never disappoints. Of the desserts, look no further than the chocolate pudding ($7).

Pepolino

Stepping upstairs and then inside Pepolino is a heady experience. One moment you're inhaling the fumes from the Holland Tunnel approach; the next, you're breathing the air of a folksy Florentine trattoria. Sooner than you and yours have had time to figure out who's sitting where at the little butcher-block table, someone arrives with crusty Sullivan Bakery bread accompanied by a garlicky tomato flan that you spread like jam. Life at Pepolino just gets better and better.

| Cost | Lunch $19–30 |
| | Dinner $25–70 |

Address 281 West Broadway, between Canal & Lispenard Sts
☎212/966-9983
Transportation A,C,E to Canal St
Open Mon–Fri noon–3pm & 5.30–11pm, Sat & Sun noon–midnight
Accepts AmEx
Reservations Suggested

Co-owner (and pastry chef) Enzo Pezone must count on one loaf of bread per diner. For the next house specialty to arrive is the terrine di cozze con burro e prezzemole ($10), a ramekin of shelled mussels in a pool of melted butter, garlic, and parsley that requires several slices of toast for sopping. And then there's the Tuscan bread soup ribollita ($8). Made with cannellini beans, cabbage, thyme, and sage, this thicker-than-thick version has no visible liquid. You could feasibly drop this soup, but you couldn't really spill it. The spinach ricotta soufflé ($10) and the polenta mousse with wild mushroom and white truffle oil ($10) also reflect the rustic, hearty, herb-packed style of chef Patrizio Siddu's cooking.

Pasta is not a strong point, excepting the malfatti (spinach-ricotta dumplings) in a butter sage sauce ($11 lunch, $14 dinner) and the daily homemade lasagna ($12) served at lunch. Among evening entrees, the chicken ($18.50) is a joy. Succulent and tender pieces of boneless breast are assembled with roasted pears, melted Pecorino cheese, and a rich wine sauce to create a melt-in-your-mouth sensation. Similarly, roast leg of lamb with artichokes ($22) is a revelation. The deboned and rolled lamb is superbly tender, if occasionally a tad dry. From the sea there is the spicy fish stew cacciucco alla Livornese ($25). And how nice of Enzo to go to the trouble of preparing such wonderful desserts (all $7) as bittersweet flourless chocolate cake, ricotta cheesecake, and panna cotta. These give the illusion of choice when in truth here is none—quite simply, bypassing the chocolate flan with caramel sauce is nothing short of a crime.

TriBeCa

Le Zinc

To truly enjoy Le Zinc, it is almost better not to know that chef David Waltuck and wife Karen are behind it. Twice the Waltucks have broken new ground for fine downtown dining, first when they opened the exacting French/New American restaurant Chanterelle in SoHo 1981, and later when they moved it to TriBeCa in 1989. Le Zinc, on the other hand, despite a few outstanding dishes, is merely a good neighborhood place. With a zinc-plate bar, Thonet bentwood chairs, and unframed art posters plastered on the high walls, the 95-seat dining room suits a high-rent district that still sees itself as arty and nonconformist. The menu seeks a comparable balance between creativity and comfort, listing Asian fusion snacks alongside bistro fare and hearty Old World selections.

| Cost | Lunch $16–50 |
| | Dinner $25–70 |

Address 139 Duane St, between West Broadway & Church St
☎212/513-0001
Transportation 1,2,A,C to Chambers St
Open Daily 8am–midnight
Accepts All major credit cards
Reservations For large groups

If you ended up with cute Asian appetizers like the chicken satay with spicy peanut sauce ($7) and pulled pork in moo shu wrappers ($7) you wouldn't run away. But with better versions of similar things elsewhere you wouldn't make a special trip, either. The cornmeal-coated duck wings ($8.50), however, are a revelation. Chewing the fried, confit-like duck meat off the bone is the closest thing you'll ever experience to a duck spare rib. The curried onion fritters ($5.25) are milder than you expect, but still very good. Aunt Fanny's chopped chicken liver ($5.50) is dry.

The onion roll used for an otherwise solid bacon cheeseburger ($12 with first-rate fries) is detrimentally large. Objections to the grilled pork chop ($20) have nothing to do with the juicy meat and everything to do with the black pepper inexplicably dominating the apple smoked bacon sauce. Better to keep that pepper to the grilled shell steak au poivre ($25). The roast chicken ($18), with fresh thyme under its crisp skin, in its sauce, and throughout the sensational stuffing made with cubes of sourdough bread and Parker House rolls, exudes true greatness. When it comes to desserts (about $6), disparities are just as marked. On a night when the ice cream in profiteroles was crystallized, the top-notch pecan pie was successfully ridding the classic of its cloying gooiness.

Wall Street & Lower Manhattan

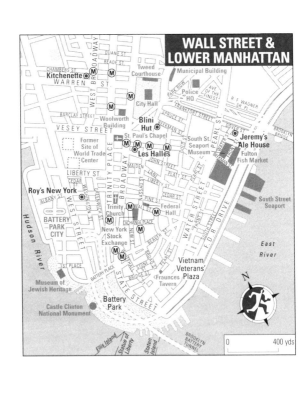

WALL STREET & LOWER MANHATTAN

CHAMBERS ST.
Kitchenette
WARREN ST.

DUANE ST.
READE ST.
Tweed Courthouse
Municipal Building
FANE ROW
Police HQ
AVE OF THE FINEST
R F WAGNER SR PL

BARCLAY STREET
City Hall
FRANKFORT STREET
Woolworth Building
Blini Hut
VESEY STREET
St. Paul's Chapel
BEEKMAN ST.
South St. Seaport Museum
PEARL ST.
DOVER ST.
BROOKLYN BRIDGE
Jeremy's Ale House
Fulton Fish Market

Former Site of World Trade Center
Les Halles
JOHN ST.
LIBERTY ST.
CEDAR ST.
MAIDEN LANE
PLATT ST.
CEDAR ST.

Roy's New York
ALBANY ST.
WASHINGTON ST.
GREENWICH ST.
TRINITY PLACE
BROADWAY
NASSAU ST.
WILLIAM ST.
PINE ST.
Trinity Church
WALL ST.
Federal Hall
EXCHANGE PLACE
New York Stock Exchange
BEAVER ST.

BATTERY PARK CITY
Hudson River
WATER STREET
F D R DRIVE
South Street Seaport
East River

1ST PLACE
BATTERY PLACE
STATE STREET
STONE ST.
BRIDGE ST.
Vietnam Veterans' Plaza
Fraunces Tavern

Museum of Jewish Heritage
Battery Park
Castle Clinton National Monument

BROOKLYN BATTERY TUNNEL
Ellis Island
Statue of Liberty
Staten Island

N

0   400 yds

Blini Hut

In immigrant Lenny Kuvykin's dreams, every interstate, suburban shopping mall, and downtown food court in America would have at least one Blini Hut, the Russian fast-food franchise that does for blini and borscht what McDonald's achieved for burgers and fries. So far there is but the original—and, since 9/11, struggling—Blini Hut, inauspiciously situated about four blocks from the former site of the World Trade Center. Kuvykin has tried to boost business by introducing such American junk as fried chicken, Buffalo wings, and mozzarella

Cost	$4–14

Address 132 Nassau St at Beekman St

℡212/233-3500

Transportation 1,2,4,5 to Fulton St; A,C to Broadway Nassau

Open Mon–Fri 7am–7pm, Sat 11.30am–5.30pm

Accepts All major credit cards

Reservations Not accepted

sticks. But these hold little appeal for the local students, city bureaucrats, and office workers who are loyal to his sixty-seat, counter-service, Russian-video-playing eatery. Regulars here depend on the sort of daily recovery only a homemade hot soup can provide. And as added compensation, the very existence of blini with sour cream and caviar for a mere $4.99 redefines the classic, rags-to-riches Wall Street success story. Blini and caviar used to be the reward for making it to the top. Thanks to Kuvykin, nowadays it's what you eat on your way there.

The Ukrainian native has only scorn for what normally passes for borscht in his adoptive country. "There's not a borscht," he says, his accent thicker than sour cream. "It's beets and water." His version is a hearty vegetable soup amply stocked with carrots, potatoes, tomatoes, and cabbage. Served with wholewheat bread, it's pretty darn good for $2.96. The same amount also buys a chicken broth with pelmenyi (ground beef dumplings) and a thick, vegetarian split pea. Russian entrees are not much more expensive. The rice and beef golubtzi (stuffed cabbage) is just $4.57; the big, juicy chicken Kiev, $4.62. (The prices are rounded once the sales tax is factored in.)

Blini are prepared fresh each morning and come in four varieties: original (with sour cream only), salmon caviar (2oz), smoked salmon (about 2oz; $4.99), and sour cherry ($2.49). The latter can be a dessert alternative to the apple or cherry blintzes ($2.49 for three). The fresh blintzes are also prepared as savory crêpes, with such fillings as chicken and potato. **149**

Jeremy's Ale House

(🍴) Jeremy Holin anticipated the 1980s boom and 1990s bust set off by the marketplace-styled redevelopment of South Street Seaport when he pitched his deep-fryers and beer taps in a vacant space beside the Brooklyn Bridge in 1981. Whereas the developers sanitized the historic waterfront area, leasing space to franchise eateries and touristy restaurants of little lasting interest to discerning locals, Jeremy's crude, raucous seafood tavern captured some of the grit and stench of the old harbor. Moreover, that colorful essence is likely to survive the still tentative construction of a Frank Gehry-designed Guggenheim Museum on four nearby piers as well as the planned move of the neighboring Fulton Fish Market from here to the Bronx. In truth, Jeremy's never depended upon the trade from the city's main wholesale fish market. The hundreds of customers' neckties and brassieres hanging from the garagehouse's high rafters are evidence of that, as longshoremen generally do not wear either to work. Those garments were presumably left behind by workers from another lower Manhattan market. After the close of trading on Thursdays and Fridays, the place is packed with Wall Street carousers.

Cost	$6–25

Address 254 Front St, between Dover St & Peck Slip
⊤212/964-3537
Transportation 4,5,6 to Brooklyn Bridge-City Hall; 1,2,J,M,Z to Fulton St; A,C to Broadway-Nassau
Open Mon–Sat 8am–midnight, Sun 8am–2pm
Accepts Cash only
Reservations Not accepted

At other times, the principal attractions are fish and beer, both of them cheap, fresh (the catch is brought in daily except weekends), and sold from the bar. For fried-to-order seafood there are few better batters—or deals—in town than those to be found in Jeremy's platters ($5.95-7.95 including coleslaw and passable fries). Best are the calamari, accompanied by a spicy tomato sauce, and the clams, which can be dipped into tartar sauce or cocktail sauce but, like the calamari, require only a squeeze of lemon. The smallish shrimp don't have all that much flavor. As a lower-fat alternative, grilled calamari ($6.95) is sensationally tender.

Some two dozen drafts, including such notables as Pilsner Urquell, Bass Ale, Pete's Wicked Ale, Harp's Lager, Double Diamond Original Burton Ale, and Saranac Black Forest Lager, are poured by the clear-plastic pint ($4.50) or the Styrofoam, 32oz "bucket" ($6.75). Disciplined lunchers sworn to a one-beer limit are generally partial to the larger option.

Kitchenette

Lower Manhattan is not entirely consumed with the business of either making money or, as is frequently the case, losing it. For all those who'd rather be tending a garden than a portfolio or sifting flour instead of paperwork, cozy, quirky Kitchenette, with its distressed-wood furnishings, flea market relics and homespun pantry, is a breath of fresh air. The 9-to-5ers or, very often, 8-to-8ers are joined at communal, enamel-topped tables by moms (and nannies) and their charges drawn from their TriBeCa apartments by Kitchenette's inviting pastry case, sweet (albeit scattered) service and vaguely Southern fare. Or maybe it's just the peanut-butter-cream-filled chocolate cupcakes.

Cost	Lunch $9–20 Dinner $12–30

Address 80 West Broadway at Warren St
☎212/267-6740
Transportation 1,2,A,C to Chambers St
Open Mon–Fri 7.30am–10pm, Sat & Sun 9am–10pm
Accepts All major credit cards
Reservations Not accepted

AMERICAN

The cafe's logo cleverly incorporates a pan of eggs, sunny side up, into the letter "K"; take the not-so-subliminal suggestion and indulge in any of the hearty egg-centric breakfast or brunch options available until 4pm. A roast eggplant omelet ($8.50) includes spinach and sun-dried tomatoes and is served with so-so breakfast potatoes and buttery biscuits. Ordering the Lumberjack ($9.25), with two eggs, bacon, and two pancakes, allows you to straddle the line between an egg selection and Kitchenette's other specialty: carbo-loaded breakfast breads and sweets. The blueberry or blackberry pancakes are fluffy and dense, and if they're occasionally a little on the dry side, there's plenty of pure maple syrup on hand.

For lunch or dinner, abandon thoughts of going healthy, as the salads (from $3.50 for field greens with balsamic vinaigrette to $8.50 for Cobb or roasted beet salad) tend to look and taste like a resented afterthought, added to the menu in an attempt to appease chronic dieters. Much more appealing are the tuna melt with tomato and cheddar ($10) or the BLT on challah ($7.25). All sandwiches and burgers are served with hand-cut fries ($2.75) whose occasional lack of crispness is made up for by their warm garlic and black pepper bite. As for the crusty-rimmed muffins and other goodies in that pastry case, there isn't a clinker in the bunch. The choice changes daily, but always includes gooey cream-filled cupcakes ($3) and rich, tangy sour cream coffee cake ($3.25).

Les Halles

In a business district where an average lunch "hour" lasts 22 minutes and the after-work dinner trade is negligible, there is purportedly no place for a stylish French brasserie like Les Halles. But try telling that to the overjoyed bankers, French expats and tourists sidling up to its ornate mahogany bar or settling into its comfy, high-backed leather banquettes. A smartly restored tavern that feels more pre-crash (1929) New York than *Belle Époque* Paris, Les

Cost	$25–70

Address 15 John St, between
Broadway & Nassau Sts
℡212/285 8585
Transportation A,C to
Broadway-Nassau;
J,M,Z,1,2,4,5 to Fulton St
Open Mon–Sat noon–midnight
Accepts All major credit cards

Halles is the Lower Manhattan offshoot of the popular bistro/butcher shop of the same name (411 Park Ave South, Gramercy Park; ℡212/679-4111) and is thus the second culinary home of chef Anthony Bourdain, author of restaurant tell-all *Kitchen Confidential*. Autograph seekers are, however, a more frequent presence than the globetrotting Bourdain.

This Les Halles has no butcher counter, but it does share with its sibling a flair for cooking with French cuts of beef, sausages, and meat fats. A little of each probably fortifies the French onion soup ($7.50) crusted with a thick layer of salty Gruyère. Bacon lardon enriches both the tartiflette ($7.50), a bubbling gratin of Reblochon cheese and tender fingerling potatoes, and the fine frisée salad. Nine varieties of moules frites ($9/$12.50) are each nobly presented in beautiful, copper-bottomed casseroles. Standouts include marinières (white wine, shallots, and garlic), billi-bi (saffron, cream, and vermouth) and portugues (garlic, cilantro, white wine, spicy chorizo, and tomato). The crisp, golden, salty, Les Halles frites are legendary.

Potato lovers will also like the duck parmentier ($14.50), with its strips of rich duck confit, although this duck shepherd's pie may arrive with a tepid center. Steak frites is cooked with precision—you wouldn't expect otherwise—either as a plate ($14.50) or on a crusty "French dip" baguette ($12.50) where the steak replaces the usual roast beef. Both are served with a red wine-and-shallot sauce for dipping. Decadent choucroute garnie ($16.50) assembles smoked pork loin, white veal sausage, smoked pork breast, boiled potatoes, and sauerkraut all slow-cooked in white wine. For dessert, tarte tatin ($6) is a good, basic expression of the classic.

Roy's New York

(🍴) The type of restaurant tip that puzzles the most goes something like this: "I'm not a big fan of sardines, but the sardines at so and so's are outstanding." If a person doesn't much care for a certain food, wouldn't his or her fondness for a particular rendition suggest its essential character had been lost Members of the "I'm-not-a-big-fan" club will worship this handsome crowd-pleaser for camouflaging its star ingredients in the most original ways. Roy is Roy Yamaguchi, the pioneer first of Euro-Asian cooking in LA and then of Hawaiian regional cuisine at the first Roy's in Honolulu. The fifteenth Roy's, tucked into the Marriott that was barely spared the attacks of 9/11, has toned

| Cost | Lunch $25–70 |
| | Dinner $30–70 |

Address 130 Washington St at Albany St

☎212/266-6262

Transportation
A,C,J,M,Z,1,2,4,5 to Fulton St-Broadway Nassau; 6 to Cortland St

Open Mon–Fri 6.30–10am, 11.30am–2.30pm & 5.30–10pm, Sat & Sun 7am–1pm & 5.30–10pm

Accepts All major credit cards

down some of the Polynesian excesses of yore. Though lamps hung from the ceiling by twisted rope do resemble pineapple slices, there are no Tahitian nudes depicted on the colorful, hand-painted columns.

Personable service and daily specials supervised by executive chef James Dangler help dodge the franchise fakeness that hounds similarly conceived spin-offs. The view from the curved food bar that faces the open kitchen is one of excitement, spontaneity, and hyperactive sauce cooks who float juicy crabcakes ($11) in a pool of spicy sesame butter sauce. The crabcakes also take a ride on a dim-sum-styled canoe-for-two ($25) with salty potstickers, Szechuan-spiced baby back ribs with little to chew on, shrimp sticks, and chicken satay.

Fish entrees ($16–25), no matter their treatments (porcini dust, lemongrass crust) and accessories (Thai curry red wine sauce, lobster basil truffle sauce), are flawlessly cooked. When the sauce really works—as with the wasabe ginger butter sauce, which counterbalances the delicacy of the ground macadamia nuts encrusting the shutome (Hawaiian swordfish)—the results are exceptional. Meats and birds, though less dependable in preparation, are unapologetically indulgent—garlic honey mustard short ribs ($18), say, braised to a mush. Desserts ($6–8) are just fine. Sure, the mascarpone cannoli could use more crunch. But the awesome hot chocolate soufflé is the volcano that Roy's sometimes tries too hard to be.

153

West Village

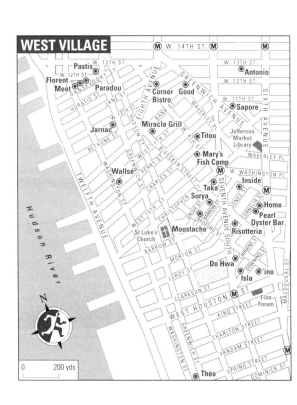

WEST VILLAGE

W. 14TH ST.

W. 13TH ST.
Pastis
W. 12TH ST.
Florent
Meet   Paradou

Antonio

W. 13TH ST.
W. 12TH ST.

SIXTH AVENUE

GREENWICH AVENUE

Corner
Bistro   Good

W. 11TH ST.

Sapore

EIGHTH AVENUE

HORATIO ST.
JANE ST.

HUDSON ST.

BANK ST.

WAVERLEY PL.

Jarnac   Miracle Grill   Titou

Jefferson
Market
Library

BETHUNE ST.

GREENWICH ST.

WEST 11TH ST.

Mary's
Fish Camp   WAVERLEY PL.

W. WASHINGTON PL.

Wallsé

PERRY ST.

BLEECKER STREET

Taka   Inside

Surya   Home

CHARLES ST.

WASHINGTON ST.

SEVENTH AVENUE SOUTH

JONES ST.

Pearl
Oyster Bar

CORNELIA ST.

WEST 10TH ST.

CHRISTOPHER ST.

GROVE ST.

BARROW ST.

BEDFORD ST.

Moustache   Risotteria

St Luke's
Church

CARMINE ST.

DOWNING ST.

MORTON ST.

LEROY ST.

Do Hwa

Isla   'ino

CLARKSON ST.

MACDOUGAL ST.

WEST HOUSTON ST.

Film
Forum

KING STREET

WASHINGTON S.

GREENWICH S.

CHARLTON STREET

VANDAM STREET

SPRING STREET

Théo   DOMINICK ST.

TWELFTH AVENUE

Hudson River

N

0   200 yds

'ino

If 'ino didn't have its picture-window view of a quaint West Village street, it would still be one of the nicest restaurants in the area. If it were forced to discontinue its long list of not merely good but also interesting Italian wines, diners would simply redirect their attentions to the origins, producers, and vintages of the sodas: limonata (lemon) and aranciata (orange). If this intriguing wine bar were not also an adorable, inexpensive, snug, neighborly cafe fit for morning crosswords, afternoon daydreaming, and midnight debates following a late screening at the nearby Film Forum, you could dream up still more excuses to claim the first open table. But change by a hair the thickness of the soppressata slices in the salami, Fontina cheese, and arugula panini and we're out of here!

Cost	$12–40

Address 21 Bedford St, between Downing St & 6th Ave
☎212/989-5769
Transportation 1,2 to Houston St; A,C,E,F,V to West 4th St
Open Mon–Fri 9am–2am, Sat & Sun 11am–2am
Accepts Cash only
Reservations Not accepted

Some New Yorkers bring back Tower of Pisa refrigerator magnets from their travels in Italy. Lupa (see p.97) co-owner Jason Denton and Jennifer Gripenberg returned with an inspiration: to open a wine bar serving the Italian bruschetta and panini they couldn't stop eating during their trip. You'll soon know how they felt. At $2 apiece, 'ino's bruschetta offer zero incentive for restraint. It's simpler to order them all than confront a Solomonic dilemma between, say, the braised fennel with tapenade or the roasted vegetables and goat cheese. The $8 panini are fundamentally pressed sandwiches, yet from this modest frame come forth the great riches of Italian salumeria and formaggiaio. Honoring the latter is a scrumptious, three-formaggio grilled cheese drizzled with white truffle oil. Cured meats appear one-to-a-sandwich, as in the classic prosciutto, mozzarella, and tomato.

Breakfast at 'ino revolves around an egg toast treat Americans know by a variety of names (knothole eggs, toads in the hole, eggs on a raft and so on). Here the egg-in-the-hole is blanketed with melted, truffle-oiled Fontina and thereby takes the name that strong men mumble in their dreams: truffled egg toast. For dessert, you could somehow survive without the Nutella panini ($5). But forego the bruschetta topped with mascarpone and berries ($5)? Impossible.

157

West Village

Antonio

Picture Mike Piazza stepping up to pinch-hit in a Prospect Park slow-pitch softball game. Imagine Martin Scorsese shooting the video for a wedding reception at the LaGuardia Airport Marriott. Such will define the magnitude of your astonishment upon meeting up with chef Michael Gilligan and his superbly chewy fresh rosemary pappardelle with oven-roasted chicken, escarole, and white beans at Antonio Ristorante. That isn't to suggest this West Village townhouse restaurant is bush-league or that Gilligan is a superstar. But the roomy and comfort-

| Cost | Lunch $18–25 |
| | Dinner $30–70 |

Address 40 West 13th St, between 6th & 7th Aves
☎212/645-4606
Transportation 1,2,3,9 to 14th St
Open Mon–Fri noon–11pm, Sat 4–11pm, Sun noon–10pm
Accepts All major credit cards
Reservations Suggested

ably appointed interior, with large front bar, high grid-paned windows, white-clothed tables, and slatted dark wood chairs, is styled more like a Buick than an Alfa Romeo. And since the sweet-tempered service and prices bear not a whiff of attitude or sophistication, you're just not prepared for Antonio's modernized Tuscan-American repertoire.

Modest or uncertain expectations only enhance the easy, rustic pleasure of the zuppa del giorno—perhaps potato, arugula, and bread ($6.50). By puréeing some but not all of the potatoes, the chef creates the illusion of the spuds melting into the garlicky, hot-pepper-oiled broth. The appetizer list also includes sautéed, tender-as-can-be calamari with garlic, white beans, tomatoes, basil, and balsamic ($9) and a knockout grilled pizza with sweet splotches of chopped tomato, basil, and Bel Paese and Pecorino cheeses ($9). Pastas are rich, engrossing, and a bit heavy, except when you expect them to be—the homemade potato gnocchi with Gorgonzola sauce ($14.95) are uncommonly light. The two surefire entrees are the exceptionally juicy and tender grilled veal T-bone with polenta and a rosemary garlic wine sauce ($22.95) and the scene-stealing braised lamb shank with ratatouille, Barolo wine sauce, and a sprinkling of chopped garlic, mint, and parsley ($20.95).

Overpriced desserts ($7–9) should be stripped of one ingredient each. The warm chocolate cake does not require vanilla ice cream, raspberry coulis, *and* crème anglaise. And an early version of the panna cotta, with cinnamon and fresh berries, was far preferable to the current one, which has caramelized apples, caramel sauce, *and* crème anglaise.

Corner Bistro

In the annals of preposterously named eateries, this ranks somewhere between the Jackson Diner, which is an Indian restaurant, and Seppi's, a French place. There's no problem with the appellation "Corner" for a dark old pub bounded by the picturesque intersection of two quiet streets. But "Bistro" is an odd thing to name a drinking establishment that serves only burgers, mild chili con carne, and fries. If its kitchen were a telephone booth, there wouldn't

Cost	$8–20
Address 331 West 4th St at Jane St	
☎212/242-9502	
Transportation 1,2,3,A,C,E to 14th St; L to 8th Ave	
Open Daily noon–3.30am	
Accepts Cash only	
Reservations Not accepted	

be room for long-distance calls. Ultimately, this is a classic West Village saloon. College students instinctively recognize the mahogany bar, stamped-tin ceiling, and frosty mugs of beer—both those etched in the stained-glass cabinet doors and the drinkable ones filled with Budweiser, Samuel Adams, and McSorley's—as a perfect literary backdrop for all those great American paragraphs yet to be written.

The pleasures of a Corner Bistro burger lead to a clear understanding of what's very right and very wrong in the New York hamburger universe. When you bite into this chubby archetype, dressed with tomato, lettuce, raw onion, and pickle on a lightly toasted sesame seed bun, the tasty pink juice squirts out of several gaps in the leaky patty and, under the best of circumstances, forms a puddle on the bottom of the small paper plate. Were it not for that plate's fluted sides, Corner Bistro would have a serious spillage situation not confronted by pretenders who make their so-called steakburgers with tightly pressed ground sirloin or some other prime, lean meat. Great burgers start with fatty, loosely packed meat. And a knowing grill man *never* presses out their juices with a spatula as they cook. The slender fries ($2), though good enough for frozen, are not in the same league.

The cozy back room is an ideal spot to cultivate your burger education in small study groups. The tiny tables in the dimly lit, brick-walled space could even be called romantic. Couples have been known to declare their love for one another (a good burger will do that to you) by scratching each other's names in the wooden banquettes.

Do Hwa

You can tell how mainstream Korean food has become by how little handholding is offered at Do Hwa. This house policy of nonintervention portends all that is very good and most of what isn't about this stylish spin-off of the East Village's wondrous Dok Suni's (see p.37). The traditional cooking speaks for itself, eloquently. But the servers' indifference can make you feel rushed, abandoned or, worse, unloved.

Cost	$25–65

Address 55 Carmine St,
between Bedford St & 7th Ave
South
☎212/414-1224
Transportation A,C,E,F,V to
West 4th St; 1,9 to Houston St
Open Sun & Mon 5–11pm, Fri
& Sat 5pm–midnight
Accepts All major credit cards
Reservations Suggested

Named after a flower, to suggest blossoming, Do Hwa—pronounced "DOE-ha"—extends the mother-and-daughter collaboration of Myung Ja and Jenny Kwak that works so well at Dok Suni. The home cooking is mom's; the downtown vibe, just as surely, is Jenny's. Architect Hassan Abouseda's dark, spare, and casual design relies on dramatic lighting, irregular geometry, and hard surfaces to create a New Age abstraction with a Korean imprint. It has just the right mix of comfort and mystery.

The menu is somewhat more adventurous than Dok Suni's. Four $25–27 per-person tasting dinners (one of them vegetarian) let groups of four or more sample a variety of the best appetizers and main courses. Financially and artistically, this is the way to go. Mandu, those fabulous crescent dumplings, come boiled or deep-fried. It's easier to appreciate the meat and kimchee (spicy, pungent, fermented vegetable) fillings when they're stuffed beneath the cleaner, softer, boiled casing. And boiling sets the dumplings apart from the golden pancakes often appearing alongside. Three barbecue dishes—kalbi (short rib), bulgogi (rib-eye), and deji bulgogi (thinly sliced pork)—constitute the main-course hooks that win over the skeptical and the squeamish. The ultra-tender meats, marinated in sesame oil, soy sauce, garlic, sugar, and kiwi juice, are luscious. The meat may be plucked off the grill or wrapped in a leaf of lettuce with various accessories and kimchee. The shellfish grill platter, with squid, sea scallops, lobster tail, and surprisingly tasty shrimp, is likewise superb. And the kimchee bokum bop, a stir-fry of kimchee, beef, and rice, quickly becomes an obsession. Unexceptional desserts range from a vaguely sweet chocolate cake ($8) to gingerbread with pumpkin ice cream ($8).

Florent

The view outside has changed drastically since Florent Morellet's arrival in 1985. Once the lone beacon for night owls on a desolate, difficult-to-find block in the Meatpacking District, this one-of-a-kind French diner is now surrounded by hip restaurants, bars, and boutiques. These days it's yellow taxis and stretch limos rather than transvestite hookers who troll the cobblestone streets for pick-ups. Some of the nocturnal pedestrians headed to Florent now approach with the aloof gait of reverse snobs who want nothing to do with the Johnny-come-latelies. But Florent the community leader and Florent the community eatery only get cooler with age. Cool as in hip. Cool as in tolerating anything but intolerance.

Cost	Lunch $16–50
	Dinner $20–60

Address 69 Gansevoort St, between Greenwich & Washington Sts
☎212/989-5779
Transportation 1,2,3,A,C,E to 14th St; L to 8th Ave
Open Mon–Thurs 9am–5am, Fri–Sun 24hr
Accepts Cash only
Reservations Suggested

When it comes to selecting what to eat, usually the choices are pretty clear: thin, golden, French pancakes in the after sunrise ($6.25). Nice basic salads ($3.95–7.95), English muffin burgers with great fries ($5.50–8), and roasted portobello baguette sandwiches ($8.75) during the midday. And in the evening, what else but steak frites ($13.50–19.50). But matters get more complicated during the wee small hours. The diners who are just beginning the day might not want to eat—and, hopefully will not want to drink—like the majority of people who are reaching the end of theirs. And of those who *are* looking for a pre-crash breakfast, there's not necessarily going to be any consensus about particular cravings.

Luckily there is a selection of stellar dishes on the decent, reasonably priced, and exceedingly diverse bistro menu, which is unconstrained by such notions as "brunch" and "supper." The moules frites ($10.50) are outstanding. And though it's hard to let go of the classic marinières version, the newfangled specials—sake, ginger, and black bean; spicy tomato and fennel—are often delightful. The rib-eye steak ($16.50), skirt steak ($13.50), and boudin noir (blood sausage) with apples and onions ($13.95) are dependable. How could they not be with those frites by their side? The creamy mashed potatoes ($3.50) are a worthy side for any dish. And several desserts—rice pudding, crème caramel, country apple tart—hit any spot you care to mention.

161

Good

(icon) This restaurant started as Campo, a Pan-American country kitchen bridging the cultural divide between north- and south-of-the-border cooking through its apparent affection for both. Unfortunately for chef/owner Steven Picker, his would-be diners didn't know what to make of the place. Plum-tired of explaining what Campo meant, Picker removed the farm tools from the brushed blue walls, repainted the place neutral beige, reversed the menu's mix from 60/40 Latin to 80/20 American, and—how's this for playing it safe?—changed the name to Good. "That," says Picker, "everyone understands." (If only it were true…) The doubly popular result is "New American" in its inventiveness, yet uncharacteristically down-to-earth for that classification. Another wonderful anomaly is Picker's affinity for brunch, the meal most of his peers loath.

Cost	Lunch $20–45 Dinner $25–60

Address 89 Greenwich Ave, between Bank & West 12th Sts
℡212/691-8080
Transportation 1,2,3 to 14th St
Open Mon 6–11pm, Tues–Thurs 11am–3pm & 6–11pm, Fri 11am–3pm & 6–11.30pm, Sat 11am–4pm & 6–11.30pm, Sun 10am–4pm & 6–10pm
Accepts All major credit cards
Reservations Suggested

Even dinner appetizers possess a brunch-like breadth. The grilled arepa (corncake) crested with a salad of julienned cucumbers, pickled red onion, and poblano pepper is gift-wrapped in the smoked salmon you didn't put on your morning bagel ($8). Tender grilled calamari are assembled with chile mint vinaigrette and the fruit salad (mango, melon, watercress) you passed over at lunch. Fried chicken tenders coated in crunchy peanut crumbs, the best of the not-really-brunch bunch, tacks on your midnight party snack to a toss of frisée and roasted corn vinaigrette ($7).

The moderately spicy baked green chile macaroni and cheese draped with melted mozzarella, Parmesan, and peppered Jack cheese and lightly dusted with tortilla crumbs and grated Parmesan ($13) is a must, even if you have to borrow from your next day's calorie rations. You'll enjoy too, but not without guilt, the juicy burger with slab Indiana bacon ($10) and the molasses-glazed tuna with a trio of carrot scallion griddlecakes drizzled with still more molasses, their sweetness barely cut by acidic balsamic vinegar and collard greens ($17). The dessert that Picker never let out of his sight—and neither should you—is a holdover from Campo: warm orange donuts with Mexican hot chocolate for dunking ($6). Delicious.

Home

It's one thing to name your restaurant Home, as David Page and Barbara Shinn did in the spring of 1993, and quite another to have your diners calling it home, as many grateful New Yorkers have been doing ever since. By decorating their unlikely venue for American comfort food with bead-board wainscoting, assorted antique wall sconces, quaint old photos, and a distressed, pine-planked floor, Page and Shinn turned a cold-water flat into something suggesting the Victorian interior of a New England walk-in closet. The full extent of their success is perhaps illustrated by recurring requests for the precise paint colors used for the walls, molded rails, wood banquettes, and tin ceiling. (Warning: their creamy colors of preference, Benjamin Moore Nos. 380 and 382, get their chartreuse cast from the yellowish lighting as opposed to any dye in the paint.) Home is, apparently, exactly what they want their own house to resemble and be.

Cost	Lunch $18–45 Dinner $28–55

Address 20 Cornelia St, between West 4th & Bleecker Sts
☏212/243-9579
Transportation A,C,E,F,V to West 4th St; 1,2 to Christopher St
Open Mon–Fri 9am–4pm & 5–11pm, Sat 10.30am– 4.30pm & 5.30–11pm, Sun 10.30am–4.30pm & 5.30–10pm
Accepts AmEx
Reservations Suggested

AMERICAN

You might expect Home cooking to be real home cooking. But the delicious irony is that most of us would only think of eating cornmeal-crusted oysters with roasted red pepper tartar sauce and a fennel, green apple, and red onion slaw ($10) or blue cheese, cream cheese, and buttermilk fondue with caramelized shallots and rosemary toasts for dunking ($8) in a restaurant. In this restaurant. The memories of those wondrous oysters and runny fondue can only be tied to a professional kitchen.

Similarly, most of us can only dream of a childhood that featured a succulent pork rib chop spiced with a house mix of cumin, coriander, and mustard and sided with mashed butternut squash and parsley salad ($16). The juicy roast chicken with braised greens, awesome onion rings, and now famous homemade ketchup ($16) is an exclusive. And who among us grew up with lemony tangerine sauce to spoon over grilled whole brook trout ($17)? Only the down-to-earth desserts—dark chocolate pudding ($6), griddle-toasted pound cake ($6), chocolate pecan pie ($6)—finally convince you that Page and Shinn's wonderful approach to American cooking is truly homespun as opposed to Home spin.

163

Inside

(🍴) It's tempting to explain away prominent chef Anne Rosenzweig's West Village retreat as an economy blend of her two prior East Side restaurants, the Lobster Club and Arcadia. But its dash of comfort from the former and drizzle of inventiveness from the latter notwithstanding, Inside is too quirky to be summed up in a soundbite. Likewise, the narrow room, with African masks and photos of trees hung on the white walls, and ceiling fans suspended from the bleached-tin ceiling, is impossible to peg. The only certainly is the recommendation that you dine at smart-casual Inside, which will appeal especially to the over-30 and under-20 crowd—referring first to the diners' ages and then to their dollar budget for entrees. The value is astonishing.

Cost	$30–60

Address 9 Jones St, between West 4th & Bleecker Sts
☎212/229-9999
Transportation 1,2 to Christopher St; A,C,E,F,V to West 4th St
Open Mon–Thurs 6–11pm, Fri & Sat 5.30–11pm, Sun noon–3pm & 5.30–9pm
Accepts All major credit cards
Reservations Suggested

The tight menu is a moving target of transient dishes that don't necessarily belong together. You can't even be sure who's supervising the kitchen at any given moment. Charleen Badman, formerly sous-chef at the Lobster Club, is officially the chef. But Rosenzweig's fingerprints are all over the tongs and saucepan handles. The duo has assuaged some of the confusion by upgrading the temporary visa of the insider's favorite appetizer, the delicately crisp salt-and-pepper shrimp ($9), to the status of permanent resident. You are also likely to stumble upon the he-man salad, a rugged toss of bacon, blue cheese, and romaine ($8).

Understated main courses are about showing off flavors and not technique. The short ribs with fried horseradish ($18) suggest a flanken (the Eastern-European Jewish boiled beef dish) with Mediterranean leanings (tomato and green olives). In a similar vein, braised lamb stew acquires Israeli couscous, cinnamon, and garlic ($18). But the slow-cooking similitude is broken by the sautéed sea bass with shiitakes ($18), which is prepared in a flash but presented without it. The garlic fries must sit in at table whether or not they fit with your entree. Finally, if you do stop in for dinner, please insist that the banana split with peanut brittle and malted milk ice cream ($6) and the visiting gingerbread-crumb-topped fruit clafoutis ($6) be issued green cards.

Isla

The azure tiles, white-leather banquettes, potted palms, and bluish opal tabletops transport diners either to a poolside cabana in 1950s Havana or to an airport lounge on a Miami-to-Rio layover. Either way, Isla is some groovy place. If the playful curves of the plastic-mesh deck chairs and suspended orange globe lights don't get to you, the "cocteleria"—a selection of nine exotic cocktails—most certainly will. And as for the amazing creations introduced by pastry chef Tricia Williams—these will have you considering the uncertain merits of a nice weight-loss program: the DOD, or dessert-only diet. The best way to order might be to go heavy on the ends (appetizers, ceviches, desserts) and light on the in-betweens (entrees, side courses).

Cost	$40–80

Address 39 Downing St, between Bedford & Varick Sts

☎212/352-2822

Transportation 1,9 to Houston St

Open Tues–Thurs 6pm–midnight, Fri 6pm–1am, Sat 11am–4pm & 6pm–1am, Sun 11am–4pm

Accepts All major credit cards

Reservations Required

Dishes, like body movements, are calibrated to Isla's compressed confines. There's plainly no room to budge, much less mambo. While most of the appetizers are cleverly put together, portions can be skimpy and, in the case of cornmeal smoked chicken and chorizo croquetas ($14), uncharacteristically bland. Steamed mussels packed with fresh garlic chips in a smoked tomato broth are a marked improvement ($15). But *the* starter to behold is "La Isla" ($32), a two-person rotated assortment of lime-marinated seafood ceviches each served on a long Lucite tray in glass cups over ice. The presentation is spectacular and a couple of the featured ceviches (scallops in coconut milk; pristine tuna sashimi with accents of ginger, chile, and soy) truly terrific. You might also be offered them prepared with lobster, calamari, or red snapper.

Despite caveats, when main courses like tamarind glazed duck breast ($25), or wine-marinated filet mignon with roasted fingerling potatoes and avocado salad ($28) are on the mark, they're truly superb. But when cooking gets either sloppy or, by the time it reaches your table, cold, then you're ready to reexamine the DOD. First course: an intensely rich cafe-con-leche flan remarkably true to its flavor ($9). Second course: a fudgy, high-octane dark chocolate cake served with guava sauce and thick vanilla cream ($12). Dessert: a butterscotch custard and ginger sponge cake with meringue kisses ($10).

West Village

Jarnac

The distance between the far west of Manhattan and the far west of central France is greatly reduced by this tranquil and informally romantic bistro. Jarnac probably has less affinity with the hip Meatpacking District to its immediate north than with its namesake city in the Cognac-producing region of Poitou-Charentes some 3500 miles away. The engaging owner Tony Powe grew up in late French President François Mitterand's birthplace and brings to his restaurant a small-town sensibility and an easy rapport between staff and customer. This intimacy might take some time to get used to—perhaps as long as five minutes. It's atypical even for a quiet corner of West Village, whose charms are seen and felt through white-paned country windows.

Cost	$37–80

Address 328 West 12th St at Greenwich St
☎212/924-3413
Transportation 1,2,3,A,C,E to 14th St
Open Tues–Thurs 6–10pm, Fri & Sat 6–11pm, Sun 6–9.30pm
Accepts All major credit cards
Reservations Suggested

The monthly changing tastes of chef Maryann Terillo run more towards Southwest France and the Mediterranean than France's mid-Atlantic coast. The sophistication of her winter menus is bold. Multiple layers of flavor are applied to hearty plates, and understatement is limited to the appetizers. Even there, the restraint is restrained. Grilled jumbo shrimp are teamed with an avocado, Maine Peekytoe crab, and grapefruit salad ($10.50). The butteriness of crisp-edged, sautéed sweetbreads is cut with lemon and spicy greens ($10). Black truffle garlic flan ($9.50)—wow!—combines two forceful obsessions in the smoothest and gentlest of packages.

Of the entrees, the bubbling, garlicky casserole of cassoulet ($22) could nourish a bear on the eve of hibernation. It's crammed with great northern white beans and tomatoes fat-fed with the drippings of pork, duck confit, and sausage. The imposing, bone-in veal breast braised in pear cider ($19.75) promises to be lighter, until you contend with the roasted butternut squash and chestnuts. The fish entrees also endure substantial embellishment, be it Puy lentils and garlic sauce for oven-roasted cod ($23) or a sauce of braised wild mushrooms and leeks for porcini-crusted Chilean sea bass ($25). This is complex stuff, and occasionally you might wish that the bistro had some of the Jarnac area's taste for simple seafood. For desserts, veer away from the chocolate and towards the fruit—warm apple crisp with crème anglaise or high-impact blueberry tart (both $8.25).

Mary's Fish Camp

For diners, splitting a bowl of ultra-creamy, bacon-laced New England clam chowder is a difficult but do-able proposition. But for Mary Redding and Rebecca Charles, co-founders of the cherished Pearl Oyster Bar (see p.173), it was a nightmarish consequence of their decision to go their separate ways. In their settlement, Charles was allowed to keep Pearl. But Redding neither signed a non-compete clause nor handed over full menu custody. She instead created a snug eatery with picture windows, pressed-tin ceiling, tin-plated counter, and comparable versions of the same signature dishes less than six blocks away. Though egos may have been damaged in the process, neither party is hurting for business. Both play nightly to overflowing crowds.

SEAFOOD

| Cost | Lunch $22–60 |
| | Dinner $35–75 |

Address 64 Charles St at West 4th St

℡646/486-2185

Transportation 1,2 to Christopher St

Open Mon–Sat noon–3pm & 6–11pm

Accepts All major credit cards

Reservations Not accepted

When first laying eyes on Mary's Fish Camp, the perspective of past Pearl patrons is distorted. To them, the cramped, eight-table space looks roomy in comparison to the one-table Pearl. Conversely, the expanded menu seems shorter than ever. Their eyes invariably focus in on the lobster roll ($18), the life-enhancing sandwich of sweet, faintly peppery, mayonnaise-saturated lobster chunks spilling out of a toasted hot dog bun and sided with a stack of rusty-golden matchstick fries. Most adults have sufficient willpower to start first with an appetizer, maybe plump Canadian steamers ($10), fried oysters and clams with scallions and cilantro ($9), salt-crusted shrimp ($10), or the fascinating lobster knuckles ($9). Why fascinating? Whereas seafood restaurants of yore featured lobster tail because it was the least difficult and messy part to eat, these sweet-meated claw joints are just the opposite. Forget a bib. What you need are rubber gloves and goggles.

The dinner menu proposes a number of fine dishes, including grilled whole fish ($24). Nevertheless, that's a lot to spend at so casual and so tough-on-the-backside an eatery. That's one rationale, anyway, for returning to the lobster roll or, during lunch, digging a fork and dipping those croutons into that bowl of linguine with clams ($11). Although the blueberry almond tart and tapioca pudding are homey delights, you may well never see beyond the monster ice cream sundae (all $6).

167

Meet

🍴 The translucent onyx bar that slashes through the front section of Meet like the curved blade of a giant hockey stick immediately confronts diners with two obstacles. One is physical; the other, philosophical. Firstly, passage from the bar to the coconut-wooded, Feng Shui-arranged sanctuaries of leatherette banquettes and cane chairs is so constricted that you must pass through sideways, not forgetting to turn your head simply to avoid banging your nose. Secondly, the primacy of the sleek design and engineering, the metallic-mesh curtains and white-washed I-beams as well as the curvilinear bodies undulating beneath them, makes you wonder if this will be yet another Meatpacking district hotspot where food succumbs to fashion.

Cost	$35–80

Address 71–73 Gansevoort St at Washington St
☎212/242-0990
Transportation 1,2,3,A,C,E to 14th St; L to 8th Ave
Open Sun–Thurs 6–10.30pm, Fri & Sat 6–11.30pm
Accepts All major credit cards
Reservations Required

Such a result would be a shame in view of chef Ten Vong's worldly, urbane, witty, and expertly executed bistro menu. First up, grilled quail with an unfried falafel "stuffing" (literally the stuff that goes into falafel) and a wolf berry syrup ($12) proves Vong can cross a bridge from China to the Middle East more smoothly than his diners gain passage from the bar to the restrooms. Puffy sweet chestnut gnocchi ($12) with their sticky, gooey, buttery, truffled chanterelle reduction are outrageously good. This is not the first you will hear from faintly sweet designer dumplings at Meet. In an entree of beautifully seared duck with shredded confit and citrus jus ($24), the "secondary" attraction is basil gnocchi of untold buoyancy. Meat dishes range from spare—wood-grilled sirloin ($28)—to ornamental. Witness the walnut-crusted, pomegranate-glazed rack of lamb ($26). Red snapper capped with baby zucchini and carrots is coddled by the saffron and cardamom in its silky broth ($25). Not everything is that expensive. Fettuccine with braised veal cheeks will set you back just $16. And all the sandwiches and things served in the adjacent Meet Café annex are less than that.

Outstanding desserts ($7–8) play with deep-rooted associations. The clever chocolate ice cream sandwiches, for example, accompanied by hot chocolate for dunking, are Oreo-esque in structure. And as for the sticky-rice pudding fritters with a passionfruit dipping syrup—stupendous.

Miracle Grill

Thumbnail reviews often praise the original Miracle Grill (112 First Ave, East Village, ☎212/254-2353) as the restaurant that launched TV *Food Network* host Bobby Flay to stardom. Others put it on their short list of best cheap eats. Founder Lynn Loflin would rather be disassociated from her first chef and first—albeit more slowly ascending—prices. No wonder her West Village outpost tries so hard to offer good food and value. Its two dining rooms are sparsely decorated with sandy, stucco-like walls, with lamps that emit a romantic glow all but neutralized by the bar's deafening din. To avoid the noise, come for weekend brunch. It's a good one, with fine blue-corn pancakes and all sorts of eggy things with Southwestern home fries.

Cost	$25–65

Address 415 Bleecker St, between Bank & West 11th Sts ☎212/924-1900
Transportation 1,2 to Christopher St
Open Mon–Thurs 5.30–11.30pm, Fri 5.30pm–midnight, Sat 11am–3.30pm & 5.30pm–midnight, Sun 11am–3.30pm & 5.30–11pm
Accepts All major credit cards
Reservations For large groups

Dinners involve lots of edible and likeable (as opposed to architectural and esoteric) food crowded on a plate, with blurred distinctions between first and second courses. At Miracle you simply can't tell the appetizers from the mains without a menu. There's no white space on the appetizer plate of ancho-chile-seared rare tuna piled over mixed greens, red bliss potatoes, olives, and green beans ($8.95). Smooth, corn-sweetened red chile polenta with sautéed kale, goat cheese, and ranchero cream ($7.50) fits its dish as snugly as five New York Knicks in the back of a taxi. The top starter, however, consists of soft tacos folded over hot serpents of corn-crusted catfish, sesame slaw garnish, and a cool, spicy ribbon of smoked jalapeno mayo ($8.95).

Entrees are imaginative without getting silly. Even the color-crazy saffron risotto with grilled shrimp and swirls of Ranchero cream, cilantro cream, and chile oil ($14.95) leaves you dazzled yet not dazed. BBQ salmon, in a molasses and ancho-chile glaze ($18.95), should delight anyone intrigued by the idea, and grilled New York strip steak charred in chipotle butter ($19.95) is a terrific take on steak au poivre. Desserts ($5-6) score high on effort, low on result: ancho-chile powder is baked into a flourless chocolate cake to no real effect. The deep-fried Mexican pastry *bunuelos* are plunged into rather than topped or sided by ice cream.

Moustache

Only a dozen or so copper-topped tables fit into this cozy West Village hideaway. Two rugs on the walls provide a colorful backdrop for bright-faced diners and vibrant tabouleh. And the Tintin poster in the restroom never fails to amuse diners, albeit one at a time. All the same, your moustache-high regard for this place probably won't jump to your arched eyebrows until you start thinking of it as something more than a Middle Eastern pizzeria baking "pitzas." So-called, of course, because the thin-crust-ed, individually sized pies are made with rolled-out pita dough.

Cost	$10–30

Address 90 Bedford St, between Grove & Barrow Sts; plus other locations
☎212/229-2220
Transportation 1,2 to Christopher St
Open Daily noon–11pm
Accepts Cash only
Reservations Not accepted

That's not to say you should overlook those pitzas ($5.50–10) or their fresh, Italian-style and Middle Eastern toppings. Quite the contrary. The spicy, garlicky chicken pitza is an explosive combo flavored with red pepper, scallions, parsley, and olive oil, while the traditional lahambajin puts forward a tight coalition of lamb, onions, tomatoes, parsley, and dry spices. And vegetarians will adore the green pitza ($9.50), a light, addictive trio of leeks, scallions, and herbs that makes a great appetizer. That said, you really should acquaint yourself with the outstanding Middle Eastern vegetable salads and spreads, namely babaganoush and hummus (both $4), each drizzled with a puddle of olive oil and served beside homemade pita bread freshly baked in the pizza oven. The pita is so good, so fluffy—so *different*—that some first-timers don't even recognize it for what it is.

It's the pita which sets apart the sandwiches. The substantial merguez sandwich ($7.50) contains a thick, spicy, ground lamb sausage (instead of the typically long and skinny affair) along with onion, ripe tomato, and superbly silky tahini sauce. The slices of lamb that stuff a meaty sandwich ($7.50) are a big improvement upon the souvlaki-style chunks that typically turn kebabs into tough-going affairs. And the falafel balls ($5.50), cleanly fried to a golden-brown crisp, are rarely dry. You can get them served as a platter for a couple of dollars more. Finally, if your check does not include a $3.50 charge for the saffron rice pudding, someone has made a big mistake.

Paradou

Dinner is pre-empted tonight and every night at Paradou, a wine bar whose idea of paradise, as its Provençal name suggests, is to put out breads and spreads for good friends, open a nice bottle of red or two, play a game of pétanque in the backyard, and forego the predictable arc of a three-course meal. Of course you're probably eating and paying nearly as much as you would at any modest bistro. But the mere act of filling up on favorite bread toppings recalls a guilty pleasure you probably haven't felt since some annoyingly observant aunt or uncle spotted a dab of grape jelly on your chin.

Cost	$20–60

Address 8 Little West 12th St, between Greenwich & Washington Sts
☏212/463-8345
Transportation A,C,E to 14th St; L to 8th Ave
Open Mon–Thurs 5–11pm, Fri & Sat noon–midnight, Sun noon–10pm
Accepts MasterCard, Visa
Reservations For large groups

In any case, when you're grouped around a bar or table pieced together out of wooden wine crates, the very idea of cutlery seems way too formal.

If you do spot some jam on a friend's chin at Paradou, it's probably the homemade fig confiture that joins sautéed foie gras atop bread slices. No PBJs here. At $15, it's the most decadent of the house tartines, as the French counterparts to Italian bruschetta are known. Other varieties include duck rillettes (chopped meat pressed into a fatty paste; $9), ricotta and asparagus ($6), and herbed goat cheese with lemon zest ($6). Taking a cue from the city's flourishing panini bars, Paradou also merges its toppings into pressed and grilled sandwiches. The duck rillettes reappear with capers, roasted tomatoes, and shallots, their fatty juices let loose by the heat of the sandwich press. A bold combo of andouille sausage, mushroom, and roasted garlic is bonded by the buttery, nutty flavor of melted Manchego ($11). Dessert crêpes could almost be mistaken for baked strudel. The one with roasted pear, Roquefort, and lavender honey is a revelation.

Real bargains on the wine list are difficult to spot. Good mid-priced options include the Domaine Henry Cru St Georges (a Languedoc red made mostly with Grenache; $39), the crisp and balanced Pouilly Fumé from Domaine Caibordin ($38), and the fruity Roches Neuves Saumur Champigny ($42) from the noted producer Thierry Germain.

FRENCH

Pastis

The exhilaration of Keith McNally's retro haunts—Odeon (see p.144), Cafe Luxembourg (p.278), Balthazar (p.130) and more—is equal parts illusion and reality. The access to 1920s Paris is make-believe; the connection to late twentieth-century New York glamor, wondrously genuine. In 1999, the mix of period furniture and somewhat younger celebrities instantly established Pastis as yet another hopelessly hip epicenter of munching and mingling, this time with a difference. Though McNally's foray into the fashionable Meatpacking district has inherited the fabulous breads and diligent co-chefs, Riad Nasr and Lee Hanson, from Balthazar, the unfussy French cooking gives it more of a bistro soul. Pastis takes its name from the anise-flavored aperitif of Marseille. Bottles of the Ricard brand line the illuminated backbar as well as walls of the kitchen entranceway. A custom-made "zinc" bar curls into the middle of the 70-seat front barroom over a starburst mosaic floor and under a tin ceiling. Up to 100 diners are crowded into the rear space's perimeter of banquettes or around a long communal table that turns strangers into either warmhearted friends or sharp-elbowed enemies.

Cost	Lunch $20–65 Dinner $25–75

Address 9 Little West 12th St at 9th Ave

☎212/929-4844

Transportation A,C,E to 14th St; L to 8th Ave

Open Mon–Thurs 9am–2am, Fri 9am–2.30am, Sat noon–2.30am, Sun noon–2am

Accepts All major credit cards

Reservations Required

The kitchen turns out a host of satisfying appetizers: deeply flavored French onion soup ($8), fatty rillettes (potted meat paste; $7) to spread over the Balthazar bread, puffy pissaladière (the Niçoise pizzette) topped with caramelized onions, black olives, and anchovies ($9).

The fatty, gelatinous, garlic-cured pork-belly meat that make the robust mini-casserole of glazed pork and lentils ($18) so succulently satisfying for some is for others a surefire turn-off. Less contentious is the sandwich of pork confit and apple-quince chutney, stuffed into a ciabatta roll ($13) which absorbs the shredded meat's luscious juices. The best steak: the thick "Butcher's Tender" with a classic shallot sauce ($19). The burger ($11), too, is solid. And Nasr and Hanson's fries ($6) are as remarkable as ever. Meaty skate well matched to its traditional accompaniment of capers and black butter sauce ($16) is another cholesterol chartbuster. Desserts ($7) are unexceptional, with chocolate mousse and crêpes Suzette beating the others hands down.

Pearl Oyster Bar

With just eleven seats at the marble counter, eight stools against the wall, and room at a single table by the front window for up to seven Lara Flynn Boyles, this New England-style oyster bar is woefully undersized. Protracted waits for those 26 choice chairs could have you thinking that chef-owner Rebecca Charles might want to sell them as co-ops or, at the very least, time shares. But she won't even commit them to reservations. As a result, folks must endure lone waits for precisely the kind of impulse seafoods—oysters on the half-shell, salt-crusted shrimp, lobster rolls—that demand instant

Cost	$25–65

Address 18 Cornelia St, between West 4th & Bleecker Sts

☎212/691-8511

Transportation A,C,E,F,V to West 4th St; 1,2 to Christopher St

Open Mon–Fri noon–2.30pm & 6–11pm, Sat 6–11pm

Accepts All major credit cards

Reservations Not accepted

gratification. The alternatives are to come in for lunch, for an early dinner (about 6.15pm), for a late supper (about 10.30pm) or anytime to hand Charles a fully paid lease for a ready-to-go 300-seat restaurant.

Opened in 1997, Pearl grew out of Charles' childhood memories of summers on the Maine coast, her reverence for San Francisco's Swan Oyster Depot, and apparently also her fondness for grayish metallic colors. Everything, from the ceiling and antique oil lamps, to the pepper mill and Champagne bottle wrappers—and, of course, the fish skins—bears a silvery tone. These contrast with the meals and their golden beginnings (fried oysters, jumbo lump crabcakes), middles (seared scallops, crisp matchstick fries, buttered and toasted hot-dog buns top-loaded with lobster salad), and finales (blueberry crumble, butterscotch praline parfait).

The mayo-creamed, faintly lemony, overstuffed lobster roll ($17) is an essential NYC sandwich. For many, not ordering it is simply not possible. The gentlest departure might be the fried oyster roll that runs frequently as a special ($15). The sensation of those big, crunchy, mushy oysters meshing with the oozy tartar sauce is spellbinding. The advantage of the outstanding Caesar salad ($6) and New England clam chowder with smoked bacon ($5) is that these appetizers don't preclude your having a lobster roll afterward. But opting for grilled whole sea bass ($25) or pan-roasted cod ($17) requires, and ultimately rewards, self-sacrifice. Besides, it's not like anyone is suggesting you forego the Callebaut chocolate mousse ($5).

West Village

Risotteria

It's not surprising that New York has an eatery devoted to the preparation of risotto. The wonder is that it took well over 350 years for it to arrive. As it happens, New Yorkers might still be living in the purgatory of a risotteria-less metropolis had Joseph Pace not signed a lease for a compact corner of Bleecker and Morton. The narrow confines ruled out the idea of specializing in anything as long as fettuccine or bucatini. Even penne was out of the question. This cute space was meant for cooking rice, prefer-

Cost	$13–45

Address 270 Bleecker St at Morton St
☎212/924-6664
Transportation 1,2 to Christopher St; A,C,E,F,V to West 4th St
Open Daily noon–11pm
Accepts All major credit cards
Reservations Not accepted

ably short grain so that sufficient room remains for the tapered kitchen, a single row of tables, and the long counter between them. A full half of the limited seating is a long cushioned sill against the picture windows. The lack of back support isn't all bad. It speeds up table turnover.

There are 45 risottos on offer, divided by rice type: Vialone Nano is shorter and thicker than Arborio and holds twice its weight in liquid. Pace recommends it for seafood and vegetables. Carnaroli, the caviar of rice, is the highest grade of superfino (short, plump, and stubby grain) and yields an ultra-creamy risotto. It's paired here with meats and hearty flavors, with a particularly successful merger of roasted pork shoulder with roasted garlic. Baldo is a versatile, quick-cooking variety of superfino presented with vegetables and cheeses. The fabulous porcini, truffle oil, and sweetcorn risotto ($10.50) brandishes the creamy consistency the Italians call all'onda, or "with waves," yet each individual Baldo grain retains its chewiness. A great Vialone nana pick blends zucchini, oven-dried tomato, parsley, and melted Fontina ($9.50). (The intense oven-dried tomato is reason enough to order any variety.)

Terrific salads grouped by greens—romaine, arugula, spinach, mixed baby lettuce—borrow judiciously from the risotto pantry. Again, the oven-roasted tomato is particularly good, perhaps combined with arugula, shaved Parmesan, and lemon vinaigrette ($5.25 for an ample small; $11.50 for a large). Tiramisu, the lone dessert, is dandy. Still, Mr Pace should realize that New Yorkers are tired of living in a city without Carnaroli rice pudding.

Sapore

The man who does the food buying at Sapore has a difficult job. He needs to keep an eye on the Weather Channel. If the forecast is for a clear and mild evening, he must plan on the sidewalk cafe staying open and thus buy sufficient provisions for seatings of 32 people. But if an unexpected shower rains down on dinner, the total number of diners may be as much as halved and several pounds of perishables could go to waste. More troubling still, the rainout would require that diners be conveyed to one of the tiny green tables inside the restaurant without the benefit of being able to remove the plate-glass window. Finding room for ballet dancers and jockeys poses little challenge. But fitting in anyone over 110lb without injury to fibula or furniture requires the skill of a wispy whizz in space management.

| Cost | Lunch $8–20 |
| | Dinner $18–45 |

Address 55 Greenwich Ave at Perry St
☎212/229-0551
Transportation 1,2,3 to 14th St
Open Daily noon–11pm
Accepts Cash only
Reservations Not accepted

You put up with the cramped quarters either because you want to eat well and cheaply or because you desire to take a relationship to a new level. Salads contain nice assortments of fresh ingredients and are large enough to share. The tre colore variety adds grilled sesame chicken breast and a honey vinaigrette to the defining assortment of arugula, radicchio, and endive ($6.95). The insalata di tonno ($6.95) has lots of everything: tuna, black olives, onions, cukes, endive, even extra virgin oil. Fried calamari ($6.95) is extremely fresh—you actually taste the squid— and profitably entangled with fried zucchini. Grilled portobellos with sautéed spinach ($7.95) are first-rate.

With pasta it's best to stick to spaghetti and keep it simple. Spaghetti al pomodoro (with tomato and basil; $4.95) and spaghetti aglio olio e peperoncicno (garlic, olive oil, and hot pepper; $4.95) are far better options than anything more complicated. The same principle extends beyond pasta. The potato-wrapped veal ($11.95) is an absurdity. But the grilled chicken breast ($7.95) is basic and fulfilling. The veal scaloppine ($11.95), pounded to be extra thin, may prove to be the perfect dish for anyone who desires to get in and out of Sapore with ease.

INDIAN

Surya

(icon) When this mod Indian bistro first opened in 1998, its Ultrasuede banquettes flanked a battlefield where the menu's destiny was being passionately fought: Anand and Pandian, the Tamil-speaking *sauciers*, were refusing to talk to Jamaican chef Denzil Richards for his having the audacity to purée their rustic masala sauce. That clash illustrated both Surya's formidable challenge and greatest strength: to provide genuine, not-strictly-vegetarian South Indian cooking with contemporary flair. And although the absurdly tall, thin, and stunning people who first packed the narrow room mostly vanished soon after the successful ceasefire, the food, furniture, and

Cost	$30–70

Address 302 Bleecker St, between Grove St & 7th Ave South
☎212/807-7770
Transportation 1,2 to Christopher St
Open Mon–Thurs 5.30–11pm, Fri 5.30pm–midnight, Sat noon–3.30pm & 5.30pm–midnight, Sun noon–3pm & 5.30–11pm
Accepts All major credit cards
Reservations Suggested

the cinnamon-dusted Tajmapolitan (Absolut, Chambord, lime juice, cranberry) have remained intact. The orange walls and lime-green pillows reflect the mid-century-modern fashion that extends to the lovely garden furnished with shapely designer stacking chairs by Arne Jacobsen.

The logical starter is the vegetable pakora ($5). Served with red chutney and coconut dips, these mildly spicy fritters are made with coarsely ground lentil flour for an appealingly crisp and gritty exterior. They may be paired with fried kaikari rolls ($6) consisting of turmeric- and cumin-seasoned potatoes wrapped in wonton skins. The most style-conscious appetizer consists of two firm, sautéed, sweet-and-spicy jumbo shrimp stacked at the center of a large plate carrying tamarind sauce, a decorative drizzle of curry oil, and a red pepper-and-dill garnish ($9). The vegetable korma ($11), a trail mix of lentil sprouts, black channa (dried chickpeas), onions, and cilantro, is more filling.

The star main courses are the megaphone-shaped dosas ($19), their fillings served seperately in a bowl. Diners tear off clumps of the delectably crisp, made-to-order pancake, and wrap it around their fillings. That Chittenad-style masala also graces grouper ($20) and rack of lamb ($26), adding to the meat its rich texture and animated flavors, among them cinnamon, chile, curry leaf, onion, tomato, and coconut milk. Desserts ($7) are perfect for post-dental-surgery dining. Everything is a pudding.

Taka

Mitch, June, Reed, and David, though no doubt proud to be among the Taka regulars honored with personalized ceramic teacups, can't be too thrilled to also see their first names in this context. They would prefer you didn't learn of this sushi spot and thus compete with them for its 32 prized seats. For years they've counted on passers-by to be dissuaded by the modest room crammed with blond bentwood chairs and unsightly green tables, some of

Cost	$25–45

Address 61 Grove St, between
Bleecker St & 7th Ave South
☎212/242-3699
Transportation 1,2 to
Christopher St
Open Tues–Sun 5–11pm
Accepts All major credit cards
Reservations Suggested

which are chipped. Moreover, additional discouragement is provided by several unremarkable cooked dishes and specials, including bacon-wrapped oysters and Japanese-style egg rolls. But finding fault with the preparation and presentation of sushi takes levels of fabrication and imagination that are beyond anybody's capabilities—and especially those of the knowing folks waiting in line nearly every night.

"Taka" is Takaka Yoneyama, the serene sushi chef and accomplished sculptress in the white hat. It's a treat to watch her carve carrots and cucumbers or simply spread a dab of wasabe with her index finger across the length of a sushi roll. Even her plastic takeout containers have a personal style. Hers is not precise, symmetrical sushi in which man imitates machine. A methodical worker, she pauses only to choose the right serving vessel. Beautiful ceramic plates and accessories in a variety of glazes and free-form shapes are all hand-crafted and signed by Taka. Particularly lovely are the long slabs that curve up at one end like water skis.

Rolls of raw fish, in turn, are inspired by the land. The "Mt. Rocky Roll" ($12) is an inside-out mountain peak of spicy tuna, yellowtail, cucumber, and avocado with flying-fish caviar, sesame seeds, and toasted seaweed flakes clinging to its surface. Another offering, the "Volcano" ($11), an improvised tuna roll, is garnished with salmon roe and gold leaf. It contains both chopped and whole tuna, creating an echo of textures. The first melts in your mouth instantly; the second, after a few chews. Alternatively, you would do well to leave the choosing to Taka, requesting either a sushi deluxe ($21) or sashimi deluxe ($25).

West Village

Théo

🍴 There are lots of places to eat in New York, but only one that's in a former UPS warehouse. Not that dining in a one-time overnight package processing center is in itself a draw, but when Jonathan Moor, co-creator of such ultra-chic locales like APT and BondSt (see p.91), is involved, you pay attention. You'll find little evidence of the dusty old mail room at Théo. Instead, a sexy, modern bistro in two parts awaits: at street level, a warm, spare dining room with oversized tan banquettes big enough to sleep on; upstairs, a dark, sultry lounge filled with long-legged lovelies and strikingly sharp men in black. Everyone up here sips Théo martinis ($9)—Cuervo Gold, Stoli Vanilla, guava and lime juices, shaken not stirred—and snacks on chef Spencer Black's affordable lounge eats including crisp, thin-crust pizzas ($9–11), zesty devil's eggs ($5), and juicy mini-burgers ($11).

Cost	$30–80

Address 325 Spring St at Greenwich St
☎212/414-1344
Transportation C,E to Spring St; 1,9 to Houston St
Open Sun–Thurs 6pm–midnight, Fri & Sat 6pm–1am
Accepts All major credit cards
Reservations Required

Here's the inside scoop on dinner downstairs at Théo: save room for dessert. This is not to disparage chef Black's inventive global fare. Quite the opposite. But pastry chef Sonia El-Nawal's desserts are off the charts, so keep that in mind as you navigate the tempting savory menu. Good choices to start include minted eggplant spread with freshly grilled flatbread ($6.75), tender charred calamari skewers with sweet, slow-roasted tomatoes ($7.50), and tuna tartare ($9.75), perfect cubes of mango-flecked ruby red fish with a soy-ginger kick. For the main course, go for Black's gigantic veal osso buco. The meat falls effortlessly off the bone with the slightest nudge of a fork ($23).

Okay, now stop eating dinner and order twelve desserts. It's possible. El-Nawal introduces after-dinner tapas (all $4): little white china cups layered with thematic flavors and textures. Lemon Lightning combines lemon curd, shortbread, and meringue. Pistachio Jubilee layers chocolate mousse, dark chocolate cake, chocolate ganache, pistachio ice cream, and brandied cherries. Banana Banana teams banana custard and milk chocolate wafers with layers of walnut brittle and brûléed bananas. Make sure to dig your spoon deep enough into the cup to reach all the good stuff buried beneath the surface.

Titou

The utter familiarity of Titou—all warm woods, lovingly worn tables and chairs, and Serge Gainsbourg and Edith Piaf on the CD player—makes you realize how naturally New Yorkers have taken to the bistro format. No fanfare. No attitude. Just an attractive neighborhood hangout that lures you in off West Fourth Street like the gracious, slightly mischievous older cousin who liked to sneak you a paper cup of red wine and tell you stories back when you were a teenager.

Cost	$25–55

Address 259 West 4th St, between Charles & Perry Sts
℡212/691-9359
Transportation 1,2 to Christopher St
Open Tues–Sat 5.30–11pm, Sun 10.30am–3.30pm & 5–10.30pm
Accepts All major credit cards

FRENCH

Chef Ira Levine, also of nearby Tartine, Titou's tiny forebear, isn't reinventing the wheel with his on-the-money bistro fare that keeps West Villagers happily, quietly well-fed. Start off with a Roquefort, pear and walnut tart ($7.95) whose base of puff pastry has a nice balance of butter and crunch. The Roquefort, rich and piquant, is ever so slightly oozing, and the fruit and nuts both decidedly fresh. Otherwise, an appetizer of thinly sliced smoked trout ($8.25) is divine when paired with a silky horseradish crème fraîche, and there are a number of salads that hit their marks, notably the salade Basquaise ($7.95) whose sweet roasted red pepper strips and silky Bayonne ham barely need the balsamic vinaigrette.

Steak frites ($16.25), a NYC French bistro litmus test, is right on the money, although those who like their meat rare are advised to say so at least twice during the height of a busy dinner service. The crispy, salty fries will make even the calorie-conscious clean their plates; they're even better coated with the meat's rich, nicely herbed Bordelaise sauce. If you prefer something lighter, pissaladière ($10.25), a lovely tart layered with sweet onions, tomato, basil, and anchovies, makes an excellent entree. Other fine choices include the juicy, well-seasoned and browned roast chicken with a truffle-oiled potato purée ($13.95) and a thick pork chop with a sweet and tart apple compote, served with mashed potatoes heaving with sugar-sweet roasted garlic cloves ($13.95). Desserts are of the standard chocolate mousse and crème brûlée variety (both $6), each now more commonplace to West Villagers than their American counterparts, chocolate pudding and vanilla custard.

West Village

Wallsé

This bistro's arrival in summer 2000 heralded not so much the rise of a trend as the end of a fizzle. The expected boom in new Austrian cuisine following the success of David Bouley's Danube had proven to be just another Y2K no-show until a disciple of that superstar chef conceived this more moderately priced alternative. Kurt Gutenbrunner was born in Wallsee, a village along the Danube, and cooked nouvelle cuisine in Vienna and haute cuisine in Munich

Cost	$40–80

Address 344 West 11th St at Washington St
☎212/352-2300
Transportation 1,2 to Christopher St
Open Mon–Sat 6–11pm
Accepts All major credit cards
Reservations Suggested

before relocating to New York. He worked at Bouley, Bouley Bakery, and, in a conceptual role, Danube before his talents caught the eye of another employer: himself. At Wallsé (pronounced "vall-see"), Gutenbrunner's approach differs from that of his ex-boss. He did not, for instance, put his surname in the restaurant's title. Probably a shrewd decision. Furthermore, the decor is as spare as Danube's is lush. Set over dark-wooded floors against white-painted brick walls, the Thonet bentwood chairs furnish merely an elegant hint of classic Art Nouveau styling.

The minimalism suits the chef's modern, Franco-Americanized take on Austro-Hungarian cooking. By preparing his dishes with great care and restraint, he effectively challenges the widespread image of this cuisine being all about leaden soups, stews, and cream sauces. Seasonal appetizers are downright dainty, even when they don't sound it. Case in point, the nearly weightless herb spätzle with sautéed rabbit ($12). Chilled tomato, pepper, and crawfish soup is a lasting thrill ($8), while wild cherries bestow just the right balance of sour and sweet upon sautéed foie gras ($16).

The uncharacteristic lightness extends to such entrees as the pristinely golden wiener shnitzel ($24); the goulash with tender but not mushy veal chunks ($24), and the tafelspitz (boiled beef) matched to a fabulous apple-horseradish condiment ($26). The roastbraten ($25), however, is no lightweight: fried onions top the gorgeously grilled hunk of sirloin (not roast beef). And roast chicken ($22) is saucy and succulent. For dessert, the nifty, three-disk mixed berry strudel ($8), stacked like a New Age Napoleon is obviously not your grandmother's strudel, while the sabayon-capped ice coffee is a real Viennese indulgence.

Midtown

Garment District & Little Korea

Ben's Kosher Deli

The jazzy, Art Deco-styled, 250-seat Ben's was conceived in 1997 to be the Radio City Music Hall of Garment District delis. A gorgeous terrazzo floor leading to the counter, bar, and sprawling dining room bears a violin, a pickle, a coffee cup, and an uncorked bottle all rendered in sweeping curves. Three unfunny deli jokes are hand-stenciled in gold bands along the handsomely wooded walls. Owner Ronnie Dragoon, who also runs one Ben's in Bayside and seven on Long Island, has the know-how needed to serve 500 kosher (but not glatt) lunches in two hours on a typical workday. That's no small accomplishment. But, sadly, he lacks either the expertise, resources or will to make a truly great deli sandwich. His restaurant is best for midday hot meals—portions are enormous—or, given that Madison Square Garden is only five blocks away, pre-game eats.

Cost	$10–50

Address 209 East 38th St, between 7th & 8th Aves

☎212/398-2367

Transportation 1,2,3,7,N,Q,R,W to 42nd St-Times Square

Open Daily 11am–9pm

Accepts All major credit cards

Reservations For large groups

JEWISH DELI/KOSHER

Ben's does pickle its own corned beef, piling enough slices of fat-glistening meat on rye to justify its $8.25 price. But rather than cure its own pastrami (also $8.25), Dragoon uses the low-impact product made by Hebrew National, which, despite its pink color, sufficient fat, and good mouth feel, lacks the smoky, peppery kick that's the whole point of pastrami. It's preferable, however, to the thick-sliced, rubbery brisket of beef ($8.25) that not even a quart of gravy and a 20lb mallet could save. The golden, crinkle-cup fries are excellent ($2.95). And the platter of "specials" ($10.95), oversized franks split butterfly-style for even grilling, makes an elegant presentation.

When it comes to Jewish/Eastern European standards and dinner entrees, Ben's is careful about not taking sides. The only passion is for consistency. Nicely textured matzoh balls ($3.75 with chicken soup) strike the perfect balance between "sinkers" (heavy and compact) or "floaters" (light and fluffy). Good roast chicken ($12.95) and chicken in the pot ($14.95) are mildly seasoned. Pâté-like chopped chicken livers ($6.95 for an appetizer portion) are neither light nor heavy on the onions. Only the extra-crisp potato latkes ($2.50 apiece) and the sweet coleslaw have a bias. For dessert, the rugelach (cheese cookie crescents; $11.95/lb) rule!

Garment District & Little Korea

Cho Dang Gol

🍴 When coaxing a companion into joining you for dinner at Cho Dang Gol, you might want to exclude from your pitch the terms "tofu" and "bean curd" and their associations with veggie burgers and simulated dairy products. Better you pique his or her curiosity by whispering the simple question: "Do you do doo boo?" Doo boo, for the uninitiated, is the Korean term for those healthy unmentionables. And the homemade doo boo, as it is prepared and understood here, is

Cost	$9–45

Address 55 West 35th St,
between 5th & 6th Aves
☎212/695-8222
Transportation
B,D,F,Q,N,R,V,W to 34th St
Open Daily 11.30am–10.30pm
Accepts All major credit cards
Reservations Not accepted

not a stand-in for something else but rather a star ingredient to be appreciated for its softness and lightness and its unique ability to absorb whatever flavors it comes into contact with.

Just get your friend in through the door and let Cho Dan Gol do the rest. The dining room is a serene blend of country classic and city modern, with vertical cherrywood beams rising from the concrete floor and an abstract forest of trees outlined on the cement walls. Servers are gracious and, though their English is limited, generally ask the right questions. They rightly warn first-time non-Koreans that appetizers are too large to order as a first course, unless you're sharing. Besides, the gratis little dishes called panchan—sesame-sauced spinach, egg cakes, assorted kimchee, crunchy miniature fish (think 1:200 scale anchovies) with soy beans—do the appetite-stimulating trick. You nevertheless want to share one of the 12-inch pancakes (pa-jun), which neutralize any lingering illusions about sanctimonious eating with the pure joy of good grease. The boo-choo-pa-jun ($12) is particularly nice: a soft, golden cake striped with glistening green leeks.

The doo boo take the form of triangular, weightless wedges of goodness in such dishes as the mo-doo-boo-oh-jing-uh bok-um (best to ask for no. 4 from the pan-fried specialties list), a sizzling iron casserole of squid, mushrooms, scallions, and noodles ($15.95). The doo boo is cut into cubes for daen-jang-ji-gae (no. 4 in the main-course column), an earthenware crock holding green chiles, scallion, potato, ground beef, and a scintillating broth. All spooned over rice, the doo boo carries the flavors—and the day!

Kansuh

The no-wool, no-cotton dress code that normally applies to down-and-dirty Korean BBQ joints does not apply to Kansuh. Those who do not tuck their hair under a rubber bathing cap will not require a triple-rinse shampoo before returning to work. That's because the peppery, garlicky, charcoal-burning smoke and grease that typically permeates such places—stinking up the clothes and hair of hapless diners—doesn't occur at this comfortable, friendly, and versatile restaurant. So effective are the ventilation hoods over each second-floor, grill-embedded table that you could easily assume the barbecue is not actually available at the time of your arrival. But because Kansuh closes only for credible bomb threats, such an hour does not exist.

Cost	Lunch $10–60
	Dinner $22–60

Address 1250 Broadway at 32nd St

℡212/564-6845

Transportation
B,D,F,N,Q,R,V,W to 34th St

Open Daily 24hr

Accepts All major credit cards

Reservations Not accepted

Lacking the trappings and gimmicks of touristy, novelty Korean barbecue, Kansuh is the restaurant you go back to for barbecue *after* you've begun to explore the other riches of Korean cuisine. The BBQ service begins without fanfare: an invariably kind waitress delivers a pedestrian assortment of panchan—the complimentary little plates of mung bean sprouts, scallions, Daikin radishes, and kimchee (pungent, spicy, fermented cabbage and turnips)—that precludes the need for appetizers. Then the guy with the cinder box delivers hot charcoals, loading them on either side of the grill. The waitress returns with the barbecue fixings—lettuce leaves, raw garlic cloves, sliced chile pepper, soy sauce, the hot fermented chile paste gochu jang, and, of course, the items to be grilled. The two standards are exceptionally tender bulkoki (rib-eye; $18.95) and succulent kalbi (boneless short ribs; $18.95), both marinated in soy sauce, sugar, and sesame oil. Adventurous second-timers may wish to try instead the pork, the ox-tongue, the shrimp, or, best of all, the squid in a spicy marinade (all $18.95). Once cooked, grilled items are wrapped with their accessories in a lettuce leaf, picked up with hands, dipped in soy sauce, and gobbled.

Besides BBQ, the menu lists an array of Korean specialties plus an extensive selection of sushi. You might forego BBQ altogether and drop by for a stone-pot bop (rice casserole) or a noodle dish, both available as $6.95 lunch specials.

Garment District & Little Korea

Mandoo Bar

True, man cannot live on mandoo alone. But near the southwest corner of 32nd and Fifth, it's worth considering. This is no place for the recovering between-meals munchaholic to be meandering. For in the storefront of Mandoo Bar is a surefire come-on: a butcher's block atop which two cooks roll, shape, stuff, and seal several varieties of mandoo—Korean dumplings— and load them row-by-row into shallow, three-sided blond-wood trays. The window must surely be cleaned three times a day just to wipe off the noseprints left by transfixed passers-by. Once prepared, the mandoo are cooked to order in a medium-sized kettle for boiling or a wok-like casserole for pan-frying.

Cost	$8–25

Address 2 West 32nd St,
between 5th & 6th Aves
☎212/279-3075
Transportation
B,D,F,N,Q,R,V,W to 34th St
Open Daily 11am–11pm
Accepts All major credit cards
Reservations Not accepted

If the window display is meant to draw you in, the Buddhist austerity inside seems intended to hurry you out. The thin seat cushions do little to pad the backless wood benches. Only devoted monks, master yogi, and circus performers manage to stay longer than thirty minutes without fidgeting like a nine-year-old in a dentist's chair. The sleek design is, however, kind of nifty, with illuminated wall recesses and such wall messages as "Why bother?" and "Divorce Leaves a Permanent Void" to ponder.

The difference between appetizers and mains is basically six dumplings and a couple of dollars. It makes virtually no sense to order an appetizer, as you're paying more for each mandoo. Better you share entrees according to the size and appetite of your group. Each order is served with a pair of pickled radishes for picking and soy sauce, white vinegar, and Vietnamese red chile sauce for dipping. The most stunning of the mandoo varieties is the vegetable mool (10 pieces $6.49). The green casing of these boiled vegetable dumplings appears so delicate and wilted that the mandoo at first resembles a stuffed green cabbage leaf. The steamed kimchee mandoo (10 pieces $7.99), filled with tofu, pork, veggies, and kimchee, make a spicier alternative. The pan-fried goon mandoo ($6.99), packed with interwoven pork and vegetables, is crisp but not greasy. Rice and homemade noodle dishes ($7.99–10.99) are little more than menu fillers, and you'll be offered no desserts.

Mr. Broadway Kosher Deli

Mr. Broadway looks like an old-fashioned New York kosher deli with all the classic trappings. The meat counter stands opposite the cash register that guards the storefront's typically narrow entrance. Wade through the crowd of takeout customers calling orders to the countermen, and the room widens to a large dining room fitted with utilitarian chairs and Formica tabletops protected by paper placemats. Many of the customers are men wearing skullcaps and designer clothes. But it is not only the Garment District's kosher/fashion crowd

Cost	$8–45

Address 1372 Broadway at 38th St

☎212/921-2152

Transportation
1,2,3,7,N,Q,R,W to 42nd St–
Times Square

Open Sun–Thurs 9am–9pm,
Fri 9am–3pm

Accepts All major credit cards

Reservations Not accepted

filling up every lunchtime seat. Mr. Broadway may smell like an old-fashioned deli, the spice of pastrami and the vapors of the excellent matzoh ball soup ($3.75) in the air, but it has something for everyone. Tucked behind the cashier is a sushi bar. The menu has a list of Chinese and Israeli/Middle Eastern dishes.

Indeed, the last thing you want to eat here is the dreadful pastrami and corned beef. Nowadays, the main meat attraction is shawarma ($7.50 as a sandwich stuffed in pita or a crusty baguette; $11.75 as a platter with two sides). The rotating cone of ground and seasoned turkey and lamb cooks on a vertical spit by the front door, literally and symbolically upstaging the hot dog grill. True, the well-spiced, kosher hot dogs ($2.50) come in natural casings with real snap, a rarity these days. But the shawarma, sliced with a flourish, is an absolute show-stopper, succulent and savory. Order it and you get your choice from a small salad bar of Middle Eastern pickles and vegetables. Also from the Israeli/Middle Eastern section of the menu—of special note to vegetarians—is an excellent plate of mezze with a stack of hot pita ($7.75): earthy hummus, garlicky babaganoush, smooth tahini, and fiery red Turkish salad.

The chicken schnitzel ($14.75)—breaded and fried cutlets—are perfect; they go particularly well with very good Eastern European side dishes like onion-laden kasha varnishkas ($3.75), properly stodgy stuffed derma ($3.75), or one of the best potato knishes ($2.50) in the city. The Chinese kitchen turns out a credible General Tsao's Chicken ($14.95), too!

AMERICAN

Pub Room at Keens Chop House

Legendary actress Lillie Langtry broke the gender barrier at Keens, the historic (1885) chop house best known for its handsome, oak-walled private banquet rooms and the 64,000 Church Warden pipes that adorn their ceilings. A fair number of those pipes are attached to the first-floor Pub Room, the sole consideration both of this review and of hungry, thirsty, weary, informed souls headed to or from Madison Square Garden, Macy's, and the Empire State Building. This gorgeous room of dark-stained mahogany and pine, with its masculine, polished-brown banquettes, bench-like tables, geometric-tiled floor, and vintage photos of sports figures, also has the classic style of an old New York men's club. But as an affordable and practical alternative to the $35 steaks and mutton chops served upstairs during lunch and dinner hours, the Pub Room offers great sandwiches and pub food throughout the day.

Cost	$18–45

Address 72 West 36th St, between 5th & 6th Aves
☎212/947-3636
Transportation B,D,F,N,Q,R,W to 34th St
Open Mon–Fri 11.45am–10.30pm
Accepts All major credit cards
Reservations Not accepted

It is difficult to walk on 36th from Sixth to Fifth Avenues without at least popping in for crisp ringlets of floured dusted fried calamari ($8.50) scattered with tiny halos of scallion and served with two dips: cold tomato and extra-garlicky aioli. The Caesar salad with large, salted anchovies ($7.50) also merits a detour. And once inside, a rationale can always be found for having the remarkably juicy, moderately sized steakburger with equally good fries ($12). The steak sandwich ($18.50 with fries) is also a marvel. The grilled beef, served on a toasted and crusty baguette brushed with meat juice, is tender enough to cut into with your teeth but not too soft as to become mushy. There is only one way to spread the accompanying horseradish cream sauce over the steak sandwich, and that's quickly. The good BBQ lamb sandwich ($10.50), with thinly sliced, sauce-drenched meat posed over focaccia with red onion, is not in the same league.

Dessert desires gravitate towards two ice cream treats, the hot fudge sundae ($7) or the coffee cantata (coffee ice cream with raspberry syrup; $7.50). But should you opt instead for a classic like the warm, deep-dish, crumb-topped apple pandowdy ($7), you still get a scoop of first-rate vanilla.

Midtown East

Brasserie

Twentieth-century throwbacks who remember the Brasserie as the place they ate French toast at 4am beware: the Frenchified coffee shop long famous for 24/7 service now goes to bed at 1am. Likewise, the celebrated birthplace of rotisserie baseball no longer serves rotisserie chicken. But if there's no stepping back in time to be done at the remade Brasserie, its invitation to step down ultimately rejuvenates more effectively than a year of Botox treatments. You escape the foyer through an open hatch and then a long, glass stairway that cuts through the center of the subterranean spacecraft stationed below. The descent beneath cascading panels of Swiss pearwood constitutes one of Manhattan's most glamorous restaurant entrances.

Cost	$30–75

Address 100 East 53rd St, between Lexington & Park Aves
☎212/751-4840
Transportation E,V to Lexington Ave; 6 to 51st St
Open Mon–Fri 6.30am–3pm & 5.30pm–1am, Sat & Sun 11am–3pm & 5.30pm–1am
Accepts All major credit cards
Reservations Required

Designers Ricardo Scofidio and Elizabeth Diller have emphasized amusement over ostentation, creating a carefree counterpart to the Seagram Building's other restaurant-in-residence, the almighty Four Seasons. Glancing left, six booths are divided by avocado-green backs that slant from seat to ceiling. At right, gel-cushioned barstools shaped like tractor seats face a line of color monitors displaying video snapshots of patrons entering the restaurant. A frosted glass backbar appears to freeze its horizontally held bottles in time. In the expanse between, open-back Saarinen chairs hug the hips of diners in soft white vinyl.

The brasserie-style French cooking is, by comparison, a low-tech and timidly spiced collection of mostly classic dishes. Start with the escargot garlic puffs or the French onion soup (both $8.50), then get serious about the standout cold lobster salad with a cabbage-and-frisée chiffonade, a wasabe-detonated ginger mayo, delectably crisp sesame chips, and plenty of meaty lobster at its fresh and firm best ($23). The pot au feu assembled with deliciously tender boiled short ribs and the standard accessory kit ($24) is great on the merits, great on the execution, and the bacon cheeseburger ($15), a perfectly pink chopped steak topped with oven-dried tomato and caramelized onion, is one of the best on the planet. It's a swell lead-in to the warm chocolate beignets or the cookie bowl (both $7.50).

Midtown East

Grand Central Oyster Bar

As the supply of oysters from beds off Long Island dried up at the end of the nineteenth century, so too did the popularity of oyster bars lodged in cellars and vaults throughout New York City. But a dependence on oysters from the Chesapeake and other "foreign" waters hindered neither the 1913 opening nor the enduring landmark status of the Grand Central Oyster Bar & Restaurant. Though the words "The Oyster Bar" alone are sufficient, this 400-seat institution is forever linked with the great railroad depot in which it resides. The tiled vaults designed by Rafael Guastavino constitute one of Grand Central Terminal's—and Manhattan's—great architectural treasures.

Cost	$10–80

Address Lower level, Grand Central Terminal, 42nd St & Park Ave
☎212/490-6650
Transportation 4,5,6,7,S to 42nd St-Grand Central
Open Mon–Fri 11.30am–9.30pm, Sat noon–9.30pm
Accepts All major credit cards

The oyster stew and oyster pan roast (both $9.95) are celebrated classics of American cookery, and the daily selection of 30-plus oysters on the half-shell ($1.45–2.75 apiece) remains the best in town—as well as the most common motive for commuters "accidentally" missing the next train back to Connecticut. Yet the oyster platters are admittedly not the novelty they once were now that brasseries all over town feature multi-tiered shellfish extravaganzas. Likewise, the superbly fresh seafood now commonplace at better bistros, seafood restaurants, and local ethnic grills make the Oyster Bar's daily catches seem more expensive and less special than before. For $26.95 it's no longer enough to serve a halibut or swordfish steak. The efforts of a highly skilled chef have to show.

Still, there is no known substitute for grabbing a seat at the winding counter and having a bowl of rich, creamy New England clam chowder ($4.75) with biscuits and oyster crackers. From this noble position you can also choose among some splendid sandwiches, notably the grilled tuna with spicy salsa ($8.75) or grilled Asian tuna burger ($9.75), or partake of the famous oyster stew and oyster pan roast. Both dishes are briskly whisked as they bubble up in double boilers so that they're exceptionally creamy at the moment they're poured into a shallow soup dish. The rice pudding ($4.50) and Key lime pie ($5.75) are the dessert equivalents of steadfast old pals.

Heartbeat

Any lactose-intolerant environmentalist with a hefty expense account should hurry along to Heartbeat in a, well, single pulsation of their blood-pumping organ. The posh commissary of the glamorously retro-fitted Hotel W New York is largely organic, mostly non-dairy, and thoroughly original. But even those whose dietary requirements and income are on the average side will admire what chef Michel Nischan and David Rockwell have come up with. The latter's mid-century modern design is at once striking and warm. Coaster-topped columns

| Cost | Lunch $30–75 |
| | Dinner $35–80 |

Address 149 East 49th St, between Lexington & 3rd Aves
☏212/407-2900
Transportation 6 to 51st St
Open Mon–Fri 7am–11am, noon–2.30pm & 6–10pm, Sat 7am–noon & 6–10pm
Accepts All major credit cards
Reservations Required

encased in a geometric stained-glass mosaic are shaped like the observation towers Philip Johnson designed for the 1964 World's Fair. Eames-era plywood chairs and wheat-straw tabletops are surrounded by walls sheathed in limestone and period fabric.

The food too is carefully designed, although devoid of nostalgia. The haute-and-healthful menu starts off with a hearty organic vegetable consommé ($11)—the first of several instances in which Nischan shrewdly and artfully substitutes pointed spices and vegetable juices for fat. Likewise, the fig-and-mushroom hash matched to the first-rate whole roasted quail appetizer ($11) expels any sense of spa-styled deprivation. Alternatively, the sliced raw tuna paired with a three-radish salad and wasabi-yuzu dressing ($12) possesses zen-like clarity.

Of the main courses, Maine lobster with "corn milk succotash" ($28) is a glorification of a sweetcorn chowder—which is somewhat dispiriting given that it's the lobster you're ostensibly paying for. But you'll have no such disappointments with the steamed black bass propped over a deceptively deep bowl filled with a saffron artichoke broth ($23). When it comes to Heartbeat's upbeat finales, the menu makes a distinction between "desserts" and "indulgences". The former category includes such low-fat inventions as poached pineapple with green tea granité ($9), goat's milk gelati ($8), and excellent homemade sorbets ($8). The latter—molten chocolate orange cake ($10), white chocolate and coconut mousse with sesame-nut brittle ($10)—are sweet and, as it happens, unearned compensations for prior so-called deprivations.

Maloney & Porcelli

Whimsical presentation, eccentric Americana, and a name lifted from a downtown law firm make high-rent Maloney & Porcelli resemble an Elks Club for $400-per-hour litigators. Wooden geese fly in a line over the balcony's balustrade, safe from hunters armed only with subpoenas. Fine steaks tagged with potato lollipops as well as seafood, sides, and desserts of Flintstones dimensions are dressed in the fanciful food fashions of corporate chef/partner David Burke. Curious diners can view the show from a counter facing the open kitchen.

Cost	Lunch $38–90
	Dinner $45–95

Address 37 East 50th St, between Park & Madison Aves
℡212/750-2233
Transportation E,V to 5th Ave; 6 to 51st St
Open Daily 11.45am–11.15pm
Accepts All major credit cards
Reservations Suggested

Among successful starters, twin béchamel-creamed crabcakes with ratatouille ($14.50) and crisp lobster spring rolls ($14.75) do not quite elicit the excitement of the filet mignon carpaccio ($11.75), the salmon pastrami ($12.50), or the terrific flat-crusted pizzas ($12.75). The round white pie topped with Robiolo cheese, truffle oil, and mushroom is so sublime that diners returning from the restroom have been known to follow its scent to the wrong table. Then there's the rectangular red pie of diced tomato and three Italian cheeses, set atop a wooden slab from a wine crate bearing the name of a Grand Cru Bordeaux—an aristocratic platform, like the restaurant itself, for childlike amusement.

With several of the steaks there is—literally and figuratively—no beef. Swordfish marinates for two days before it meets its portobellos, caramelized onions, lemony sauce, and mushrooms in a fish London broil ($24) while mustard-crusted tuna steak ($27.50 lunch/$29.50 dinner) is sliced into four squares and set in an elegant Japanese context. For a poultry steak, roast boneless breast ($19.50/$22.50) is wrapped with dark meat and flavored with thyme and a knockout punch of garlic. Red-meat hankerings are handled by a thick, tasty sirloin ($33.75) which looks better in the company of whipped potatoes, stubby fries, or tempura onion rings. Narrowing down the selection of ten desserts ($8) to a single choice is no easy affair. We can get you down to three— chocolate burnout cake, warm apple tart, "drunken donuts" (a paper bag of warm powdered cake donuts with liquored fruit jam)—but you'll have to take it from there.

Marichu

With its location just west of the UN and its status as the city's foremost culinary ambassador from the Basque Country, Marichu could well have been envisaged by chef/co-owner Teresa Barrenechea and her husband Raynold von Samson as a diplomatic mission, or at least a restaurant on one. They instead fashioned a self-confident import which, precisely because it has nothing to prove, proves to be charming, genuine, and special. The candlelit walls are decorated with ceramics and color photos, including one of another New York-Basque connection, the Guggenheim Museum in Bilbao.

| Cost | Lunch $27–50 |
| | Dinner $35–75 |

Address 342 East 46th St, between 1st & 2nd Aves
☎212/370-1866
Transportation 4,5,6,7,S to 42nd St-Grand Central
Open Mon–Fri noon–2.30pm & 5.30–10pm, Fri noon–2.30pm & 5.30–11pm, Sat 5.30–11pm, Sun 5.30–9pm
Accepts All major credit cards
Reservations Suggested

BASQUE

The courtyard garden, with its terracotta tiling and zigzagging glass canopy, is appropriately spare. Thus nothing comes between your nose and the sizzling, snap-happy gambas (shrimp) al ajillo ($12), whose garlicky component could stop traffic on First Avenue. Other must-try appetizers include the lettuce-wrapped monkfish with béchamel and a sensuous black (squid ink) vinaigrette ($11) as well as the beautifully arranged leaves of endive cradling sharp Cabrales cheese, almonds, and yogurt sauce ($10). Two specials also merit your nose's undivided attention: ajo blanco, a cold soup of almonds, grapes, and olive oil infused with garlic ($8) and the white asparagus served over sweet, olive-oil-immersed piquillo peppers (pimentos)($14). Befitting the cuisine from Spain's "Region of the Peppers", the piquillos return for the next course, this time stuffed with salt cod and draped with an outstanding, slightly bitter roasted pepper sauce ($18). Among entrees it is second only to the delicate, slow-cooked chipirones (baby squid) en su tinta ($24), with a classic ink sauce centered by a ring of white rice. This is Basque cooking at its most basic and elegant.

The kitchen also excels at grilling for maximum impact, either with salty and succulent lamb ribs over scalloped potatoes ($22), tuna steak with a laurel of greens ($24), or filet mignon ($28). The selection of desserts ($7–8) is best represented by the leche frita, three deep-fried squares of eggless milk custard in a honey-like glaze, and tarta de arrese, a custard pie with nantillas (crème anglaise) and raspberry sauce.

Naples 45

(🍴) The traditional Neapolitan cooking so close to our moonstruck hearts gets stylishly reworked at this 260-seat, louder-than-a-locomotive lunch factory near Grand Central Terminal. The arcaded ceiling and back bar, with its cool white finish and abstractly floral lighting fixtures, suggest a modern take on the nearby Grand Central Oyster Bar (see p.194). Clubby wooden booths centered on the modish terrazzo hold suits sipping tall pink Napolis—cocktails of Champagne and blood orange purée.

Cost	$18–55

Address 200 Park Ave South
at 45th St
☎212/972-7001
Transportation 4,5,6,7,S to
Grand Central-42nd St
Open Mon–Fri
7.30am–10.30am &
11am–10pm
Accepts All major credit cards
Reservations For large groups

To bestow its dough with authenticity, Naples 45 uses a special wet brewer's yeast, a low-gluten durum wheat, and bottled water close in hardness to the H_2O of Napoli. The bakers are less exacting, pulling out pies from the wood-fired brick oven that are either underbaked as a whole or blackened on one end and raw beige on the other. When baked evenly, the pies are crisp, chewy, and sublime. A drizzle of extra virgin olive oil does wonders for the mozzarella-heavy Margherita, the quattro formaggi (Pecorino Romano, Parmigiano-Reggiano, provolone, mozzarella), and the funghi pie with mushrooms, tomatoes, and mozzarella. Small individual pizzas proportioned for a single meal or shared appetizer cost between $11.95 and $13.95. Beautiful and superior ovals measured by the half-meter (serving three to five) go for $26.50–29.

Appetizers, pastas, and entrees can be as unreliable here as the service. Still, a $13.95 combination plate of three salads makes a solid lunch, while at dinner there's an impressive antipasti for $15.95. And there are some chances worth taking: the polpettone de verdure miste side (moist, pleasantly coarse vegetable croquettes with a spicy kick; $5.50); the baked pastas ($14.75)—try arugula, spinach, potato, and Caprino layered with pasta sheets or béchamel-sauced artichoke lasagna—and, in the meat category, the lemon-roasted chicken audaciously detonated with garlic ($16.95). Desserts (around $5) such as the seductive fruit and almond tart with zabaglione gelato and a cannoli shell stuffed with orange-scented ricotta ensure an upbeat return to the office.

Pershing Square

Only a homesick pigeon could object to what transpired under the Pershing Square Viaduct extending south from Grand Central Terminal. Between massive granite walls, restaurateur Buzzy O'Keeffe (The River Club, The Water Club) installed a decorative framework of green steel beams and cork bricks which, in their herringbone pattern, take after the Guastavino tiles in the Grand Central Oyster Bar (see p.194). Cherrywood banquettes and mahogany-and-iron tables enhance the period feel. Meanwhile, a custom-made vestibule of steel, aluminum, and glass leads to a cafe/bakery section and the wooded "Buzz Bar,"

| Cost | Lunch $25–$70 |
| | Dinner $35–80 |

Address 90 East 42nd St at Park Ave
☎212/286-9600
Transportation 4,5,6,7,S to 42nd St-Grand Central
Open Mon–Fri 7–10am, 11.30am–3pm & 5–10.30pm, Sat & Sun 8am–11am, 11.30am–3pm & 5–10.30 pm
Accepts All major credit cards
Reservations For dinner only

AMERICAN

equipped with a brass foot rail so that commuters can get a leg up under Park Avenue. Still, the most distinct—and least appealing—architectural feat is one of acoustics. Put a dozen diners in the 220-seat dining room, close your eyes, and it will sound like a full house during Happy Hour.

Were Pershing Square a television series, it would be broadcast on HBO, not PBS. Chef Russell Rosenberg's twists and flourishes are aimed at instant gratification rather than long-range enlightenment. The pleasure principle is apparent in the rich French onion soup ($8). Its crusty melted cheese topping is garnished with fried red onions—a frivolous exploit that delights. All efforts to disparage the salmon tasting appetizer ($13) consisting of smoked salmon, gravlax, tartare, toasts, and homemade crème fraîche are doomed to failure.

Most main courses are solid: sweet-glazed sea bass set against a delicioius scallion-green potato purée ($26). Soft and succulently sweet braised short ribs ($26). A thick, buttery filet mignon au poivre with truffle risotto ($27). And let's thank Buzzy for the chicken pot pie that recalls the great one served at his defunct Cafe at Grand Central. It's offered as an alternative to the short ribs in the compelling $30 prix fixe. In this rendition, a croissant-wrapped duck leg protrudes through the center of the pastry. You're entitled to study the entire dessert card (about $7 apiece)—the cookie plate is fab—prior to selecting the bananas Foster and its coming together of bananas, sugary rum syrup, vanilla ice cream, and pure joy.

The Prime-Burger

The Prime-Burger is a relic to relish on the midtown lunchscape. The circa 1965 coffee shop started as an off-shoot of Hamburger Heaven, a pre-War chain of burger joints. When the HH fleet perished, new proprietors redesigned two of the flagship stores and reopened as The Prime-Burger. This, the last surviving locale, opposite St Patrick's Cathedral, recalls a more optimistic age when urban designers and architects endeavored to satisfy the needs of working people. As an alternative to sitting at the long counter, parties of one have the grander option of occupying one of the 24 box seats collectively known as "the track". Arranged in groupings of six, these large, blond-wood sectionals are divided by wide armrests equipped with highchair-like trays. What fun!

Cost	$5–25

Address 5 East 51st St, between Madison & 5th Aves
☎212/759-4729
Transportation E,V to 5th Ave
Open Mon–Fri 5am–7pm, Sat 6am–5pm
Accepts Cash only
Reservations Not accepted

As forward-thinking as this seating-system was, it's doubtful that the designers thought its appeal would not only last through but also reach a new peak in the twenty-first century. Yet the shop's 1960s modernism, with its groovy lamps and mineral-textured dropped ceiling, is in vogue. Whereas both first-time and longstanding customers used to beg owner Tony DiMiceli to renovate, now they plead with him not to. The mere changing of a spent lightbulb causes a stir. Among the throwbacks painstakingly maintained by DiMiceli and his sons Michael and John include gentlemanly waiters in white jackets and bow ties, a change maker rather than a cash register, and soft, juicy, fresh-tasting hamburgers ($3.65) machine-shaped on the premises with 4oz of—what else—prime meat. The steak fries are cooked to a well-done crisp; the home-made onion rings ($2.95), just scrumptious.

The preparation and presentation of the standard coffee shop fare—challah French toast ($2.35 as a breakfast special), say, or golden chicken-in-a-basket with fries ($9.95)—could fairly be described as reliable. George David has worked the broiler since 1954. At the time of head-waiter Arthur Ward's 1955 arrival, Russell Teal already had five years under his belt as prep man. And Ed Adams has baked his signature apple crumb and sweet potato pies (both $2.95) at this address for more than half a century.

Teodora

You don't open a restaurant on East 57th and name it after a Byzantine princess without creating expectations of something slick and glitzy. Accordingly, the homey setting and the plethora of knick-knacks that must have been snatched from some grandmother's attic can cause a little confusion. While New York Italians in the art, fashion, and wine trades are clearly in their element here, the Americans don't always get it. Italians may be the design kings of the world, but when it comes to dining they could care

Cost	$30–80

Address 141 East 57th St, between 3rd & Lexington Aves
☎212/826-7101
Transportation 4,5,6 to 59th St; N,R,W to Lexington Ave
Open Mon–Sat noon–11pm, Sun noon–10pm
Accepts All major credit cards
Reservations Suggested

less about decor if the food is excellent and genuine. No wonder everyone you pass at the bar seems to be conversing in fluent Italian. "That's not true," protests host Salvatore Nasello, insisting his countrymen make up just under a third of the diners. "Thirty percent is a lot of Italians for New York. But without Americans we can close tomorrow."

Whether or not the newyorkese representation ever gets as high as Nasello's wishful estimate doesn't really matter. Teodora will speak Italian with the glorious accent of the Emilia-Romagna region for as long as chef-owner Giancarlo Quadalti is preparing piadina romagnola ($12). The Ravenna native tops Romagna's semi-crisp, griddle-baked flatbread with Stracchino cheese, broccoli rabe, or salumi (prosciutto, coppa, and salami). The appetizer role of Parmigiano-Reggiano, his region's world-famous cheese, varies from supporting (a mini-lasagna of eggplant, zucchini, and tomato-basil; $9.50) to starring (sformato, a cheese soufflé with porcinis; $11.50).

Teodora's native pasta is tagliatelle alla Bolognese ($14.50), a definitive pairing of the region's preferred pasta shape and ragu. Also good is the ricotta-and-spinach filled fazzoletto (a homemade, raviolo-like triangle; $13.50) with a simple sauce of butter and sage. The remarkable fritto misto ($23) is a fried basket of waffled potatoes filled with zucchini, eggplant, calamari, and shrimp. Other fish entrees (from $19 for salt cod to $32 for whole fish), whether daily or on special, are dependably fresh. Highlights from the rotated dessert collection ($7) include a splendid millefoglie (like a Napoleon), a whipped-creamy tiramisu, heavenly profiteroles with vanilla or hazelnut ice cream, and a runny warm chocolate cake to remember.

MEXICAN

Zarela

🍴 The name Zarela is cut out of decoratively patterned sheets of tissue paper that hang in banners from one end of this benchmark East Sider to the other. These custom displays of *papel picado*, as that Mexican art of paper-cutting is known, bring fiesta colors and crafts to a very serious dining duplex masquerading as a frolicsome bar. But since 1987, the Margarita-ministered merriment has been no match for the combination jab-and-clinch of cooking star Zarela Martinez, a native of Sonora, Mexico. Behind every sharpened dart of fiery flavor she loads into her dishes is an underlying warmth. Something smooth or creamy coddles and comforts the area around the burn without diminishing the residual flavors.

Cost	Lunch $25–50
	Dinner $30–60

Address 953 2nd Ave, between 50th & 51st Sts
☎212/644-6740
Transportation E,V to Lexington Ave; 6 to 51st St
Open Mon–Thurs noon–3pm & 5–11pm, Fri noon–3pm & 5–11.30pm, Sat 5–11.30pm, Sun 5–10pm
Accepts All major credit cards
Reservations Suggested

Forget about the coarsely mashed guacamole ($8.95) serving as your exclusive source of gloppy bliss. The chilaquiles are a creamy, bubbling, molten mass of baked chicken shreds, tortilla strips, sour cream, and tomatilla sauce ($9). Try to spoon a small portion of that appetizer from its little casserole dish and the whole thing slowly oozes out. Same goes for the queso fundido (baked white Cheddar; $8.95) that disarms its pickled jalapenos and spicy chorizo ammunition. Savory spices do the same for Martinez' signature red snapper hash with minced garlic, chiles, scallions, and fresh cilantro ($9.95). A crisp tortilla chip never had a better friend.

The Martinez jab-and-clinch works to best effect in the chiles en nogado ($10.95), a renowned dish from the state of Puebla. A single large poblano chile is stuffed with shredded chicken, chopped dried fruit (apricots, prunes), and green olives in a creamy pool of roasted tomato sauce. The chile bites. The sauce soothes. Over and over again. The principle is similar in pollo borracho ($14.95), which is braised chicken in a spicy fruit sauce. But the only side effect of an alapeno sauce with the anis-like buzz of hoga santa is cool, citrusy serenity. Pastry chef Ed Bonuso's desserts lay it on thick. The Aztec Treasure ($7) is a warm pecan pie with Kahlua and dark chocolate inside and chocolate sauce and vanilla bean ice cream outside.

Midtown West

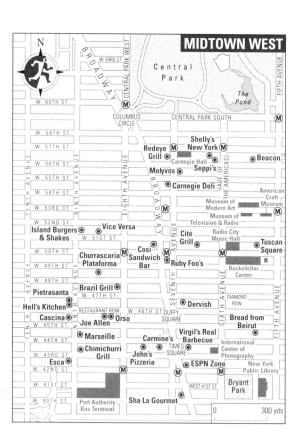

MIDTOWN WEST

N

W. 63RD ST

W. 60TH ST

W. 58TH ST

W. 57TH ST

W. 56TH ST

W. 55TH ST

W. 54TH ST

W. 53RD ST

W. 52ND ST

W. 51ST ST

W. 50TH ST

W. 49TH ST

W. 48TH ST

W. 47TH ST

W. 46TH ST

W. 45TH ST

W. 44TH ST

W. 43RD ST

W. 42ND ST

W. 41ST ST

W. 40TH ST

BROADWAY

CENTRAL PARK WEST

TENTH AVENUE

NINTH AVENUE

EIGHTH AVENUE

BROADWAY

SEVENTH AVENUE

SIXTH AVENUE (AVE. OF THE AMERICAS)

FIFTH AVENUE

Central
Park

The
Pond

COLUMBUS
CIRCLE

Central Park South

Shelly's
New York

Redeye
Grill

Carnegie Hall

Beacon

Molyvos

Seppi's

Carnegie Deli

American
Craft
Museum

Museum of
Modern Art

Museum of
Television & Radio

Island Burgers
& Shakes

Vice Versa

Cité
Grill

Radio City
Music Hall

Tuscan
Square

Churrascaria
Plataforma

Cosi
Sandwich
Bar

Ruby Foo's

Rockefeller
Center

Pietrasanta

Brazil Grill

DIAMOND
ROW

Hell's Kitchen

Dervish

Cascina

Restaurant Row

Orso

Joe Allen

DUFFY
SQUARE

Bread from
Beirut

Marseille

Virgil's Real
Barbecue

International
Center of
Photography

Chimichurri
Grill

Carmine's

TIMES
SQUARE

Esca

John's
Pizzeria

ESPN Zone

New York
Public Library

Port Authority
Bus Terminal

Sha La Gourmet

WEST 41ST ST

Bryant
Park

0   300 yds

Beacon

For chef Waldy Malouf, the rotisserie marks a turning point away from fussy fusion food. He relies on that spinning roaster, along with a wood-fired oven and grill, to draw out the essential character of the finest meats, seafood, and vegetables. These rustic ways, as common in Italy and Spain and as they are fashionable in California, have rarely been undertaken on such a large scale. With more than 35 foods cooked nightly on the open fire, Beacon's menu possesses the bounty of a Lucullan feast. Oddly, this prodigious output does not prevent the odd diner from asking if there are any specials. (How demanding New Yorkers can be.) You might choose to sit a few steps down from the main dining room, where an eight-table section faces the exposed terracotta kitchen. If a view of people is what you're after, try sitting on the perimeter mezzanine. The clubby room with circular pin-striped booths is also nice, though the condom-shaped hanging lamps do take the masculine thing too far.

Cost	$30–85

Address 25 W 56th St, between 5th & 6th Aves
℡212/332-0500
Transportation F,N,Q,R,W to 57th St; E,V to 5th Ave
Open Mon–Thurs noon–2pm & 5.30–10.30pm, Fri noon–11pm, Sat 5.30–11pm
Accepts All major credit cards
Reservations Required

NEW AMERICAN

Listing which of the dishes are perfectly cooked and which are a bit off is a pointless endeavor, as its usefulness presupposes consistency in the kitchen's inconsistency. But when Beacon beams it is truly a splendid thing. For starters, the roasted artichokes and asparagus ($10) practically explode with flavor. The wood-roasted oysters ($12) are divine, even if the shallots and buttery white wine sauce obscure some of the briny oyster taste.

Main-course standouts include a roasted lobster garnished with curlicues of fennel ($30), its sweet meat wading in a buttery stock enriched with fennel oil and extra virgin olive oil. Knockout venison chops ($30) glisten from red-wine jelly and profit from the grit and pungency of crushed peppercorns. And each serving of the rotisserie-roasted, mole-rubbed suckling pig ($28) contains all the essential parts: leg, loin, shank, and, most crucially, crackling skin. Sandwiches in the $18 range entail no compromise. The exceptional dessert lineup is led by the chocolate chocolate chip soufflé ($9) and the caramelized apple pancake ($8).

Brazil Grill

The bare-faced, full-bellied carnivores who regularly compete in rotisserie steakhouse marathons (see Churrascaria Plataforma; p.212) are apparently too young to remember the archetypal midtown Brazilian chowdowns of yore. Back in the twentieth century Brazilian gluttony was restricted to small, mid-block eateries where big appetites for garlic chicken, Linguica sausage, salt cod croquettes, and feijoada (the national black bean stew) were both whetted and washed down by multiple caipirinhas (the definitive cocktail of cachaca and lime). Brazil Grill is a likeable throwback to that simpler time, except that the theater district bistro rests on a corner and also rests on individual portions too small to feed the entire Brazilian national soccer team. The setting, with harlequin tiling and Dalí-esque canvases, is pleasant enough, providing you don't mind the invisible—not to be confused with unobtrusive—service.

| Cost | Lunch $25–50 |
| | Dinner $25–65 |

Address 787 8th Ave at 48th St
℡212/307-9449
Transportation C,E to 50th St
Open Daily noon–midnight
Accepts All major credit cards

The shock of not being able to start by attacking an all-you-can-eat buffet is allayed by the tried-and-true appetizers. The fried Linguica sausage ($6.95) either recalls or creates a lasting taste memory. A bite into the blokinhos de bacalhao (salt cod croquettes; $6.95) exposes fresh, steaming-hot but not greasy goodness, as do the variations filled with beef, chicken, or, better still, yuco. And the salada Copacabana with hearts of palm, tomatoes, roasted red peppers, and a lovely house vinaigrette ($6.95) is wonderfully constant.

Many of the grilled meats of the style carved tableside at the churrascarias are featured here as a la carte entrees priced between $10.95 for sausage to $21.95 for filet mignon. But chances are you would be there and not here if that's how you wanted to eat. Better to try one of the seafood specialties ($17.95–18.95), even if those coconut-milk sauces evoke the curries of Southeast Asia more than the casseroles of South America. One sure bet is the outstanding house feijoada ($15.95). The pork-enriched black bean stew is already broth-like, yet additional broth is served to spoon over the rice. Cheese desserts ($4) with condensed milk and guava paste are intensely sweet.

There's another Brazil Grill at 102 MacDougal St, Greenwich Village (℡212/777-7637).

Bread from Beirut

(icon) Breadwinners from the Diamond District, the midtown banking and publishing houses, Rockefeller Center office buildings, and Broadway theaters converge at this diminutive, corrugated-tin-topped Lebanese eatery/takeout for—what else?—winning breads. At lunchtime, the line stretches out the door. Those who rightly insist on having their breads fresh from the cylindrical, colorfully tiled brick oven have two alternatives: they can carry their trays back to the tiny L-shaped dining area bounded by whimsical murals and squeeze into one of eight tables, or they can get a job on this block so that the foil-wrapped breads are still warm when they get back to the office.

Cost	$7–20

Address 24 West 45th St, between 5th & 6th Aves
☎212/764-1588
Transportation B,D,F,V to 47th–50th Sts-Rockefeller Center
Open Mon–Sat 9am–8pm
Accepts All major credit cards
Reservations Not accepted

MIDDLE EASTERN

Of course not all takeout customers manage to wait that long. For a quick, filling, eat-as-you-walk lunch it's hard to beat the crisp-edged, golf-ball-sized felafel ($4.50) made with chickpeas and fava beans and packed with tahini sauce and pungent pickled turnips in home-baked flatbread that's a more like lavosh than a pocket-less pita. Equally tasty and portable is the juicy beef shawarma carved off the spit ($6.50). The beauty of both made-to-order wraps is that their contents are melted together under the weight and heat of a sandwich press. The bright, lemony, mostly parsley tabouleh salad ($5) you must eat sitting down. In an outstanding version of the lentil salad known here as moudardra ($5), the tender brown beans are interspersed with fragrant rice and topped with sweet, crisp, fried onions. The counterman will scoop from under the onions and thus leave them out of your serving, unless you instruct him—twice if necessary—to do otherwise.

Energetic young cooks are continuously sliding out such steaming hot, freshly baked breads as keshik ($4), a chewy yet buttery flatbread heartily stuffed with dried goat cheese, crushed wheat, and sesame seeds, and arayess ($6), a flaky, paper-thin dough folded over ground beef, onions, tomatoes, and pine nuts. The latter eats like a full meal. Perhaps the best freshly baked Bs-from-B are the flat, pizza-like rounds ($4) that are rubbed with Moroccan olive oil and topped with zaatar, a spice mixture containing sumac, thyme, and sesame seeds.

Carmine's

ITALIAN

No New York restaurant cuisine varies as widely in quality, cost, and refinement as Italian. At the high end are temples of truffles and Barolo; at the low end, pizza counters that offer garlic knots and massive tubs of soda to wash down your greasy, cheese-globby slice. Somewhere squashed into the vast middle lies Carmine's, an Italian-American fantasyland that is honest about what it is (unrefined, noisy, glutton-friendly) and isn't (to be taken too seriously). Mismatched chandeliers crowd the high ceilings, walls are jammed with black and white family photographs, and you'll even see a wonderfully passé display of old Chianti bottles in wicker baskets.

Cost	$25–65

Address 200 West 44th St, between Broadway & 8th Ave
☎212/221-3800
Transportation
1,2,3,7,N,Q,R,W to 42nd St–Times Square
Open Sun–Thurs 11.30am–11pm, Fri & Sat 11.30am–midnight
Accepts All major credit cards
Reservations For large groups

An oversized bread basket will hit your table before you open the menu. Choose carefully: some, like the squares of focaccia with thinly sliced onions or a layer of tangy tomato, basil, and Parmesan, are satisfying; others, like the sesame-seed roll, will merely fill you up. Wine, chosen from a succinct list, is poured into juice glasses. The Etna Rosso from Sicily ($23) makes an ideal complement to the heavily red-sauced menu. All dishes are meant for sharing, including the appetizers. The Caesar salad ($16), with crusty garlic croutons and optional anchovies straight from the can, serves six adults. Fresh clams on the half-shell ($12/dozen) are perfect for dipping into an uncommonly potent cocktail sauce.

Five types of dried pasta (spaghetti, linguine, angel hair, penne, and rigatoni) are available with a variety of sauces from simple marinara ($18) to vodka ($22). Stray if you must to a massive osso buco special ($35) or a juicy veal saltimbocca ($21) surrounded by buttery prosciutto and redolent of sage. But the real game is a plate of spaghetti with red sauce and a side of meatballs ($7) the size of tennis balls and the weight of cannonballs. At the risk of needing a stomach pump, close with the strawberry shortcake ($9)—a massive pyramid of whipped cream covered with syrupy strawberries atop dense, sugary shortbread—which is, like everything else at Carmine's, more than enough for everyone.

There's another Carmine's at 2450 Broadway, Upper West Side (☎212/362-2200).

Carnegie Delicatessen

Reports of this legendary deli's lowered standards are not so much exaggerated as they are tiresome. Although drops in the quality of the food and the consistency of the deli meat appeared to coincide with the passing in 1988 of the great deli king Leo Steiner, it is in all fairness difficult to identify specific things that Leo insisted upon that his successors do not. That the pastrami is no longer cured on the premises could be a factor. Regardless, the pastrami and

Cost	$12-60

Address 854 7th Ave at 55th St

☎212/757-2245

Transportation B,D,E to 7th Ave; N,Q,R,W to 57th St

Open Daily 6.30am–4am

Accepts Cash only

Reservations Not accepted

JEWISH DELI

corned beef are good—occasionally superb—if admittedly not, as they once were, the best in New York. And the excellent, golden, crisp-edged crinkle-cut French fries ($3.95), introduced some five years ago, are infinitely superior to the frozen steak fries served throughout King Leo's reign. Some things stay constant, however: the service staff is as grumpy and unsmiling as ever.

The main draw, and drawback, of the Carnegie, both then and now, is the enormity of the sandwiches. The combination sandwich ($18.95) named after the prior owner, "Leo's Delightin," is a fat, triple-decker, tourist-trapping tower of turkey, corned beef, tongue, coleslaw, and Russian dressing. You can be reasonably certain Leo never touched the darn thing. (Fearful of cholesterol overdose, his daily ration was a roast chicken whose crisp skin was a minefield of garlic.) The widely accepted belief that Jewish deli is largely about unspeakable excess is wrongheaded.

It's highly recommended that you pay the $3 sharing fee to split with your partner the corned beef sandwich ($11.45), the pastrami sandwich ($11.45), or the combination "Woody Allen" ($14.45). With six extra slices of rye bread, the Woody can easily be divided into four slender sandwiches. In that way, each of you can sample the corned beef, with its glistening beads of oily juices, as well as the peppery, appropriately fatty, and tender to the point of crumbly pastrami. For dessert, split an order of nut and raisin sourcream rugelach ($5.95), a wedge of splendid New York cheesecake ($6.45), or the shameless combination of the two, the rugelach-crowned cheesecake draped with creamy milk chocolate ($6.95).

Cascina

To speed the gentrification of Hell's Kitchen, the rough-and-tumble district portrayed in *West Side Story*, property owners adopted the less incendiary name of Clinton. The mixed success of their campaign is apparent inside rustic-chic Cascina, named after co-owner Mikele DeNegri's Cascina Ordolina winery in Piedmont. Italian for "farm estate," the name suits a countrified venue of brick and brushed walls lit by candles and antique brass chandeliers. The young and hip diners who refill the tables emptied by the pre-theater crowd are instantly embraced by the old-world warmth of the stone-domed, wood-burning brick oven. The ensuing charms confirm the wisdom of their moving to the neighborhood, but not their acceptance of its sanitized name. Everyone still calls it Hell's Kitchen.

Cost	$21–70

Address 647 9th Ave, between 45th & 46th Sts
☎212/245-4422
Transportation A,C,E to 42nd St
Open Mon–Sat noon–midnight
Accepts All major credit cards

The charisma exuded by the host seems slicker with each visit. When he persuades lovers to sit at the handsome but very public communal table up front, you suspect he's only trying to make the place look busier to curious passers-by. And when he elicits your response to a failed special like the tepid lasagna ($15), his subsequent expressions of astonishment and regret come across as patronizing. Happily, the opportunities for these are few. The gratis sundried tomato and olive oil dip has you eating well even before the fried calamari ($10) and wonderful grilled vegetables ($8) arrive. And the thin pizzas are splendid whether basic (cheesy Margherita; $12.50) or uncommon (sweet chicken sausage with roasted red, green, and yellow peppers; $16).

The best entrees come from that pizza oven, too. The oven-roasted, Chianti-sauced veal shank ($18.50) is doubly special because it comes with a creamy risotto perfumed with pure saffron threads. Oven-roasted double pork chop ($17), lamb shank ($17.50), forgivably dry chicken in apricot sauce ($16), and whole fish (market price) serve you well. Off the grill come two fabulous, reasonably priced, truffle-sauced steaks, the rib-eye ($19.50) and, as a special, filet mignon ($22). Anyone partial to upside-down desserts will adore the sundae dish of a bourbon-like sauce topped first with sweet banana and then hazelnut ice cream ($7).

Chimichurri Grill

Chef Jorge Rodriguez is forever eager to leave his confined workspace. He exits his kitchen more often than his homemade pastas and fat steaks to grab a discreet smoke at the tiny bar, greet first-timers, and share a laugh with old friends. When a host expresses such warmth for his guests it doesn't take much time or effort for them to reciprocate. The reassuring presence of Horacio Badaraco, the gracious waiter with the black vest, quickly transforms the exotic into the familiar. It's a throwback to a pre-1970s generation of small theater-district bistros that first introduced office workers, tourists, and daytrippers to foreign cuisines.

| Cost | Lunch $20–40 |
| | Dinner $30–60 |

Address 606 9th Ave, between 43rd & 44th Sts
℡212/586-8655
Transportation A,C,E to 42nd St
Open Tues–Thurs noon–3pm & 5–11.30pm, Fri noon–3pm & 5pm–midnight, Sat 4pm–midnight, Sun 3–10pm
Accepts All major credit cards
Reservations Suggested

ARGENTINIAN

The name comes from the thin green sauce of parsley, oregano, pepper, vinegar, olive oil, and especially garlic that forms the tango rhythm of Argentine cooking. The workhorse condiment may be administered to the plump chorizo appetizer ($7.50) and the incomparably flaky empanada ($3) filled with ground beef, minced olives, and raisins. Excellent appetizer alternatives include the chilled quail with a cold onion, carrot, and pepper relish ($9) and the flawlessly grilled baby calamari ($8.50). The polenta of the day ($7.50) might be a crisp-rimmed round of soft corncake with a wild mushroom ragu.

Most of the beef comes from grass-feeding Argentine cattle. Rodriguez informs anyone who'll listen that his steaks puff out on the grill and cook in half the time without shrinking back to size. In reality, you may wish his 16oz shell steak ($21) *did* reduce itself by a good third. Down the whole thing and a taxi could charge you for extra baggage on the ride home. One favorite steak is the grilled prime Argentine Angus ($21) after it's been slathered with chimichurri, while others may prefer the plump, tender filet mignon served with grilled mushrooms ($23). Herb-crusted rack of lamb ($24) is luscious to the bone. Among hoofless alternatives are assorted pastas and grilled chicken breast, duck, or Chilean sea bass. The uneven dessert selection ($6.50–7.50) does feature a wonderful lavender flan and a thin, caramelized apple tart that Rodriguez himself flambées at your table.

Midtown West

Churrascaria Plataforma

Anyone planning a celebration at the Theater District's Brazilian-style rotisserie steakhouse can count on several things. No one will feel rushed. No one will go underfed. And no one will leave before he or she has heard "Feliz Aniversario" sung at least six times. Those repetitions, performed by a bossa nova trio, are appropriate regardless of the occasion, since every diner is fed as if it's their birthday. The salad bar, buffet, and endless barbecued meats indulge celebrants of any age who can't seem to get too much of a bad-for-you thing. The arena for these fixed-price excesses ($27.95 for lunch, $38.95 for dinner) is a swank, lofty banquet hall graced with a slate-tiled floor, white leatherette chairs, and brick walls punctuated by mahogany capitals. A circular bandstand divides the bar area from the dining room.

Cost	Lunch $35–55
	Dinner $48–75

Address 316 West 49th St, between 8th & 9th Aves
☎212/245-0505
Transportation C,E to 50th St
Open Daily noon–midnight
Accepts All major credit cards
Reservations Required

Subtle lighting over the centerpiece salad bar casts a golden glow over the likes of beef carpaccio, sliced ham, octopus salad, stuffed artichokes, and, the most recent addition, sushi. Four silver domes contain such tempting hot dishes as a saffron-scented calamari paella. One salad-bar favorite is tutu de feijao, a delectable mush of red beans, bacon, and yuca flour.

When seated, diners are given a coaster with a red rim ("stop") on one side and a green rim ("go") on the other. By keeping the red side up, diners are telling the waiters who carry around pit-barbecued meats on spits not to carve anything for them. By flipping to green, they signal them to begin the stampede. The mouth-watering variety of rotated meats is as vast as the seasoning is limited. Nearly everything is salty, a bit garlicky, and, in the case of beef, tender and medium-rare. Fattier options—brisket, lamb, skirt steak, fork-tender short ribs, top round dripping with juices—are a cut above. Among other choices are pork sausage and ribs, chicken hearts and thighs, roast beef, flank steak, and turkey wrapped in bacon. Some view the array of side dishes, including decent fried potatoes and plantains, yuca flour, black beans, and addictive fried yuca tots, as mere fillers, threatening their meat-gorging capacity.

Cité Grill

Traveling second class has its advantages. Though this, the annex to Cité, may lack some of the breeding of that steakhouse, its informality and lower prices make it one of the better options for relaxed meals near Radio City Music Hall and various Rockefeller Center attractions. The handsome setting, with its Mediterranean tile and vine-engraved, L-shaped bar, doesn't make you feel in the least bit slighted, especially since wine lovers may order the $60 Grape Wine Dinner for which Cité is justly prized. Sign on for that complete dinner and they keep pouring any or all of four specially selected wines until you say stop, or a caring friend says it for you. Before 8pm, when the unlimited pour is uncorked, there are good wines to choose from in the $30–40 range. You can't go wrong matching the full-bodied 1999 St. Joseph Domaine du Chene to red meat for as long as that $39 bottle is available.

Cost	$20–80

Address 120 West 51st St, between 6th & 7th Aves
☏212/956-7262
Transportation B,D,F,V to 47th/50th Sts-Rockefeller Center; 1,2 to 50th St; N,R,W to 49th St
Open Mon–Fri noon–2.30 pm & 5–11.30pm, Sat & Sun 5–11.30pm
Accepts All major credit cards

The flexibility to choose just about whatever you want for the $44 prix fixe dinner rewards strategic decision-making. There's little reason to start with a sweetcorn chowder with bacon and leeks ($8 a la carte), or any other soup du jour, when you can have instead the pan-seared crabcake ($15 a la carte) or, better yet, the astonishing lobster cocktail Dijonaise ($16 a la carte)—no more or less than a whole, firm, and deliciously sweet 1lb, meal-in-itself lobster served cold with a Dijon mustard dressing. Likewise, unless you're mad for sauerkraut, there's little sense in choosing the $16 pastrami Reuben sandwich as a main course under the prix fixe over the $22 English-cut prime rib or the impeccable pink and uncharacteristically unsmall $27 filet mignon.

Then there's the burger factor. At $11 with chips (or, as a wise substitute, long and slender fries), this chubby, charbroiled, and lean beauty entails no sacrifice. Paired with the lobster cocktail it becomes a surf-and-turf of distinction. Follow that duo with the marble cake and its sidecar of Maker's Mark or banana dolce de leche ice cream ($9) and you truly are living large.

AMERICAN

Cosi Sandwich Bar

Some day there may well be too many Cosi Sandwich Bars. But for the moment, the proliferation of this Paris import continues to brighten the shadowed canyons of Manhattan's sometimes dreary lunchscape. All sandwiches are made to order using the bread that makes Cosi so much better than "cosi cosi"—Italian for "not so bad." The delectably chewy and crusty flatbreads are freshly baked on the premises in an iron-clad brick drum that fronts the stylish eat-in/takeout/delivery cafe. Directly in front

Cost	$7–25

Address 1633 Broadway at 51st St; plus other locations
℡212/653-1600
Transportation 1,2 to 50th St; N,R,W to 49th St
Open Mon–Sat 7am–9pm, Sun 7am–6pm
Accepts Cash only
Reservations Not accepted

of that oven, a baker usually sets out a bowl of warm bread scraps—gratis nibbles to occupy those waiting patiently on the sandwich assembly line. Presumably the sneaky folks who grab a few scraps, suddenly discover they are no longer hungry, and then walk out are not among those concerned about Cosi's aggressive expansion both in and outside New York.

The worry resulting from Cosi's growth, and its merger with the Zando coffee bar chain, is that the quality of the sandwich fillings will suffer. When you order one of eight combination sandwiches containing tomatoes, you're already likely to get slices cut from an insipid winter tomato, even in July. Fortunately, most other ingredients are decent and some are really quite good, notably grilled eggplant, roasted red peppers, and caramelized onions. You can ask for all three in the same sandwich or order instead a pre-selected combo. Best bets are the no.22 (tandoori chicken, roasted red peppers, and vinaigrette; $6.95), the no.38 (roasted turkey, Swiss, and honey mustard; $6.95), and the no.53 (ham, grilled eggplant, roasted red pepper, romaine, and Dijon mustard; $6.45).

The idea of baking bagels with the Cosi bread dough and oven was an inspired one. But the recently introduced, square-shaped "squagels" (95¢) are a bit too bready and lack the hard lid produced from boiling. The sorry name (the precaution of trademarking it was probably unnecessary) doesn't help matters. Still, those who can think of squagels as breakfast rolls rather than bagels will appreciate the granular crust of the cinnamon raisin (good toasted), Parmesan, and Asiago cheese varieties.

Dervish

Near Times Square, where kilowatts are counted by the millions, this restaurant's green neon sign hardly seems glaring. Yet few theater displays are so eye-catching as the one that climbs two stories to spell "Dervish." The sign heralds the latest venue for hit-and-run chef Orhan Yegen. He's the talented and smug dervish who opened, guided, then sold two of the best Turkish addresses from the last millennium: Turkish Kitchen and Deniz à la Turk. His challenge here was to convert the retro

Cost	Lunch $20–40
	Dinner $30–55

Address 146 West 47th St, between 6th & 7th Aves
☏212/997-0070
Transportation B,D,F,V to 47th-50th Sts-Rockefeller Center; N,R,W to 49th St
Open Daily 11.30am–11.30pm
Accepts All major credit cards

TURKISH

woodwork, handsome booths, and kitchen at Teatro Grill from Italian to Turkish in two days. While the resulting set-up succeeds in transplanting Turkish dining from the realm of the ethnic eatery to that of a Broadway classic, there is one drawback: the bar/smoking section is much livelier than both the rear and mezzanine dining rooms.

The gap between front and back extends to the menu, in which, quite simply, appetizers rule. Yegen's mastery in food-wrapping is evident in four starters elegantly transferred from serving dish to plates by the courteous waiters. Icli kofte ($6.50) are delectably nutty stuffed meatballs enfolded in a cracked wheat crust and tahini dressing. Similarly appealing are the soft and sweetly fragrant topik ($5.50)—rolls of kneaded chickpeas and potato stuffed with shallots, pine nuts, and currants. Pristinely pan-fried boregi ($5.50) arrive as golden, feta-cheese cigars hand-rolled in phyllo, while the grape leaves parceling grilled sardines ($7.50) take the edge off their fishiness.

A superior example of cooking *en papillote* is the entree of brook trout baked on a brick stone ($14.50). The dainty fish effectively steams under the cabbage-leaf wrapping that shields its flavors and juices from the intense heat. You cannot go wrong, either, with whole char-grilled striped bass ($17.50) or the casserole of octopus, mushrooms, garlic, and tomatoes ($14.50). Scooped over a rice pilaf, its pleasures are rhapsodic. Desserts ($5) are delectable. The halvah and the almond pudding boast choice textures, but it's the custard-smooth rice pudding that should have its name in neon. The lunch prix fixe is $13.95; the pre-theater prix fixe, $20.

Esca

The yellow walls, plush fabrics, and centerpiece vegetable/antipasti table are lovely enough, but they are clearly not the *esca*—Italian for "bait"—that has schools of foodies snapping at the end of the reservations line. Esca's lure is in fact the uncooked bait that the partners behind Babbo and Lupa (see p.88 and p.97), superstar chef Mario Batali and restaurateur Joe Bastianich, are dangling. *Crudo* (Italian for "raw food") is new to New York and much of the world, although the owners insist the raw fish specialty has a widespread and distinguished Italian past. In addition to being a great cook, chef-partner Dave Pasternak is a fanatical weekend angler. In the diner room, host-partner Simon Dean runs a tight ship with too few seats.

| Cost | Lunch $30–75 |
| | Dinner $40–90 |

Address 402 West 43rd St at 9th Ave

℡212/564-7272

Transportaion A,C,E to 42nd St

Open Mon noon–2.30pm & 5–10.30pm, Tues–Sat noon–2.30pm & 5–11.30pm, Sun 4.30–10.30pm

Accepts All major credit cards

Reservations Required

Each individual crudo is proposed as an appetizer ($11–13), much as you would have a single piece of sashimi in a Japanese restaurant. (The comparison also applies to their direct, pronounced flavors.) But it's perhaps better to order a tasting of six ($30 per person) as a first, second, or sole course. After all, this is why you and Esca are here. The exquisitely fresh fish are ingeniously marinated in a variety of spiced, infused, or garnished olive oils. Recent selections on the menu, which changes daily, have included Boston mackerel in Gaeta olive aioli, black bass with toasted pine nuts, Arctic char with pink peppercorns, and hamachi with two fennels.

Before or after the crudo you may have a sensationally clear-cut seafood pasta. Happily, the linguine with clams, hot pepper, and pancetta ($19 lunch/$22 dinner) and spaghetti with fresh mint, chiles, and 1lb of lobster ($22/$24) are available most days. The selection of baked, roasted, fried, pan-seared, or stewed fish entrees is staggering, as the prices can be when it comes to exotic (Columbia River sturgeon; $28) or imported (baked, salt-crusted branzino; $50 for two) selections. The salty frito misto ("mixed fry"; $20/$24) is awesome. If panna cotta with caramelized pineapple is the featured dessert ($8), take the *esca*.

ESPN Zone

To forestall a child's pleas to be taken to a madly popular theme restaurant, besieged parents could usually count on food critics to hang the latest Planet-Harley-Hard Rock-Hollywood by its velvet ropes. This time, however, Disney's slick sports-themed eatery is tough to knock for food, value, and service. A three-story, interactive amusement park/restaurant inspired by Disney's all-sports cable network, ESPN Zone might even merit *you* pleading with your kids to let you take them. Its commitment to the total sports nut is apparent not only in the giant screens, scoreboards, and Sports-Center studio set against the back wall of its spectacular two-tiered atrium but also inside the restrooms. They're equipped with cable-wired video monitors so fans can do their business without missing any action. New York purists may initially object to the menu's lack of local partisanship. Even when the Knicks play on the big screen, it doesn't quite feel as though you are eating on the home court. But, that said, nowhere does it say this is supposed to be New York food. Rather, these are dishes that will live up to any American child's wildest food fantasies.

Cost	$20–55

Address 1472 Broadway at 42nd St

☎212/921-3776

Transportation 1,2,3,7,N,Q,R,S,W to 42nd St–Times Square

Open Mon–Thurs 11.30am–11pm, Fri–Sun 11.30am–midnight

Accepts All major credit cards

Reservations Not accepted

Take, for example, the cheeseburger pizza ($10.95). While most grown-ups have no use for such an animal, the result, topped as it is with ground meat, chopped onions, Cheddar, mozzarella, lettuce, tomatoes, bacon, pickles, and Thousand Island dressing, is masterful. A kid will recognize exactly what it is supposed to be. Similarly, the Cajun fettuccini ($12.25) is perfect for any brat who wants both a pasta dish *and* a couple of blackened chicken breast cutlets tossed with andouille sausage, onions, and peppers. There's little point distinguishing between appetizers and mains. This is impulse grub. Order the ferociously spicy Asian chicken wings ($10) and the tender, tangy baby back ribs ($18.95) and pass them around.

Desserts, naturally, are sizeable and, in the case of the "Sudden Death" brownie-in-a-skillet ($7.49) and the Zone pancake ($6.95)—a batter cake topped with good vanilla ice cream, berries, and maple syrup and served hot in a skillet—well worth the exertion.

Hell's Kitchen

Hell's Kitchen is one of those neighborhoods that's seen more change in the past five years than Joan Rivers' face and, by and large, to better effect. Once truly deserving of its notorious title, today it is home to a Starbucks, a Blockbuster, and other depressingly stable standards of community sanitization. The area's upswing does get a welcome and recurring kick from its namesake restaurant—a casual, local favorite for strong Margaritas (frozen or on the rocks with fresh-squeezed lime juice and premium tequilas) and Sue Torres' distinctive brand of modern regional Mexican cuisine. This joint starts jumping early and stays that way all night long. The one hitch: the reservations policy can lead to long backups for tables.

| Cost | Lunch $18–45 |
| | Dinner $25–65 |

Address 679 9th Ave, between 46th & 47th Sts
☎212/977-1588
Transportation C,E to 50th St
Open Tues & Wed 11.30am–3.30pm & 5–11pm, Thurs & Fri 11.30am–3.30pm & 5pm–midnight, Sat 5pm–midnight, Sun 5–11pm
Accepts All major credit cards
Reservations Required for pre-theater dining; not accepted at other times

Patience is rewarded by the basket of grilled homemade corn bread with chile-spiked black bean spread. Don't feel constrained by the traditional, three-step eating plan (appetizer, main, sweet). While entrees like duck breast with cranberry mole and sweet potato-chipotle purée ($18) and grilled salmon with fresh corn tamale and salsa de morita ($17) flaunt Torres' skill and creativity, her talents really shine in the appetizers. So don't hold back. Order a boatload. Embark with the duck confit empanadas ($8)—scrumptious mini-pastry pockets busting at the seams with luscious, sweet-spicy shredded duck. The puddle of fig mole is a clever twist on the classic chile-based sauce. Mini-tacos stuffed with spicy chorizo and apple scotch bonnet salsa ($8) fit snugly into the palm of your hand and can be devoured in three, two, or, for the truly ambitious, one bite.

Cilantro-crusted tuna tostadas ($8) are one of Torres' signatures. Perfectly seared slices of deep, garnet-colored tuna are served on crisp corn tortillas and topped with a lively pineapple salsa and a pretty dollop of guacamole. At the other end of the scale, skip the frisbee-like quesadilla of leaden black bean epazote and goat cheese ($15). Desserts ($6) merit your resisting the pressure put on you by the hungry eyes of waiting diners.

Island Burgers and Shakes

Nobody makes a bigger deal about not serving french fries than William Brown, the guilt-ridden proprietor of Island Burgers and Shakes. His menu carries a feeble, 114-word explanation of why he doesn't serve them. "We've been hammered on it [not having fries] for years," says Brown. "We had to put an end to it." Strangely, most people would not give a hoot about the fried potato issue had Bill not made such a big deal about it. Diners adore his colorful eatery, which would be the perfect surfers' burger joint if a/you could fit a board in the narrow shop sideways, and b/there was a beach anywhere near Hell's Kitchen.

Cost	$8–23

Address 766 9th Ave, between 51st & 52nd Sts

☎212/307-7934

Transportation C,E to 50th St

Open Sat–Thurs noon–10.30pm, Fri noon–11pm

Accepts Cash only

Reservations Not accepted

The burgers ($5.25–8.25) are fine. An ample amount of satisfactorily fatty beef is spread over such breads as pita, rye, dark rye, Pullman sourdough, sesame bun, and absorbent ciabatta. The last is worth the 50¢ surcharge, especially if you're going heavy on the extra toppings, which seem to number in the hundreds (in fact there are 38 combinations). Contrary to the widely held less-is-more policy regarding New York burgers, Islands' take well to piling-it-on. The pre-selected burger combos like the "Saratoga" (bacon, Cheddar, horseradish, sour cream) and "Marco's" (pesto, ranch dressing, bacon, Parmesan) are highly recommended. These improbable breakthroughs are presumably the survivors of a nasty trial-and-error process no one but a fryless entrepreneur should put themselves through.

But burgers, however good, are not up to the standard of the grilled chicken sandwiches, also known as churascos ($6.50–8.75). Your choice of extras for these is the same as it is for the burgers, and indeed many of the spicier ones—jalapeno, habanero, Cajun spices—seem to go better with the chicken. Really, everything except the horseradish goes better with the chicken. Considering all the sandwich extras, it's surprising the not-too-thick milk shakes ($3.75) only come in three or, if you're feeling bighearted, four flavors: vanilla, chocolate, strawberry, and black and white (vanilla ice cream and chocolate syrup). That's one fewer than the number of potato chip varieties.

Joe Allen

The theater directory printed on the front page of Joe Allen's menu helps pre-theater diners navigate their post-meal route to the appropriate Broadway house. The irony of this convenience is that most theatergoers already acquainted with this venerable haunt pretty much know where they're going and how to get there. What's truly needed is a map on the cover of *Playbill* leading uninitiated theatergoers to Joe Allen. The brick walls, framed posters (of spectacularly miscast flops), and waiter-playing actors of this long-running, Restaurant Row hit formed the template for theatrical pubs everywhere, among them Joe Allen outposts in London, Miami Beach, and Paris. Certain fixtures cannot be easily reproduced, however, in particular the famous people that regularly occupy its bentwood chairs. If management framed all its credit-card receipts since 1965, it could display one of Broadways best autograph collections. Better still, we'd discover who was a bigger tipper, Al Pacino or Nathan Lane.

Cost	$20–60

Address 326 West 46th St, between 8th & 9th Aves
℡212/581-6464
Transportation A,C,E to 42nd St
Open Sun & Wed 11.30am–11.45pm, Mon, Tues & Thurs noon–11.45pm, Fri noon–midnight, Sat 11.30am–midnight
Accepts Visa & MasterCard
Reservations Suggested

No one would bother to copy the second and third pages of the menu, with their lists of basic American bistro fare with some contemporary flourishes. The finest of these, a corn leek pancake with smoked salmon and sour cream ($10), works best as a shared appetizer or bar snack, maybe accompanied by a glass of sparkling wine (Mumm Napa is $7). Other good bets include the decent Caesar salad ($6 as a prologue; $12 as the main act) or black bean soup ($6).

Ordering the burger (at $10, the least expensive entree) does not label you as an unemployed actor or bankrupt impresario. It shows only that you recognize quality. A request for the grilled sirloin ($24), on the other hand, could be more easily taken as a faux pas. The kitchen does stage a surefire turkey, as contradictory as that sounds—a roasted breast with country-style cornbread stuffing and cranberry relish ($18)—and there are a couple of sure-ticket sandwiches (both $11): meatloaf on sourdough, and grilled chicken with Cajun mayo and grilled onions on ciabatta. As encores, the upstart hot fudge pudding cake a la mode upstages the immortal banana cream pie (both $7).

John's Pizzeria

Several years ago, a young Belgian tourist boarded a Manhattan-bound A train at the Howard Beach-JFK Airport station, set down his two-ton backpack, and asked a passenger for directions. "Does this train go to John's Pizza?" he asked, only mildly surprised the Transit Authority cartographers had pinpointed Central Park and Yankee Stadium but not Bleecker Street's landmark pizzeria on its subway map. "Will Woody Allen be there tonight?" How joyful he would be today, seated in the newest location of that Village eatery which, spectacularly housed in the old Gospel Tabernacle Church in the heart of

Cost	$15–40

Address 260 West 44th St, between 7th & 8th Aves; plus other locations
℗212/391-7560
Transportation
1,2,3,7,N,Q,R,S,W to Times Square-42nd St; A,C,E to 42nd St
Open Mon–Sat 11.30am–11.30pm, Sun noon–11.30pm
Accepts All major credit cards
Reservations Not accepted

PIZZA

the theater district, is revered by Broadway's pizza apostles as their Cathedral of St John the Divine. The Belgian zealot, like other locals and foreigners making the same pizza pilgrimage, might not notice, much less care, if John's classic Margherita pie topped only with mozzarella and tomato and baked in a coal-fired oven had slipped a notch or two.

The pizza pies ($10 and up) at the Times Square John's, like that at the other branches, are still pretty good. The 400-plus diners who, during pre-theater hours, vie for seats in the tables and booths below its stained-glass cupola, are not knuckleheads. But, sadly, the reputation of this institution far exceeds its performance. The the tomato sauce is runny and a tad bland. And the mozzarella, though adequately soft and creamy, needs a sprinkling of grated Romano or Parmigiano *before* the pie is baked. Fortunately, the four brick ovens do still turn out the beautifully charred crusts that have been a hallmark of John's since 1929. When a John's pie is right you have to tear off bitefuls with your teeth. At its best it is crisp, not brittle. Its air pockets compress to the chew. It's irresistible with no more coverage than a drizzle of olive oil.

Desserts ($6) brought in from the Little Pie Company, including a superb ricotta cheesecake and three-berry pie, show a pursuit of excellence and consistency less evident at the pizza stations.

Marseille

In 1940 and 1941, New Yorker Varian Fry secured safe passage to America for more than 1200 refugees holed up in Marseille. Had Warner Brothers turned his exploits into a Humphrey Bogart movie, its clandestine activities might have revolved around a grand cafe in the mold of Francophile restaurateur Simon Oren's West Side bistro fantasy. Nancy Mah, a hot designer whose restaurants (Ruby Foo's, see p.227, and Lotus) resemble Hollywood movie sets, transformed a corner bank space in the Film Center Building into a beguiling period set suggestive of French-Mediterranean style and intrigue. With vaguely Moorish arches bending over burgundy banquettes and exquisite Moroccan tiling, the only omission is a wholesome Nordic beauty to play the Ingrid Bergman role.

| Cost | Lunch $22–60 |
| | Dinner $30–70 |

Address 630 9th Ave at 44th St
℡212/333-3410
Transportation A,C,E to 42nd St
Open Mon noon–3pm & 5.15–11pm, Tues–Fri noon–3pm & 5–11.30pm, Sat 11am–3pm & 5.15–11.30pm, Sun noon–3pm & 5.15–10pm
Accepts All major credit cards
Reservations Suggested

Chef Alex Urena's depiction is likewise loose and romanticized. The enduring ties between Provence's seaport city and its Mediterranean neighbors serves as his pretext to merge and modernize French, Spanish, Italian, and North African flavors. His skilled approach is first reflected in single-nibble mezze platters cleverly plated in rectangular rows. The seafood mezze ($6) might contain boquerones (Spanish anchovies), oysters, and mussels matched respectively to tapenade, Sherry raspberry mignonette, and pesto oil. Its meat counterpart may achieve similar feats for Serrano ham, poached foie gras, and chorizo. The same artifice imbues superior appetizers like wild mushroom soup with Parmesan foam ($7), rock shrimp falafel ($10), and sautéed sweetbreads with caramelized leeks ($7).

The bouillabaisse ($24) wants to be genuine, but as good as this fish stew is, its seafood assortment and soup are simply too clean. They've got no grit. Olive-crusted salmon ($17); poached duck breast ($16); roasted lamb chop with braised lamb leg ($22); and braised short ribs and beef cheeks with hummus and horseradish jus ($18) are rooted only in the kitchens—Blue Hill (see p.000), Bouley, El Bulli—listed on Urena's impressive resumé. How the chocolate peanut butter tart with celery sorbet found its way to Marseille is a mystery. But you'll be glad it did.

Molyvos

With its $34.50 pre-theater menu served one-half block from Carnegie Hall, Molyvos is a superior option for dining before a performance. Still, it's painful to relegate a visit here to the role of preliminary entertainment. From the food to the decor to the service, few restaurants get it as right as this urbane Greek taverna. With considerable passion and apparent wherewithal, the Livanos family decorated the deep space of terracotta-brushed walls and Mediterranean tiling with collections of vintage photographs, colored bottles, ceramics, and curios. And by dividing the dining area into smaller zones, the effect is at once intimate and expansive, casual and well turned out. The two things Molyvos is not are cheap and sexy.

| Cost | Lunch $30–65 |
| | Dinner $35–80 |

Address 871 7th Ave, between 55th & 56th Sts

☎212/582-7500

Transportation F,N,R,Q,W to 57th St; 1,2,A,B,C,D to 59th St–Columbus Circle

Open Sun–Fri noon–2.30pm & 5–11.30pm, Sat noon–2.30pm & 5pm–12.30am

Accepts All major credit cards

Reservations Suggested

GREEK

The cuisine is a combination of classic and what top young chefs like Molyvos' Jeff Botsacos like to call "progressive" dishes. The latter are not in this instance fusion or Frenchified inspirations so much as inventive ways to approach, associate, and animate traditional regional ingredients. The menu neither offends old purists nor bores young trendies who, at Molyvos, frequently sit at the same family table. It's tempting to make an entire meal out of mezedes (small plates). Grilled asparagus stands in for gigante beans in a classic combo of exceptionally creamy skordalia (whipped potatoes and garlic) set against unusually crunchy beets ($8.25). The wood-grilled baby octopus with fennel, lemon, and greens ($10.50) is a fragrant standout. The $7.50 charge for the sampler of the customary but hardly ordinary spreads—roasted eggplant, fish roe mousse, cucumber-yogurt—should be as certain a dinner-check fixture as sales tax.

You may choose to zero in on seafood entrees, perhaps a special of pan-seared black bass with fava beans and sautéed wild mushrooms folded into spring onions ($25), steamed salmon wrapped in grape leaves ($19.50), or simply grilled whole fish ($25–30). But grilled baby lamb chops ($23.50) will also delight. Desserts ($7.50), like creamy rice pudding topped with sour cherry preserves and foamed milk or semolina cake saturated with a orange-vanilla syrup, epitomize the rare blend of new and old that is Molyvos.

223

Orso

🍴 To best absorb the backstage buzz of this Theater District haunt, you need to reserve weeks in advance for a pre-curtain or post-applause table. To reassure yourself that the trattoria of Restaurant Row co-habitant Joe Allen (see p.220) has not actually been buried in a 1980s time capsule, it's better to dine off-peak, between 8pm and 10.30pm. Without the cast of luminaries to blur your starry-eyed vision, Orso reveals itself to be a cozy, tasteful, and densely staffed stomping ground. When, during the pre-theater rush, the waiter who's just uncorked your Montelpulciano recites, "We let you serve your own wine," it's easy to assume that the hurried staff cannot be bothered with refilling glasses. Only during quieter hours can the policy be appreciated as a welcome informality.

Cost	$35–80

Address 322 West 46th St, between 8th & 9th Aves
☎212/489-7212
Transportation A,C,E to 42nd St
Open Mon, Tues, Thurs & Fri noon-11.45pm, Sat, Sun & Wed 11.30am–11.45pm
Accepts MasterCard & Visa
Reservations Required

Sandy walls and pale gray wainscoting give the low, narrow room a bleached-out look. It's as if the sunburst lamps were emitting color-fading UV rays. Fronting the kitchen, four terracotta planters are over-stuffed with the crusty breads that will be grooved (but not sliced through) before they and their white bean spread reach your table. Tables are set with colorful Solimene ceramics; the slow revelation of their colorful, vibrant design stems somewhat the sadness of clearing slice by slice one of the crisp, divinely light, thin-crusted pizzas ($14.50). These are typically ordered as a shared appetizer in lieu of or in addition to one of several interesting salads ($8–10).

When Orso first opened, pastas like the ravioli filled with minced salt cod, raisins, and artichokes ($19) or fusilli with porcini, broccoli rabe, hot peppers, and shaved ricotta salata ($17.50) were new and exciting. Now they're merely good. It has become harder, too, to get worked up about the perfectly fine Prosecco sauce for roasted tilapia ($23) or the gorgonzola polenta purée that sits under crumbling pieces of braised chicken ($21). It's no real fault of Orso—perhaps the dishes are simply too familiar. If you prefer your desserts sweet rather than cloying, take risotto pudding ($7.50) over caramel bread pudding ($8.50).

Pietrasanta

In review blurbs covering the Italian restaurants around the Theater District and Hell's Kitchen, "great value" generally means cramped and rushed; "rustic" translates as trendy, pricey, and overbooked; and "quaint" is a euphemism for twenty-minute pastas and straw-bottle Chiantis. But an entirely separate glossary is required to explain the appeal of affordable, friendly, and hopelessly unfashionable Pietrasanta. In a strange instance of reverse restaurant psychology, the faux marble walls and unsightly dropped ceiling manage to entice rather than ward off hungry, pre-theater passers-by. The assumption is that if a place as unconcerned with appearances as Pietrasanta is crowded, it has to be for the food, value, and service. In this instance at least, the assumption is correct.

Cost	$20–55

Address 683 9th Ave at 47th St

☎212/265-9471

Transportation C,E to 50th St

Open Sun & Mon noon–10.30pm, Tues noon–11pm, Wed 11am–11pm, Thurs noon–11pm, Fri noon–midnight, Sat 11.30am–midnight

Accepts All major credit cards

Nary a table goes without the homemade mozzarella, either fresh with roasted peppers ($6.95), pan-fried ($5.95) within the spinach fettuccine alla pietrasanta (with zucchini, peas, and a tomato cream sauce; $13.95), or melted atop a pizza ($10.95). The pizzas, though decent, are hard to classify, falling as they do somewhere between a classic New York pie and a more generic variety. The extra zip of the Gorgonzola and grilled eggplant pie has the edge over the flatter-tasting Margherita. Grilled eggplant also brings allure to the baked bread topped with olive and tomato ($6.50).

If you're going to have a homemade pasta (that's a given) and a cream sauce (debatable), the pre-eminent pairing is the gnocchi with wild mushrooms ($10.95). Alternatives can be overproduced or basically too rich, as is true of the farfalle with salmon, basil, and sage ($14.95). But any inclination to favor simpler main-course options is challenged by the giddy pleasure of sautéed chicken breast with pancetta, smoked salmon, and a pink vodka sauce ($14.95)—a dish once accurately praised by a kind waitress, a third-year student of Pietrasanta's reverse psychology, as "weird and misleadingly good." Otherwise, the variations on veal scaloppine ($14.95—15.95) are sure bets, as is the grilled and commendably straightforward salmon ($19.95).

Midtown West

Redeye Grill

Redeye is a high-flying brasserie ideally suited for anytime, any-appetite, any-way-you-are suppers. It has partially supplanted Petrossian, the Russian Tea Room, and Carnegie Deli (p.209) as the haven around Carnegie Hall for late-night smoked fish. Its pastrami smoked salmon club ($16.95) takes on two Carnegie Deli titans—pastrami and smoked salmon—in a single, overstuffed bagel. Decadent seafood platters and muraled columns painted with lascivious New York fantasies seem inspired by another legendary haunt, Paris' La Coupole. The intelligentsia can go ahead and debate the symbolism in the mural of three nudes romping atop the Chrysler Building with a toy globe. We're hungry.

Cost	$30–85

Address 890 7th Ave, between 56th & 57th Sts

☎212/541-9000

Transportation F,N,Q,R,W to 57th St

Open Mon 11.30am–3.30pm & 5.30–11.30pm, Tues–Sat 11.30am–3.30pm & 5.30pm–12.30am, Sun 11am–11.30pm

Accepts All major credit cards

Reservations Suggested

Appetizers assembled at the "Dancing Shrimp" carpaccio/sushi/salad bar include seven kinds of smoked fish ($10.95–18), none more dazzling than the smoked sturgeon drizzled with white truffle oil. That sturgeon can get to be an expensive habit. Sashimi and smoked fish are combined in four irresistible maki rolls ($10.75–12.75). The tuna spring roll ($11.95) is tame compared to the grilled shrimp and chorizo quesadilla ($9.75) and the popped rock shrimp with spicy coconut sauce ($13.50).

The kitchen is especially adept at keeping grilled fish moist and tender. Each fish entree, ranging in price from $21.95 for Atlantic salmon to $24.95 for Gulf red snapper, comes with a stuffed baked potato, a vegetable, and a trio of sauces: tomato-basil, lemon pesto, and green herb sauce. Lobster comes five ways: in a bouillabaisse ($32.95), and, more cheaply, in an open-faced pot pie, grilled, steamed, or stuffed with crabmeat and baked. If you don't feel like fish, the steaks, chops, and main-course salads (some of them smoked fish extravaganzas), are huge. Atop a dessert tray, a scoop of Crisco-simulated cream and a whole, unpeeled banana stands as a figurative representation of the truly outstanding banana cream pie ($8.95). The strawberry shortcake and the warm apple pie (both $8.95) are great too, despite their whimsical displays—some people are here more for the whimsy than the food in any case. There's live jazz Tuesday through Sunday after 9pm and during Sunday brunch.

Ruby Foo's

R-U-B-Y F-O-O'-S is a block-lettered blockbuster heralding a new Broadway adaptation of an old Hollywood fantasy of a Chinese dining palace. More than fifty years ago, the restaurateur Ruby Foo opened Chinese joints in Boston, Miami, and New York, and today the name awakens a sentimental longing for a notorious, palatial icon that exists only in our collective imagination. In a spectacular, 300-seat, 7000-square-foot interior distinguished by mah-jong-tiled walls, dynastic statues on lacquered displays, and magnificent, orange-glass lanterns with hanging tas-

Cost	$30–75

Address 1626 Broadway at 49th St
☎212/489-5600
Transportation 1,2 to 50th St; N,R,W to 49th St
Open Sun & Mon 11.30am–11pm, Tues–Thurs 11.30am–11.30pm, Fri & Sat 11.30am–12.30am
Accepts All major credit cards
Reservations Suggested

PAN-ASIAN

sels, designer Nancy Mah surpassed anything Fu Manchu-creator Sax Rohmer or Charlie Chan-author Earl Derr Biggers might have envisioned.

Opened in 2000, the self-defined "dim sum and sushi palace," like the year-older original on the Upper West Side (2182 Broadway; ☎212/724-6700), exhibits its executive producer's amazing knack for knowing what and how a particular demographic of New York wants to eat. Stephen Hanson Atlantic Grill and Ocean Grill; see p.255 and p.284) figured he'd run up checks faster with sushi and Chinese-Thai-Malaysian-Japanese "dim sum" than with straight Chinese. You can find better and cheaper interpretations of yellowtail-scallion maki ($8.95) and steamed vegetable dumplings ($5.95) elsewhere, but not together in a tourist magnet as singularly entertaining and convenient to the Theater District as this.

Waitresses rightly counsel you to eat tapas-style, sharing such appetizer plates as toothsome teriyaki-sesame sea bass with wakame seaweed salad ($7.95); tamarind-glazed baby back ribs ($7.95—too bad the tangy flavors don't penetrate the tender meat); delectably puffy wedges of goat cheese tempura with greens and a tart-spicy sesame-chile dressing ($8.50), and a side of soft tofu cubes with a hot, chile-spiced garlic sauce ($4.95). From "main plates," wok-fried jumbo shrimp with pepper lime sauce and coconut sticky rice ($19.50) is exactly the kind of scrumptious junk you want to be eating here. Same for the ingenious dessert sampler ($7.50), a bento box of chocolate cake, cherry sundae, and sushi-shaped morsels (wasabe marzipan, for example) to dip in chocolate sauce. **227**

Midtown West

Seppi's

What is Seppi's doing with a name like Seppi's? And why is Seppi's dong whatever it's doing with the name Seppi's at the Parker Meridien Hotel? Such questions are unavoidable when you choose an Italian name and Carnegie Hall/City Center location for a SoHo-styled French bistro. Yet the moniker and address are somehow appropriate for a fish-out-of-water restaurant that maintains an island of late-night, downtown cool in a sea of midtown uptightness. The stamped tin walls, black-and-white leather booths,

| Cost | Lunch $25–75 |
| | Dinner $35–80 |

Address 123 West 56th St, between 6th & 7th Aves

☎212/708-7444

Transportation F,N,Q,R,W to 57th St

Open Daily 11.30am–2am

Accepts All major credit cards

Reservations Suggested

slate-board menus, butcher-paper-topped tables, and informal service certainly suit a spin-off of the perennially popular SoHo bistro Raoul's. Seppi's is named after the father of brothers Serge and Guy Raoul.

While the bulk of Seppi's menu is classic French prepared with flair, chef/co-owner Claude Alain Souilliard honors his partners' Italian heritage with several dishes, most notably a melt-in-your-mouth osso buco with saffron risotto ($25). Sadly, his once celebrated forays into Turkey, in the form of manti (dumplings) and Ottoman rice have been suspended. For starters, a mint-accented celery root remoulade cradled in endive leaf enlivens lamb pâté ($8). Escargot in buttery garlic sauce ($9) reaches the table piping hot in its baking dish. Among entrees, the shiitake-stuffed baby chicken ($20) is sawed in half to give you a peek at the juicy filling, while succulent duck breast ($24) is advantageously plated with a sweet potato gratin, and a black-peppercorn-slathered steak au poivre ($26) comes with first-rate frites. In a stellar fish dish, two grilled daurade fillets are propped over cumin-dusted root vegetables on a plate painted red with a beet-and-sumac sauce ($24)—the last vestiges of Seppi's Middle Eastern period.

Downtown dessert impulses and excesses ($7-12) are as uninhibited as ever. A chestnut Napoleon is layered with the densest chestnut cream imaginable and garnished with a sticky-sweet fig sauce. Crème caramel is flanked by two big balls of ultra-rich whipped cream. And both chocolate options—warm, nearly flourless cake and a Black Forest tower—possess a shameless degree of cocoa pleasure.

Sha La Gourmet

(icon) Wholesome, homey food on Broadway, just steps away from 42nd Street? Sounds highly unlikely, which is why denizens of the Theater and Garment Districts treasure this little shop, which from the outside looks no different from so many other takeout shops that clutter Manhattan. It is, for sure, mainly a sandwich, salad, and hot-table business, sending luncheon orders to the fashion showrooms and shops on the surrounding streets. The difference here is Abe and Vera, the owners. They run Sha La as

Cost	$6–20

Address 1435 Broadway, between 40th & 41st Sts
☎212/869-9414
Transportation
1,2,3,7,N,Q,R,S,W to 42nd St-Times Square
Open Mon–Fri 7am–5pm
Accepts Cash only
Reservations Not accepted

a personal canteen, with five tables for two set against the wall opposite the food cases. Of course no one will mind if you pull up a third chair. You can't miss Abe. He is generally sitting at his desk at the back of the long, narrow storefront, often eating his own food. A good sign.

Vera, presiding over the hot table, knows most of her customers by name. To one she will recommend the vegetable burgers ($5) that "just came out of the fryer." To another, she'll say "the brisket [$5] is particularly good today." Vera knows who dotes on her creamy macaroni and cheese ($4); who habitually takes a slab of the moist baked salmon ($9); who likes turkey meatloaf ($7); who orders corned beef ($5) only when the meat is fatty; and who is willing to chance a new creation. There is always hot, freshly roasted turkey breast with a crust of rosemary—for sandwiches ($5) or to be customized into a plate with salad and/or vegetables ($8).

Further down the line is the cold station, where Sha La's manager, Salim, supervises the sandwich and salad making. On any kind of bread, including lavosh wraps, you can have freshly cooked strips of chicken breast dressed with nothing but Hellmann's mayonnaise and diced celery ($5), or shrimp salad, cold cuts, or cheeses. Besides green salad, there are several bean and grain salads, tomato and onion, and cucumber with dill. Don't ignore the bakery counter as you leave. Stop for an espresso or soft-serve ice cream, and some of the best cakes, pastries, and cookies in midtown.

Shelly's New York

If restaurants could be evaluated by how successfully they indulge their owners' whims, Shelly Fireman's flights of fancy (Redeye Grill, see p.226) would hover in the four-star stratosphere. This brasserie firmly establishes the Bronx native as Manhattan's crown prince of upper-crust cravings. Local kids of advancing age recognize Shelly's as the birthday-bash venue their parents could neither afford nor endure. The one-time Automat and, most recently, Motown Café has been transformed into a triplex emblazoned with what teenagers, current and former, consider to be great art. Peter Max abstracts adorn the walls behind the dining room's comfy banquettes and half-moon booths. A circular mural painted by Red Grooms shows a motley ensemble of voracious New York characters.

| Cost | Lunch $30–70 |
| | Dinner $40–80 |

Address 104 West 57th St, between 6th & 7th Aves
℡212/245-2422
Transportation F,N,Q,R to 57th St
Open Mon 11.30am–10.45pm, Tues–Fri 11.30am–12.30am, Sat 11am–12.45am, Sun 11am–10.45pm
Accepts All major credit cards
Reservations Suggested

The kitchen pampers grownups with longstanding, deep-rooted aversions to the word "no." Among its many nutritionally incorrect highlights is a thick and exceptionally buttery New England clam chowder ($7) and, as starters or sides, gooey, crusty, ham-fortified macaroni and cheese ($8) and the creamiest of creamed spinaches ($7). To satiate seafaring fantasies there are tiered platters ($65/$122) displaying lobster, jumbo shrimp, Alaskan king crab legs, oysters, and stone crabs over ice. The sweet and meaty stone crabs, air-freighted up from Florida, may be ordered a la carte for a small fortune—$21–41/pound. Entrees include a 30oz porterhouse ($39) and rib chop for two ($65). Good, leaner options include tuna steak encrustd with roast garlic ($24) and miso-glazed halibut ($23). The showstopper dessert is a large glass bowl containing ice cream, chocolate ganache, cookie crumbs, a massive dollop of whipped cream, and a jumbo wooden spoon for mixing and mashing them together. It can be ordered as part of the $35-per-person sharing deal, which encludes an oyster platter or seafood salad and the porterhouse.

The best thing about brunch (entrees $12–24) at Shelly's is the breakfast pantry, with its zucchini cheese mini-muffins and crispy puff-pastry palmiers. The chocolate chocolate-chip French toast ($13) is marvelously frivolous, and the banana cream pie is outstanding.

Tuscan Square

No one need ever again schlep all the way over to Italy to enjoy the untold riches of Florence and Siena and their surrounding vinegards, olive groves, and marble quarries. Today the Tuscan countryside has been assembled in a midtown food mall. The mogul behind this Planet Tuscany is restaurateur Pino Luongo (Le Madri, Coco Pazzo). Here his core business expands from wines and prepared foods to include clothing, table linens, and beauty products. It's one-stop shopping for Tuscan totebags, tagliolini, towels, and toothpaste. But as easy as it is to ridicule this theme park, there's no

Cost	Lunch $15–70
	Dinner $35–85

Address 16 West 51st St at Rockefeller Plaza

℡212/977-7777

Transportation B,D,F,V to 47th–50th Sts-Rockefeller Center; E to 5th Ave

Open Mon–Fri 7.30am–4pm & 5.30–9pm, Sat 11.30am–3pm & 5.30–9pm

Accepts All major credit cards

ITALIAN

denying the good taste of Luongo and his team. Nearly every inch of the two-level, 12,000-square-foot space has style. The casual 120-seat restaurant is squeezed in behind a grand, curving staircase leading down to the marketplace, gourmet takeout counter, and open kitchen below. And if you like what you're eating or, better still, what you're spilling it on, you can buy practically all of it on your way out.

The marketplace centers on a handsome salad bar where bottles of extra virgin olive oil hang on an iron rod and swing down like foozball men to give your salad a kick. There's a brick pizza oven and a pasta station where fresh ravioli is cut from long sheets, and an eating counter where video terminals allow you to watch your lunch being prepared. No one is sticking pinkies into saucepans here! The marketplace's weekend lunch options are handier and less expensive than the restaurant's. Pizzas are $9.50 and up, while lunch boxes with two of the following—soup, fruit, pasta salad, antipasto plate, half-sandwich—cost just $10.

At the restaurant prix fixe lunches and dinners have recently been replaced with an a la carte menu. The flexibility better suits the needs of Rockefeller Center office workers, shoppers, and tourists. A grilled squid and radicchio lunch plate ($10) or, at dinner, penne with garlic-roasted eggplant, plum tomatoes, and smoked mozzarella ($17) is often enough. Note the early closing time, which perhaps better than anything demonstrates that this is no 32-oz, $34 rib-eye sort of dinner destination.

ITALIAN

Vice Versa

The Italians have marched into Paris, or at least the Theater District's version of it. Years from today, Franco Lazzari, Daniele Kucera, and Stefano Terzi, all alumni of Central Park South's San Domenico, may be remembered as the brave rivoluzionari who infiltrated the north side of West 51st Street's 300 block and ended decades of dominance by pre-theater escargots and after-the-curtain chocolate mousses. And quite apart from breaking the Gallic time warp, Vice Versa's lasting contribution may be affordable sophistication. Superior in quality, comfort, and service to the pasta cafes on Ninth Avenue and more economical than established favorites like Orso (see p.224), Vice Versa fills an important gap.

| Cost | Lunch $25–55 |
| | Dinner $40–75 |

Address 325 West 51st St, between 8th & 9th Aves
☎212/399-9291
Transportation C,E to 50th St
Open Mon–Fri noon–2.30pm & 5–11pm, Sat 5–11pm
Accepts All major credit cards
Reservations Suggested

The dining room, with its dark-wood floor, green limestone columns, glass-walled garden, and dramatically lit cream-colored walls, is sleek and stylishly understated, and the Italian cooking is rustic, flavor-focused, and of the moment. Chef Terzi borrows from all the right places: tonnato (tuna sauce) from Sicily, duck ragu from Tuscany, warm flourless chocolate cake from NYC. His antipasti collection is led by the pan-fried tortino (pie) of artichokes and calamari loosely bound by flour and garlic ($11.50). Other pleasing starters include arugula salad with bresaola (dried beef) rolled goat cheese ($10.50) and codfish and olive oil purée ($12.50) served over crisp, thinly sliced rounds of potato.

As befits a San Domenico veteran, Terzi prepares three sensational pastas: long twists of strozzapreti ("strangled priest") tangle with a fabulously chunky duck ragu laced with carrots, fennel, and black olives ($13.50). The ravioli-like casoncelli are stuffed with ground veal and, for a hint of sweetness, amaretto cookies, and then topped with brown butter, sage, and Parmigiano ($14). Spinach tagliatelle take on the sweetest possible mussels, Manila clams, scallops, and tomato ($13.50). One meat dish of comparable quality is the thick veal medallions bronzed to perfection and plated with a dreamy Parmigiano cream sauce ($22.50). When it comes to desserts ($6–7.50), you'll be safe with tiramisu and pear tart. But who cares for security when balsamic-sauced banana semifreddo and a devilishly creamy panna cotta with kiwi sauce have broken the French frontier?

Virgil's Real Barbecue

The 10,000-mile fact-finding tour that took the founders of Virgil's to 100 barbecue joints from Tennessee to Texas was surely one heck of a road trip, but it may not have been the wisest way to formulate a recipe. The best regional styles don't always travel easily across a county, let alone a country, and don't take well to the democratic premise of amalgamation: smoked ham from Maryland, beef brisket from Texas, mustard sauce from South Carolina. Such give and take, however commendable, ultimately comes off as a phony and noncommittal. In the end, the crucial piece of Virgil's geography is Times Square. You won't find any place accommodating larger groups with bigger food and finer brews for more moderate prices in a better party atmosphere any closer to the crossroads of the world.

Cost	$20–65

Address 152 West 44th St, between Broadway & 6th Ave
☎212/921-9494
Transportation 1,2,3,7,N,Q, R,S,W to Times Square-42nd St; B,D,F,V to 42nd St
Open Sun & Mon 11.30am–11pm, Tues–Sat 11.30am–midnight
Accepts All major credit cards

BARBECUE

The two-level space is a handsome shrine to American barbecue, with photos on the walls and a map delineating the owners' favorite BBQ joints printed on the placemats. (Out of modesty or, more likely, honesty, they've excluded their own.) Make no mistake, Virgil's favorably fatty, beautifully crusted, hickory-, oak- and fruitwood-smoked meat that falls off those ribs ($18.50) is tender and smoky, almost too smoky. It's darn decent barbecue and clearly preferable to the dry and tough brisket ($16.50). The pig-out portions both of the entrees and the sides (good potato salad, fries, beans) that come with them push your digestive capacity to the breaking point.

Better to stick with appetizers and sandwiches. The crisp, cornmeal-coated, scallion-specked hush puppies with maple butter are great ($4.50) and the loopy buttermilk onion rings with creamy blue cheese dip ($6.50) are pretty good if delivered fresh from the frying hopper. Pulled pork on a sesame seed bun ($10.50) is gently spicy and smoky and can be easily doused to taste with Memphis hot sauce. With desserts ($5.95) you need to choose carefully. The fluffy peanut butter pie is exactly what you want it to be, whereas the gooey, cloying pecan pie and doubly dense chocolate cheese pie are unyielding.

233

Murray Hill & Kips Bay

MURRAY HILL & KIPS BAY

Ⓜ E. 42ND ST
New York Public Library
Grand Central Station
Chrysler Building
E. 41ST ST

MURRAY HILL

E. 40TH ST
E. 39TH ST
E. 38TH ST

Asia de Cuba ◉

PARK AVENUE

Josie's ◉

E. 37TH ST
E. 36TH ST

Pierpont Morgan Library

FIFTH AVENUE
MADISON AVENUE
LEXINGTON AVENUE
THIRD AVENUE
SECOND AVENUE
FIRST AVENUE

E. 35TH ST
E. 34TH ST

Empire State Building

E. 33RD ST

Artisanal ◉

Ⓜ

E. 32ND ST

Hangawi ◉   Tony's ◉ Burger

Melissa Blue ◉

KIPS BAY

E. 31ST ST

PARK AVENUE SOUTH

E. 30TH ST

0   200 yds

E. 29TH ST

Artisanal

🍴 Who would have thought the combined stench of 250 different cheeses could lure capacity crowds to one of Manhattan's notoriously cursed restaurant spaces. Terrance Brennan, that's who. The chef of the acclaimed Mediterranean restaurant Picholine made his fromagerie the centerpiece attraction at what became, seemingly seconds after its spring 2001 opening, one of New York's most bustling brasseries. Adam Tihany's Deco design bestows jazz age romance upon aged Gouda, Berkshire blue, Colston Bassett Stilton, and—would you believe it?—fondue. The

Cost	Lunch $18–70
	Dinner $32–80

Address 2 Park Ave at 32nd St
☎212/725-8585
Transportation 6 to 33rd St
Open Mon–Thurs noon–3pm &
5–11pm, Fri noon–3pm &
5pm–midnight, Sat 11am–3pm
& 5pm–midnight, Sun
11am–3pm & 5–10pm
Accepts All major credit cards
Reservations Required

FRENCH

upbeat mood for the 160 diners seated on cane chairs and banquettes is set by amusing vintage posters, moderne lighting fixtures, and, underfoot, the black, gold, and burgundy syncopation of the geometric tiles.

Brennan takes fondue to the limit, with six varieties (among them Stilton with Sauternes and Fontina with white truffle oil) and, to supplement the bread cubes, six "baigneuses" (beef tips, potatoes, kielbasa, etc). Served in enamel-coated pots, these fondues ($22 and up) may be superior to any you've ever tasted. Still, the intrinsic fondue problem—diminishing returns—persists. The second bite never tastes as good as the first, sadly. Better to relegate the fondues to the bar and, if you must get an early cheese fix, order the sensational, three-fromage French onion soup ($9), a basket of gougères (cheese puffs; $6/$9) or, at lunch, one of the grilled cheese sandwiches ($12–16.50). Even if you choose to ignore cheese altogether you can have a truly great meal, starting perhaps with the moules marinières ($10) or the garlicky escargot pastries ($11.50).

Though limp frites detract from the steak options, the brasserie fare, with its French-Mediterranean accents, can be exceptional: pan-crisped skate with a blood orange butter sauce ($17.50), say, or venison steak au poivre with a grain of squash and prune ($24.50). As for the delectably crisp yet succulent chicken cooked under a brick ($19.50)—you could sample thirty cheeses at Artisanal and still leave talking about this one dish. If concluding with a cheese plate at America's greatest cheese restaurant is not already a no-brainer, the bland desserts make it so.

Murray Hill & Kips Bay

Asia de Cuba

Better to surrender to the seductions of a glamorous hotspot like the Morgans Hotel's Asia de Cuba, we say, than fight them. Leave the rational considerations—do you get your money's worth? Are there dishes you'd go back for? Would you enjoy the coffee-lacquered duck chow-chow as much if you tried it at a Polynesian supper club in Piscataway?—to the spoilsports. Designer Philippe Starck and dining impresario Jeffrey Chowdorow have devised a stylish platform for some very amusing "Chino-Latino" experiments.

Cost	$40–90

Address 237 Madison Ave, between 37th & 38th Sts
☎212/726-7755
Transportation 7 to 5th Ave; 4,5,6 to 42nd St-Grand Central
Open Mon–Fri noon–3pm & 5.30–11pm, Sat 5.30–11.30pm, Sun 5.30–10pm
Accepts All major credit cards
Reservations Required

The 50ft marble slab that slashes the center of this balconied exhibition hall is less a two-sided communal dining counter than a fashion runway. With leatherette chairs and crescent-shaped booths surrounded by white curtains, it's either Starck's vision of heaven or merely a way station on the steep ascent. Waiters in Maoist jackets are a diner's best friend. Throughout dinner they bring you technicolor cocktails, repeatedly change your grease-absorbing napkins and rightly advise you that all servings are sized to be shared family-style.

The menu does not divide the two cultures in the same way as the Cuban-Chinese eateries of Upper Broadway (see Flor de Mayo; p.280). The fusion here has no trade barriers, dealing freely in wonton chips and plantain crisps, Asian mushrooms and Caribbean spices. The standout starter is Thai beef salad with seared rounds of beef carpaccio, oranges, avocado, crisp curls of twice-baked coconut, and a lightly creamed chipotle dressing ($18). Fried calamari salad is a trove of tiny ringlets buried in chicory, banana, and chayote ($16.50), while the excess of the five-spice, pan-fried foie gras ($25) is only to be applauded.

Entrees should be shared and shared just once. Their fascination fades quickly. The duck breast and confit (leg-thigh) with a coffee-and-vanilla bean sauce ($29) is yummy, but also cloying. Succulent, grilled, mojito-glazed rib steak tingles with a sake- and foie gras-enriched mango sauce ($42). Multi-spiced fried chicken is set against crunchy kimchee slaw ($27). For dessert, surrender if you must to the guava mousse in a chocolate tuile or the towering chocolate coconut layer cake.

Hangawi

🍴 Usually when you are advised to dine on the late side, it's to correspond with the time when the energy and noise levels of some stylish haunt are nearing their peak. Here, the advantage of reserving for 9pm or after is just the opposite. The zen-like tranquility of this vegetarian shrine, with its low tables, colorful seat cushions, New Age folk music, antique artifacts, heavy ceramics, and framework of wood, stone, and copper, is defeated by the dinner-hour din. True balance between yin and yang or, in Korean, um and yang, is not achieved until the crowd thins and the clamor fades. Only

Cost	Lunch $12–50
	Dinner $30–60

Address 12 East 32nd St, between Madison & 5th Aves
☎212/213-0077
Transportation 6 to 33rd St
Open Mon–Thurs noon–3pm & 5–10.30pm, Fri noon–3pm & 5–11pm, Sat 1–11pm, Sun 1–10pm
Accepts All major credit cards
Reservations Suggested

KOREAN/VEGETARIAN

when you can hear the patter of the servers' slippered feet against the wood-planked walkway does Hangawi begin to feel like the remote, peaceful, mountain retreat it was so meticulously designed to resemble.

Chef Steven Chung's menu can be appreciated at any hour, providing your inseam is 36 inches or less (legroom is minimal) and you're wearing the appropriate hosiery (shoes must be checked at the entrance). The most comprehensive introduction to his cuisine, with its emphasis on carrots, radishes, root grains, potatoes, and tofu, are the multi-course, prix fixe lunches and dinners ($29.95 or $34.95). A la carte ordering, however, gives you more flexibility. Either way, few diners skip one soothing porridge ($3.95) or another, in such clear-flavored varieties as pumpkin and delicious black sesame. By eschewing the spoon and instead picking up the bowl, the rice-thickened texture seduces your upper lip as the hot soup slides in under. Among the other appetizers, all of them elegantly assembled, are skewers of oyster mushrooms and scallions ($8.95) and a crunchy salad with bean paste, lemon dressing, and the gently bitter perfume of shredded ginseng root ($8.85).

A new and hopefully permanent addition to the popular, main-course stone rice bowls ($19.95) is the one laced with stuffed eggplant and mushroom. The marvelous kimchee wraps ($15.95) are a must, if only to watch the server secure the kimchee stuffing into the fragile, potato-vermicelli pancakes. For dessert, the gelatinous tofu puddings (lemon or chocolate) are good for what they are.

Murray Hill & Kips Bay

Josie's

Rare is the restaurant that can delight both a carnivorous Capricorn and the leaf-loving Libra he or she is meeting. But at Josie's, a loud, see-and-be-seen playroom sleekly designed in the style of vintage diner, chef/owner/ juice maven Louis Lanza satisfies dietetically mismatched couples with what he calls "conscious cuisine." In conscious English, this means that all dishes are certified organic and dairy-free without resorting to serious deprivation. Pleasure-wise, the Latin- and Asian-accented contemporary American food is worth every certified bite—as the sexy singles slurping the sangria of the day (pineapple-cantaloupe-grape, pear-apple-citrus) by the liter ($17) will attest.

Cost	Lunch $15–40
	Dinner $22–50

Address 565 3rd Ave at 37th St
☏212/490-1558
Transportation 6 to 33rd St; 4,5,7 to 42nd St-Grand Central
Open Mon–Wed noon–11pm, Thurs & Fri noon–11.30pm, Sat 11.30am–4pm & 5.30pm–midnight, Sun 11am–4pm & 5.30–11pm
Accepts All major credit cards
Reservations Recommended

It's best to begin by sharing such creative small plates as ginger-grilled calamari with feisty pineapple-red pepper salsa ($8), nori "sushi" rolls stuffed with brown rice, julienned portobellos, and steamed spinach ($6), and pan-seared spicy black soy bean dumplings with mango miso sauce ($7). Then move on to main courses divided into thematic sections. "Earth Friendly" (100 percent vegetarian) options include roasted "meatloaf" with rosemary jus ($12). Made from lentils, wild rice, red beans, mixed veggies, and seitan, this savory loaf has no off-taste or mushiness to offend meat eaters. Under "Ravioli & Pasta," the sweet potato ravioli with Gulf shrimp, sweetcorn, and roasted peppers in a white wine leek sauce is stellar ($15). Stir-fries are fairly ho-hum compared to sesame seared tofu ($13), grilled teriyaki chicken ($14), and lemongrass-curry shrimp ($16).

The "Market Seafood" section boasts a world-class tuna burger ($16) as imposing as its red meat counterpart ($11). The dairy-free, wheat-free pies ($6) are not chalky or cement-like, as such things often are. Deep-dish, three-berry ginger pie topped with a butterless walnut-oat crumble is truly impressive—the perfect way to end a (virtually) guilt-free meal. (Let's not count that third liter of sangria.)

There's another Josie's at 300 Amsterdam Ave, Upper West Side (☏212/769-1212).

Melissa Blue

It's hard to get a handle on the food politics of the spare, modern, and very likeable bistro Melissa Blue, which is named for a butterfly found in small colonies in New York State. Owner/co-chef Gabriel Pellegrini may try to use organic vegetables bought from local farmers and support sustainable agriculture whenever possible, but he is not an absolutist. Additionally, his ability

Cost	$20–45

Address 575 2nd Ave,
between 31st & 32nd Sts

℡212/481-4844

Transportation 6 to 33rd St

Open Daily 4pm–midnight

Accepts All major credit cards

to come up with something as outlandish as vegetarian Buffalo chicken wings made with seiten (wheat gluten) dumplings-on-a-stick on a non-vegetarian menu makes him difficult to peg. Ultimately, what's oddest about Melissa Blue is what's best: it's not preachy. The idea is to eat well with no frying, no fatty meats and very limited dairy.

Those seiten dumplings don't taste anything remotely like chicken, but they are crisp and firm and their butter-free hot sauce and blue cheese dip are fine ($6.95). Serving "yesterday's soup" as opposed to a soup du jour is a brainwave. Pellegrini's suggestion is that soups like tomato basil ($4.95) taste a lot better the day after their base has been prepared. Happily, the grilled shrimp quesadilla overstuffed with vegetarian chorizo, Jack cheese, roasted peppers, and cilantro yogurt ($8.95) is not more than a few seconds old. Be sure to share it as an appetizer. You get all you need out of it from a quarter triangle.

Main courses are always changing, and not always in the way you would like. The least desirable entree, the clunky and overwrought turkey osso buco with sweet potato cobbler and roasted vegetables ($14.95), has outlasted the superb "not-fried" chicken with mashed potatoes and truffled corn chowder ($14.95). Fortunately, mushroom Wellington with its spinach and vegetable pâté filling and unsoggy puff pastry ($14.95) are intact. And two fish entrees with loyal followings, crisp herbed salmon ($14.95) and tamari almond trout ($14.95), have had only minor adjustments in their accompaniments. The trout's nutty coating brings to mind the taste of smokehouse almonds. Among desserts, crisp oats and sugar make a pleasantly crunchy topping for the warm apple crisp ($5.95), while the oatmeal crème brûlée ($5.95) is an interesting take on the classic.

Tony's Burger

Forget the four tables at this drab greasy spoon near the Empire State Building. To absorb the Tony's experience you must plant yourself on one of the nine stools covered in worn black leatherette, lean your forearms on the lunch counter topped with marble floor tiles, and watch the skilled short-order cook and his burgers sweat under the sizzling heat. Above his confined work space, a range hood traps a good 95 percent of the greasy smoke emanat-

Cost	$4–15

Address 34 East 32nd St, between Park & Madison Aves
☎212/779-7191
Transportation 6 to 33rd St
Open Mon–Fri 7am–8pm, Sat 7am–4pm, Sun 8am–noon
Accepts Cash only
Reservations Not accepted

ing from the grill and griddle. The remainder infuses every inch of space above belt level with what only urban romantics would term "ambiance." Some regulars know to do separate laundry loads for clothes worn at Tony's. Others have taken to twice shampooing their hair and eyebrows at the earliest opportunity.

The Tony's burger is champ in the sphere of wide, flat patties which know no color gradations between deep-red rare and well-done gray. The soaking-wet surface of a cooked, 6oz burger, its toasted sesame-seed bun left open, is marked with charred dashes like a highway divided by dotted lines. It's a thing of beauty. A basic burger with iceberg, tomato slices, and pickle is $4.05; a deluxe with a thimble of coleslaw and a heap of frozen (but good for their type) fries, $5.30. You'd do best to spring for the bacon burger or bacon cheeseburger deluxe ($6.05/$6.50). Each comes with six or seven strips of crisp-edged but neither brittle nor curled bacon. With the layered bacon as thick as the burger pattie itself, the chew is extraordinary.

The subject of bacon brings to mind Tony's other superlative sandwich, the BLT ($3.75), its bacon strips flattened with an iron as they cook. In this instance it might be preferable to sit at the table. You don't really want to see just how much mayo is spread over the toast. Also worth a look are pocketless pita sandwiches like the tuna melt ($4.95). At breakfast, it is possible to order eggs wiht a side of gyromeat in place of bacon. But no one you know and admire would do that.

Uptown

Harlem & Hamilton Heights

Amy Ruth's

(🍴) When, during summers spent on his family farm in Alabama, Carl Redding was warned that cooking was for girls, the Harlem native did not heed his grandfather's advice. Strangely, he preferred cooking and tasting alongside his maternal grandmother to cleaning the pigpen and picking cotton (hello?). It may be a vestige of granddaddy's thinking that influenced the naming of this wonderful Southern-style cafe. True, it's likely Redding first thought of pasting a sepia

Cost	$8–35

Address 113 West 116th St, between Lenox & 7th Aves
☎212/280-8779
Transportation 2,3 to 116th St
Open Daily 8am–11pm
Accepts All major credit cards
Reservations Not accepted

SOUTHERN

portrait of Amy Ruth Bass throughout his restaurant as a loving tribute to his grandmother, who died in 1987. Many of the recipes are hers. But surely he knew the restaurant's feminine persona would help him compete with Sylvia's, the doyenne of Harlem restaurants (see p.249). It isn't girls we think feed us better than boys; it's the mothers of their mothers.

To offset its homespun image, Amy Ruth's incorporates touches of refinement, sometimes to comic effect. When the manager scurries over to prevent people from seating themselves at one of many unoccupied marble tables, the waitresses roll their eyes. And when an eatery that serves Sanka instead of brewed decaf pushes bottled water instead of NYC H2O, it's the diners who do a double take. The atmosphere is otherwise classy, easy-going, and popular with the politicians, religious leaders, and dignitaries who have dishes named after them. Redding sure knows how to play the name game.

Whenever a restaurant serves waffles throughout the day, the message is clear: order them. These golden, deep-grooved, fluffy but not bubbly waffles ($4.95) are served with a variety of co-stars—the "Rev. Al Sharpton" comes with fried or smothered chicken ($8.50)—but never without pure maple syrup. Should you, acting against your best interests, want to consider something else, the salmon croquettes ($7.50) and corned beef hash ($7) are swell breakfast items accompanied by hot grits and warm biscuits. The fisherman's platter ($15.95) boasts a generous assortment of fried jumbo shrimp, crabcakes, catfish fingers, and, like all entrees, a choice of two sides (fried okra and candied yams are good). The only dessert superior to sweet potato pie ($2.75) is—what else?— the w-a-f-f-l-e-s.

247

LATINO/AMERICAN

Café Largo

Just west of the City College's North Campus, this Latin bistro brings an unexpected mix of understated sophistication and good eating to the historic but gastronomically neglected West Harlem precinct of Hamilton Heights. Easily spotted from the window of a Broadway bus, the shapely awning and red French doors are incentive enough to disembark and investigate. Inside, the bistro's casual elegance, extending from the copper-plated bar to the black-and-white nudes hung on brick walls lit by steel-colander sconces, is almost too good to be true. You begin to wonder if Café Largo truly belongs here and was not the victim of some terrible mix-up? (Who knows? The contractor may have been working on a modest bodega and got the addresses mixed up.) Actually, the restaurant is the fulfilled dream of the February 27th Partnership, an extended family enterprise named for Dominican Independence Day. Its members wanted to do something special for themselves, their neighborhood, and us.

Cost	$11–50

Address 3387 Broadway, between 137th & 138th Sts
☎212/862-4570
Transportation 1 to 137th St
Open Mon 5pm–midnight, Tues–Sun noon–midnight
Accepts All major credit cards
Reservations For large groups

The cooking is not easy to place. Although its foundations are Caribbean/Latino, the menu accumulates Mexican, Italian, Cajun, and American tastes. Only the red and black beans, side dishes spiced with cilantro and aromatic Dominican oregano, are purely Caribbean. Given that the profuse entrees come with a green salad, appetizers may seem to be superfluous. But overlooking the camarones al ajillo ($6) means missing out not only on deliciously sweet shrimp but also on a great garlic-driven parsley white wine butter perfect for bread-dunking. And the appetizer portion of exceptionally meaty, dry-rubbed, mildly spicy BBQ ribs ($7) gets you to thinking that it might be the main courses that are expendable.

Pollo Largo ($12), despite its Spanish name, shows off the bistro's Italian accent by placing pounded, lightly floured, sautéed chicken breasts ankle-deep in a lemony white wine butter sauce. Half the liquid would do. Blackened catfish fillets ($14) are too gently spiced, but at least you can taste the fresh fish. The garlic mashed potatoes-vs-fries face-off is a wash. Both are perfectly decent. The lone homemade dessert—thick, creamy, ultra-rich, coconut vanilla flan ($3)—is so good that it too could stop a bus.

Sylvia's

🍴 It was more grit than grits that got Sylvia Woods her start in the food service industry a half-century ago. The South Carolina farm girl who had never set foot in a restaurant lied about her work experience to land a waitressing job at a Harlem lunch counter. She was found out on the first minute of her first shift. When the boss asked for a coffee, she pulled the wrong lever and put the cup—and herself—in hot water. The boss was impressed. "He told me, 'If you have that much nerve, I'm gonna teach you, I'm gonna make you the best waitress,'" recalls Woods. Eight years later, she and

Cost	Lunch $11–40
	Dinner $15–50

Address 328 Lenox Ave, between 126th & 127th Sts
☎212/996-0660
Transportation 2,3 to 125th St
Open Mon-Fri 11am–10.30pm, Sat 8am–10.30pm, Sun 11am–8pm
Accepts All major credit cards
Reservations For large groups

SOUTHERN

her husband, Herbert Woods, bought the eight-stool eatery, expanded the menu of Southern down-home cooking (the description "soul food" was coined a few years later), and changed the name from Johnson's to Sylvia's. A legend was born.

The publication of a Sylvia's cookbook in 1992 was initially looked upon as the most significant disclosure of classified documents since the Pentagon Papers. But home cooks soon learned what many longstanding diners already knew: it's the woman who made those sweet, spicy, tangy spare ribs ($12.95) and gravy-smothered chicken ($10.95) famous and not the other way around. Sure, the collard greens ($2.50) were solid, especially before the kitchen surrendered to nutritional correctness by replacing the pork skins and bacon drippings in that classic side dish with smoked turkey wings. Certainly, the candied yams ($2.50) and sweet potato pie ($3.50) have always been terrific. But personal warmth and not recipes have established Woods as the toast and taste of Harlem for 40 years. When the Queen of Soul Food says she likes to rub shoulders with her customers, be they politicians, movie stars, neighborhood regulars, or Japanese tourists, she means it in the literal sense.

Another quality that makes fried catfish ($11.95) and twin smothered pork chops ($12.95) taste better is the on-site music. Saxophonist Lonnie Youngblood plays on Saturday afternoons, while the sweet voices of Ruth and Clay Simpson animate the rousing Sunday gospel brunch.

Upper East Side

UPPER EAST SIDE

Museum of the City of New York
Mount Sinai Hospital
Islamic Cultural Center
Harlem River
Jewish Museum
92
Cooper-Hewitt Museum
Ruppert Park
National Academy of Design
Guggenheim Museum
Sassy's Sliders
Gracie Mansion
Café Sabarsky
Comfort Diner
Neue Gallery
Le Pain Quotidien
Zócalo
Carl Schurz Park
Metropolitan Museum of Art
Brasserie Julien
Q Café
Cherokee Apartments
Brother BBQ
Jimmy's BBQ
John Jay Park
Atlantic Grill
Taperia Madrid
Whitney Museum
Candle Cafe
Spice
Payard Bistro & Patisserie
Asia Society
Trata
Frick Collection
Hunter College
Seventh Regiment Armory
L'Absinthe
New York Hospital-Cornell Medical Center
Temple Emanu-El
Maya
Jo Jo
East River
Gino
Metropolitan Club
Roosevelt Island Tram
Guastavino's
Bloomingdale's
QUEENSBORO BRIDGE

Central
Reservoir
Park
TRANSVERSE ROAD NO. 4
TRANSVERSE ROAD NO. 3
TRANSVERSE ROAD NO. 2
TRANSVERSE ROAD NO. 1
CENTRAL PARK SOUTH
EAST DRIVE

FIFTH AVENUE
MADISON AVENUE
PARK AVENUE
LEXINGTON AVENUE
THIRD AVENUE
SECOND AVENUE
FIRST AVENUE
YORK AVENUE
FRANKLIN D ROOSEVELT DRIVE

E 103RD ST
E 102ND ST
E 101ST ST
E 100TH ST
E 99TH ST
E 98TH ST
E 97TH ST
E 96TH ST
E 95TH ST
E 94TH ST
E 93RD ST
E 92ND ST
E 91ST ST
E 90TH ST
E 89TH ST
E 88TH ST
E 87TH ST
E 86TH ST
E 85TH ST
E 84TH ST
E 83RD ST
E 82ND ST
E 81ST ST
E 80TH ST
E 79TH ST
E 78TH ST
E 77TH ST
E 76TH ST
E 75TH ST
E 74TH ST
E 73RD ST
E 72ND ST
E 71ST ST
E 70TH ST
E 69TH ST
E 68TH ST
E 66TH ST
E 64TH ST
E 63RD ST
E 62ND ST
E 59TH ST
E 58TH ST

0   400 yds

92

For the post-preppy neurotics of the Upper East Side's well-heeled Carnegie Hill district, breakfast, lunches, and dinners at 92 have become their equivalent of eating in. The rapid routinizing of so polished and far-from-cheap a restaurant in Woody Allen's backyard was no accident. By furnishing family-friendly 92 with burgundy banquettes and Art Moderne woodwork and hardware, owner Ken Aretsky essentially dressed up his everyday diner-with-counter like a swank brasserie-with-bar so his clientele could dress it right back down. If anything, the undertaking is too successful.

| Cost | Lunch $25–75 |
| | Dinner $30–85 |

Address 45 East 92nd St at Madison Ave
☎212/828-5300
Transportation 6 to 96th St
Open Mon–Fri 8–11am, noon–3pm & 5–11pm, Sat 9am–3pm & 5–11pm, Sun 10am–4pm & 5–10pm
Accepts All major credit cards
Reservations Suggested

With interlopers from distant zip codes stopping by after visits to the nearby Cooper-Hewitt, Guggenheim, and Jewish Museums, nowadays locals must suffer the indignity of needing to make a reservation to dine at home.

The first edible brought to the table is a baguette in a wax paper bag bearing the trademark designer-logo of Carnegie Hill resident Eli Zabar. It's a perfect touch. In these parts, the Eli's Bread logo is as sure an emblem of good breeding today as the polo-shirt alligator was some twenty years ago. Starters like fried calamari ($10), solid Caesar salad ($9), and a sweet French onion soup ($11) are neither memorable nor uninteresting, which is to say they're just right for 92's needs. As is often the case with old TV shows, it's the predictable things that hold up best to repeat viewing. Deciding about the steamed saffron mussels ($12 as an appetizer, $18 as a main) is a tough call. Plenty of fresh dill and leeks but negligible saffron turn up every time you pluck a mussel or sink a hunk of Eli's into the broth.

The easy pleasure of bacon-wrapped meatloaf ($20) notwithstanding, the top daily entree is pan-roasted chicken ($21) with the crisp, golden coating of the finest roast duck. If you can take the high salt quotient it's a keeper. The pretty lean steakburger ($15 at lunch, $16 at dinner) begets thick, beautiful fries; the homemade-mayo-slathered lobster roll ($23), the crunchy shoestring variety. Exercises in ice cream excess—banana split ($9), root beer float ($6), hot fudge sundae ($8)—bring it all home.

FRENCH

L'Absinthe

L'Absinthe could qualify as one of the finest places east of Brittany to eat classic French cooking—if only chef Jean-Michel Bergougnoux could rein in his own inventiveness. But then, who's complaining? L'Absinthe could also solve a variety of everyday dining dilemmas—if the cuisine and moderate-to-high prices (up to $32 for main courses) remotely resembled what most of us think of as "everyday." But again, who's complaining? Few restaurants so successfully straddle the line between traditional and inventive, dressy and informal, local and worldly, an April Tuesday and New Year's Eve. With its brass-railed banquettes, zinc bar, vintage floor tiling, high mirrors, and efficient yet congenial service, L'Absinthe could be the perfect compromise dining destination—if its standards were not so uncompromising.

| Cost | Lunch $30–60 |
| | Dinner $40–90 |

Address 227 East 67th St, near 2nd Ave
☎212/794-4950
Transportation 9 to 68th St; F to Lexington Ave-63rd St
Open Mon–Sat noon–3pm & 5.30–11pm, Sun noon–3pm & 5.30–10pm
Accepts All major credit cards
Reservations Required

Rotated appetizers meticulously assembled to camera-ready perfection have encompassed a cold terrine of quail and foie gras in a Port wine aspic ($12.50); a lobster salad with black truffle celery root remoulade and a Port truffle vinaigrette ($15), and a snail fricassée with prosciutto chips, shaved Parmesan, and sautéed salsify. Shellfish trays ($44/$88) might include not only oysters but also whelks, razor clams, periwinkles, Jonah crab, Little Neck clams, and jumbo shrimp. Main courses can be as contemporary and fusion-like as steamed jumbo shrimp in coconut lemongrass broth with basmati rice ($28) or as classic French as a pot au feu with slowly poached meats and winter vegetables ($32). The latter comes from Bergougnoux's menu of brasserie classics, which can make the place feel like another sort of establishment, if not an entirely different restaurant. Should you choose to dine in *that* L'Absinthe, the free-range chicken poached in broth with thinly sliced black truffles is a revelation ($22).

Desserts (mostly $10) too display great versatility and artistry. They can be as straightforward as the thin, crusty apple tart with a sweet buttery finish or as stylized as a frozen praline ice parfait in a bittersweet chocolate shell. The pumpkin nut soufflé and the warm chocolate cake with cardamom orange marmalade find that dangerously sensuous place between solid and liquid. But then, who's complaining?

Atlantic Grill

Replicating his successful formula at Ocean Grill (see p.284), owner Stephen Hanson created this large, stylishly appealing fish house with a menu to match. Factor in smooth service and prices as low as anyone visiting this high-rent location could hope for and it's easy to understand why the place became so wildly popular so quickly with so broad a cross section of East Siders. True, few dishes live up to the promise offered by the handsome, wood-and-chrome-detailed bar lined with Jacques-Henri Lartigue's dreamy photos of the French Riviera. Yes, nothing you put fork to is as fabulous as the studded ecru chairs and brown-velour Hollywood booths in the main dining room. And yes, no appetizer welcomes you as enticingly as the caned chairs and long banquettes in the tiled oyster bar room. But the kitchen does most things quite well and a few things extremely well, and that is apparently well enough.

| Cost | Lunch $28–50 |
| | Dinner $35–75 |

Address 1341 3rd Ave, between 76th & 77th Sts
☎212/988-9200
Transportation 6 to 77th St
Open Mon–Fri 11.30am–11.30pm, Sat 11am–midnight, Sun 11am–11pm
Accepts All major credit cards
Reservations Required

SEAFOOD

So what if you wouldn't travel here exclusively for the decent sushi maki rolls ($6.50–8.95) and the sushi and sashimi platters ($19.50–31). It's nice to have them available in a restaurant that can also launch your meal with a salad of seared, five-spice yellowfin tuna with micro greens and aged balsamic vinaigrette ($9.50). The sesame-crusted lobster roll ($8.95) with two dips—the citrus soy sauce is nicest—is also outstanding.

Often the fashionably treated New American seafood entrees ($18–21)—porcini-dusted swordfish, potato-crusted trout, pan-seared sea bass with cumin polenta and gummy fried onions—are executed with too much restraint. But the buttery, herb-crusted salmon served with mushy risotto ($18.50) is a happy exception, as is the Thai red curry bouilla-baisse ($22)—a clay pot of shellfish and glass noodles in a sweet-and-spicy coconut-infused broth. Moreover, two sides (both $5), a spring-roll-like vegetable strudel and horseradish mashed potatoes, are simply amazing. Come dessert time there's no regretting the warm, crunchy-almond-topped apple crisp with honey cinnamon ice cream ($6) and, for sheer frivolity, the caramelised banana ice cream tower with toasted marshmallow sauce and hot fudge ($6.50).

FRENCH

Brasserie Julien

(Ⓟ) Accomplished French chef
Philippe Ferret runs his and his
wife Cecelia's neighborhood brasserie
with the unremitting perfectionism of a
home improvement fanatic. He is always
taking on an interior design project, be it
creating stained-glass panels for a backbar of hand-finished woods, gilding the
classical capitals of the tall columns, or
crafting an Art Deco partition for the open
kitchen doorway to match the cherry-
wood-and-bronze elevator doors of the

Cost	$28–75

Address 1422 3rd Ave,
between 80th & 81st Sts
℡212/744-6327
Transportation 6 to 77th St
Open Sun–Thurs
5.30–10.30pm, Fri & Sat
5.30pm–midnight
Accepts All major credit cards

Chrysler Building. The upshot, assuming the irrepressible remodeler has
not already started all over again, is an informal yet plush backdrop for a
suitor who wants to romance an existing love interest or, on weekend
nights especially, meet a new one either at the bar or the innovative
chef's table reserved for communal, family-style dining. A jazz duo plays
on Fridays and Saturdays.

Ferret's continuous menu-tinkering mostly entails adapting French
classics for American tastes. He is far less concerned with dazzling technique and fussy presentation, though he is capable of both, than setting
down lots of likeable food. The homemade pâté ($9.50) and marinated
smoked herring with potatoes ($11) are both served à volonté, meaning
diners can have as much of these two appetizers as they want. You could
easily make an entire meal with repeated servings of the herring and
potato salad. But no one with an eye on a main course will require seconds of the copious salads ($7.50-10.50), the foie gras terrine ($14.50),
or the pastis-flambéed escargots with garlic parsley butter ($12).

Entrees may lack for finesse but never size. Whatever free space there is
on a plate of tender lamb shank braised in red wine ($19.50) is occupied
by whipped potatoes impossible to leave unfinished. Moroccan chicken
bisteeya ($19.50), a sweet-and-savory phyllo pie, is accompanied by a high
pile of mesclun greens. And the grilled striped bass ($22), flambéed in
pastis and stacked high over green and white asparagus, fennel, sun-dried
tomato, and black olives, is a long-distance delight. Chocolate lovers will
adore the hot-sauced profiteroles and the molten-centered Valrhona
chocolate cake with pistachio sauce and vanilla ice cream (both $8).

Brother Jimmy's BBQ

The fact that Carolinian Manhattanites are routinely critical of the hickory-smoked ribs at Brother Jimmy's should not be immediately interpreted as an indictment of their quality and authenticity. Kvetching about local translations of foods from back home is an immutable consequence of moving to the world's great melting pot. It's one way transplanted New Yorkers of diverse origins convey their ethnic pride. Though it's unlikely that the BBQ is as good here as at the famed North Carolina joints it was inspired by, the slow-smoked, vinegary-sauced, tart-and-tangy ribs are pretty darn tootin' good. Furthermore, it's a good bet that some of the postgraduate regulars are wearing Duke Blue Devils, Wake Forest Demon Deacons, or University of North Carolina Tar Heel boxer shorts under their beer-stained jeans.

Cost	$11–45

Address 1485 2nd Ave, between 77th & 78th Sts; plus other locations
☎212/288-0999
Transportation 6 to 77th St
Open Mon–Wed 5pm–midnight, Thurs–Sun noon–midnight
Accepts All major credit cards
Reservations Not accepted

Brother Jimmy's is above all an endurance challenge. For the frat-party refugees, it's a raucous marathon of boozing, scarfing, and belching. For everyone else, it's a test of just how much of that boozing, scarfing, and belching they can stand. Some synchronize their visit with the quiet lull between happy hour and televised basketball games that begins at around 7.16pm and concludes at 7.35pm. Others ask to sit in the side dining room away from the bar. This room too is cluttered with the odd collectibles—vintage soda pop bottles, old BBQ menus, rabbit seed sacks—that give Jimmy's make-believe shack its southern character.

The meaty ribs ($16.95 with two sides) come three ways: northern (with a sweet glaze), southern (spicy and with a sour ting), or, best of all, the deep and complex, 21-spice dry rub (spicy and, as the description implies, no sauce). Don't fret about missing the moist marinade. A squeeze bottle of runny, spicy, and wickedly tart sauce is at the ready. Other options to look at are the pulled pork sandwich ($7.50), the BBQ half-chicken ($11.95), and assorted finger foods/starters: stuffed jalapenos, Buffalo wings, hush puppies, fried onion "straws" (a single $4.95 order feeds five). To finish, the warm pecan pie has just the right proportions of nutty crunch and sweet gooeyness.

Upper East Side

Café Sabarsky

The short stroll from the entrance of the Neue Gallery New York to the elegant staircase leading up to its galleries of early twentieth-century German and Austrian art can be negotiated in anywhere from seven seconds to four hours. In fact, some people never make it to the staircase. Without paying admission they detour to Café Sabarsky, take possession of an Adolf Loos black bentwood chair and a white marble table, pull out the necessary reading or writing materials, and nurse a kleiner brauner (espresso) until the lights beneath the Joseph Hoffman sconces are extinguished. Art collector Ronald Lauder opened the Neue Gallery in 2000 and named the in-house cafe in memory of its co-founder, the art dealer and curator Serge Sabarsky.

Cost	$18–55

Address 1048 5th Ave at 86th St
☎212/288-0665
Transportation 4,5,6 to 86th St
Open Mon & Wed–Sat 8am–7pm, Sun 1–6pm
Accepts All major credit cards
Reservations Not Accepted

Café Sabarsky is housed in the beautifully restored drawing room of a Fifth Avenue mansion dating from 1914. Furnished with reproductions of classic pieces from the Viennese Secessionist and Arts and Crafts movements, it is an elegant evocation of a grand Viennese coffeehouse without the tobacco smoke and intellectual fire. But passions are stirred by the soups, sandwiches, and pastries and, it must be added, the clueless service. The Austro-Hungarian menu of Kurt Gutenbrunner, chef-owner of the superlative Austrian bistro Wallsé (see p.180), sets a new standard for museum cafes.

Open-face rye bread sandwiches like ham with grated horseradish and chives ($11.50) and liverwurst dabbed with minced onion confit ($11.50) are so good you almost have to slow yourself down to fully appreciate their individual parts. The rich and creamy chestnut soup ($9.50) has already stimulated discussion groups. The quality of the entrees justifies their high prices. Few savory pastries are as delicate and unsoggy as the one encasing cod strudel with Reisling-tempered sauerkraut ($25). And the tafelspitz (boiled beef) with creamed spinach and potatoes ($25) is every bit the standout here as it is as Wallsé. You can also come in at any time to enjoy one of Gutenbrunner's splendid Viennese tortes or a kaffee mitt schlag ($5) without having a savory. Oh, and the galleries are said to be great too.

Candle Café

The rosy-cheeked, East Side thirty-somethings sitting at the dark-wood tables come with the territory. But few past experiences in the organic-vegan dining realm prepare you for the mass of folks crowding the sidewalk, or the booze that awaits them. Unlike most eateries of its ilk, the sleek and casual Candle Café has a liquor license and serves a thoughtful, modest selection of organic and sulfite-free wines and organic beers. The organic Samuel Smith lager is a smooth and balanced reward for waiting it out.

Cost	$12–45

Address 1307 3rd Ave, between 74th & 75th Sts
☎212/472-0970
Transportation 6 to 77th St
Open Mon–Sat 11.30am–10.30pm, Sun noon–3pm & 5.30–9.30pm
Accepts All major credit cards
Reservations For large groups

Start with a plate of edamame ($6.50), the steamed, sea-salted soybeans that have become a favorite healthful snack addiction. Since service can be slow and there's no breadbasket, these little pods—and a Sam Smith lager or two—will tide you over until your food arrives. Appetizers are hit or miss, with Asian dumplings ($7.95) falling into the latter category. The bright green spinach envelopes, though pretty, are doughy and filled with an insipid vegetable mixture. The Caesar salad ($6.95), with crisp piles of romaine and a creamy, caper-accented dressing, hits the mark. The south-of-the-border seitan sandwich ($10.95) is a between-the-bread feast. A multigrain hero is stuffed with chile-rubbed grilled seitan and smoky-sweet caramelized onions and then slathered with spicy vegan chipotle mayo. A gigantic slab of tempeh lasagna ($12.95) layered with spinach-herb tofu ricotta, tomato sauce, and soy mozzarella is as good as it is huge. The BBQ seitan burrito ($14.95) is another sizeable treat. Packed to capacity with portobellos, zucchini, kale, black beans, basmati rice, and soy cheese, and topped with roasted tomato sauce and a chunky cilantro-laced avocado salad, this dish alone could explain the line snaking out of the door.

Dairy-free desserts are massive, too, and happily so. The cocoa-coated double layer chocolate cake ($5.25) is one rich, gooey, duplex slice of devil's food heaven. Alternatively, you could turn to the fruit drinks, smoothies, and soy protein shakes that fall under the category of "Fruition Nutrition." The apple Betty ($5.50), with apple, pear, banana, and cinnamon, takes America's classic dessert and lets you suck it through a straw.

Comfort Diner

You could hardly call Ira Freehof a fashion victim. The diner historian opened this affectionate tribute to the classic American diner years *after* the 1980s retro diner craze had swept in and out of town. As a result, the Comfort Diner's terrazzo tabletops, streamlined chrome details, red tail lights, and kitschy 1950s wall sconces appear dated—just not in the way they were intended. Nevertheless, it's always nice to come across a restaurateur motivated by love rather than opportunism. Indeed, the challenge for Freehof is in assembling and maintaining a staff able to put his child-like enthusiasms (Mom's Meatloaf "On Her Best Day", the "Imagination Burger") into practice. And though the Comfort Diner is fun, consistency and versatility—hallmarks of a New York diner—are wanting.

Cost	$10-35

Address 142 East 86th St, between Lexington & 3rd Aves
☎212/426-8600
Transportation 4,5,6 to 86th St
Open Sun–Wed 8am–11pm, Thurs 8am–midnight, Fri & Sat 8am–2am
Accepts MasterCard and Visa
Reservations Not accepted

What's never lacking is quantity. Even Jim Carrey would have difficulty fitting the above-par sandwich standards—BLT ($6.95), grilled chicken club ($8.50), tuna melt over a toasted English muffin ($7.95)—in his mouth. "Large plates" are way over the top. "Thanksgiving Every Day" ($12) is a self-defeating concept, reminding us why we only eat that way once a year. The plate stacks piles of roast turkey breast over stuffing and somehow fits a heap of excellent mashed potatoes, cranberry sauce, *and* fresh vegetables on the same plate. The best side, shoestring onion rings ($3.95), is big enough for three. And there is no letting up with desserts: the fabulous house take on s'mores ($4.95), melted marshmallows and chocolate sandwiched between graham crackers, is enhanced with chocolate sauce and a double scoop of vanilla ice cream.

The peak times to seek out Comfort are February and August. In February the Great Grilled Cheese meltdown features a different grilled cheese sandwich—grilled Cubano (Swiss, turkey, pork, pickles, and mustard); melted Gorgonzola with pears on baguette—daily. (It's a pity that there are only 28 days in February.) August is Milkshake Madness, when you can go crazy for a huge variety of shakes from chocolate chip cookie to Key lime.

There's another Comfort Diner at 214 East 45th St, Midtown East (☎212/426-8600).

Gino

Central casting could find Italian character actors to fill the roles of the bow-tied waiters. The costume guy could outfit them in the signature gray jackets with red cuffs. The set designer could recreate everything from the red, zebra-print wallpaper to the warped, fluorescent-lit wall panels. A Neapolitan chef could be found to prepare a red sauce of comparable quality. And still you would not have Gino. They simply don't make 'em like this anymore and they couldn't if they tried. The clatter, energy, and swagger of this circa 1945 haunt and

| Cost | Lunch $25–65 |
| | Dinner $30–75 |

Address 780 Lexington Ave, between 60th & 61st Sts
℡212/758-4466
Transportation 6,N,R,W to Lexington Ave-59th St; F to Lexington Ave-63rd St
Open Daily noon–10.30pm
Accepts Cash only
Reservations Not accepted

ITALIAN

former rat-pack hangout benefit from renewable sources of energy: regulars bring their kids and friends who bring their kids and friends and so on.

Do not try to bribe Mario or Sal to quickly get a table. They wouldn't like that. If you don't care to wait at the bar, you have perhaps three options: 1) Come very early, maybe after a shopping jaunt to nearby Bloomingdale's. 2) Shower a regular with gifts from Bloomingdale's and come in later with him or her. 3) Return often enough (say three times a week for five years) to merit the VIP treatment.

The grub, like the service, is agreeably gruff and habit-forming. No-nonsense appetizers like the watery chopped salad ($9.50) and the piping hot clams oreganato ($8.75) are not so much served to you as they are shoved at you. It's as much a part of the show as keeping secret the contents of the house sauce (lightly creamed tomato) that goes out with good gnocchi ($13.50) and paglia e fieno (a $13.50 weave of egg— "straw"—and spinach—"hay.") Linguine with clams ($13.50) has all the clams you need in a sauce great for dunking that mediocre Italian bread, while broiled chicken "Gino" ($14.95) is indiscriminately slathered with chopped garlic (you decide if that's a good thing). Veal Parmigiano ($16.95) is appealing, the cheese, sauce, and breading clinging to the tender meat. The pleasing cheesecake ($3.95) and tiramisu ($3.95) notwithstanding, the thick and soused zabaglione ($4.95) is a must. It's too big by half for its tall glass dish.

Upper East Side

Guastavino's

Opened on February 14, 2000, Sir Terence Conran's Valentine to New York was named for Rafael Guastavino, the Catalan architect who designed the tile vaulting for the Grand Central Oyster Bar (see p.194), and the soffit soaring over the restaurant and beneath the Queensborough Bridge. Once occupied by the produce vendors of Bridgemarket, the arcaded space languished as a storage facility until investors led by London's lord of home design and restaurant development leased a 25,000-square-foot share for the 300-seat brasserie and the dressier, 100-seat Club Guastavino. The tile vaults, limestone walls, and 40ft columns that support them were left bare to dwarf the sleekly sculpted fixtures, both in furniture and flesh, of the sexy, loud, elongated bar.

Cost	$22–80

Address 409 East 59th St, between York & 1st Aves
℡212/980-2455
Transportation N,R,W to Lexington Ave; 4,5,6 to 59th St
Open Mon–Wed 11.30am–2.30pm & 5.30–10.30pm, Thurs & Fri 11.30am–2.30pm & 5.30–11.30pm, Sat & Sun 11.30am–3.30pm & 5.30–10.30pm
Accepts All major credit cards
Reservations Suggested

The disappointment of downstairs dining is that the overhead mezzanine—where you'll find Club Guastavino—cuts off the view and expanse of the arcades. Consolation comes with the knowledge that the brasserie shares with its upscale companion the same executive chef, Daniel Orr, a small-town Indiana boy who made his New York name at the venerable French restaurant La Grenouille. His history suits a menu that blends sophistication with down-home values in such appetizers as portobello stuffy (a vegetarian riff on Rhode Island stuffed clams; $9.50) and fried, cornmeal-coated green tomatoes with pickled pepper sauce and Indiana goat cheese ($8). For a spin on New York Jewish soul food, he makes one great matzoh ball for his chicken soup ($7.25).

Low-end main courses pick up on similar themes. Fried catfish, a Southern classic, acquires Northern outerwear, namely a batter of Brooklyn ale, to go with hand-cut fries ($13.75). The center-cut pork chop ($18.50) spends days in a brine of bourbon, maple syrup, and orange juice before it acquires its oven-roasted glaze. And the potato-chip-crusted, pan-roasted chicken cutlet ($17.50) is terrifically trashy. To close in a similar vein, there's the burnt vanilla ice cream ($8.25), a New Orleans hybrid of British Trinity cream and French crème brûlée.

Jo Jo

Jo Jo is short for Jean-Georges Vongerichten as well as the name of the townhouse duplex where, beginning in 1991, he blazed a new East Side trail for worldly and wily French cuisine. Although the Alsatian had already substituted vegetable juices and herb-infused oils and vinaigrettes for creamy sauces and heavy meat stocks at a luxurious midtowner called Lafayette, it was in this snug and, for a while at least, reasonably priced bistro that he pioneered his penchant for spare but flavor-concentrated dishes with Asian intonation. The same minimalism is not quite true of the million-dollar, 2001 makeover. Velours, silks, and brocades in reds, oranges, and plums outfit its rooms like those of a *Belle Époque* bordello too tiny for double beds. Waitresses are dressed in lacy black slips.

Cost	Lunch $30–90
	Dinner $45–100

Address 160 East 64th St, between Lexington & 3rd Aves
℡212/223-5656
Transportation F,N,R,W to Lexington Ave; 4,5 to 59th St; 6 to 68th St
Open Mon–Fri noon–3pm & 6–11pm, Sat & Sun 11.30am–4pm & 6–11pm
Accepts All major credit cards
Reservations Required

FRENCH

Only on the East Side, where the two economic classes are old money and new money, is it not a stretch to term an establishment with a $35 entree a "bistro." Still, the sensational $20 prix fixe lunch gives bargain access to world-class cuisine. Chef de cuisine Alex Powell directs a team that turns out distinctive dishes which get better the better you know them. Two longstanding starters are Peekytoe crabmeat with cumin crisps, mustard tarragon butter, and diced mango ($14), and faintly sweet, orange-dusted shrimp ($14). Pumpkin and mascarpone ravioli with fried sage and brown butter ($10) are a temporary show.

With entrees, Jean-Georges augured the trend whereby side attractions command as much attention as star ingredients. In one take on duck breast ($26), the accompaniments are a honeyed, gingered shallot confit and a phyllo-pouch of ground duck leg and foie gras. Pepper-crusted venison ($29) is impeccable, yet it's the poire au lard, a hash of pear and bacon, that you will tell your grandchildren about. Jo Jo also set off the national craze for warm, underbaked chocolate cake. Though divine as ever, better to get in on the ground—or second—floor with the roasted pineapple bread pudding ($9) or the sour cream cheesecake done up with blueberry compote and kumquat sorbet ($9).

MEXICAN

Maya

This East Sider Mexican has the look and lineage of greatness. Chef-owner Richard Sandoval knows where he comes from and where he's going. At two prior restaurants (Savann and Savann East), the 1992 winner of Mexico's National Toque D'Oro possessed an uncommon understanding of the contemporary cooking that mid-range diners want and the price they are willing (long waits, squeezed tables) and not willing ($15 appetizers, $20-plus entrees) to pay in order to get it. At Maya

Cost	$35–75

Address 1191 1st Ave, between 64th & 65th Sts
℡212/585-1818
Transportation F to Lexington Ave-63rd St; 6 to 68th St
Open Sun–Thurs 5–10pm, Fri & Sat 5–11.30pm
Accepts All major credit cards
Reservations Suggested

he's gone for shorter waits, well-spaced tables, and bigger checks. In a comfortable dining room, Mayan masks are bordered by blue frames painted onto coral-colored walls. Earthenware, candlesticks, and the volcanic-rock mortars called *molcajetes* (for guacamole) were commissioned from renowned silver designer Emilia Castillo. How you feel about the guacamole service will define how you feel about Maya and its somewhat polished take on Mexican food. Rather than serve the dip directly in its native mixing bowl, they place it in a silver cup propped inside. While some may see this as bringing uptown elegance to south-of-the-border tradition, others see a pricey ($9) order of guacamole.

Fortunately, not all appetizers are so confined. The chile relleno ($11.50), a stuffed and roasted poblano pepper cushioned with superb black-bean purée, is bursting with shrimp, scallops, and calamari that spill out into a cilantro oil salsa. The tamal al chipotle ($8.50), a moist tamale filled with shredded chicken, is diagonally striped with delightfully smoky chipotle sauce and crema fresca. Pan-seared tuna ($11.95) has you eating the crunchy, spicy jicama slaw before the rare strips of fish.

Main courses feature impressive architecture and color, sometimes at the expense of the star ingredients. You remember the tampiquena ($23.95) more for its poblano-peppered potato gratin and mole poblano enchilada than its filet mignon. Choose instead the grilled shrimp with a goat cheese-stuffed roasted Anaheim chile ($22.95) and the steak chilaquiles ($22.50) layered with sliced tortillas, black bean purée, crema fresca, and Manchego cheese. The okay desserts ($6.50) may be as simple as a rich flan or as dramatic as sweet bananas flambéed with tequila.

Le Pain Quotidien

Despite the flourishing presence of five additional locations in Manhattan and another 24 stores in Belgium alone, it is hard to believe that the Pain Quotidien just two blocks from the Metropolitan Museum of Art is not the only one of its kind. Its long wooded communal table, aged floorboards, sienna walls, country-style antiques, and rustic baskets of freshly baked breads and rolls are not the stuff of which food chains are usually made. Somehow, Alain Coumont, who opened the Brussels flagship in 1990, has managed to duplicate

Cost	$14–35

Address 1131 Madison Ave
between 84th & 85th Sts; plus
other locations
☎212/327-4900
Transportation 6 to 86th St
Open Mon–Fri
7.30am–7.30pm, Sat & Sun
8am–7.30pm
Accepts All major credit cards
Reservations Not accepted

his cafe/bakery without sacrificing its local charm. Quite the contrary. Le Pain Quotidien is the un-Starbucks, a gathering place that, like a skilled painter who adores his subject, both absorbs and greatly enriches the collective character and color of the surroundings.

Little actual cooking is done on the premises, excepting a soup du jour ($4.95/$6.95). What the kitchen knows how to do best is assemble superior ingredients on tartines (open-faced sandwiches), in beautiful salads, and atop charcuterie platters and cheeseboards. Several sandwiches are habit-forming, among them a thick-cut pleasantly salty jambon de Paris (cooked pressed ham) with three separate fine mustards ($7.95); Scottish smoked salmon with fresh dill ($12.75); and the subtle combo of ricotta, radishes, and scallions ($7.75) that ought to be a rite of spring. Among the platters there is no surer way to transform a thirty-minute lunch into a picnic than the assiette Toscane (Tuscan platter; $14.50) from which ricotta, pesto, black olive tapenade (that's Provençal, but no one would dare send it back), sundried tomatoes, prosciutto, and Parmesan may be spread atop a long sliced baguette.

Served with butter and jam, slabs of the fabulous breads ($2.95)—baguette, wheat levain, peasant rye, walnut, five-grain—are a natural for French-style breakfasts with a café au lait ($2.50) for dunking or, during museum breaks, with a Belgian hot chocolate ($3.25). The flaky croissant and brioche (both $2.95) are among the best in town, but it's the pain au chocolat ($2.95) of which there can be no other.

Upper East Side

Payard Bistro & Patisserie

To meet the public's growing appetite for homey desserts, many top pastry chefs are turning to grandparents rather than grand masters for inspiration. Fruit crumbles and bread puddings abound. François Payard has long been following his grandfather's example—the distinction being that *his* papi ran a celebrated pastry shop on the French Riviera. Forget cozy and quaint. Payard the patisserie is a boutique on the level of FAO Schwarz and Tiffany, its precious toys—chocolates, pastries, candies, cakes, breads—tantalizingly displayed in look-but-don't-touch show-

Cost	Lunch $25–75
	Dinner $45–80

Address 1032 Lexington Ave, between 73rd & 74th Sts
℡212/717-5252
Transportation 6 to 77th St
Open Mon–Thurs
noon–10.30pm, Fri & Sat
noon–11pm
Accepts All major credit cards
Reservations Required

cases. The goodies even shape the decoration of the mezzanine bistro. Croissant forms are molded into classical friezes. Blown-glass globe lights are shaped like cream puffs. How fortunate for Payard that his pastries are world-class. Anything less than spectacular would be a spectacular letdown.

With the dot-encircled "P" logo imprinted everywhere but on the toilet paper, it was initially difficult for the bistro's chef, Philippe Bertineau, to make a name—or even an initial—for himself. His first appetizers were too fussy and intricate, as if he were trying to match the stylized precision of the pastries. But he soon made the transition to rustic and robust, instilling Payard with the soul if not the humility of a bistro. There is no comfier kick-off to a winter dinner than celery root, chestnut, and mushroom soup ($7) or a twice-baked upside down cheese soufflé with Parmesan sauce and truffle oil ($12).

It took only a couple of years for several entrees to become signature dishes. If Monsieur B erased the braised lamb shank ($26) or four-peppercorn-sauced sirloin ($29) from the menu there'd be hell to pay. There was practically a riot when he replaced the halibut that enriched the bouillabaisse ($25) with Chilean sea bass. The $34 pre-theater prix fixe, with seatings at 5.45pm and 6pm, makes the prices more palatable. And the lunchtime Croque Monsieur ($12 with a seasonal salad and herb vinaigrette) is hardly a lesser pleasure. Desserts ($9) are great, from the warm banana tart and white chocolate mousse combination to the passion fruit gratin, after which a dot-encircled P will be forever emblazoned on your heart.

UPTOWN

Upper East Side
UPTOWN

Upper East Side

Q Café

(icon) Don't be alarmed by the apparent radioactivity of the house mojito or what it says about Q Café. The Cuban cocktail of rum, fresh mint, sugar, and soda gets its uranium-like fluorescence from a glow stick. More to the point, that neon swizzle should not be seen as an indication this is yet another singles bar masquerading as a restaurant. Q Café has a real chef and a setting to inspire her. Broad-paddled ceiling fans spin slowly over a warmly modern dining room with dark-wood tables, geometric-patterned banquette fabrics, and a series of modern yet earthy art abstractions. One such wall piece has a waterfall that drips down the front, inevitably necessitating an extra trip to the powder room.

Cost	$30–70

Address 244 East 79th St, between 2nd & 3rd Aves
☎212/717-6500
Transportation 6 to 77th St
Open Sun noon–4pm & 5–10pm, Tues–Thurs 5–11pm, Fri & Sat 5pm–midnight
Accepts All major credit cards
Reservations Suggested

NEW AMERICAN

Chef-owner Myriam Corboda, easy to spot with her beet red hair, has put her native Venezuelan cooking on the back burner. Her intelligent and concise menu is a worldly collection with Latin, Mediterranean, and tropical accents. Even her oyster ceviche appetizer ($10) seems to have been uprooted from its South American foundation. The yummy crêpes filled with corn and melted goat cheese ($7) have no nationality. Neither does the mango tango ($7), a chunky toss of mango and cucumber that picks up a North African rhythm from its cilantro harissa vinaigrette. Entrees are no easier to peg. Macadamia-crusted mahi mahi ($18) matches its nutty crunch to a truffled potato purée and a spicy Thai sauce. Ravioli Q ($14) is a smoky powerhouse of ravioli filled with an innocent white bean purée. Only the grilled sirloin ($18) accompanied by chorizo, chimichurri sauce, and long-and-lean fries has a continental identity. The best dessert is the deep, coconut-infused crème brûlée ($6) served in a hollowed coconut shell over ice. But the warm chocolate cake ($6) with hot chocolate ganache and superfluous strawberry sauce will not disappoint, either.

   One aspect of Q that is unmistakably Latin is the $10 prix fixe Sunday brunch. If the menu's name—"Sunday Latin Brunch"—doesn't convince you of this fact, the cachapas (sweet corncakes with white cheese), emapanadas (beef, black bean, and cheese), arepas and huevos rancheros surely will.

267

Upper East Side

Sassy's Sliders

Naming the three colloquialisms for the bite-size burgers of the pre-McDonald's era—"belly bombers," "belly busters", and "sliders"—is no problem. But explaining the origin of those terms is a difficult task valiantly undertaken by Sassy's co-owner Michael Ronis. "It was called a slider for the way it slid down your throat," he explains, "and actually for how it slid out the other way, too." The same goes for the other terms, which accurately describe an attack by these deliberately greasy burgers on our sys-

Cost	$4–12

Address 1530 3rd Ave,
between 86th & 87th Sts
☎212/828-6900
Transportation 6 to 86th St
Open Sun–Thurs
11.30am–10pm, Fri & Sat
11.30am–11pm
Accepts Cash only
Reservations Not accepted

tems. The pioneer who first launched this digestive assault on America was J. Walter Anderson. In 1916 he divided unwieldy amounts of ground meat into smaller patties, mashed in shredded onions, seared them quickly on both sides, and thus invented what soon became the White Castle belly bomber. Exhibiting a flash of genius, he placed freshly baked buns atop the puny patties as they cooked to absorb the beef flavor, the onions, and, yes, the grease.

Sassy's revives the spirit of belly-busting burger joints put to pasture by franchises like McDonald's and Burger King. (White Castle is still around, but it long ago stopped making quality sliders, partly due to its substituting frozen meat for fresh.) Sassy's 89¢ sliders are made with freshly ground beef, turkey, or, in the veggie version, grated carrots, zucchini, Chinese cabbage, soy, and pickles. Like silver dollar pancakes, these sliders somehow taste different to their larger forebears, possibly because they're a hoot to gobble down. The skinny fries ($1.59/$1.99) are dandy; the sweet potato fries ($1.89/$2.39), uncharacteristically crisp. A $16.99 combo with fifteen burgers and three large fries easily feeds five children or one inebriated undergraduate.

Situated seconds away from several multiplexes, this reasonably fast food outlet is ideal for a quick snack before or during a screening. They're certainly less noisy to consume than a box of popcorn. The brightly lit joint's curvy blue Formica counters, enamel-like white wall panels, and cheery menu graphics represent an inviting, 1950s celebration of J. Walter Anderson's easy-in/easy-out legacy. But the absence of public restrooms on the premises can be somewhat less amusing.

Spice

🍴 With the advent and spawning of Spice (there are branches in the Village and Chelsea), Thai food finally attains the junky status of face-stuffing Chinese takeout. But order this cheap chow to go and you're missing half the noisy, stinky, crispy fun. In a loud, funky, post-industrial cafe redolent of soy sauce, the twisted legs of a spidery lighting fixture point low-wattage bulbs toward stainless-steel tables and a cement floor. For self-respecting diners concerned with outward appearances

| Cost | Lunch $10–20 |
| | Dinner $18–40 |

Address 1411 2nd Ave, between 73rd & 74th Sts; plus other locations

☏212/988-5348

Transportation 6 to 77th St

Open Daily noon–10.45pm

Accepts All major credit cards

Reservations Not accepted

and inward consumptions, the cool, dark and somewhat austere setting provides stylish cover for an hour of spicy, sweet, sour, salty, greasy, and near-instant gratification.

Constructing a meal without fried foods is possible. You could conceivably start with steamed vegetable dumplings ($4) and move on to a credible steamed fish with vegetables, ginger, and black beans ($16). But such a noble act would require skipping all the compulsory appetizers: crisp, hot spring rolls packed with carrot, cabbage, and vermicelli ($4); ground shrimp and crab fritters with sweet-and-sour dip ($4); Thai crêpes filled with shredded chicken, peanuts, and sweet chile sauce ($5); fabulously crunchy calamari ($5). Even the imaginative Caesar salad ($4) with miso ginger dressing owes its appeal to fried wonton croutons.

Likewise, big portions of noodles are nobody's idea of spa cuisine. The peanut-packed pad Thai ($8) and broad "drunk man" noodles with basil and shrimp ($8) satisfy the all-important junk quotient with a doggy bag's worth to spare. For theatrical excess, you can't improve upon the crispy duck ($13), a vertical sphere with broccoli, celery, carrot, baby corn, pineapple chunks, Thai basil, and fresh ginger piled over fatty slices of duck breast—that is, of course, unless you were to spoon it over a side of "six o'clock" fried rice with chile, onion, and basil. Dessert brings the dinner full circle: sweet banana is rolled in a spring roll wrapper and cooked to order in hot oil ($3). See now why it may be better to enjoy this good-and-greasy stuff within the obscurity of Spice, where the delicious guilt is shared, than do takeout and risk going public.

SPANISH

Taperia Madrid

(🍴) Taperia Madrid could pass for a classic Spanish tapas bar of the type favored by Ernest Hemingway. With its decorative hams that seem to predate the hand-painted mosaics, its rustic candelabra, and old-fashioned matador portraits, Antonio Francesco needed only to carve the initials EMH into one of the communal tables to complete the delightful deception. He might have done away with another piece of authenticity, however—the roguishly cramped seating. Yes, hardwood benches are as traditional of this institution as the tapas (hors d'oeuvres or small "raciones") served to accompany a glass of sherry, wine, or beer. But the cellar's kindergarten stools could give even a master yogi tendinitis in both knees. Perhaps Francesco's greatest success is in understanding that many of his young and restless Upper East Side clients would rather gulp flavored vodkas than sip imported sherries.

Cost	$25–60

Address 1471 2nd Ave, between 76th & 77th Sts
☎212/794-2923
Transportation 6 to 77th St
Open Mon–Thurs 5.30pm–midnight, Fri & Sat 5.30pm–2am, Sun 5pm–midnight
Accepts All major credit cards
Reservations Not accepted

Ordering from chef Diego Gonzales's menu of 25 tapas is challenging on two counts: firstly, though winners greatly outnumber losers, the variation in quality is staggering. Secondly, as you shout in your order above the Excedrin-grade clamor, your request may be misinterpreted. This could be calamitous—the difference between "abuela" (blood sausage) and "angiulas" (eels) is $24.50. The cold dish to avoid at all costs is the salad of tough-to-swallow bacalao (salt cod) tossed with roasted pimiento peppers. Fortunately, Spain's national racion, tortilla Espanola ($5.45), is superbly realized. The cubes of this Spanish potato omelet are as fresh and moist as can be. Its only competition in the cold category comes from the marinated fresh anchovies ($9.45).

Two hot tapas elevate the entire experience. Gambas a la sal de mare ($9.45) consists of eight sizzling prawns blast-sautéed over coarse sea salt. The snappy, skin-on, piping-hot prawns are packed with sweet pleasure. The pan-seared chipirones ($7.45) are remarkably tender baby squid delivered with the light tang of sherry vinaigrette. Another hit is the bocadillo ($8.95), a sandwich of grilled beef buried in onions and roasted peppers. And the casserole of unshelled Manila clams and fava beans ($7.45) is appealing, if only to sop up its peppery, garlicky sauce. Desserts are dreadful.

Trata

🍴 It would be all too easy to fall in love with Trata, as you might an alluring companion with Aegean-blue eyes, on the first dinner date. This hit spin-off of the Greek seafood house Milos duplicates its model's market-style, you-pick-it/we-grill-it system, only it doesn't require you raid your savings to pay for it. Sadly, however, Trata's handsome informality notwithstanding, it is almost as easy to become disillusioned on the second date. The trouble is, when you see an ice chest of trophy fish displayed in the middle of a restaurant named after a Greek fishing boat and decorated with photos of Greek fishing villages, anything less than consummately cooked seafood can bring about distress. Luckily, the happy memory of several winsome appetizers ultimately wins over conflicted diners.

Cost	Lunch $20–40
	Dinner $30–65

Address 1331 2nd Ave, between 70th & 71st Sts
☎212/535-3800
Transportation 6 to 68th St
Open Sun–Thurs noon–4pm & 5–11pm, Fri & Sat noon–midnight
Accepts All major credit cards
Reservations Required

GREEK

Smooth, bread-thickened taramasalata (fish roe dip; $6.75) and equally solid tzatziki (yogurt and cucumber dip; $6.75) are indispensable starters. To that duo you should add a golden triangle of saganaki (fried kefalograviera cheese; $8.50), a crabcake ($15.50) so packed with crabmeat it barely holds together, impossibly tender grilled octopus ($11.95), and a quintet of fresh imported sardines ($9.50) that are grilled to perfection. The entree list is dominated by whole fish hand-picked from the display and grilled to order. Mostly seasoned with capers, lemon, and olive oil, the daily catches are priced by the pound (up to $20) and may include such Mediterranean imports as the delicate loup de mer or the versatile royal dorade. Looking for the best specimen? A loup de mer would be singled out for the tautness and brilliance of its gray-silver skin; a royal dorade for the brightness and color of its eyes and the firmness of its flesh.

The kitchen does not do as well with alternative main courses, whose ubiquitous mix of veggies makes things seem repetitive. For a sweet finish there is an enormous wedge of good baklava ($6.50). And two desserts will have you falling in love with Trata all over again: an ultra-rich and creamy Greek yogurt with Greek honey ($6.75) and delectably warm loukoumades (fried honey balls; $7).

Zócalo

(🍴) The fixation on authenticity that dogs most commentary on Mexican food is a cliché, be it from the Mexicophile who resents seeing one of the world's great cuisines reduced to cheesy slop, or the tequila-toting tourist who gets off a plane from Mexico and alerts every passing motorist on the Van Wyck Expressway that the Mexican food up here is nothing like it is down there. But who among us can really tell what is authentic anymore? Every moderate-to-upscale Mexican restaurant has a style and regional focus totally different from

Cost	$35–75

Address 174 East 82nd St,
between Lexington & 3rd Aves
☎212/717-7772
Transportation 4,5,6 to 86th
St
Open Mon–Thurs 6–11pm, Fri
& Sat 6–11.30pm, Sun
5.30–10.30pm
Accepts All major credit cards
Reservations Suggested

the next. Zócalo's regional feel is unmistakably Upper East Side, from the front bar holding fifty tequilas to the cozy middle room and the comfortable, high-ceilinged, stucco-walled rear dining room painted to match the color of the blood orange Margaritas. Service is solicitous, even on frenzied weekend nights.

Chef Ivy Stark's food is both robust and stylish without overreaching for refinement. Chomp on warm, freshly fried tortilla chips and smoky chipotle salsa while you choose. You can forget the usual chicken stuffing for flautas. Zócalo's are rolled over braised short ribs and sided with guacamole and charred tomato salsa ($7.50). When crab comes into play in a full-plate-sized quesadilla ($8.95), the fresh lump crabmeat is found both inside and outside the tortillas. And sautéed calamari acquires Spanish chorizo, white beans, piquillo peppers, *and* grilled bread ($9).

Tampiqueña, a chile-rubbed grilled hanger steak with a wine-cured goat cheese quesadilla, guacamole, rice, and beans ($22.50), is just the beginning of the beefy excitement. Should the unbelievable roast garlic-and jalapeno-stuffed rib steak ($28.95) with chimichurri sauce and smashed potatoes be running the night of your visit you're in luck. As for fish, red snapper over banana leaves with coconut rice has a pleasantly sour passion fruit sauce ($24) that's not the least bit cloying, and the great mahi mahi tacos ($21) are terrific. The must-have dessert is a smooth and rich flan ($6.50).

There's another Zócalo in Grand Central Terminal, Midtown East (☎212/687-5666).

Upper West Side

Artie's Delicatessen

Red neon letters set against a gleaming white porcelain backdrop spell out the ultimate tribute to a late great restaurateur. Artie's represents the unrealized dream of Artie Cutler, co-creator of the seminal Upper West Side eateries Carmine's (see p.208), Dock's Oyster Bar, and Ollie's Noodle Shop. The hidden subplot behind this Jewish deli involves a secret pastrami formula bought at a close-out auction by co-owner Jeffrey Bank. The uncertain quality of the recipe said to be from the old Lower East Side deli Schmulke Bernstein is almost beside the point. That Artie's is curing its own pastrami, a rarity nowadays, is alone cause for celebration.

Cost	$10–35

Address 2290 Broadway at 83rd St

☎212/579-5959

Transportation 1,2 to 86th St

Open Sun–Thurs 9am–11pm, Fri & Sat 9am–midnight

Accepts All major credit cards

With solid Eastern-European Jewish (non-kosher) cooking from chef/co-owner Chris Metz, Artie's has become a valuable neighborhood resource with the obligatory hanging salamis, frankfurter grill, and appetizing display case. The dining area's Formica tables, mirrored walls, and snug booths are the modest trappings of a retro coffee shop distinguished by oblate globe lights.

Thin, uniform, peppery, deep-pink slices of house-cured pastrami are piled high on rye bread ($7.75). The sandwich is best when carved fresh out of the steamer, which is not always guaranteed. It's worth insisting your pastrami be warm. The corned beef sandwich ($7.50) is a tender compromise between juicy and lean, and the terrific hot brisket of beef sandwich ($7.50) is gratifyingly undry, meaning that the meat does not absolutely need to be doused in gravy, lathered with mustard, or detonated with horseradish. A pot of sensationally tender flanken ($13.95), the boiled beef dish that is the Jewish version of short ribs, is combined with hearty mushroom barley soup. Chicken in the pot ($12.95) contains smooth hunks of white and dark meat, lightly salted chicken soup, and terrific matzoh balls of the floater (soft and light) rather than sinker (firm and dense) variety. Satisfying sides on top of the gratis coleslaw (great!) and smallish, uncrunchy pickles include golden French fries in the traditional half-inch-square cut ($2.50) and semi-smooth chopped liver ($4.95). Homemade chocolate ruggelach ($3.25) and diner-style rice pudding ($2.95) get the dessert nods over ordinary cheesecake ($3.95).

Avenue

With something in its product line for every conceivable appetite, Avenue once aspired to be the Microsoft of Upper West Side neighborhood eateries. It was something of a surprise that the combination pastry shop/lunch counter/gourmet takeout/terrace cafe/tapas bar/French bistro/bakery wasn't also equipped to handle the dry cleaning. Since Christina Kelly replaced Scott Campbell as chef, ambitions have become more realistic. Avenue's versatility is reflected in a decor that shifts according to one's perspectives. Some may look at the brick walls, old photos, and homespun fabrics and see a New England country cafe. Others will view the antique chandeliers and mirrors, dark-wood furnishings, and see a sophisticated Manhattan restaurant.

| Cost | Lunch $10–30 |
| | Dinner $35–75 |

Address 520 Columbus Ave at 85th St
☎212/579-3194
Transportation B,C,1,2 to 86th St
Open Sun–Fri 10am–4pm & 5–11pm, Sat 10am–4pm & 5pm–midnight
Accepts All major credit cards
Reservations Suggested

Kelly's cooking is characterized by rich, deep flavors and multiple textures, perfectly demonstrated in the panko-crusted cod with butter roasted potatoes and fava beans ($20). Her playful side comes out in homemade cinnamon donuts and orange, lemon, and cherry lollipops. Basically, if you see something you like the look of, go for it: some people change their bed linens less frequently than she does her menus. The grazing menu, divided between baby bear (appetizer), papa bear (main course) and mama bear (either-or) portions has wisely been abandoned but not, thankfully, the salty fried calamari ($9) lifted from it. The golden rings are gathered in a metal cup and paired with a spicy lemongrass cilantro dip. Most other seasonal starters and mains (24 in all) have been replaced a few times over the years.

Avenue is a great place to bring kids for lunch and brunch, when the blasé service is less of an issue. For lunch, the grilled chicken club with avocado, hickory-smoked bacon, and haricots verts on focaccia ($7.75) is fantastic. Choose-your-own salad combos ($7.75 for two; $9.50 for three) might encompass Asian cucumber, curry chicken with Granny Smith apples, and a Caesar dense with homemade garlic focaccia croutons. For brunch, the asparagus Benedict is a smart alternative to the standard version, with house-smoked salmon and dill sauce substituting for hickory-smoked ham and Hollandaise.

Barney Greengrass

The last remnants of wallpaper depicting the New Orleans French Quarter are now taped to the walls of the drab Barney Greengrass dining room. Third-generation owner Gary Greengrass wisely has no intention of papering over the homely and incongruous covering before he has to. Likewise, the wood-grained Formica tables and wainscoting are not going anywhere anytime soon. These homely, fluorescent-lit fittings are so closely associated with "The Sturgeon King" that the devoted throng waiting outside for a weekend table could easily turn into an angry mob were any renovations proposed. Tellingly, when the second Barney Greengrass opened in Beverly Hills in the 1990s, it was outfitted with sleek, stylish decor—and employees. For the anti-snob snobs (forgive them their acronym) of the Upper West Side, it's an unsettling harbinger of what could happen here if Gary did not hold the line.

Cost $9–25

Address 541 Amsterdam Ave, between 86th & 87th Sts
℡212/724-4707
Transportation 1,2,B,C to 86th St
Open Tues–Fri 8.30am–4pm, Sat & Sun 8.30am–5pm
Accepts All major credit cards
Reservations Not accepted

JEWISH DELI

The furnishings inside the adjacent retail deli date back to 1929. Behind vintage marble counters, a wide array of high-quality, premium-priced goods are stocked in white-enamel, black-trimmed Art Deco cabinets, shelving, and refrigerator cases. On weekends, diner-style chairs and tables are set up on its terrazzo floors to increase seating capacity. Still, the buttery, thinly sliced, oil-glistening Nova Scotia smoked salmon somehow tastes better in the New Orleans room. It may be ordered as a single-person appetizer sandwich ($10 including cream cheese and a bagel) or within spectacular, two-to-three-person smoked fish platters—Nova solo ($21), Nova and smoked whitefish ($23.50), Nova and world-class smoked sturgeon ($29.50)—including two bagels, cream cheese, black olives, sliced tomatoes, sliced onions, and coleslaw. Another Nova specialty is the "LEO" scramble of lox (smoked salmon), eggs, and onions ($12).

Among non-fish selections, the coarse-textured chopped chicken liver ($6.75 with rye bread or a bagel) is deservedly legendary. Whatever their order, a few discerning Greengrass regulars address the quandary of increasingly large, bready, and bloated bagels by asking to have them sliced in thirds rather than halves. The three-piece bagel happens to be a perfect fit for the three-slice Nova appetizer.

277

FRENCH

Cafe Luxembourg

In a dining guide organized by location, it's natural for many of the restaurants to be singled out for the way they reflect the personality of their surroundings. This bistro is extraordinary for the extent to which its character differs from that of a neighborhood disparaged for its dearth of both fine and hip dining. It's surprising that the Postal Service will even deliver mail addressed to Cafe Luxembourg within the Upper West Side's 10023 zip code. The food itself is somewhat overpriced and sometimes less than wonderful. But the glamor radi-

| Cost | Lunch $20–65 |
| | Dinner $30–80 |

Address 200 West 70th St, between Amsterdam & West End Aves
☎212/873-7411
Transportation 1,2,3 to 72nd St
Open Daily 9am–midnight
Accepts All major credit cards
Reservations Required

ated by this very downtownish translation of 1930s Montparnasse is a two-decades-old constant. The fantasy of Cafe Luxembourg is depicted in its own Brassai-like postcard of three plump, naked women standing against the zinc bar. The reality comes alive in a beige-tiled room of caned chairs, terrazzo flooring, arched windows, and Deco blinds whose soft, tawny lighting flatters the complexion of smartly attired New Yorkers, some of whom work at nearby Lincoln Center and ABC News.

It's always fashionably correct to order dinner from the "brasserie" menu no matter the depth of your pockets. It features a commendable lobster roll ($16) and smoked salmon sandwich ($13.50) as well as the thick, juice-dripping Luxemburger ($12.75 with amazing fries). The $38.50 prix fixe is peculiar, as you'd pay no more if you chose its best selections—cornmeal-crusted oysters with saffron aioli ($9.75) and lightly crisped, succulent, herb-roasted free-range chicken with sautéed spinach and creamy mashed potatoes ($18.50)—a la carte. A solid alternative is the grilled and silky salmon with lobster vinaigrette, fennel, and fava beans ($21).

Among lunch and brunch enticements there is an excellent and crusty BLT sandwich made with smoked Danish bacon and arugula ($11 with fries or salad), a superb salade Niçoise made-to-order with fresh tuna, and the same Luxemburger and desserts (about $8)—crème brûlée, German chocolate cake, lemon tart—that you find in the un-West Side-like evening.

Cooke's Corner

The name doesn't sound any better after you hear the story behind it. Chef James Yacyshyn and his wife Maggie Long met Brian Cooke aboard an Antarctica cruise and later named their restaurant after the cartoon that the British writer had penned for the London Daily Mail. (Lucky thing Charles Engelhard wasn't the cartoonist they befriended, or the bistro might be called "Absolute Tripe.") Copper-colored silk curtains at the storefront window and beige leatherette banquettes behind the tightly spaced, oak-inlaid tables were meant to import a downtown modern feel. But Cooke's Corner works better if you place it firmly in its Upper West Side context and praise it as a casual, scaled-down alternative to neighborhood phenomenon Ouest (see p.285).

Cost	$25–75

Address 618 Amsterdam Ave at 90th St
℡212/712-2872
Transportation 1,2,B,C to 86th St
Open Mon 5–10pm, Tues–Thurs noon–3pm & 5–10pm, Fri & Sat noon–3pm & 5–11pm, Sun 5–9pm
Accepts All major credit cards
Reservations Suggested

NEW AMERICAN

Local residents Yacyshyn and Long were frustrated by the dearth of dining options in these parts in the late 1990s, and decided to open a place where they themselves would want to eat. (Perhaps it would have been easier to move?) Though ethnic and theme eateries flourished, not many local kitchens were then devoted to the straightforward, contemporary American cooking thriving elsewhere in the city. Today, starters like sizzling tiger shrimp in garlic ($9), house-cured gravlax with mustard dill sauce ($7), and a trio of crisp goat cheese cakes with a salad of endive, tomato, black olive, and garlic croutons ($7) would stand out in any precinct. Yacyshyn knows the flavor associations he's after and won't allow himself—or his diners—to get distracted.

Servers rightly push the "four-hour" braised beef with red wine horseradish sauce and spätzle ($15). The time-softened meat is their boss' resonant response to Ouest's braised short ribs. But if there's crooning to be done, why not for the maple-glazed, pan-seared salmon and melange of steamed greens ($15) that answers to no one? The maple body treatment adds just the right measure of sticky sweetness. At $24, the herb-crusted rack of lamb is a tad pricey. But should a plate of this perfectly pink version pass by you, you are unlikely to do the same to it. Lemon tart tops off the okay desserts ($5).

Upper West Side

Flor de Mayo

No one could possibly confuse this budget eatery with the chic fusion restaurant Asia de Cuba (see p.238), even though their personalities are split along the same cultural lines. Still, when this lunchtime stalwart moved to its present location more than ten years ago, the polished parquet floor and oak-trimmed laminate signaled a major upgrading of a fading cheap-eats genre. Today, the color television stays tuned to CNBC, allowing diners and waiters to follow the fortunes of their stock portfolios as they consume or serve $4.95 lunch specials. And Flor de Mayo is different too from most of the remaining cheap "China-Latina" joints—unlike the Cuban-Chinese who had twice fled Communist revolutions, Flor de Mayo's owners immigrated from Peru.

Cost	Lunch $8–35
	Dinner $12–35

Address 2651 Broadway, between 100th & 101st Sts
☎212/663-5520
Transportation 1 to 103rd St
Open Daily noon–midnight
Accepts All major credit cards
Reservations Not accepted

Many don't even bother to open the menu, much less pay attention to its Chinese half. They request such Cuban standbys as ropa vieja (shredded beef; $8.15), picadillo (chopped beef; $7.75), or unexpectedly moist pernil asado (roast ham; $8.15). All are served with sweet plantains or a steaming-hot heap of rice (white or yellow). Pink or black beans ($1.20) you order on the side. The dry-spiced but not spicy pollo a la brasa is one of the best rotisserie birds ($6.50 for a half-chicken). You apply the heat yourself by dunking bites of chicken into a Peruvian dip of minced onions, chile, lime juice, and vinegar. Whatever you order, you will need an avocado and lemon side salad ($3.50).

The Chinese food is actually far better than most give it credit for. Ask for sautéed bok choy ($6.75), even when ordering Cuban (there's not much greenery in that neighborhood), and choose if you want it cooked with garlic or ginger and scallions. Of the Hong Kong specials, king do gai ($8.95) delights as much for the sweet-and-sour dipping sauce you can spoon over the rice as for the crisp and moist fried chicken nuggets. And nostalgic hankerings for greasy roast pork lo mein and shrimp chow mein ($8.35) are indulged in a New York minute.

There's another Flor de Mayo at 484 Amsterdam Ave, Upper West Side (☎212/787-3388).

Gennaro

Gennaro Picone needs a wake-up call. As the man behind an Italian restaurant that makes nearly every published short list of affordable places to eat, the Sicilian immigrant is something of a living legend on the Upper West Side. True, nobody has been seen kissing his ring. But there are probably devout diners who would throw their raincoats over a puddle he was about to step in if it got them a table pronto. All that said, the price of dining-on-the-cheap at Gennaro

Cost	$20-40

Address 665 Amsterdam Ave, between 92nd & 93rd Sts
℡212/665-5348
Transportation 1,2,3,B,C to 96th St
Open Daily 5.30-11pm
Accepts All major credit cards
Reservations Not accepted

ITALIAN

is climbing. The waits of up to an hour are part of the deal. People expect it. But the slapdash and arrogant treatment you're apt to experience once seated is deplorable. During one recent visit, a busboy asked permission to move a table and chairs a few feet to open up a clogged service lane. Three minutes later, a waiter dragged the table back to clear the narrow path the prior action had closed off. Voicing their frustration got the hapless diners only a shrug, a smirk, and a tepid ricotta and spinach tortellini in a lukewarm butter and sage sauce.

So why the nightly lines? Are these folks masochists? Is treating-'em-bad-and-making-'em-like-it part of the successful formula? Well, they certainly don't come for the terracotta tiling, unvarnished wainscoting, and decorative ceramics. Brisk Mediterranean flavors and the accomplished, though at times sloppy, Italian cooking is the draw. Indeed, it's hard to hold a grudge and also manage the antipasto della casa ($21.95), a captivating collection of hot and cold vegetables, prosciutto, mozzarella, shellfish, and other rotated specialties. As alternatives, the $8.50 alliances of potato and portobello (in a tart) and grilled calamari and couscous (Sicilian-style, with pine nuts and raisins) are advantageous ones.

The fine pastas (around $9) and roast Cornish hen ($12.50) notwithstanding, the second most compelling reason for tolerating random table shifts is the tender braised lamb shank in a rich red wine sauce. The first is the $14.95 that you'll pay for it. The tiramisu you can live without.

Good Enough to Eat

(logo) On weekend mornings the cow-bell chimes hanging over the door-way ring at 9. At 9.08am it is already too late. All the unvarnished wood tables are filled and a line of young families, students, and assorted combinations of chirpy early risers and the morning-after mopers they've dragged out of bed is already forming next to the fence that surrounds the small sidewalk terrace. Soon the wait to be seated and sipping java will exceed an hour, defeating the whole point behind the rural wallhangings, recurring cow motif, homespun pies and cakes, and understated name: to transport the quaint, and presumably serene charms of a small-town breakfast nook to the Upper West Side. Still, even if you can drive to the country in the time it now takes to get a brunch-time table, the schmoozing, eavesdropping, and people-watching out here in the heart of Seinfeld country is certainly more diverting than it is on the Long Island Expressway.

Cost	Breakfast $10–15
	Lunch $18–30
	Dinner $18–55

Address 483 Amsterdam Ave, between 83rd & 84th Sts
⊤212/496-0163
Transportation B,C to 81st St; 1,2 to 86th St
Open Mon–Thurs 8am–10.30pm, Fri 8am–11pm, Sat 9am–4pm & 5.30–11pm, Sun 9am–4pm & 5.30–10pm
Accepts All major credit cards
Reservations Not accepted

Good Enough to Eat appreciates that burnt toast does not a great day begin. That when your fluffy but not airy flour-grain pancakes are both topped and filled with blueberries ($8.75), only good things can come after. Patience has no better reward than the "Lumber Jack" ($8.50), a plate of two plain pancakes, two scrambled eggs, and two thick, desirably chewy strips of outstanding slab bacon. Eggs are special too, perhaps loosely scrambled with red onion, chopped tomato, and dill ($5.50); in overstuffed omelettes ($7.75–8.50) or soaked into homemade cinnamon-swirl bread for French toast ($8.75). A warm biscuit with strawberry butter accompanies all egg dishes. Oddly, the waffles ($7.50–9.50) don't cut it.

American comforts listed on the lunch and dinner menus are more iffy. The buttermilk onion rings ($4.75 as starter or side) and the main course, four-cheese macaroni and cheese ($10.75) are splendid. But the veggieburger ($10) crumbles apart, the BBQ chicken sandwich ($10.50) is all sauce, and the pizzas ($13) are barely good enough to eat. But with the rustic pies (apple, blueberry, pecan, lemon meringue) and cakes ($5–5.50) it's almost impossible to go wrong.

Miss Mamie's Spoonbread Two

Formica meets gingham at this countrified urban diner where northerners get to sip lemonade from mason jars and order up down-home food. What fun! The restaurant grew out of *Spoon-bread and Strawberry Wine*, a family memoir written by sisters Carole and Norma Darden that traced their African-American ancestry largely through home-grown formulas for cosmetics, medicines, and Southern cooking. Norma, formerly a successful Wilhemina fashion model who did not know the difference between sautéeing

Cost	$18–30
Address 366 West 110th St at Columbus Ave	
☎212/865-6744	
Transportation 1,B,C to 110th St	
Open Sun 10.30am–10pm, Mon–Thurs noon–10pm, Fri noon–11pm, Sat 10.30am–11pm	
Accepts All major credit cards	

SOUTHERN

and pan-frying, used the book's recipes as the basis first for a catering company, Spoonbread, and then for this restaurant named after her mother (as well as a Harlem spin-off, Miss Maude's, honoring her aunt). The ruffled strawberry curtains and red-and-white checkerboard floor were patterned after Mamie Jean Sampson Darden's kitchen in Alabama.

One peek at the ample-times-two portions tells you this is no place for a present-day or future Wilhemina model to nourish her willowy assets. Two practices do put a lid on the caloric and cholesterol overloads, however. Firstly, the collard greens are fortified with smoked turkey wings instead of pork fat. Secondly, there is, thank heavens, no foreplay. Without appetizers to trouble with, diners get hot and heavy in a hurry with falling-off-the-bone BBQ ribs stuck to a gooey sauce of honey and molasses ($12.95); long-simmered short ribs dripping with tangy, cayenne-revved juices ($12.95); gravy-smothered chicken ($10.95); and splendid fried chicken ($10.50) and well-seasoned fried Louisiana catfish ($11.95) that both benefit from frequent oil changes. All orders come with cornbread and a choice of two sides.

Sensational desserts (mostly $3.95) are large enough to be registered as real estate properties. Some of the cream pies don't appear to have been cut or sliced. Rather, each portion is transferred to a plate in one big blob. The cobbler is always luscious, no matter the fruit filling (peach, pear, mango), and the coconut cake and sweet, creamy, banana pudding will have you running out—check that, lumbering out—to find the Darden cookbook and copy the recipes.

Upper West Side

Ocean Grill

With its ocean liner styling, of-the-moment seafood and raw bar selections, and prime location opposite the American Museum of Natural History, the Ocean Grill has many things going for it. Trend-surfing owner Steve Hanson (Ruby Foo's, see p.227, and Atlantic Grill, p.255, as well as Blue Water Grill, Isabella's, and Park Avalon) runs a noisy neighborhood cruise. Service is energetic; prices, fair.

| Cost | Lunch $20–50 |
| | Dinner $30–65 |

Address 384 Columbus Ave, between 78th & 79th Sts
☎212/579-2300
Transportation 1,9 to 79th St; B,C to 81st St
Open Daily 11.30am–4pm & 6–11.30pm
Accepts All major credit cards
Reservations Suggested

Beyond the suspended silk beachball that lights the foyer is a long dining room with coffered ceiling, hardwood floor, leatherette booths, banquettes, and a porthole view of the kitchen. In another, clubby dining room, an undulating, 1950s chandelier illuminates a busy gallery of seashore photos. One night you might sit beneath a beach shot of Brigitte Bardot. Another time, it may be Marilyn Monroe filling a swimsuit.

The "ocean" theme is sometimes carried a bit too far in dishes as salty as the Atlantic. But though seasoning may be a little off, most of the food is at least pretty good and some of it is really rather special. There are two large salad plates that are good enough to make regulars out of anyone. You could devote Tuesdays to the warm goat cheese salad with baby greens and country bread croutons ($8.50); Thursdays, to the gorgeous chopped salad with cucumbers, feta cheese, tomatoes, Kalamata olives, chickpeas, and roasted peppers ($8.50). The thin lobster bisque ($6.50) and heavy steamed shrimp dumplings ($7.95) are appetizer alternatives. Among entrees, a thick slab of wood-grilled yellowfin tuna ($16.95) is far superior to the same high-quality fish in a pepper-crusted, shake'n'-bake-like version with a sad absence of any peppery kick ($19.50). Wood-grilled mahi mahi ($19.50) and tender filet mignon ($22.95) confirm that the kitchen does right by the grill. Desserts ($4.75–6.75) require little intuition. The drop-dead chocolate fudge brownie sundae, the homemade ice creams and sorbets, and the warm baked apple crisp with cinnamon ice cream make it easy to pick a winner, whatever you go for.

Ouest

Named for the direction of the setting sun and pronounced as it is translated, Ouest thrives in a dining-deprived part of town where sophisticated restaurants are as scarce as right-wing Republicans. Exactly why the cultured, prosperous Upper Ouest Side has failed to adequately support the few influential chefs it has attracted remains a mystery. More apparent are the factors that enabled this particular breakthrough. When you pass from the squeeze of the tapered bar to the dark-wooded expanse

Cost	$35–80

Address 2315 Broadway at 84th St

℡212/580-8700

Transportation 1,2 to 86th St

Open Mon–Thurs 5–11pm, Fri & Sat 5pm–midnight, Sun 5–10pm

Accepts All major credit cards

Reservations Required

NEW AMERICAN

of the high-ceilinged dining room, the effect is of a hip, trendy, noise-maker. But the large, red-and-orange lampshades and comfy crescent-shaped red leather booths befit a restaurant that is ultimately as bourgois as its core diners. The distinction is that co-owner Tom Valenti, perhaps the least glamorous of New York's celebrity chefs, projects the same hippie-lefty image that many a self-deceiving Upper West Sider still sees when he looks in the bathroom mirror.

Valenti's cooking is robust both in content and technique. Most plates give the impression of depth and volume, even when portions are stingy (see: short ribs). He may be the only chef who can turn both a sweet-pea broth ($9) and an endive and Roquefort salad (more like a cheese course; $8) into star turns, while turning even the nutritionally correct on to mustard-crusted pork rillettes ($10) and silky, creamy oyster pan roast ($11).

Limiting your signature dish to specials status is cruel. Choosing Mondays and Tuesdays as the days to release those braised lamb shanks from slow-cooking captivity shows pure chutzpah. How does he get away with it? By offering lush daily distractions like braised short ribs with fava beans and white polenta ($25); roasted and beautifully crisped bacon-wrapped capon with roasted barley and foie gras-enriched jus ($24); a duck ragout with potato gnocchi and Parmesan ($19); and a great filet mignon with Parmesan flan that, at $27, could be the best buy in the place. Among Michael Moorhouse's terrific desserts the plum tart ($7) has the edge—though it's likely Valenti himself is a chocolate cake with peanut crunch and banana ice cream kind of guy.

Upper West Side

Rosa Mexicano

The opening in 2000 of a second Rosa Mexicano had devotees of the East Side favorite (1063 First Ave, Midtown East; ☎212/753-7407) hoping for the best and fearing the worst. Would its arrival bring dependable dining to a food-cursed part of town? Or would the offshoot be a disappointment that managed only to drain valuable resources from the original? Most of those hopes and only a few of those fears have been realized: this snazzy Rosa belongs near the top of the city charts in the categories of "Best Mexican" and "Best Near Lincoln Center." Designer David Rockwell played to the weaknesses of a difficult two-story space. Against the constrictive main wall he installed a striking 30ft, blue-tile water wall that serves as the diving cliff for 240 white figurines. The staircase alongside this abstract Acapulco is composed of terrazzo slabs matched to the hues of the belt-woven chairs. Windows facing the State Theater add continuity and splendor to the upper level.

| Cost | Lunch $30–55 |
| | Dinner $40–75 |

Address 61 Columbus Ave at 62nd St
☎212/977-7700
Transportation 1,2,A,B,C,D to 59th St-Columbus Circle
Open Daily 11.30am–3pm & 5pm–midnight
Accepts All major credit cards
Reservations Suggested

The menu, a 40/60 mix of new and established dishes, is supervised by chef Jorge Quintana. With this gig must come the acceptance that his most accomplished appetizers will invariably play second avocado to the guacamole ($14 for two) prepared tableside and served with chips, silver-dollar corn tortillas, and, ideally, a frozen pomegranate Margarita. Still, it is starters like hongos ($8), a garlicky sauté of meaty wild mushrooms propped over a polenta-like mush, and the desirably chewy chicken ravioli wading in a shallow pool of smoky poblano pepper sauce and melted manchego that distinguish this from other moderate-to-upscale Mexican eateries.

Perhaps the best of the *platillos principales* is the mixióte de cordero (chile-rubbed lamb shank; $24). Staged within the rumpled round rim of its open parchment casing, the smoky lamb juices are deeply flavored. Another kind of roasted chile flavor, this one dark, heavy, and spicy, imbues every tender bite of the braised chilayo (pork loin; $20). Service fumbles may vanish in time, which is the best that could be hoped for most of the desserts ($8). Okay, the chocolate mousse pastry on a chocolate-peanut pedestal could stick around.

Sarabeth's

Pretty, pricey Sarabeth's is a mid-block fantasy world bursting at its wainscoted seams with not only city folk but also suburbanites who drive into town merely to be transported back out to some country cottage in either of the two Englands—New or old. Were Martha Stewart and Laura Ashley contemporaries, you could see them fitting in just fine here, admiring the sheaves of wheat and jam jars displayed in the centerpiece hutch. Soon they'd get around to the serious business at hand: sitting down with Sarabeth Levine and devising interesting new ways to enjoy poppyseeds. If, emboldened by each other's company, they felt like being naughty, they could order the "green and white" (scrambled eggs with scallions and cream cheese; $7.75), the lemon ricotta pancakes with berries and warm pure maple syrup ($9) or any of the delightful breakfast items as late as 4pm.

Cost	$20–65

Address 423 Amsterdam Ave, between 80th & 81st Sts; plus other locations
☎212/496-6280
Transportation 1,2 to 79th St; B,C to 81st St
Open Mon–Fri 8am–10.30pm, Sat & Sun 8am–4pm & 5.30–10.30pm
Accepts All major credit cards
Reservations For dinner only

Not since the Great Depression has New York witnessed such long lines of people waiting for bowls of oatmeal as outside this leader on the breakfast and brunch circuit. The most seasoned cynic could not, however, fairly ridicule the quality of the homemade jams, omelets, muffins, and, yes, oatmeal. The porridges (from $4.25 for the "Baby Bear" bowl to $5.50 for the "Big Bad Wolf") are at once creamy and granular, with honey, fresh cream, bananas, raisins, and wheatberries counted among the accessories. The Goldie Lox ($9.50), a scramble of smoked salmon and cream cheese, is an egg thing that some Upper Westsiders see more often than their spouses. Jams and breakfast breads, all available for carryout, deserve their fame.

The cuteness peaks at lunch, most notably with the crisp-edged, moist-centered polenta logs ($4), arranged like the megaliths of Stonehenge, and the salad of poached salmon, corn, tomato, and chopped lettuce ($13) set out in perfect bands of pink, yellow, red and green. Still, their composition, like that of the smoked mozzarella sandwich ($10.50), the Virginia ham and Vermont Cheddar club-style sandwich ($11.75), and the soupy chicken pot pie with a puff-pastry lid ($14) undeniably first-rate.

Brooklyn

Bay Ridge & Bensonhurst

BAY RIDGE & BENSONHURST

SHORE PARKWAY

SHORE ROAD

BAY RIDGE AVE

88TH ST

86TH ST

BAY RIDGE PARKWAY

3RD AVE

4TH AVE

HAMILTON PARKWAY

85TH ST

86TH ST

UTRECHT AVE

BAY RIDGE

86TH ST

Provence en Boite

Tuscany Grill Ⓜ

Mambo Italiano

Embers Ⓜ

GOWANUS EXPWY

7TH AVE

Dyker Beach Golf Club

BENSONHURST

18TH AVE

Tommaso's Ⓜ

Dyker Beach Park

BAY 8TH ST

CROPSEY AVE

SHORE PARKWAY

VERAZZANO NARROWS BRIDGE

N

Gravesend Bay

0   500 yds

Embers

You almost have to leave Brooklyn entirely to get to the borough's "other" steakhouse. Situated at the end of the R subway line and near the approach to the Verrazano Narrow Bridge, Embers is cherished as the working-man's Peter Luger's in that its location and prices are miles south of that famous Brooklyn steakhouse. You don't need to look far to figure out how owner Louis Rocanelli can charge as little as $32.95 for a 60oz T-bone steak-for-two. He owns the butcher shop next door and

| Cost | Lunch $15–30 |
| | Dinner $30–60 |

Address 9519 3rd Ave, between 95th & 96th Sts
℡718/745-3700
Transportation R to 95th St
Open Mon–Sat noon–2.45pm & 5–10.30pm, Sun 2–9.30pm
Accepts MasterCard & Visa
Reservations Not accepted

STEAKHOUSE

probably gives himself a good bulk price on those well-aged Brooklyn hunks. But only an Arthur Andersen accountant could see a profit in selling a Ruffino Chianti Classico 1997 Ducale Riserva Gold for $54 when other restaurants are getting $75–85 for the same bottle. Whatever the explanation, you can be reasonably sure Rocanelli's wine supplier does not wait as long as ordinary mortals do for a Saturday night table.

Dated stereotypes about Embers' bejeweled, helmet-headed customers are regrettably sustained by the odd diner dressed for a hot date in a designer jogging suit. That said, workout garb is not that ridiculous in view of the cramped conditions both at the bar and in the two dining rooms as well as the physical exertion required when taking on a steak. Besides, the marble wallpaper and suspended acoustic ceiling are hardly the decorative counterparts of a smart, black leather blazer.

The menu is shorter than it appears at first glance. Much shorter. You basically want to concern yourself with three superb, absurdly affordable steaks (in order of preference): the juicy T-bone (a 32-ouncer is $21.95), the New York sirloin ($18.95), and the filet mignon ($19.95). They're why you're here. The rest is window dressing. Even the potato choice is a charade. While the potato pie—smashed potato with grated Parmesan, prosciutto bits, and butter—is justifiably revered and an absolute must, the frozen fries are a joke. The fine frutti di mare (cold seafood salad appetizer; $8.95) is the single exception to the steak-only rule. Ordering any dessert once is a mistake. Ordering one twice is a crime.

Bay Ridge & Bensonhurst

Mambo Italiano

To your left, in a caricaturist's mural of Italian movie stars, native daughter Marisa Tomei asks Joe Pesci whether he can mambo. Overhead, a signora's long-dried undergarments dangle from a clothesline. To your right, Patricio, a tenor who happens to be your co-waiter, serenades your table with a Neapolitan love song as he fills your glasses with Chianti. So goes your introduction to the mondo of Mambo Italiano, a campy, hand-clapping, family-forging, diet-destroying dining destination that's ideal for bachelor—or bachelorette—parties, birthday celebrations, and other boisterous bashes. Besides the crooning servers, nightly entertainment is provided by the likes of Johnny Lala, who does a great Al Green, and Jeannie, a red-headed Aretha.

Cost	$30–65

Address 8803 3rd Ave at 88th St

☎718/833-4432

Transportation R to 86th St

Open Mon–Thurs noon–11pm, Fri & Sat noon–midnight, Sun 2–10pm

Accepts All major credit cards

Reservations Suggested

Mambo Italiano differs from other singing restaurants in that the place actually has a kitchen. While the food is good enough to please Brooklyn sophisticates, plates are large enough to stretch even the most voracious diners to their limits. Family-style platters portioned and priced for two people can feed at least three regulation-sized adults. Appetizers include cleanly fried calamari with spicy red sauce ($16.95), an imposing cold antipasto ($17.95), and an all-encompassing frutta di mare ($18.95) with cold shrimp, calamari, and scungili (a cousin of conch) marinated in olive oil, garlic, and lemon juice.

Mambo's pastas are stirring illustrations of creativity and overkill. Fettuccine Mambo ($27.95) piles shrimp, lobster, scallops, peas, artichokes, and a creamy tomato sauce over its pasta. In spirali arragosta ($30.95), the short-cut pasta takes on lobster, Serrano ham, arugula, and a sundried tomato cream sauce. But all this is child's play in relation to the shameless glut of the special lobster Stoli for two ($45.95)—two lobsters with pink vodka lobster sauce, shrimp, and fusilli pasta. And then there are the veal, chicken, and steak entrees, including a 32oz porterhouse topped with sautéed onions and mushrooms ($39.95). Best advice for dessert, after ogling a cart topped with the likes of chocolate cheesecake, tiramisu, and a Napoleon, is to take two shorts and one long: an espresso and a walk on the short side, and then a nap on the long.

Provence en Boîte

The name Provence en Boîte—
"canned Provence"—features two
out of three great French passions
brought to Bay Ridge's main dining strip
by charming hosts Leslie and Jean-
Jacques Bernat. The shelves in their
endearing bistro/pastry shop are crowded with a vast collection of vintage
boîtes, meaning "tins" or "cans," for such
old-time Gallic groceries as Aiguebelle
cocoa and Maggi bouillon cubes. Hung
just beneath those shelves and draped

| Cost | Lunch $12–35 |
| | Dinner $27–60 |

Address 8303 3rd Ave,
between 83rd & 84th Sts
℡718/759-1515
Transportation R to 86th St
Open Sun–Thurs 8am–11pm,
Fri & Sat 8am–midnight
Accepts All major credit cards

FRENCH

over the tables are fabrics and tablecloths in Provençal colors and patterns. The third Bernat passion—pastries—may not be present in the
name, but they are prominently arranged in a glass display case just
inside the front door so that they are the first, last, and, as it happens,
most lasting images of a visit for breakfast, lunch, dinner, brunch, or
something in between.

The pre-dessert cooking is two-thirds Provençal and one-third classic
French. The former is best represented by escargots à la Provençale ($9),
a traditional preparation in which the snails are sautéed with chopped
mushrooms, parsley, and garlic and simmered with white wine to create
a richly flavored but not thickened sauce. Classic French flavors find
expression in the French onion soup ($7.50), admirable less for the dilut-
ed soup than the crusty cheese topping, and the tartiflettes savoyardes
($8), a cheese-topped potato gratin. Entree highlights include herb-roast-
ed chicken smothered in mushroom sauce and paired with good frites
($15), a small salmon fillet with a lightly sour sorrel cream sauce prepared
according to the recipe of Pierre and Jean Troisgros ($16), and a pretty
good bouillabaisse of shrimp, mussels, scallops, monkfish, and haddock in
a pale, fennel-scented broth with rouille-smeared toasts afloat ($19).

Jean-Jacques Bernat is a pastry chef by trade, a fact made plainly obvious by his delectable, camera-ready pastries (all about $3.50). The apri-
cot tart, chocolate-mousse-filled porcupine, and hazelnut nougat praline
pastry figure among the best options. But Bernat is proudest of his
Lafayette, a triumph whose integral parts—almond dacquoise, chocolate
mousse, fresh raspberries—may be drawn out by a glass of dessert wine
like Muscat Beaume de Venise or Muscat de Rivesaltes (both $5).

Bay Ridge & Bensonhurst

Tommaso's

Tommaso Verdillo doesn't look like the Brooklyn treasure he is any more than his renovated, kitsch-congested dining room resembles a multi-starred restaurant. You simply don't expect to be serenaded with the finest Italian food, wines, and arias by a guy dressed for a trip to the Laundromat. But Verdillo's casual garb, the old family photos, and the standup piano make more sense once you think of this as his home and not his place of business. This requires some imagination, as few domiciles have 14,000 bottles of wine in their basement. Though a diner's checks, aspirations, and body weight may be fattened somewhat by the likes of foie gras gently sautéed with bittersweet caramelized orange peel ($13.95), there is no compromise in opting for the most basic Southern Italian dishes that also pepper the menu. As Verdillo likes to say when comparing a $20 and $200 wine: "They're both excellently made. There are just different things going on."

Cost	$35–75

Address 1464 86th St, between 14th & 15th Aves
☎718/236-9883
Transportation W to 18th Ave
Open Tues–Sun noon–midnight
Accepts All major credit cards
Reservations Suggested

Not that he is above snobbery. He regarded requests for his $20 prix fixe dinners as social blunders and eventually took them off the menu. Now there's no choice but to start with such appetizers as the stuffed artichokes ($8.50) and deep-fried mozzarella in carozza ($6.50). Two pastas prepared with unusual finesse merit serious consideration: cannelloni fruitti di mare with crab sauce ($14.95) and veal-and-Swiss chard agnolotti in a heady leek, mushroom, and veal sauce ($14.95).

As for entrees, succumbing to the breast of veal stuffed with spinach, ground veal, raisins, pine nuts, and bread ($16.95) is almost like being adopted into an extended family. It's challenged in scope only by the osso buco ($23.95), a veal shank braised to tender perfection and portioned by the cubic acre (half a shank per order). Other alluring possibilities include calf's liver sautéed with onions, figs, and pancetta ($17.95) as well as grilled duck breast in the same bittersweet orange sauce used with the foie gras ($18.95). Settling upon one of two outstanding desserts—semi-freddo topped with chocolate sauce ($4.50) or panna cotta ($3.50)—assures a creamy, melt-in-your-mouth finish.

Tuscany Grill

Festive, multi-colored lights are strung from the outside of this Bay Ridge trattoria. The Verrazzano-Narrows looms in the distance, a twinkling if steely stand-in for the Ponte Vecchio. Inside, John Conforti, perched at the wooden bar, warmly greets all-comers. Throughout the evening, he casually makes his way from farmhouse table to farmhouse table between the deliberately distressed walls of the softly lit dining room, chatting with regulars and first-timers alike. His wife Marny is mostly confined to the kitchen, turning out her partially Tuscan, wholeheartedly rendered Italian cuisine which, together with seamless service and portions as big as the locals' hair, packs the house even on weeknights.

Cost	$30–70

Address 8620 3rd Ave, between 86th & 87th Sts
☎718/921-5633
Transportation N to 86th St
Open Sun–Wed 5–10pm, Fri & Sat 5–11pm
Accepts All major credit cards
Reservations Required

Marny previously cooked at Al Forno in Providence, Rhode Island, and it was she who introduced Brooklyn to that restaurant's claim to fame: wood-grilled pizza. Cooked over an open fire, Marny's extremely thin, light, crisp-crusted grilled pizzas ($12 and up) pose not a question of if, but only how, and when. Shared appetizer? Entree? Side dish? Cheese course? All of the above. Combinations ranging from the standard Margherita—tomato, mozzarella, basil—to Gorgonzola, roasted peppers, and onions, are all sparingly topped so that the dressings neither soften nor overwhelm the crust. A pizza appetizer may be supplemented with the rustic salad of warm red cabbage ($9) or, if you're not opposed to bread-on-bread, bruschetta ($6) with a mix of ripe tomatoes, fresh basil, and fine extra virgin olive oil heaped onto grilled Tuscan bread.

Pasta comes in first-course half-portions or as a sizeable entree. Tripolini Toscana ($8/$13.50) is a robust bowl of bow-ties, fresh tomatoes, radicchio, grilled sausage, and black olives. Grilled chicken filled with herbed goat cheese and served over spinach alongside rosemary potatoes ($18) is a hearty invention, playing the perfectly charred and crisped skin against the succulent meat and oozing cheese. Other laudable entrees include a trio of sausages from Faicco's Pork Stores (the Brooklyn branch is on 11th Ave) served with sautéed bitter greens and garlic mashed potatoes ($17.50), and balsamic-glazed oven-roasted pork tenderloin. As a coda, the wild berry tart ($6.50) bears a scrumptious overflow of sweet, tangy fruit.

Brooklyn Heights & Downtown Brooklyn

BROOKLYN HEIGHTS & DOWNTOWN BROOKLYN

East River

BROOKLYN BRIDGE

PLYMOUTH ST

WATER ST

FRONT ST

Grimaldi's

OLD FULTON ST

BROOKLYN-QUEENS EXPRESSWAY

SANDS ST

NASSAU ST

PROSPECT ST

PEARL ST

JAY ST

CONCORD ST

PRINCE ST

FLATBUSH AVENUE

ASHLAND PL

EDWARDS ST

Noodle Pudding

ADAMS ST

TILLARY ST

MYRTLE AVE

BROOKLYN HEIGHTS

CAMDEN PLAZA

DOWNTOWN

Metro Tech Center

Long Island University

Brooklyn Historical Society

HICKS ST

CLINTON ST

BROOKLYN

Junior's

MONTAGUE

HENRY ST

St. Ann's Church

WILLOUGHBY ST

Fulton Mall

FULTON ST

DEKALB AVE

REMSEN

BROOKLYN HEIGHTS PROMENADE

New York Transit Museum

Gage & Tollner

LIVINGSTON STREET

JORALEMON ST

SCHERMERHORN

N

STATE STREET

BOERUM PL

BOND ST

0   400 yds

ATLANTIC AVENUE

PACIFIC ST

Gage & Tollner

When Charles Cage opened his restaurant in 1879, Brooklyn was still an independent municipality of roughly 600,000 inhabitants, the third largest city in the US. When he moved it to its current address in 1882, the Brooklyn Bridge was still a year away from opening. Now, the entrance to the exquisitely restored Gage & Tollner is a direct passage to that glorious time and place. The solid mahogany tables, bentwood chairs, velvet brocade, and gaslit chandeliers of cut glass reflected in long rows of arched mirrors distinguish with Victorian elegance the first restaurant interior to be designated a landmark by the city Brooklyn joined in 1898. Yet this is no museum, even if the mannered, uniformed servers do recall a long-lost era. A magnet for business and political lunches by day, at night the restaurant attracts an effervescent, well-dressed, and diverse crowd from the surrounding communities.

| Cost | Lunch $22–70 |
| | Dinner $32–80 |

Address 372 Fulton St at Red Hook Lane & Smith St
℡718/875-5181
Transportation M,N,R to Lawrence St; 1,2 to Hoyt St; A,C,F to Jay St-Boro Hall
Open Mon–Thurs 11.30am–3.30pm & 5–10pm, Fri 11.30am–3.30pm & 5–11pm, Sat 3–11pm
Accepts All major credit cards
Reservations Suggested

AMERICAN

The menu spoils any lingering illusion of time travel with words like "balsamic" and "lemongrass." But it does feature some of the throwback seafoods and chops that once defined grand New York dining. Chef Louis Garces performs faithful covers of the venerable southern-style dishes of his legendary predecessor Edna Lewis, among them crabmeat Virginia ($12.95), a potato galette with spinach and fresh, spicy, crabmeat; outstanding Maryland she-crab soup or lobster bisque (both Sherry-creamed and $6.50); and clam bellies ($8.95 as an appetizer; $17.95 as a main course), breaded and broiled Ipswich clams fitted with buttered vegetables into unrelated Cherrystone shells before you slurp those soft, sweet babies down.

Among entrees, grilled salmon ($18.95) is close to perfect, nicely set up with mashed potatoes and a mustard dill sauce. A pat of not quite melted butter compensates for the sporadic dryness of mammoth steaks ($23.95 for a sirloin; $29.95 for a T-bone) as do rotated sauces for veal chops ($27.95). You're better taken care of with a grilled whole fish like orata ($22.95). The dual chocolate mousse ($6.50) is the cake to pluck from the fine dessert cart.

PIZZA

Grimaldi's

It isn't for tiring that Brooklyn's pizza-loving romantics get weak at the knees while waiting in line at Grimaldi's. The pizzeria is perched at the foot of the Brooklyn Bridge, affording standees a breathtaking view of the Brooklyn waterfront and the Lower Manhattan skyline. Their hearts are further stirred by the old Sinatra recordings spilling out the door, accompanied both by the Nelson Riddle Orchestra and the waft of garlic emanating from the brick oven. Inside, an entire wall is covered with photos of Ol' Blue Eyes. Oh, baby, this is how pizza was meant to be.

Cost	$6–25

Address 19 Old Fulton St, between Front & Water Sts
☎718/858-4300
Transportation A,C to High St; 1,2 to Clark St
Open Sun–Thurs 11.30am–11pm, Fri & Sat 11.30am–midnight
Accepts Cash only
Reservations Not accepted

Once seated, the only thing that can come between you and your pizza is the antipasto ($9) of mozzarella, salami, Sicilian olives, and roasted peppers. Better to skip it entirely and have those sweet roasted peppers atop your pie, either a six-slice small ($12 and up) or eight-slice large ($14 and up), both baked and spottily charred in the coal-fired oven. The result is a delicately chewy and divinely thin crust save for the outer rim, whose air bubbles are so large it looks as though the pizza has sprouted mushrooms (such pockets should probably be deflated by the baker). The pizza is crisp enough to support its thin layers of milky mozzarella and zesty plum tomato sauce, but not so stiff as to prevent easy folding of each slice, according to the native practice.

The best additional toppings are the crumbled fennel sausage ($2) and extra grated cheese ($2). Avoid the anchovies (for some bizarre reason they're served with capers—and you get more capers per portion than the anchovies themselves) and see if you can get them to put the fresh basil on the pie *after* it is baked. The blackened, shriveled basil has the pungent aroma of marijuana—presumably not what you want on a masterpizza such as this. For some, the overstuffed cannoli is a perfect dessert. For others, the departing view of lower Manhattan is sweet enough.

Junior's

The black shopping bag of Barney's New York invariably carries gifts of style and distinction. A mere glimpse of the egg-blue bag trademarked by Tiffany makes women quiver with anticipation. But no gift bag will excite a knowing and cholesterol-indifferent dinner host more than the orange-striped white bag imprinted with the oval logo of Junior's. It typically holds New York's most famous cheesecake and an emotional reminder of Brooklyn's landmark and still flourishing bakery/coffee shop/restaurant/deli.

Cost	$10–60

Address 386 Flatbush Ave at DeKalb Ave
☎718/852-5257
Transportation M,N,Q,R,W to DeKalb Ave; 1,2 to Nevins St
Open Sun–Wed 6.30am–12.30am, Thurs 6.30am–1am, Fri & Sat 6.30am–2am
Accepts All major credit cards
Reservations Not accepted

Mediocrity, the pitfall of wearing so many hats, does not escape Junior's. Those who opt for ambitious seafood platters, barbecue dishes, or Italian specials are gluttons for disappointment. Those who stick to a narrow rotation of old standards leave happy. Breakfast is close to a sure thing, as all eggs and omelets ($4.95–8.50) come with a prodigious assortment of rugelach, mini-Danish, and rolls. Similarly, no lunch or dinner is served without a setup of pickles and coleslaw. Nothing bests the broiled steakburger ($6·50–9.25)—a 10oz mound of ground meat oozing juices with every squeeze. Citing the hot open roast beef sandwich ($10.25) as a standout may be a surprise even to the waiters, who are unaccustomed to taking orders for the large platter of pink meat. Lastly, the combination sandwich pairing lean and prim corned beef with fatty and depraved pastrami ($9.25) makes perfect sense.

So just how good is that famed cheesecake? It can be difficult to know what to make of the thin, cursory layer of spongy crust that now serves as its graham-cracker foundation. Each wedge ($4.50–5.25) is not so much a cake as it is several inches of blended cream cheese topped with nuts and fruit. And, as it happens that turns out to be a very good thing. The egg cream ($2.50) is stirred in a measuring glass showing exactly how much milk, chocolate syrup, and seltzer to pour into it. You can buy egg cream kit and take it to a loved one in a striped plastic bag.

There's another Junior's in the lower level dining concourse, Grand Central Terminal, Midtown East (☎212/983-5257).

ITALIAN

Noodle Pudding

(🍴) There's never been a name posted outside this establishment and for good reason. An Italian restaurant that never has and apparently never will serve noodle pudding cannot possibly in good conscience flaunt the name "Noodle Pudding." It's painful even to write those words atop this review. The Brooklyn Heights trattoria is so-called because the proprietor answers to the family name of Migliaccio and is known to his Jewish friends as Mr Kugel. *Migliaccio* is Italian for *kugel*, you see, which is Yiddish for a

Cost	$25–60

Address 38 Henry St, between
Cranberry & Middagh Sts
☏718/625-3737
Transportation A,C to High St;
1,2 to Clark St
Open Sun 5–10.30pm,
Tues–Sat 5.30–10.30pm
Accepts Cash only
Reservations For large groups

baked pudding often made with noodles. So, neither Antonio Migliaccio nor his restaurant is Jewish. But his family did prepare its namesake dish Neapolitan-style (recipe: fettuccine, eggs, butter, milk, ricotta, raisins, sugar, and vanilla all baked until golden) back on the island of Ischia in his native Campania. "It's a sin to throw out leftover pasta," he recalls. "So we made noodle pudding."

It is also a sin, Mr Kugel, not to serve your migliaccio di Ischia at a low-priced, otherwise unassuming neighborhood restaurant called Noodle Pudding. Diners take home only warm memories of your fried calamari ($8.50) and stuffed crimini mushrooms ($9). They like the way your lamb Bolognese clings to the bucatini ($12) and how your crusty slices of grilled lamb ($16) deliver their rosemary scent. They're also impressed with the Reagan-era price of your grilled filet mignon and the option of having it in two sizes ($14 and $20). They adore too your veal Milanese with arugula and mozzarella, though it's not always possible to tell how hot, cold, or tepid each ingredient should be. They're even mildly amused to learn that bread pudding ($5) has surpassed tiramisu and seasonal fruit tarts in popularity and is now your signature dessert. Good for you!

Nevertheless, no one will fully appreciate the modest elegance of the spare and comfortable dining room you decorated, the romantic sounds of the Italian and French music you play, or the beautiful view out the wrought-iron picture window you built until the family dish is added to the dessert menu. It's either that, Signore Kugel, or a name change.

Carroll Gardens, Cobble Hill & Boerum Hill

CARROLL GARDENS, COBBLE HILL & BOERUM HILL

SCHERMERHORN ST

STATE STREET

BOERUM HILL

ATLANTIC AVENUE

PACIFIC ST

PACIFIC STREET

Brawta Caribbean Cafe

AMITY STREET

DEAN STREET

Bar Tabac

COBBLE HILL

Restaurant Saul

BERGEN STREET

WYCKOFF STREET

WARREN ST

WARREN ST

BALTIC STREET

Sam's

Sherwood Café

CLINTON STREET

KANE STREET

BALTIC ST

Cafe LULUc

Osaka

BUTLER ST

Banania Café

HOYT STREET

BOND STREET

DOUGLAS CT

DOUGLAS ST

Patois

COURT STREET

DE GRAW STREET

SMITH STREET

DE GRAW STREET

BROOKLYN-QUEENS EXPRESSWAY

SACKETT STREET

SACKETT STREET

The Red Rail

UNION STREET

UNION STREET

PRESIDENT ST

CARROLL

Carroll Park

CARROLL ST

GARDENS

CARROLL ST

1ST PLACE

HENRY STREET

SUMMIT ST

1ST ST

2ND PLACE

2ND ST

3RD PLACE

3RD ST

HAMILTON AVE

4TH PLACE

4TH ST

Gowanus Canal

COLUMBIA STREET

LUQUER STREET

NELSON ST

HUNTINGDON ST

W 9TH ST

9TH STREET

0   200 yds

N

Banania Café

FRENCH

In retrospect, it was probably not the most brilliant idea to name the place after a French brand of cocoa powder made with banana flour and closely associated since 1915 with its caricature logo of a smiling Senegalese infantryman in a red fez. The use of that advertising image, though racially insensitive to some, reflected only the noble intention of a new kid on the block to be as welcoming to young children as a mug of hot Ovaltine on a Sunday morning in January. To warm the hearts of their parents it took something more. Copper sheeting installed as wainscoting casts a

Cost	$22–50

Address 241 Smith St at Douglass St
☎718/237-9100
Transportation F,G to Carroll St
Open Mon–Thurs 5.30–11pm, Fri 5.30–11.30pm, Sat 10.30am–3pm & 5–11.30pm, Sun 10.30am–3pm & 5–10.30pm
Accepts Cash only
Reservations Not accepted

soft amber glow over the tin-ceilinged room of paper-clothed, candlelit tables, while chef-owner Danforth Houle's Mediterranean and Asian flourishes distinguish Banania from other budget bistros nearby, Houle's own Cafe LULUc (see p.310) among them. The outcome, somewhat ironic given the cramped conditions and frequently brusque service, is the most grownup, romantic, family-friendly (especially for brunch), and, to many, refreshingly unhip French bistros of the Smith Street lot.

If Houle's cooking can be faulted, it's for being too ambitious, which can make it difficult to execute the menu with consistency. It's nice that he wants to do something a little different with escargots ($6) besides the usual garlic and butter. But the lemon juice makes them too tart. Moroccan spiced calamari with frisée ($6) is more successful, however, and the cornmeal-crusted oysters with celery root purée ($6) offer a becoming play of flavor and textures. And sautéed foie gras with rhubarb mango chutney is quite a trip for eight bucks.

Among main courses, the overproduced vegetable Wellington ($12) resembling a giant, browned empanada filled with roasted tomatoes, garlic, spinach, and melted goat cheese ($12) is frivolous fun. Who cares if the first bite is ten times more pleasurable than the last? You can also get a darn good steak frites for $15. And the Provençal-style, pan-roasted cod with black olive potato purée ($13) is a winner. The dessert to try at least once is the fried banana ravioli in chocolate sauce ($5)—an unobjectionable tribute to the namesake Banania.

Carroll Gardens, Cobble Hill & Boerum Hill

Bar Tabac

The faded fantasies (Jules in the East Village, Café Noir in SoHo) that Georges Forgeois pieced together out of old furnishings, advertisements, and collectibles were convincing because he managed to leave each effort one vintage Dubonnet ashtray short of theme-restaurant sentimentality. That knack for knowing when to quit failed him, however, when he moved to Brooklyn's bistro-dotted Smith Street. Perhaps overly eager to outstrip his able competitors, Forgeois filled his exquisitely ripened period piece with

Cost	$25–55

Address 128 Smith St at Dean St
☏718/923-0918
Transportation F,G to Bergen St
Open Sun–Tues 11.30am–1am, Wed & Thurs 11.30am–2am, Fri & Sat 11.30am–3am
Accepts AmEx
Reservations Suggested

every trite trapping in his retro bistro treasure trove. The old mirrors, aperitif placards, and illuminated red "carrotte" (the lozenge-shaped signpost seen outside all French bar-tabacs) mounted on the tobacco-stained walls would have been sufficient. But Forgeois couldn't help himself, and went ahead and parked a vintage scooter and old foozball inside the restaurant.

The phoniness is happily lost on locals delighted to have this breezy brunch spot and easy-going late-night haunt in their midst. And Bar Tabac does exhibit some originality where it counts most: in the kitchen. A selection of ten grilled brochettes grouped under the heading "Bistro Bites" suggests new possibilities for aperitif nibbling, tapas-style dining, or wee-hours munching. At $5 a pop for everything from marinated beef to Burgundy snails to pastis-and-parsley-buttered-mushrooms-on-a-stick, they're pretty much irresistible.

Good standards like onion soup gratinée ($5) and warm goat cheese salad with beets, frisée, and raspberry walnut vinaigrette ($7.50) pave the way for a more conventional meal with French sauce and soul. While a New York strip admirably fulfils the steak-frite duties ($16.50), the duck leg stew ($15.50), beef bourguignon ($15.50), and braised lamb shank ($15.50) go deeper to the bone. Others may find no reason to wander from the steamed mussels with white wine, shallots, and, to the side, gilded frites ($11). The French wine list describes bottles by their place of origin but not their producers and vintages. This would be acceptable were the choice limited to carafe-style table wines. But with ten bottles at more than $35, it's arguable that Georges Forgeois chose the wrong facet in which to hold back.

Brawta Caribbean Cafe

🍴 The thing to do upon entering Brawta is to follow your nose and ears but not immediately your eyes. Up front, the sterile stainless-steel open kitchen, along with the young Brooklyn professionals waiting for their carry-out orders, do nothing to evoke the superb little West Indian restaurant this is. But follow the unmistakeable reggae rhythms of Bob Marley to the color-splashed, candlelit cafe just to the rear and that unflattering first impression vanishes like Jamaican punch on a sweltering summer's day. To accompany the soundtrack, Marley's image is deeply carved into each of the round, glass-covered tabletops. Look up and there he is again, portrayed in one of the oil paintings hung over the L-shaped banquette.

Cost	$18–40

Address 347 Atlantic Ave at Hoyt St

☎718/855-5515

Transportation A,C,G to Hoyt-Schermerhorn; 1,2 to Hoyt St

Open Sun noon–10pm, Mon noon–10.30pm, Tues–Thurs noon–11pm, Fri & Sat noon–11.30pm

Accepts All major credit cards

Reservations Not accepted

CARIBBEAN

Hospitable servers help first-timers surrender to the relaxed island mood and pace. The tropical fruit drinks are a major component of the Brawta—"something extra" in the native patois—experience. The fruit punch ($2/$4) is a rich, resonant, honey-sweetened mix of strawberries, mango, pineapple, papaya, and banana. The invigorating pine-ade ($1.50/$3), blending tart pineapple and spicy ginger, is a perfect foil for an appetizer or snack of beef patties ($2)—soft, peppery ground beef encased in a flaky pastry. As starter or side dish, macaroni and cheese ($4) is distinguished by shredded carrots and sweet red peppers.

Beware the deviously surreptitious heat within the unmatched main course, jerk chicken ($9.50). Marinated overnight in pimento, hot pepper, onions, thyme, and, naturally, secret spices before being slowly cooked (at Brawta, even the grilling is unhurried), the fall-off-the-bone tender meat releases an atomic burn not fully felt until the ninth bite. Bodies are also subjected to an unexpected crescendo of flesh-reddening heat by the shrimp sautéed with broccoli and carrots and bathed in a coconut curry sauce ($15). All entrees are served with a large side of chopped cabbage steamed with green peas, carrots, corn, and onions. From the "Sweet Tings" menu, the moist bread pudding ($3.50) is a revelation, made with pineapple and creamy, lip-smacking rum sauce.

FRENCH

Cafe LULUc

The younger, hipper, stunted sibling of Banania Cafe (see p.307) reduces the economy bistro to the bare essentials: whitewashed walls, tin ceiling, red banquettes, pine floorboards, short menu, eye-level mirrors, and fast waiters who snub French arrogance rather than their diners. Space is so tight at this teensy-weensy place that you may end up sitting on top of someone at the next table—not necessarily an unpleasant notion considering the attractive crowd. Singles can make a more conventional introduction for themselves at the tiny bar or, better still, out on the the sidewalk, which is crowded

| Cost | Lunch $11–35 |
| | Dinner $18–45 |

Address 214 Smith St, between Butler & Baltic Sts
☎718/625-3815
Transportation F,G to Bergen St
Open Mon–Thurs 7.30am–midnight, Fri 7.30am–2am, Sat 8am–2am, Sun 8am–midnight
Accepts Cash only
Reservations For large groups

with folks waiting—or merely pretending to wait—for a coveted table. (Show up before 7pm to avoid a delay.) During weekend brunch, baby-stroller gridlock thwarts such socializing beneath a sign that originally read "Cafe LULU." After a Fort Greene restaurant called Loulou protested, the "c" was painted on, echoing the co-owner's first name, Jean-Luc.

Frogs' legs à la meunière ($7), pan-roasted with lemon, butter, and parsley, may seem a modest notion for so modest an eatery, but the meat is tender and plump and there is enough of it on this starter for a main course. Still, orders for the nice salad of cold roasted beets tossed with Granny Smith apples and a soothing goat cheese dressing ($6.50) outnumber those for grenouilles by about ten to one. Some don't bother with an appetizer at all, going straight to the very good, if a little too lean, burger ($7.50, $8.50 with cheese) served over a rich brioche bun with superbly crisp, salty fries.

LULUc somehow manages a convincing grilled hanger steak with caramelized shallot sauce and frites for $12.50. The homey, fairly juicy grilled pork chop with thyme-scented wine gravy ($13.50) is outfitted with a frisée salad and always fashionable garlic mashed potatoes. The astonishingly good pistachio-crusted baked cod ($14) comes with asparagus and mashed potatoes that are this time infused with basil. While all the desserts look special, flaky-crusted, beautifully caramelized tarte tatin ($5) tastes especially so.

Osaka

Just as guys called Tiny are rarely mistaken for jockeys, eateries named after giant metropolises seldom accommodate the population of a single brownstone. The oversized ambition suits a clever sushi joint, named after a city known as "the kitchen of Japan", which aspires to be both better than and equal to a trusty neighborhood restaurant. Osaka safeguards the honored status of a local favorite through its friendly feel and improvised informality. The clientele consists largely of drop-ins from the Cobble Hill Cinemas. But much of the food,

| Cost | Lunch $11–30 |
| | Dinner $18–50 |

Address 272 Court St,
between Butler & Douglass Sts
☎718/643-0044
Transportation F,G to Bergen St
Open Sun–Thurs 11.30am–
3pm & 5–10.30pm, Fri & Sat
11.30am–3pm & 5–11pm
Accepts MasterCard & Visa
Reservations Not accepted

JAPANESE

cooked or raw, is too good to be dismissed by destination diners, and the decor—circular metallic place mats, blond-wood benches, washi-lined panels suspended below halogen fixtures—is stylish enough to welcome wayfarers from foreign zip codes.

The three-man sushi crew is headed by Kenny Li, a craftsman with a knack for reptilian-looking rolls. The spicy Osaka roll ($7.95), with extra-crisp salmon skin, fine strands of crab, and ground seaweed salad, is a long scorpion wrapped in wide swirls of green (avocado) and orange (flying fish roe). The sweet dragon roll ($8.95), containing eel and wondrously thin slices of ripe avocado, is a cucumber-tailed monster breathing cool flames of ginger. The rice-heavy black pepper roll ($6.95) is an inside-out sensation of tuna, avocado, and a spicy special sauce. No roll, however, can surpass the complex pleasures of the salmon skin salad ($5.50)—a leaf-lined glass bowl of candied salmon skin countered by a mildly spicy salad of cucumber, seaweed, and sesame seeds. Panko-crusted tempura, ordered as an hors d'oeuvre ($4.95) or main course ($10.95–14.95), revitalizes the tired, often soggy standard.

There are a few wrong notes. Teriyaki shrimp ($11.95) may be sweet and snappy, but the sauce is thick and gooey. Chewy meat in the beef sukiyaki ($13.95) detracts from the exquisite arrangement of glass noodles, gently cooked vegetables, and fragrant broth. Fried banana with honey sauce ($3.50) would be a hit in any locality. But tempura (fried) ice cream, with a hardened crust that breaks off its frozen filling, should be categorized as a NAMBY (Not In My Back Yard) dessert.

Carroll Gardens, Cobble Hill & Boerum Hill

Patois

Many years from today, walking tours of historic Brooklyn will no doubt stop at this, the cozy *fin-de-siècle* bistro where chef Alan Harding and partners Jim and Paul Mamary ignited the Smith Street restaurant boom. We can practically hear the guide recalling service so friendly it was hokey. How when the recorded voice of the late French songstress Barbara met the hot-garlicky scent of the buttery spinach-cushioned escargots in mid-air, the effect was of some make-believe Paris occupied by Brooklynites. Peeking inside, tour groups will see the red banquettes, missile-shaped lamps, and old tin ceiling, and wonder how the premises could date from the late 1990s and not some fifty years earlier. The guide will explain all about retro fashions and the ensuing dining renaissance during the first decade of the twenty-first century.

Cost	$27–60

Address 255 Smith St, between Douglass & DeGraw Sts
☎718/855-1535
Transportation F,G to Carroll St
Open Mon–Thurs 6–10.30pm, Fri & Sat 6–11.30pm, Sun 11am–3pm & 5–10pm
Accepts All major credit cards
Reservations For large groups

Thankfully, back in the present, we can taste the appetizers for ourselves. Tangy mussels steamed in beer and fresh thyme ($8). Thick split pea soup with pancetta crisps and croutons ($7). Duck liver mousse ennobled with poached pears and a braised-fig vinaigrette ($8). A cutesy leek, potato, and blue cheese tart ($7.50). Rustic, piping hot entrees are presented as integrated ensembles rather than as main courses with two accompaniments. There are at least four standouts. Superbly succulent roast chicken au poivre ($14), luscious to the bone, is perfectly matched with wilted, peppercorn-dotted greens, and lumpy mashed potatoes. Rigatoni is tossed with Swiss chard, white beans, sausage, and fresh garlic ($14). Fabulous duck confit and pumpkin ravioli in a buttery cream sauce ($14) are al dente at their jagged seams, but softly translucent in their puffy middles—two chews in one pasta. The lamb and bean casserole ($17) is a delight.

Sloppy cooking spoils both the grilled porkchops ($16) with cabbage and roast apple compote as well as the grilled slab of tough sirloin with sodden fries. And desserts ($6), ranging from the jelly-textured tarte tatin to the leaden profiteroles, are too mediocre to be remembered for fifty minutes, much less fifty years.

The Red Rail

AMERICAN

You won't find steep hills, dense fogs, or Tony Bennett's heart on the streets of Carroll Gardens. Yet approaching the deceptively familiar Red Rail neon sign, the atmosphere is so suggestive of San Francisco that you can practically feel the heaviness in your tired thighs, the misty sky, and Anthony Benedetto's signature lament. The neighborhood blend of bedrock Italians and freshly rooted bourgeois bohemian Brooklynites—BoBoBros—echoes the changing demographics of North Beach, the San Francisco enclave that gave New York Joe DiMaggio. The laid-back mood inside this sentimental luncheonette, coupled with its taste for tofu and grits, goat cheese and Monterey Jack, Formica tables and old plastic radios, transports you to northern California quicker than United Airlines. Still not convinced? The Red Rail offers valet stroller parking, a kid-friendly amenity that's a natural extension of the easygoing, sweetheart service. This is the kind of place that when you can't decide between the goat cheese salad and the Caesar, warmhearted waitresses will passionately debate the merits of each as if their rent money—no small amount in these parts—were riding on your decision.

| Cost | Lunch $8–20 |
| | Dinner $20–40 |

Address 502 Henry St at Sackett St
☎718/875-1283
Transportation F,G to Carroll St
Open Sun–Thurs 9.30am–3.30pm & 5.30–10pm, Fri & Sat 9.30am–3pm & 5.30–11pm
Accepts Cash only
Reservations Not accepted

The crackling home-fried potatoes offer reason enough to brave the sizeable crowds that show up for weekend brunch ($10 prix fixe). But you can better experience those spuds and the solid burrito stuffed with eggs, vegetarian chili, and Jack cheese ($7.50) amid the West Coast calm of breakfast. Otherwise try lunch and one of two superb sandwiches assembled on bread baked by Brooklyn legend Paul Cammareri. The triple-decker portobello club sandwich ($8), with bacon, roasted pepper, and pesto mayo, is stacked between thick slices cut from a Pullman loaf. The Sacramento cheesesteak sandwich ($8.50) squeezes a real steak (it takes some chewing), goops of melted cheese, mushrooms, and clandestine hot pepper into a garlic-slathered ciabatta roll.

Dinner is less consistent, though you can't go wrong with the cold linguine and smoked salmon salad ($8). The inch-thick pork chop ($14) with truffle mashed potatoes and broccoli rabe is fabulous, too. Desserts, however, disappoint.

NEW AMERICAN

Restaurant Saul

The alternately challenging and modest designs of Saul and Lisa Bolton are in perfect sync with a community that is thrilled about but also a little fearful of its gentrification and accompanying explosion of new restaurants. Tin ceiling tiles, stamped with a retro motif, constitute a blend of both the quaint and newly resourceful Brooklyn. One exposed brick wall has a varnished sheen; the other, left untreated, is without luster.

Cost	$35–70

Address 140 Smith St,
between Bergen & Dean Sts
☎718/935-9844
Transportation F to Bergen St
Open Sun, Mon, Wed & Thurs
5.30–10.30pm, Fri & Sat 5.30-
11pm
Accepts MasterCard & Visa
Reservations Suggested

Saul the chef also wants his short, cloth-bound menu both ways. The high-quality ingredients and meticulous preparation distinguish a cooking alumnus of Bouley and Le Bernardin. But the sweet excesses, as well as the prevalence of devilishly good mashed potatoes, reflect the personal tastes of a self-indulgent home cook. If he likes crème anglaise *and* caramel sauce poured around a superb warm apple tart that requires neither, that's how it is to be served. It's not for nothing that Saul gives the place his first name.

Dinner begins with a gratis amuse bouche, ideally the Pecorino-dusted wild mushroom soup sipped from a sake cup. Its pointed saltiness makes for a consummate tickler. If you're doubly lucky, the steamed mussels in a white wine broth gently seasoned with tarragon will then make a guest appearance as the special appetizer of the day ($9). The best nightly starter is the duck confit ($10), as much for the Gorgonzola-stuffed poached pear as for the crisp, succulent, beautifully bronzed, sufficiently fatty duck. The bacon and onion tartlet ($8), with fromage blanc standing in for an eggy, quiche-like filling, inspires lasting loyalties. But the tuna tartare ($11), handsomely plated with avocado purée, is saturated to disadvantage in almost syrup-sweet soy sauce. This forfeits the feel of the tuna.

Sweet main courses like the juicy roast loin of pork with a white wine shallot sauce ($21) and the garlic-sauced roast chicken with a splendid mix of veggies ($18) benefit enormously from the piping hot dishes on which they are served. For closers ($6-7), the lemon custard soufflé and the frilly baked Alaska mated with a chocolate cookie are yummy.

Sam's

In the heart of Brooklyn's bistro boom and in a classic neighborhood beset by surges of gentrification and Manhattanization, how nice it is to have a homely but oh-so-homey place to fall back on. When the new and prosperous locals see the wine list at this old Italian place for the first time, they might easily assume its prices—$11 to $17—are per glass rather than per bottle. Those with young children soon come to cherish the low ceiling, wood paneling, plastic-covered and kid-friendly tables, and the florescent-burning time warp those dated fixtures represent. Where's the fun in moving to Brooklyn without the opportunity to drink a cheap red out of a juice glass and slurp large platefuls of red-sauce-smothered, fifteen-minute spaghetti at a moment's notice?

Cost	$10–45

Address 238 Court St at Baltic St

☎718/596-3458

Transportation F,G to Bergen St

Open Daily noon–10.30pm

Accepts Cash only

Reservations For large groups

Sentimentality aside, there are two very good reasons to include Sam's on your essential dining list. The first is pizza. Walk through the front dining room to the rear of the back one and you will reach a trapezoidal opening offering a peek into the kitchen—and history. Inside is a free-standing pizza oven made of Philadelphia brick that was installed at this address, like Sam's itself, in 1930. The old man who's been baking pizzas here for some fifteen years is named Mario, but if you call out "Sam" he will turn his head and say, "What?" The crusts he bakes in that oven are phenomenal. Thin in the middle, a little puffy on the ends, crisp but not hard, delectable to the chew, nice bend. It would be great with just olive oil, but Mario/Sam loads them with runny, unspiced tomato sauce and divinely oozy mozzarella. A large, eight-slice pie is $15; a single slice, $5 (no kidding). Any additional toppings or, for that matter, Italian appetizers and entrees are too dicey to endorse. The $6.50 antipasto is hapless.

The second great thing about Sam's is the Italian (ricotta) cheesecake ($3.25). Dusted with powdered sugar, the crunchy, soaking-wet wedge may look forlorn, but that's how it's supposed to be. This is one of the greatest ugly cheesecakes of them all.

Sherwood Café

Sherwood Café is an apt name for such a fairy tale of a restaurant. An impressive antique crystal chandelier fills the room with dancing light produced by the kind of flicker bulbs you find at 99¢ stores. A shabby six-foot-tall Madonna and Child acts as the room's centerpiece. You almost forget that baby Jesus is missing his left arm as your attention is stolen by the non-rotating disco ball hung in the right corner of the room. It appears as though each fixture is trying to out-kitsch the next. Every item with a little

Cost	$18–40

Address 195 Smith St,
between Baltic & Warren Sts
☎718/596-1609
Transportation F,G to Bergen
St
Open Mon–Fri noon–midnight,
Sat & Sun 11am–midnight
Accepts Cash only
Reservations For large groups

orange sticker on it is actually for sale. Now if only the patrons would do some buying and relieve some of the clutter. Cobble Hill's slacker-bohemian counterpart to cafe society sits for many moody hours drinking cafés au lait and espressos, only to be interrupted by their most feared vision of their future selves: yuppie mommies and daddies trying to negotiate their fully accessorized, twin-engine baby strollers through the overcrowded dining room.

As the waiter seats you, he'll probably ask if you'd like a coffee. When in Rome… or France… that is to say, Brooklyn… why not skip the java and have a $5-6 glass of the house red (Côtes de Rhône) or white (Pinot Blanc). The rillettes ($5) comprise a hearty portion of very good shredded goose pâté served with a garnish of cornichons, pickled pearl onions, and olives. It's great spread on the crusty French (or Brooklyn?) bread. Or try one of the large cheese planchons ($15), samplers of French (decidedly *not* Brooklyn) cheese that are great for sharing.

The open-faced Croque Monsieur ($8.50) is a ham and Swiss sandwich loaded with rich béchamel sauce and thoughtfully served with a mesclun salad. For even heartier fare, try the roasted free-range chicken ($12.50) served with garlicky string beans and incredibly rich mashed potatoes. After cutting into the crisp, perfectly browned chicken skin, a cloud of trapped steam escapes screaming praise of the luscious meat below. For dessert, put a buy order on the chocolate cake decked out with fresh raspberries and real whipped cream ($4.50).

Coney Island, Brighton Beach, Sheepshead Bay & Homecrest

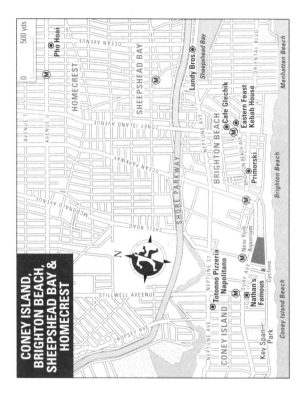

**CONEY ISLAND,
BRIGHTON BEACH,
SHEEPSHEAD BAY &
HOMECREST**

0   500 yds

Pho Hoai

HOMECREST

SHEEPSHEAD BAY

Sheepshead Bay

Lundy Bros.

Cafe Glechik

BRIGHTON BEACH

Eastern Feast
Kebab House

Primorski

Brighton Beach

New York
Aquarium

CONEY ISLAND

Totonno Pizzeria
Napolitano

Nathan's
Famous

Key Span
Park

Cyclone

Coney Island Beach

Manhattan Beach

AVENUE T

AVENUE U

OCEAN AVENUE

CONEY ISLAND AVENUE

OCEAN PARKWAY

MCDONALD AVENUE

SHELL ROAD

SHORE PARKWAY

STILLWELL AVENUE

CROPSEY AVE

NEPTUNE AVE

NEPTUNE ST

SURF AVE

NEPTUNE AVE

BRIGHTON BEACH AVE

ORIENTAL BLVD

Cafe Glechik

RUSSIAN

You need to take a deep breath before stepping from the dark gray of Coney Island Avenue into the blinding whiteness of Cafe Glechik. Though just a block from the Russian shops, markets, and nightclubs of bustling Brighton Beach Avenue, this rustic eatery seems a world apart from an ethnic enclave that is itself a world apart. The scene between walls adorned with traditional, hand-embroidered white linens and blouses does not appear any less exotic once your narrowing pupils have adjusted to the snug storefront's bright light. Nearly every square foot of the animated dining floor is covered with tables, every square inch of which is covered with pots, crocks, pans, bowls, clay casseroles, and plates, every millimeter of which is heaped with foods not immediately recognizable to even the most cosmopolitan American. Explanations in broken English don't help all that much. What the heck is "green borscht" anyway? As New York eating adventures go, Cafe Glechik is one amazing ride.

Cost	$8–35

Address 3159 Coney Island Ave, between Brighton Beach & Oceanview Aves
☏718/616-0494
Transportation Q to Brighton Beach
Open Daily 11am–11pm
Accepts Cash only
Reservations Not accepted

And is it cheap! A big hearty bowl of that mildly sour green borscht, stocked with rice, chopped hard-boiled eggs, and sorrel (the green part) is $4. The steaming hot, dill-seasoned, curative chicken soup loaded with chewy, mini-pelemyi (dumplings) just $4.50. And the pot of country-style mushroom, barley, and bean soup provides a meal for $5.50. Round one of your meal should also involve herring and potato ($4), smoked mackerel ($4), and vareniki, which are large, half-moon dumplings filled with potato, cabbage, or meat and served in a large crock ($4–4.50 for an order of 25).

The prospect of entrees may have you phoning friends for reinforcements. This is more than you and your dinner companions bargained for. Stuffed cabbage packed with minced pork and carrots ($6.50) is substantial enough even without the swathe of sour cream. The beef stew in-a-pot sweetly enriched with prunes ($8.50) is a challenge for two to knock off. And that's not factoring in the salty, garlicky, dill-flecked new potatoes swimming in butter. For dessert, the vareniki return, this time with bubbling farmer cheese and a sour cherry-jam sauce.

Eastern Feast Kebab House

The magnificent domes and minarets of Samarkand depicted in the large murals are echoed in the tapered patterns of the artificial brickwork. The pink-patterned stonework cast onto the laminate tables is yet another humble indication of cultural pride. And the new tin ceiling and exposed ventilation duct are the trimmings of an eatery firmly planted in modern-day Brooklyn. Still, the most prominent and noble display of Eastern Feast's identity past and present is both in the glass display cases up front and atop the large charcoal grill

Cost	$7–25

Address 1003 Brighton Beach
Ave at Coney Island Ave
☎718/934-9608
Transportation Q to Brighton
Beach
Open Sun–Thurs noon–10pm,
Fri noon–10.30pm, Sat
noon–11pm
Accepts Cash only
Reservations Not accepted

in the window. Speared onto metal skewers that make the ordinary wooden ones look like toothpicks, the lamb, beef, pork, and chicken kebabs look fit for a man—a very large man—who would be king. When the wind is blowing in from the south and the grill is fully engaged, the charcoal smoke travels all the way up the boardwalk to entice French and German tourists as well as resident Russian sunbathers with the smells they associate with summer vacations by the Black Sea.

Once drawn in, it isn't only the kebabs that demand attention. A wonderful combination plate ($8) may be assembled from such cold appetizers as finely grated carrots sharpened with lemon and black pepper; firm white beans with crunchy red onions; assorted pickled vegetables; pepper-red couscous; hummus; eggplant caviar, or babaganoush. Alone they are just $3. Among soups there is the option of Ubeki lagman ($6), with lamb chunks, vegetables, and thick homemade noodles in a meat borscht, and the Russian alternative of a meaty hot borscht ($4). The cheburekas ($2), parsley-spiced meat turnovers, are best when still fresh and not subjected to a microwave reheat.

Kebabs may be ordered as single skewers ($3.50 with a pedestrian salad and rice or fries) or as part of a two-skewer platter ($10). Although some diners take on two and even three kebabs, even one constitutes a hard night's work for most people. Forget the paprika-dusted chicken version and stick to the tender, juicy, charred chunks—actually, they would have to be cut in four to be called chunks—of lamb.

Lundy Bros

Ask a dozen Kings County kibitzers for the inside dope on the circa 1995 Lundy's and you're liable to hear the same refrain. "The food stinks," they groan. "Except maybe the biscuits, the steamers, the Boston chowder. And the crabcakes. And the fries. And the rice pudding." Imagine what they'd say if they actually liked the place? That's not to poke fun at sentimentalists who see the futility of trying to relive their most cherished memories from the original Lundy's, which closed in the late-1970s. Nor to downplay the unpardonable seriousness of frequent service lapses and overcooked lobsters. But it sure is swell to reencounter the stucco archways, stained-glass windows, and iron-railed stairway of this great Mediterranean villa on Sheepshead Bay.

| Cost | Lunch $20–50 |
| | Dinner $25–75 |

Address 1901 Emmons Ave at Ocean Ave
☎718/743-0022
Transportation Q to Sheepshead Bay
Open Sun–Wed 11am–2pm & 5–9pm, Thurs 11am–2pm & 5–10pm, Fri 11am–2pm & 5pm–midnight, Sat 11am–2pm & 5pm–2am
Accepts All major credit cards
Reservations Suggested

SEAFOOD

The updated menu faithfully preserves a few essentials, namely the Southern biscuits, the steamers, and special "Shore Dinners." Baked with White Lily flour, the biscuits, when served warm (if they're not, send them back) are as good as the originals. Just think, immigrants who can no longer take their kids to see the Dodgers at Ebbets Field can at least give them a Brooklyn welcome to America through Lundy's biscuits. Meaty steamers accompany the Deluxe Shore Dinner, along with a cup of creamy clam chowder (forget the thin, Brooklyn red version), a half-steamed lobster, a piece of fish, two sides (you probably want creamed spinach and the long, bronzed deli fries), dessert, and coffee for $25.95.

Fried fish—calamari ($7.95 as an appetizer), shrimp ($18.95), diver sea scallops ($19.95), flounder ($16.95), a fisherman's platter containing all four ($21.95)—are better than mediocre grilled or broiled choices ($16–22). Among other options, the thin-crusted pizzas ($7.95–11.95), linguine with white clam sauce ($15.95), and chopped steak ($10.95) are all pretty good. Enormous desserts (about $6) don't merit blowing your monthly calorie budget in a single night. You might share the blueberry pie four to six ways.

The Manhattan Lundy's, opened in 2001, is pretty much a disaster. It's at 205 West 50th St, Midtown West (☎212/586-0022).

Coney Island, Brighton Beach…

Nathan's Famous

The sentimental strollers along the Coney Island boardwalk all have the same fantasy. They close their eyes for a moment, then reopen them to see the world's playground in its heyday. Suddenly, all the vanished arcades, rides, funhouses, and restaurants are back. A Brooklyn kid flips his last nickel in the air. If it lands heads, he uses it to buy a subway token; tails, he grabs yet another frankfurter at Nathan's and walks home. The pinch that awakes everyone from this nostalgic dream is the $1.50 subway fare, the $2.15 price of a frankfurter, and, alas, the disappearance through age, neglect, or vandalism of most of Coney's storied attractions. Still, there is reason for optimism. The opening in 2001 of a minor league baseball stadium, KeySpan Park, has revitalized the area. Nathan's has for the first time set up outdoor picnic tables for on-site munching. And nothing short of a happy ending to Hamlet could match the timeless thrill from the first explosive bite of a juicy, garlicky, naturally encased Nathan's frank.

Cost	$3–15

Address 1310 Surf Ave at Stillwell Ave
☏718/946-2202
Transportation F,Q,W to Coney Island-Stillwell Ave
Open Daily 8am–midnight
Accepts Cash only
Reservations Not accepted

The traditionalists who claim the franks are better at the original emporium than at the franchises are not romantic fools. The snappy casing and luscious spices may be the same, but there's no way to duplicate the surroundings. Location affects how things taste and it's silly to think otherwise. It's why the very red wine you adored at a Parisian brasserie doesn't taste the same at home. In the instance of Nathan's, the ocean breeze that whistles down from the boardwalk, the classic neon signs above the landmark, and the dexterity of the pros who work the grills are factors that cannot be duplicated. Even the Nathan's franks served during Brooklyn Cyclones games inside KeySpan Park taste different. Perhaps it's because they're about double the price. Or maybe it's that classic "baseball" taste—another factor that's impossible to explain.

Franks get lonely without an order of crisp-edged, golden-brown, crinkle-cut, half-moon French fries ($1.83, $2.37, or $2.91). They're fried in corn oil, usually very hot, and rarely soggy. Other items rate well below the franks and the fries.

Pho Hoai

The delighted diners from a distant Q-train depot regarded a pause between courses as a welcome chance to rewind their appetites. Anthony, the assistant manager of Pho Hoai, was happily surprised to catch their chopsticks in the resting position, and seized the moment to satisfy his curiosity. "How," he asked, "does our food compare to Chinatown?" That query was the only thing the Vietnamese eatery and its capable staff got wrong all evening. The question should have been, "How does Chinatown's food compare to ours?" The superiority of this informal, utilitarian neighborhood eatery is probably due to the fact that it is geared towards Vietnamese students who live nearby and seem to care as much about what they eat as how they look.

Cost	Lunch $7–25
	Dinner $10–35

Address 1906 Ave U, between East 19th & East 20th Sts
℡718/616-1233
Transportation Q to Ave U
Open Daily noon–11pm
Accepts Cash only
Reservations Not accepted

VIETNAMESE

The crunchy, ungreasy cha gio (Vietnamese spring rolls; $3.25) and the thin layer of clean-tasting oil on the fried crab plate ($8.95) prove that anything fried merits consideration. The joy of those crabs ranges from the sweet meat tucked into the top shell to the last tasty bits of fried onion and scallion. Even these are surpassed by the so nuoc dua ($6.95), incomparably meaty mussels wrongly translated on the menu as clams. The sweet, spicy, and buttery components of the mussel broth epitomize a kind of balanced ensemble cooking that eludes other Southeast Asian kitchens. The same harmony is even apparent in fresh, nicely cut squid sautéed with lemongrass, onions, crunchy green pepper, and spicy red chile sauce ($6.95).

While powerful hits of lemongrass, chile, or cilantro can provide great action, it is also a thrill when delicate flavors are drawn out but not drowned out by the dominant notes. Such is the case with table-grilled beef ($10.95), barbecued shrimp on sugar cane ($7.95), beef fondue (thin slices of raw meat that you cook in broth at the table; $10.95), and seventeen varieties of rice noodle beef soup ($3.95–4.95). Each big bowl is a meal in itself. Forego dessert and close instead with a hot or iced coffee with sweet condensed milk.

Primorski

Faced with stiff competition from the glitzier nightclubs in and around Brighton Beach, Primorski endures as the affordable and now quaint option for Russian-style banquets with a Georgian-Jewish slant. Its ballroom is flanked on both sides by illuminated, painted-glass wall plaques bearing colorful seascapes and the scripted word *Primorski*—"by the water." On a bandstand sheathed in sheets of reflective yellow plastic, a quartet of three vocalists and one keyboardist performs Russian, American, and Continental pop deep into the night. Only the food is more relentlessly entertaining.

| Cost | Lunch $9–30 |
| | Dinner $25–65 |

Address 282 Brighton Beach Ave, between Brighton 2nd & Brighton 3rd Sts
☏718/891-3111
Transportation Q to Brighton Beach
Open Mon–Thurs 11am–5pm & 7pm–midnight, Fri 11am–5pm & 7pm–2am, Sat 11am–4pm & 7pm–2am, Sun 11am–4pm & 7pm–1am
Accepts All major credit cards

The customary way to eat at Brooklyn's Russian nightclubs is from a pre-set banquet menu. Primorski's prix fixe (from $25 per person on weeknights to $35 on weekends) includes overlapping onslaughts of warm yeasty flatbread, hot appetizers, pickled vegetables, smoked fish platters, cold vegetable salads, cold cuts, Russian crêpes, several hot entrees, assorted shashlik, fresh fruit, desserts, coffee or tea, bottomless soft drinks, and one bottle (per five diners) of Kremlovskya vodka. For anyone unfamiliar with the cuisine, the advantage of the banquet is that there's no difficulty communicating with the waiters and you get to try many things without any nasty surprises when the bill comes. The disadvantage is that you probably don't want all that food, and that the superb appetizers fill you up long before the shashlik arrives. Mind you, nothing about those mediocre kebabs will have you regretting any initial lack of restraint.

Should you choose from the extremely inexpensive a la carte menu, the starters you don't want to miss are the potato dumplings with grilled onions ($3.90), the basturma (thinly sliced dried beef; $3.90), the gefilte fish (Primorski's version of the Jewish poached fishcakes are pâté-like; $5), eggplant caviar ($2.50), and khachapuri (a warm, lightly salty, fabulously flaky, and gently crusty Georgian cheese bread; $3). If entrees are still relevant, consider the wonderful stuffed cabbage ($6.25) or stuffed grape leaves ($6.75) instead of the grilled meats. Daily soup-and-entree lunch specials are $5.99, vodka not included.

Totonno Pizzeria Napolitano

All eyes were on Joel Ciminieri's hands as he slid out what appeared to still be New York's finest pizza from the old brick oven. He pretended not to notice when his wife Louise, known to the cognoscenti as Cookie, inspected the pie's underside and noticed a tiny pop hole. Through coded messages perfected only through years of happily married life, Cookie gave Joel a look that said, "what the heck is this?" He glared back paragraphs about

Cost	$7–30

Address 1524 Neptune Ave, between 80th & 81st Sts

☎718/372-8606

Transportation F,Q,W to Coney Island-Stillwell Ave

Open Wed–Sun noon–8.30pm

Accepts Cash only

Reservations Not accepted

PIZZA

the joys of working alone. Indeed, the greatest challenge then for Joel and now for his son and successor Lawrence is not in sustaining a 75-plus-year tradition. Rather, it's getting their pizzas past the very tough Cookie who is respectively the niece and granddaughter of the legendary pizzaiollos Jerry Pero and Anthony "Totonno" Pero.

The original shop (the Upper East Side satellite, 1544 Second Ave, ☎212/327-2800, lacks the same quality control) is hidden among auto-repair lots in a rundown residential area far removed from the Coney Island beach and boardwalk. Only a screen door separates you from the aromas and emotions of 1924. Not much has changed inside the tin-and-wood, table-service eatery since then, except that some of the yellowed newspaper clippings heralding war and baseball victories have been replaced by glowing framed reviews.

The pizza ($15 and up for a large pie) is elemental. Nothing to it, as Lawrence says. Just good handmade mozzarella, imported tomatoes, and a coal oven. Yet there is magic in the hands of a baker who turns out a crust so thin, chewy, crisp, and lightly charred as his. Furthermore, something supernatural happens when the tomatoes and cheese melt under the volcanic heat of that oven. Interestingly, the true flavor of the classic, New York-style Margherita is not tomato. It's the salty tang acquired from a dusting of Pecorino Romano. Extra toppings (sausage, pepperoni, anchovies, etc) are minimal, as they should be. Instead of doctoring this pizza, the best policy would be to strip it down. Requesting a red pie (no mozzarella) or a white pie (no tomato) garners a nod of approval from Cookie.

Fort Greene

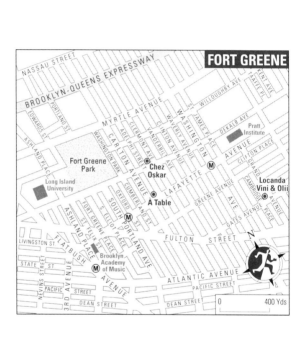

FORT GREENE

NASSAU STREET

BROOKLYN-QUEENS EXPRESSWAY

EDWARDS ST

PORTLAND ST

MYRTLE AVENUE

WILLOUGHBY AVE

JAMES PLACE

WASHINGTON

WAVERLY AVENUE

CLINTON AVENUE

VANDERBILT AVE

CLERMONT AVE

ADELPHI STREET

CARLTON AVENUE

WASHINGTON PARK

DEKALB AVE

AVENUE

Pratt Institute

CLIFTON PLACE

GRAND AVENUE

ASHLAND PLACE

PORTLAND ST

Fort Greene Park

Chez Oskar

Ⓜ

LAFAYETTE

GREENE AVENUE

Locanda Vini & Olii

Long Island University

OXFORD ST

CUMBERLAND ST

A Table

ST FELIX ST

S. PORTLAND AVE

GATES AVENUE

GRAND AVENUE

FORT GREENE PLACE

S. ELLIOT PLACE

Ⓜ

FULTON STREET

LIVINGSTON ST

FLATBUSH

Brooklyn Academy of Music

Ⓜ

AVENUE

ATLANTIC AVENUE

STATE ST

NEVINS STREET

3RD AVENUE

PACIFIC STREET

PACIFIC STREET

DEAN STREET

DEAN STREET

N

0   400 Yds

À Table

(icon) First-time diners from distant precincts who pop in before or after a performance at the Brooklyn Academy of Music would be wrong to imagine that the corner of Lafayette and Adelphi was always like this. With its high wooden ceiling, plaster of Paris walls, old communal tables, and 8ft winged "A" (part of a vintage advertisement), the circa 1999 restaurant looks old enough to be its own grandfather. Given the current fashion for French retro throughout Brooklyn's burgeoning communities, that

Cost	Lunch $12–35
	Dinner $28–65

Address 178 Lafayette Ave at Adelphi St

☎ 718/935-9121

Transportation G to Fulton St; A,C to Lafayette Ave

Open Daily 8am–11pm

Accepts All major credit cards

Reservations For large groups

FRENCH

in itself is hardly unusual. But the absurdly friendly À Table doesn't feel much like a new old bistro either. When a waiter practically sits down at your table while taking an order, you have the feeling he and others before him have done this for decades. When one of the many kids who come in for brunch pulls out a plaything from the toy box, you could easily assume—incorrectly—that his or her smiling parents are reliving a memory from their Fort Greene childhoods.

Chef-owner Jean-Baptiste Caillet, formerly manager at Balthazar (see p.130), pays no mind to trendiness, fuss, or presentation. Good eating is what matters. The baby spinach, sliced avocado, and pine nut salad is an unwieldy heap drizzled with lemon vinaigrette ($9). Likewise, ham, saucisson, country pâté, and garlic sausage are hastily arranged on the abundant charcuterie platter ($8). Small wonder then that monkfish, universally recognized for its ugliness, has become the signature entree. It is served Provençal-style with black olives, pistou, cherry tomatoes, sautéed mushrooms, and potato purée. The next best options are steaks—shell steak au poivre with very good frites ($20) or hanger steak with shallot sauce and a potato gratin ($17).

The wine list features 17 wines under $27. The 1999 Cuvée de Boisfleury from the Pouilly Fumé producer Alain Caibourdin is fruity, mineral-like, and great value at $26. The 1998 Madiran from Chateau Barrejat ($24) is lush with red fruits. A glass of Sauternes or Banyuls may accompany the oozy chocolate soufflé cake ($5), depending on whether you're matching the pistachios, the strawberries, or the chocolate.

Fort Greene

Chez Oskar

(icon) In a jazzy, 17-foot-long mural above a row of red banquettes, painter Charlotta Janssen has portrayed Chez Oskar as an idealized French colonial cafe packed with bohemians, hipsters, refugees, and black marketeers. If you were exiled to Casablanca and desperate for a forged exit visa granting passage to America, this is exactly the sort of place you'd come to get it. All that's missing from Chez Oskar is a guy named

Cost	$25–55

Address 211 Dekalb Ave at Adelphi St
(icon)718/852-6250
Transportation C to Lafayette Ave; G to Fulton St
Open Daily 5pm–midnight
Accepts All major credit cards

Oskar. The proprietor is Charles Sorel, a Parisian who worked as a waiter at three Manhattan bistros and named his first place after the son of his partner. He asked Janssen to fashion a casual and comfortable haunt appropriate for a quiet coffee, a noisy supper, or anything in between. It is she who is responsible for the oval lightshades and blue, gold, and burgundy patinas of this classic corner space with its wood casement windows, terracotta-tiled floor, and stamped-tin ceiling.

Always regard the words "fresh tuna in the Niçoise" as an indicator of good things to come. That and three other composed salads ($7–9.50) reveal a kitchen with a true bistro soul that doesn't bother with pretty presentation. The chef's concern is with getting as much and as many of his favorite foods on a single plate as possible. For openers there's no topping the mussels marinières ($10) with plenty of onions, fresh tomatoes, and white wine broth to sop up with crusty bread from Sullivan Bakery.

Of the entrees, the poached cod ($15) arrives as a Provençal festival with a chunky, ratatouille-style stew of vegetables, potato gratin, and a rich tapenade draped over half the fish. This is overkill of the best kind. The sirloin steak au poivre ($18.50), with its back-kicking peppercorns and decent fries, is, like a true friend, always there for you, even while the gently seared duck breast ($18) vies for your undivided affection. Then there's the Dijon-sauced roast chicken ($14), which is as juicy as you have the right to expect. By dessert time, only the homemade crème caramel ($6) will prevent you from taking an early exit visa.

Locanda Vini & Olii

🍴 *Locanda* suggests an old Italian inn and the promise of a good meal and a good bed. *Vini & Olii* harkens back to stores that carried wines, olive oils, and produce from local growers. Taken together and today, Locanda Vini & Olii is more than a place of business based on old-world hospitality. It is the libretto for a labor of love staged inside Lewis Drug Store, a 130-year-old Brooklyn pharmacy set among the handsome brick and limestone houses of the nascent Clinton Hill district. Meticulously restoring the stun-

Cost	$25–65

Address 129 Gates Ave at Cambridge Place
☎718/622-9202
Transportation C to Clinton-Washington Aves
Open Tues–Thurs 6–10.30pm, Fri & Sat 6–11.30pm, Sun noon–3pm & 6–10pm
Accepts MasterCard & Visa

ning mahogany woodwork down to every last apothecary display case, drawer, and compartment, Catherine de Zagon Louy and husband François Louy now dispense rustic Tuscan remedies and Italian liquid cure-alls for all kinds of chronic New York ailments.

With chefs Michele Baldacci and Luigi Ghidetti in the kitchen, the goal, according to the Louys, is to assemble the foods a Tuscan housewife might prepare for guests. Everything from the heart and home, even when traveling outside the region for inspiration. The quality of the food, frankly, is not quite as high as you want it to be given that the place is so beautiful and the people are so nice. The cooking is uneven. And blandness seems an occasional consequence of authenticity, especially with the bread and home-baked cakes. That said, you can have a wonderful time passing around such shared plates as the cheeseboard ($9.95), the charcuterie platter ($10.75) and its seafood counterpart (octopus soppressata and tuna salami; $10.75), and the crostini assortment ($12.50), along with such appetizers as sardines in a sweet-and-sour marinade ($8) and wild boar carpaccio ($9.75).

The great second-act aria is the chestnut lasagnette ($9.50), white ribbons of pasta with chickpeas and a Luganega pork sausage ragu. It's just one of several pastas, along with chewy bigoli (thicker than spaghetti) with porcini ($9.75), and melt-in-the-mouth eggplant ravioli with tomatoes ($9.75), that upstage the meat and fish entrees. The wine list, pasted on a bottle, proposes well-chosen reds—the complex but rounded 1999 Costa Vecchia Pietra Pinta ($25) is especially good—at low markups.

Park Slope

PARK SLOPE

Al Di La

The last thing on your mind when dining in Al Di La is *l'al di la*—"the life beyond." For what mortal can train his thoughts on the afterlife while the dizzying aroma of sage-scented garlic soup is in the air and the broth's silky finish is lingering on the palate? What living soul can obsess about destiny with spoon-shaped, gnocchi-like malfatti constructed of Swiss chard, ricotta, and Parmigiano-Reggiano in play? And what true New Yorker can utter even one sentence in the future tense before Mrs Di Rosa's meatballs have been polished off?

Cost	$25–50

Address 248 5th Ave at Carroll St

☎718/783-4565

Transportation M,N,R to Union St

Open Mon, Wed & Thurs 6–10.30pm, Fri & Sat 6–11pm, Sun 6–10pm

Accepts MasterCard, Visa

Reservations Not accepted

ITALIAN

By suspending a Murano blown-glass chandelier from the varnished tin ceiling of an old Brooklyn storefront, Italian-born cooking teacher Emiliano Coppa and American chef Anna Klinger (formerly of Lespinasse and the Union Square Cafe, p.83) have fashioned an enchanting marriage of Venetian and Brooklynese design. Theirs is a neighborhood place superior to 99 percent of all destination restaurants.

Some of the rotated dishes on the hand-printed menu used to be listed only in Italian, requiring explanations from Coppa. This was fortunate, as he is a gracious host whose soft voice and accent could make canned peas sound irresistible. People have been known to ask him twice what the "bigoli" in duck ragu are, just to hear him repeat his description of that delectably chewy, whole-wheat spaghetti. Typical of the fine antipasti options are mussels steamed in white wine with grilled bread, shallots, garlic, and tomato ($8.50); and a nice pairing of baccala mantecato (salt cod whisked with oil in the manner of a mayonnaise) and grilled polenta cake ($8).

Among main courses, the braised veal cheeks ($18.50) are so tender and unctuous they may have begun to cook even before the lease for Al Di La was signed. Gently seasoned whole orata fish ($20) baked in a hard crust of coarse salt is as juicy as can be, and sliced hanger steak served with balsamic-tossed arugula ($13.75) is sensational. Desserts (all $6), never Al Di La's strong suit, encompass a chocolate hazelnut ice cream, a ricotta tart, and a warm pear cake with bittersweet chocolate chips.

Park Slope

Bistro St Mark's

Park Slope may have been seeking in a bistro what many of us look for in a mate: an appearance that is contemporary and attractive, with a down-to-earth nature underneath it all. The sleekly modern and mirrored Bistro St Mark's, with its comfy banquettes and neighborly ways, is exactly that. Finding true love is nevertheless a tricky business. Some locals find the place too noisy; its service, too slow. But most are grateful to have a restaurant that understands them and takes time to listen.

Cost	Lunch $15–45
	Dinner $30–65

Address 76 St Mark's Ave, between 6th & Flatbush Aves
☎718/857-8600
Transportation 1,2,4 to Bergen St
Open Mon–Thurs 5.30–11pm, Fri 5.30pm–midnight, Sat 11am–4pm & 5.30pm–midnight, Sun 11am–4pm & 5.30– 11pm
Accepts All major credit cards
Reservations Suggested

Chef Johannes Sanzin cooks for a community that's predominantly liberal in politics but conservative about food. His menu reads as sophisticated and fussy, but the dishes it outlines ultimately come across as accessible. He truly knows how to work that trendy/down-to-earth thing, especially when it comes to appetizers. Jalapeno-infused scallop carpaccio ($7) has more of a spicy tickle than burn. In the lemon-cilantro accompaniment for grilled sardines ($9), each flavor is distinct but none overpowers. The mushroom salad with fresh herbs and Asian pears ($6) startles mostly by its freshness. And caramelized sea scallops with pasta and tomato cilantro sauce ($8) is a short story with the depth of a novel.

Seasonal main courses are firmly in the bistro mold. The relationships between meats/fish and their sides are splendid; witness the leg of lamb with potato-leek gratin and flageolet beans ($16), the braised beef cheeks with fresh horseradish nosing into the lush meat and mashed potatoes ($15), and the monkfish medallions with two olive sauces and pistachio oil ($16). Even pastry chef Jean Marc Hardy manages to be at once fashionable and grounded. Ricotta tart with green tomato jam and lemon sorbet ($5) fools you into thinking it's exotic. On the other hand, it could easily be mistaken for the inspiration of a country gardener trying to figure out what to do with all those green tomatoes. The pairing of yogurt ice cream with Grand Marnier-marinated strawberry ($7) replays familiar flavor associations. And the volcano-hot molten chocolate soufflé with fine vanilla ice cream ($7) is among the best of its kind.

Cafe Steinhof

The late actress Hildegard Knef was hailed by critics as "the thinking man's Marlene Dietrich" and described by Ella Fitzgerald as "the greatest singer in the world without a voice." That solves the mystery of the haunting beauty in that old movie poster and eliminates the only distraction to keep you from loving Cafe Steinhof. Few would dare call this the thinking man's Wallsé (see p.180) or Café Sabarsky (p.258). It's not half as serious or expensive as those Manhattan eateries. But Paul Goebert's spin-off of Max & Moritz, his nearby French-American bistro (see p.342), is indisputably the world's greatest Austrian pub in Brooklyn. Brick walls, bench-style mahogany banquettes, and Austrian-German memorabilia transport this Park Slope corner to Vienna's Bermuda Dreieck. You'll soon believe it once you've established a rapport with such house draughts as Jever (an Austrian pilsner), Gosser (an Austrian lager), and Schneider Weisse (a German wheat beer).

Cost	$20–45
Address 422 7th Ave at 14th St	
☎718/369-7776	
Transportation F to 7th Ave	
Open Mon 5–11pm, Tues–Thurs 11am–4pm & 5–11pm, Fri & Sat 11am–4pm & 5pm–midnight, Sun 11am–4pm & 5–11pm	
Accepts All major credit cards	
Reservations Not accepted	

Within Steinhof the friendly pub is a pretty good little bistro welcoming to children and other beings who do not drink alcohol. That said, those who drop in on a presumably quiet Monday night are in for a surprise. Sure, early-week spaghetti promos or chicken-wing giveaways are commonplace. But only here does *montag nacht* turn into a rockin' $5 goulash party. Actually, it's the drinkers in particular who may want to steer clear of that one, as there's always the risk of things turning ugly with a five-buck, all-you-can-eat goulash in the offing.

The daily menu lists both snacks and more substantial satisfactions. The assorted cheese and charcuterie plate ($9) ably fills both needs. Or you could start with the terrific smoked trout and potato salad appetizer before moving on to such meats as the split and grilled bratwurst ($8.50), the agreeably pink and unusually moist smoked pork loin ($12), or tender sauerbraten with red cabbage purée ($12). The mushroom fricassée with bread dumplings ($9) makes a nice meatless alternative, as do three dynamite desserts: apple bread pudding ($5), linzer torte ($5), and crêpes filled with quark cheese ($5.50).

PERUVIAN

Coco Roco

The price of co-ops in Park Slope is affected by the quality of the nearby public schools. But it's surprising that a large premium is not put on any real estate within delivery reach of Coco Roco. It's not that anyone minds dining elbow-to-elbow with the diverse mix of Brooklyn couples, families, and work buddies. The votive-lit brown paper bags add a touch of romance to an informal space of brush-painted walls, exposed brick, and folkloric decoration. But when you're waiting twenty minutes to place an order that may take thirty minutes to

Cost	$10–50

Address 392 5th Ave, between 6th & 7th Sts
☎718/965-3376
Transportation F to 4th Ave; M,N,R to 9th St
Open Sun–Thurs noon–10.30pm, Fri & Sat noon–11.30pm
Accepts All major credit cards
Reservations For large groups

reach your table, the prospect of glistening rotisserie chicken dropped off at your doorstep is an enticing one. In addition, becoming familiar with pollo a la brasa is crucial to any child's education and thus could very easily fall into the realm of homework.

Coco Roco does many things well besides chicken. Peruvian standards like papa rellena (meat-stuffed potato pies; $5.95), papa a la huancaina (boiled potatoes in spicy cheese sauce; $5.25), and the Lima barbecue addiction anticuchos (skewered beef heart; $6.95) are first-rate. Fresh seafood runs hot (fried squid, steamed mussels, grilled octopus) and cold (eight ceviches). Standouts from the cevicheria are a bracing cocktail of mussels, shrimp, squid, red snapper, cancha (toasted corn), and sweet potato in a spicy lime marinade ($10.95) and a red snapper with only papaya ginger juice as backup ($12.95).

The fact that some mains seem Manhattanized—potato-crusted red snapper ($13.95), say, or grilled salmon with couscous-styled quinoa ($12.95)—is not such a bad thing. Neither is the Argentine lean of the charred sirloin slathered with scallion-powered chimichurri ($13.95). No breath mint can conquer its alliance of scallion and garlic. But it's still a cause for celebration that the chicken spins in a window-front rotisserie kept apart from the cosmopolitan kitchen. It's served in quarters ($3.25), halves ($4.50), whole ($8), or shredded into a thick baguette sandwich with ripe avocado and jalapeno mayo ($4.95). Each dessert ($3.95) is sweeter than the next. Gummy bread pudding is sauced with tres leches, while banana fritters come with amazing tropical fruit ice creams.

Convivium Osteria

The Brooklyn address is a cunning disguise. Convivium Osteria is the sort of family-run inn you dream of coming across on a journey through the Mediterranean countryside. Mom and pop live above a cozy dining room festooned in farmhouse rustic. The lower-level tapas lounge takes after an Iberian wine cellar connected to a charming patio and moon-lit garden. More enchanting still, the dizzy-ing aromas throughout recall three-quar-ters of the owners' origins. Carlo Pulixi was born in Sardinia and raised in Rome. Michelle Pulixi is of Portugese and Irish descent. Accordingly, the robust cooking

Cost	$30–75

Address 68 5th Ave, between Bergen St & St Mark's Ave
☎718/857-1833
Transportation 1,2,4 to Bergen St; B,M,N,R,W to Pacific St
Open Tues–Thurs 6–10.30pm, Fri & Sat 5.30–11.30pm, Sun 5.30–10pm
Accepts AmEx
Reservations Suggested

PORTUGUESE/ITALIAN

incorporates Portuguese, Sardinian, and Roman specialties with great finesse and care. The missing 25 percent of their combined heritage? As of this writing there's been no evidence of an Irish stew.

Any permutation of appetizers turns into an immersion course in clas-sic Mediterranean flavors. From land there's Roman-style artichokes dressed with olive oil, mint, and garlic ($10), and a refreshing salad of fen-nel, orange, red onion, and olives ($7.50). All salads are fabulous. From the sea there's grilled baby octopus with a chopped celery salad and black olives ($11), charred Portuguese sardines ($9), roasted prawns with sea salt ($16.50), and soft and puffy, milk-soaked, batter-fried salt cod fillets ($9).

The salt cod returns for the second act, most impressively in the casse-role with sherry, green olives, onion, and mashed potatoes ($18). The Pulixis' devotion to salt cod, rare by New York standards, is matched by their diners' unexpectedly positive response to it. The widespread appeal of the seafood stew ($18), on the other hand, packed as it is with prawns, mussels, clams, and monkfish in a tomato cilantro white wine broth, is hardly a shock. And only the spice-averse put up a fight against the grilled baby chicken with the Portuguese hot pepper sauce piri-piri ($16). Pappardelle with a savory, Roman-style oxtail ragu that contains tomato, cinnamon, nutmeg, and chocolate ($14) is joyfully hearty. Chocolate returns in the more traditional role of melt-in-your-mouth cake. And panna cotta with berry compote or apple pie with vanilla cus-tard cream won't disappoint. Desserts go for $6 to $8.

Dizzy's

If you can navigate the hodge-podge menu—"Would you like a side of cheese fries with your Oriental grilled chicken salad, madam?"—you'll quickly discover that finding a good meal at Dizzy's is an effortless pursuit. A true new-old neighborhood joint, the diner stands as a toxic colored testament to yuppified Park Slope. Regulars pile in, meal after meal, to order chocolate-stuffed French toast ($7.50) for dinner or a traditional grilled cheese sandwich ($5.95) for a mid-afternoon snack. The fluorescent green and yellow walls and fire-engine-red banquets imbue the busy premises—and premise—with whimsy. Crisp linen tablecloths, flickering candles, and bud vases filled with delicate flowers soften their edges.

Cost	$12–40

Address 511 9th St at 8th Ave
☎718/499-1966
Transportation F to 7th Ave
Open Mon–Thurs 7am–10pm,
Fri & Sat 9am–11pm, Sun
9am–10pm
Accepts Cash only
Reservations Not accepted

To get things off to a fine start, try the house sangria ($5 a serving) poured into juice glasses which, left over from breakfast, are pressed into night duty. (Not to worry, they're clean.) For beverage therapy of the nostalgic kind, try instead an old-fashioned Brooklyn chocolate egg cream ($3.25) or a thick, rich, chocolate shake ($4.50)—just the thing to wash down an order of ultra-spicy but amazingly un-messy Buffalo wings ($6.95). This gentrified version of classic Buffalo wings is not dripping with toxic-looking orange sauce swimming in butter. A shrewd choice for appetizer or main course is the macaroni and cheese ($7.45). Served with a noncomformist Caesar salad, this hearty bowl of rigatoni swims in a soupy sauce made from five cheeses. The entire bowl is then topped with Rice Crispies and broiled to create a real juvenile joyride.

Substantial burgers ($8.95) deposit eight ounces of charbroiled ground sirloin on a very good brioche roll. Be careful not to order too many additional toppings. At a dollar apiece, you could easily end up with an expensive jawbreaker. Also, beware of the cranberry chutney on the turkey club ($8.95), which seems overwhelmed by the sassy condiment. Ask your well-meaning but easily distracted waiter either to go easy on the chutney or put it on the side. If you still have some digestive capacity in reserve, gaze over to the dependable dessert case.

Long Tan

The great thing about this new sort of Thai place for a new sort of Brooklyn is its versatility. With four distinct environments—bar, lounge, patio, and dining room—you can spend an entire Saturday evening in one place and still feel as though you've made the Fifth Avenue rounds. The cement-floored dining room itself is divided by an open kitchen sided by a counter and a row of red-padded stools shaped like flattened lollipops. It also happens that each eating area is subdivided by successions of wood-block booths attractively back-lit

Cost	$20–45

Address 196 5th Ave, between Union & Berkeley Sts
☎718/622-8444
Transportation M,N,R to Union St
Open Sun–Thurs 5.30pm–midnight, Fri & Sat 5.30pm–2am
Accepts MasterCard & Visa
Reservations For large groups

with Japanese-paper sconces. And those tables themselves are effectively split between those who favor green tea martinis and those who prefer ginger-kamikazes.

Long Tan only opened in 2001 and already chef Jeff Hardinger is treated like a rock star asked to play the same couple of hits over and over again. An old hand at pan-Asian pop, the alum of Ruby Foo's (see p.227) has put together a balanced menu of noodle dishes, curries, salads, and appetizers. But requests keep coming back to the kitchen for his crispy little squid rings with chile sauce ($5) and grilled duck breast ($12). The great appeal of the latter is not lost on the servers. Ask a waiter near the end of his shift where the rest room is located and he's liable to answer "grilled duck breast." Sliced on the bias and offset by sautéed bok choy, the crisp-skinned, tamarind duck is tart, tender, and sweetly succulent.

Good alternatives abound. Among appetizers, the tasty crab and mango summer roll ($7) is cut like a sushi maki into five bite-sized coils striped with colored mayo squiggles. Poached squid ($5) boasts a nice lime-drizzled toss of tomato, greens, and carrots. Among mains, the rice noodles with stir-fried vegetables ($7) and lamb chunks with a richly spiced coconut curry ($9) both prove good value. And crusty, pan-roasted salmon ($13) with a salad of julienned raw papaya, pepper, and leeks is just splendid. Finally, the sticky rice pudding ($5) and fudge-like chocolate cake ($5) are merely okay; the caramelized banana ($5), pale and syrupy.

Park Slope

Max & Moritz

This quirky, French-American bistro—named by its Austrian co-owners for the German cartoon characters—is easy enough to find, but difficult to place. Its passion for pumpkin surely comes from chef Anselmo Bello, who has created a seasonal menu of French favorites cunningly accented with ingredients from his native Mexico. There are even monthly French-Mexican dinners, when Chemo, as he's known to staff and regulars, really lets loose. The dining room's decor is eclectic, too. A pair of retired church pews serves as a makeshift banquette dotted with small romantic tables softly lit by votives. Beautifully tarnished ceiling fans lethargically spin as if they're slowing down to match the 33rpm recordings of Ella Fitzgerald and Frank Sinatra. The young, relaxed, almost over-attentive wait staff makes each diner feel as if no request is a nuisance.

Cost	$26–65

Address 426A 7th Ave, between 14th & 15th Sts
☎718/499-5557
Transportation F to 15th St-Prospect Park
Open Mon–Fri 5.30–11pm, Sat & Sun 11am–3pm & 5.30–11pm
Accepts All major credit cards

The wine list also takes its cue from the restaurant's conceptual and culinary diversity, offering everything from Rioja to Riesling. Appetizers, however, tend to fall into the classically monotonous category. Chemo does jolt things a bit by offering a crab and bay scallop tamale ($8) or by adding poblanos to his escargots ($7). It's probably best, however, to save the adventure for the entrees and start with a hearty slice of the excellent house pâté ($7) garnished with sweet-and-sour pickled pears and served with crusty French bread. The salad of mixed baby greens ($5), livened up with tart cranberry vinaigrette, makes for an admirable palate teaser.

The crispy skin and succulent dark meat beneath it are reasons enough to order the roasted duck breast ($17), but the lush and very-of-the-moment pumpkinseed sauce and brown basmati rice rule out any possible indecision. Another fashionable dish is the dense pumpkin gnocchi ($14). Served in a sauce featuring purple kale and chicken, the dumpling-style pasta is contemporized for cold-weather comfort. Whole arctic char ($19) is filleted tableside with great fanfare. It would be an utter shame if an all-pumpkin dinner were not possible and M & M does not disappoint. Even so, the pumpkin cake ($6) is second dessert choice to the rich chocolate hazelnut torte ($6).

Park Slope Chip Shop

When British expat Chris Sell said the only thing he missed from home was proper fish and chips, it's small wonder he moved to New York in the first place. But this slight to his motherland—and perhaps also his mother—turned into a great boon for fellow expats, anglophiles, and nutritionally incorrect Brooklynites. It led him to open this amusing, extremely kid-friendly, and, in a manner of speaking, healthy showcase for Britain's national dish. Of course "healthy" here refers to the size of the portions and not the nutritional benefits

Cost	$15–35

Address 383 5th Ave, between 6th & 7th Sts
☎718/832-7701
Transportation F to 4th Ave; M,N,R to 9th St
Open Mon–Wed noon–10pm, Thurs & Fri noon–11pm, Sat 11am–11pm, Sun 11am–10pm
Accepts Cash only
Reservations Not accepted

of, to take one example, the chip butty—salted chips (for the uninitiated, these are french fries, not potato chips), vinegar, and ketchup sandwiched between slices of buttered bread ($5).

Sell's recipe for fish and chips was inspired by his favorite chippie in London, the dearly departed Upper Street Fish Shop. While we don't dare compare the results to that Islington legend, the battered cod is jolly good and the chips are, as the menu maintains, bloody lovely. The crust is crisped to a golden-brown shell thick enough to conceal the superbly moist fish. The chips, sliced with an imported cutter to the regulation size of twelve centimeters, are hot, unsoggy, and, by design, not crisp. The $9 pairing can be bought to stay or to go, the latter wrapped in a sheet from the New York Times.

It turns out Sell's sentimental longings do not stop at fish and chips. The whimsical shop is furnished with imported wood dining tables and adorned with boyhood posters (Beatles, James Bond, Pink Floyd) and tacky royal memorabilia. The selection of canned draught English brews ($4-5) is outstanding. And he and his compatriot waitstaff proudly serve shepherd's pie ($9), bangers and mash (sausages and mashed potatoes; $9), Welsh rarebit (baked cheese toast; $4), and mushy peas, a traditional accompaniment whose best application, according to American opinion, is as a substitute for baseboard. It would probably be best if Sell's enthusiasms stopped at dessert. The crumbles and rice puddings are drowned in runny custard.

Sunset Park

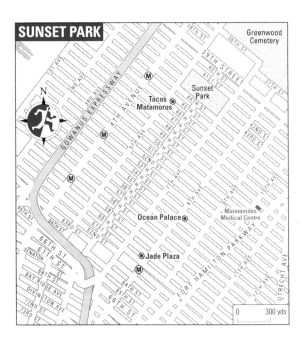

SUNSET PARK

Greenwood Cemetery

GOWANUS EXPRESSWAY

Sunset Park

Tacos Matamoros

Maimonides Medical Centre

Ocean Palace

Jade Plaza

FORT HAMILTON PARKWAY

UTRECHT AVE

N

0   300 yds

Jade Plaza

(🍴) As the boundaries of Manhattan's Chinatown slipped deep into Little Italy and the Lower East Side, new immigrants from the southern provinces of China looked east. Today, more than 60,000 Chinese make their homes and run more than 500 businesses in Brooklyn's Sunset Park. Development along a fifteen-block stretch of Eighth Avenue, the community's commercial center, has included a plethora of food markets and restaurants, each of them more prosperous than the last. Jade Plaza represents the summit of Sunset Park glitz, an enormous, carpeted banquet hall bearing three symbolic displays of opulence: a framed art piece posing shark fins against a violet backdrop; a glass display case of fine Cognacs; and two enormous tanks filled with live fish and prawns. The message is clear: Brooklynites need not cross the East River for an opulent, banquet-style Chinese dinner.

| Cost | Lunch $12–25 |
| | Dinner $20–55 |

Address 6022 8th Ave, between 60th & 61st Sts
☎718/492- 6888
Transportation N to 8th Ave
Open Daily 7am–midnight
Accepts MasterCard & Visa
Reservations Not accepted

Stepping into Jade Plaza at 11am on a weekend is one of the great thrills in the contemporary Brooklyn dining experience. Upwards of 200 diners are here for dim sum ($2–5 per item) to rival any in Manhattan's Chinatown. Har gow—the shrimp dumplings that are the test of any dim sum—contain large pieces of fresh shrimp beneath their delicate, translucent skins. The rice noodles, too, pan-fried to order at the roving carts, are outstanding.

The English-language dinner menu lists routine dishes and too few of the seafood specialties that distinguish the kitchen. (You can get a peek at that mysterious warren through an open door on 60th Street.) For non-Chinese diners, ordering is therefore a frustrating negotiation, involving gestures and jabs at dishes on neighboring tables. You'll be tempted by the bird's nest of woven taro filled with glistening scallops, shrimp, and conch rimmed with Chinese vegetables ($22.95) and the monstrous, salt-baked Dungeness crab (roughly $20/lb) with its crisp, glistening, chile-spiced, salt-encrusted body, and its sweet, meaty interior. Steamed whole fish (carp, bass, cod; $12–16/lb), topped with slivered scallions and fresh cilantro, rests in a ginger broth so good that you'll want to continually spoon it over the fish, as if basting, or even directly into your mouth like a soup.

Sunset Park

Ocean Palace

(icon) The popularity of this glittery, two-floor Cantonese restaurant and banquet hall within Brooklyn's Chinese community comes in waves. Some new place opens to great fanfare in Sunset Park, everyone flocks over to try it, and sooner or later they return to trusty, hospitable, user-friendly Ocean Palace until the next big thing is ballyhooed in the Chinese newspapers. Actually, it's not all that different from the city's fickle restaurant scene at large. Ocean Palace may also fall victim to another vagary of the public taste. New Yorkers seem to love new eateries that look old but not old eateries that look new.

Cost	Lunch $8–45
	Dinner $15–45

Address 5421 8th Ave, between 54th & 55th Sts
☎718/871-8080
Transportation N to 8th Ave
Open Daily 7am–midnight
Accepts All major credit cards
Reservations For large groups

Fortunately, there are always enough diners who care only about good food and good value to keep Ocean Palace running at high tide. You can come in at any hour and be assured of getting superb, dim-sum-quality dumplings (all $2 for four)—steamed mixed vegetables, steamed shrimp (har gow), or even deep-fried pork—as well as the highest quality lacquered-style roast meats—duck ($5.95), pork ($5.95), quail ($9.95), and suckling pig ($6.95). And you are almost sure to hear a pitch for the egg-white-battered jumbo shrimp topped with a citrusy, mayonnaise-like sauce and scattered with honey-sesame walnuts ($16.95). Though repeatedly described as "the number one" dish both here and at the second Ocean Palace (1414 Ave U, Homecrest; ☎718/376-3838), you may find you care little for the soft, puffy batter or the whipped sauce.

A far superior, if less novel, jumbo shrimp preparation is with black beans and crunchy Chinese broccoli ($12.95). Among other time-tested bets to come back for are braised whole sea bass with vegetables, bean curd, and ginger scallion broth (market price; $15–18); and hyper-tenderized steak with black pepper sauce ($8.95). The Peking duck service ($26 for a whole) with pancakes rather than buns is fine, but they're stingy with the scallions. Ocean Palace is receptive to special requests. For example, instead of a side of bok choy ($6.25) and another of pan-fried noodles ($5.95), you could have them combine the two into a $7.25 combo that provides enough for three.

Tacos Matamoros

It would be a mistake to judge Tacos Matamoros by its minimal comforts and humble accoutrements. Instead, take your reading by peering into the open kitchen, where tortillas are being warmed on the griddle, and cooks are busy chopping cilantro and onions and carving up huge slabs of meat. With the accommodating and efficient waitresses and Sunset Park locals speaking only Spanish, it's exactly the sort of authentic scene you would hope to encounter on a Mexican road trip.

Cost	$5–25

Address 4503 5th Ave, between 45th & 46th Sts
☎718/871-7627
Transportation N,R to 45th St
Open Daily 8am–1am
Accepts Cash only
Reservations Not accepted

At just a buck (that's half the going rate), each taco consists of a double layer of soft corn tortillas folded over the deliciously moist meat of your choice, along with chopped onions and cilantro. Once you've ordered, a bowl of hot sauce and a plate of lime wedges arrive at your table. The carnitas tacos are a inspired mix of fatty, juicy, crackling-crisp pork bits sure to enthrall those with no compunction about consuming such scrappy, cholestorol-loaded meats. Queasy diners are apt to prefer the cabeza taco, at least until they learn that the tasty, marinated beef comes from the cow's head parts. The pork taco boasts marvelously tender strips of meat. If your budget allows an increase of 50¢, that pork is at its best cooked in a mole sauce, hidden in a pocket of rice, reddened by a fiery chile sauce, and wrapped in a corn husk—namely in the dish called rojos y mole tamale.

The traditional posole stew ($5) contains a substantial hunk of superbly tender pork, an abundance of whole garlic cloves, and a dollop of creamy hominy all submerged in and slowly infiltrated by a pork broth. Garnished with the chopped onion and cilantro, it's absolute satisfaction. The chiles rellenos ($7.95)—cheese-stuffed Poblano peppers—are splendid, too, though just occasionally the filling is not fully melted. The rice that accompanies entrees like sizzling steak fajitas ($7.95) and plump burritos ($5) is moist and fluffy; the refried beans, utterly creamy. Sticky-sweet fruit shakes may be too sugary to sip with dinner, but the mango-papaya shake ($2.50) makes an excellent finish.

Williamsburg & Greenpoint

Amarin Cafe

The young bohemians may take some responsibility for the climbing rents in Greenpoint, but they have little to do with the clang that hits you over the head upon entering their favorite Thai luncheonette. Conversation is in fact laid-back and low-key. Rather, the racket is made by the cooks as they jiggle their woks over gas burners turned up to the max. The constant rattle establishes the rhythm of this modest eatery and the rapid rate at which you get served. When the chef in the open, behind-the-counter kitchen transfers a steaming pad Thai from wok to plate, it is garnished with bean sprouts and fresh cilantro by one woman and delivered to the table by another in a matter of seconds.

Cost	$10–30

Address 617 Manhattan Ave, between Driggs & Nassau Aves
℡718/349-2788
Transportation G to Nassau Ave
Open Sun–Thurs 11am–10.30pm, Fri & Sat 11am–11pm
Accepts Cash only
Reservations Not accepted

THAI

Appetizers are greatly enhanced by this speedy delivery. The crisp, tightly wrapped Thai spring rolls ($2.95) arrive too hot to handle, as tempted as you will be to do so. They're served with the same syrupy chile garlic sauce that accompanies the superbly crisp, bordering-on-crunchy fried calamari ($3.50). Delectable fried wontons stuffed with with chicken, potato, and onion ($2.95) are endowed with a cool cucumber dip. Those who prefer to stay clear of the frying oil can opt for one of three salads ($5.95–7.25)—easily mistaken for main courses.

The joy of the pad Thai—shrimp ($6.25), chicken ($5.95), or mixed vegetable ($5.95)—is not only its two levels of heat, as key as their hot chiles and hot serving temperature are. The coarsely chopped scallions found in most of the noodle and rice dishes act as flavor activators, their fresh, pungent crunch setting off the entire ensemble of co-ingredients. Broad spicy noodles with chicken or beef ($5.95) put forward an inspired mix of sweet (brown bean sauce) and spicy-pungent (chile and onions). On the meatless side, describing the auspicious mix of sautéed veggies teamed with tofu ($5.95) as al dente would be imprecise. They're downright chunky. Dessert is up close and personal. Order a crème brûlée ($2.75) and the vanilla custard is sugared and torched in full view. Impressive stuff, though its caramelized lid could be crispier.

AMERICAN

Diner

Diner appears to subsist in a no-man's-land of vacant trash-strewn lots and warehouses gloomily shadowed by the trestle of the Williamsburg Bridge. The dining car itself has long been concealed beneath a ruinous resurfacing sadly typical of the neighborhood's tin-siding and brick-facing saboteurs. But step inside and you encounter a great American classic bursting with martini-swilling geeks and mussel-slurping Manhattan exiles. The diner now occupied by Diner is a 1920s model with the barreled roof, long granite counter, and

| Cost | Lunch $10–30 |
| | Dinner $15–60 |

Address 85 Broadway at Berry St

☏718/486-3077

Transportation J,M,Z to Marcy Ave

Open Sun–Thurs 11am–midnight, Fri & Sat 11am–11pm

Accepts MasterCard & Visa

Reservations Not accepted

hardwood interior typical of the pre-Art Deco period of diner design. The six vintage booths beside the windows are always in great demand and worth waiting up to thirty minutes for. The rear dining pen, though fun, funky, and tobacco-(un)friendly, has none of the movement and exhilaration of the mosaic-filled main room.

The original diner at this site, The Broadway Diner, no doubt served up a hamburger and fries (what diner didn't?), but it was surely nothing like the outsized fare served here today. The twenty-first-century burger ($8) at the hip, bistrofied Diner that stands in its place is a fat, rounded, blackened, juicy mass of loosely packed, none-too-lean beef slipped into a seeded bun with lettuce, tomato, and raw onion. You'll come across grapefruits smaller and drier. The long fries ($2.50) are sliced and bronzed in the manner of the great Jewish deli fries of yore. Sized between frites and steak fries, they merit being called french fried potatoes, with added emphasis on *potatoes*. Other mainstays include the steamed mussels ($8), the hanger steak ($15), and enormous rib-eye ($17).

Co-owner Andrew Tarlow worked at Odeon (see p.144) where he absorbed their lots-of-good-food-on-a-plate, to-heck-with-presentation philosophy. Servers recite the list of specials to diners while simultaneously scribbling on the butcher paper that covers their tables. It's a nice touch. An off-menu meal might start with grilled crostini of roasted red peppers, anchovies, shaved Parmesan, and olive oil ($7.50); continue to tapenade-topped tortilla Espanola with wilted escarole ($9.50), and conclude with chocolate bread pudding and whipped cream ($5).

DuMont

Your first clue that there's something odd and wonderful about DuMont may initially have you thinking you've lost your way. Imprinted on the old awning out front, once a prop for the movie *Godfather II*, is a telephone number, a trade ("paints and blinds"), and, most disorienting of all, a street number ("241") that have nothing whatsoever to do with the current tenant or its address. This is but one of several found objects with which owner Colin Devlin, formerly a bartender at Balthazar (see p.130), has

Cost	$15–45

Address 432 Union Ave,
between Metropolitan Ave &
Devoe St
☎718/486-7717
Transportation L to Lorimer St
Open Mon–Fri 6–11pm, Sat &
Sun 11am–3pm & 6–11pm
Accepts MasterCard & Visa
Reservations Not accepted

AMERICAN

patched together his dream bistro. Pressed-tin walls, a beehive mosaic floor, an L-shaped dark wood bar, and wooden restroom doors with frosted glass panels (think Sam Spade) bring old Brooklyn charm to this former plumbing store. Red banquettes that could have been salvaged from a 1960s Pontiac provide funky cushioning for the mostly young, shabby-chic diners. The commonality between the served and the servers translates into a carefree vibe that is less Manhattan than Berkeley.

Appropriate, then, that co-chefs Chris Wei and Stephanie Sugawara were co-workers at Chez Panisse in Berkeley. Their low-priced menu is deliberately brief, with just a couple of appetizers, entrees, and desserts augmented by nightly specials. Your choice is essentially between something basic like the solid burger with good fries ($8.25) and something a little more daring, like the truly special special of pan-roasted red snapper topped with salsa verde and balanced on a warm salad with sautéed mushrooms and crispy potatoes ($14.25). While the DuMont salad ($7.50) with pickled haricots verts, radishes, pecans, crumbled blue cheese, bacon lardons, and balsamic vinaigrette is the logical appetizer, there's something to be said for sharing the macaroni and cheese ($8.50). Its radiatori are uniquely qualified to trap the bacon bits and gooey Gruyère, white Cheddar, and Parmesan cheeses. The steak frites cost just $15.95. Well-chosen wines—all two of them—are either $22 or $26.

Weekend brunch dishes ($6–7) include baked eggs with tomato, andouille sausage, and white beans; brioche French toast with sautéed apples; a Gruyère-and-egg scramble with fries; and a pressed ham-and-cheese sandwich with fresh herbs and side salad.

Williamsburg & Greenpoint

Lomzynianka

(🍴) The humble hominess of Lomzynianka gratifies both the working-class, immigrant Polish families and the fashionably thrifty East Village émigrés-with-trust-funds who live side-by-side in the trendily déclassé neighborhood of Greenpoint. Painted landscapes of Colonial-era Americana are hung on the faux-brick walls beside a stuffed deer festooned with a floral garland. In one corner of the narrow room is a tribute to the most famous Pole of our time, Pope John Paul II. The tables are tightly spaced, each cov-

Cost	$7–20

Address 646 Manhattan Ave, between Nassau & Norman Aves
☎718/389-9439
Transportation G to Nassau Ave
Open Daily noon–9 pm
Accepts Cash only
Reservations Not accepted

ered with a mauve tablecloth and a thick protective plastic cover à la grandma. Somehow, the owners managed to find small lamps in exactly the same shade of mauve as the tablecloths. The boiled pierogi are just about the only other things that match on the entire premises.

Order a cherry-flavored Polish soda ($1) in two varieties, red or white, and the friendly waiter will pour you a tall glass straight from a two-liter bottle pulled out of the fridge. Every entree includes a mixed salad plate loaded with sweet sauerkraut, vinegary shredded red cabbage, and a nicely balanced coleslaw. The red borscht ($1—let's write that out, one dollar) is a bowl of hearty, chunky beet-based vegetable soup filled with potatoes and white beans. Deep-brown potato pancakes already larger and puffier than those you find elsewhere—they're batter-fried—come five to a $3.50 order.

Fluffy-textured veal balls in creamy dill sauce ($4) are served alongside mashed potatoes without discernible butter or cream. Don't despair. The plain spuds are profoundly improved simply by using your fork to sweep the dill sauce into them. The $5.50 "Polish Platter" is the ultimate in bargain samplers. It encompasses stuffed cabbage—tender layers of wilted cabbage encasing a veal and rice mixture similar to that of the veal balls; bigos—the traditional hunter's stew of stringy meats and sauerkraut in a glistening gravy; intensely flavored if overcooked (and dried out) kielbasa; and three doughy pierogi. For dessert or brunch, blueberry blintzes ($3) baked to order with a generous topping of stewed blueberries arrive as soft, delicately rolled crêpes with sweet cheese oozing out the sides.

Planet Thailand

Good, cheap chow built a name for this arty Thai luncheonette. But it was the loss of that name through a trademark dispute with Planet Hollywood that made the rechristened "Plan-Eat Thailand" famous. In 1999, the fortunes of these adversaries took some unexpected turns. As the celebrity-backed bully announced bankruptcy proceedings, the underdog was moving to a large, two-winged industrial loft around the corner from its original, coffee-shop-like digs. And though no identifying sign was posted anywhere, the pre-litigation name was printed on the menus. The

Cost	Lunch $9–25
	Dinner $15–45

Address 141 North 7th St, between Bedford Ave & Berry St

☎718/599-5758

Transportation L to Bedford Ave

Open Sun–Thurs 11.30am–1am, Fri & Sat 11.30am–2am

Accepts Cash only

Reservations Not accepted

new Planet Thailand can be entered from metal-and-glass entrances on both North Seventh and Berry Streets. The latticed garage door on North Seventh opens to an immense assembly plant that, with its cafe tables, arcing counter, and partly open kitchen, constitutes the Thai sector. Up a few stairs from a funky bar inlaid with colored beer bottles is artist John Kessler's cleverly mechanized fountain. The Berry Street entrance leads to an equally large Japanese section equipped with a sushi bar and hibachi bar. But while it's easy to applaud the retro spirit behind the hibachi grill and the chef's parody of Benihana dexterity, those Japanese dishes aren't really so great. Whether seated in Japan or Thailand, it is wisest to choose from the Thai menu.

Ideal places to start: fresh spring rolls with apricot sauce ($2.95), spicy smothered chicken wings ($2.95), and anything answering to a word search for squid—fried ($3.50), grilled ($3.25), or tossed in a spicy salad ($3.50). Grilled beef ($3.50), like most beef options, is unremarkable. Of the several low-priced entrees, you'll do fine with shrimp curry in sweet, spicy, and fabulously silky coconut sauce ($7.50), sautéed frogs legs with basil and chile ($7.95), or sliced chicken with basil, onion, and pepper ($6.95).

Still, the great Planet Thailand constant is its pad Thai: shrimp (6.95), chicken ($5.25), or vegetable ($5.50). The steaming-hot noodles are woven with bean sprouts, scallion, Thai spices, and large egg pieces. The Frenchified desserts don't really work—the ginger crème brûlée's caramelized topping is massacred—so it's best to have ice cream.

Queens

Astoria & Long Island City

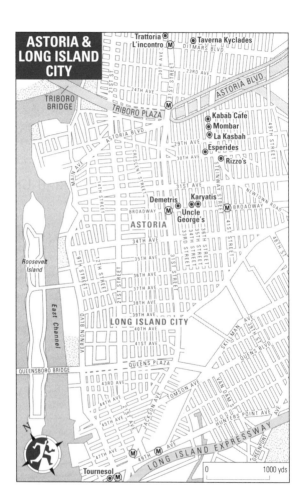

Demetris

The market-style seafood grills that rule Astoria's Greek dining scene certainly feed us better and more healthily than the kitschy tavernas that once characterized this Hellenic enclave. But even so, many people lament the loss of those plate-smashing, bazouki-playing, table-dancing, ouzo-guzzling, moussaka-scarfing feasts of times past. For them, no eatery bridges the gap between sophistication found and innocence lost more effectively than Demetris. (The former Syros was renamed in 2001 after its new owner, gyro and pita-bread tycoon Demetris Astin.) The iced fish case and thick-barred grills just inside the window assure us that fresh whole fish and blazing charcoal are at the ready. But the weekday keyboardist and weekend bazouki-led band that perform in the glass-roofed, vine-strewn, blue-and-white patio sustain a festive atmosphere. And the Adriatic murals, nautical ornamentation, and Greek-key friezes are hopelessly sentimental.

| Cost | Lunch $10–45 |
| | Dinner $25–60 |

Address 32-11 Broadway, between 32nd & 33rd Sts
☎718/278-1877
Transportation N,W to Broadway
Open Daily noon–midnight
Accepts All major credit cards
Reservations Suggested

There's nothing sappy, however, about the fresh cold dips and charred pita that start the banquet. The creamy tatziki (yogurt with cucumber), tangy taramasalata (fluffed fish roe), unapologetically bitter melitzanosalata (puréed eggplant), and forceful skordalia (whipped potato and garlic) included in the pikilia antipasto ($8.95) are all vividly rendered. The surest return, though, to Greek salad days is—predictably—the Greek salad ($5.75) topped with fistfuls of crumbled feta (though you do want to keep the waiter away from the oil, vinegar, and lemon). The spanakopita ($5.50) is another wonderful throwback, though the delicate phyllo layers of this home-baked spinach pie are superior to the greasy ones we used to know.

Sadly, personal growth and increasing girth preclude a béchamel-enriched return to moussaka and pastitsio. Chargrilled whole fish ($17–21, including two sides) is the way to go. Hankerings for something behind the times and over the top *can* be satiated, probably for good, by the Demetris combination special ($23). But those who can polish off its broiled scallops, lobster tail, and sole, its jumbo shrimp and clams with crabmeat and breadcrumb stuffing, *and* its side oval of potatoes, should not be too quick to gloat. There's still the cinnamon baked apple and honeyed pastries (both served gratis) to conquer.

363

Esperides

Esperides strikes just the right balance between homey taverna and elegant restaurant. While its terracotta tiles, teak chairs, blue cloth napkins, and concealed blue neon are dressier than anything at the nearby tavernas, its $10.95–14.95 dinner specials, including an outstanding, full-bodied avgolemono (egg, lemon, and chicken) soup make it sufficiently casual and affordable for large family dinners. Owners Gregory and Steve Soldatos, veterans of the diner

| Cost | Lunch $20–30 |
| | Dinner $25–70 |

Address 37-01 30th Ave at
37th St
☎718/545-1494
Transportation N to 30th Ave;
R,G to Steinway St
Open Daily noon–midnight
Accepts All major credit cards

trade, know how to please a diverse clientele. They've hired Greek hotel chef Constantinos Athens to do grilled fish and meats for the simple-is-best crowd, more elaborately prepared and sauced dishes for fussier appetites, and baked standards for moussaka/pastitsio traditionalists. Vigilant waiters help you navigate the varied menu by giving useful advice. Instead of the usual noncommittal nonsense ("everything our chef does is fabulous"), they'll talk you out of a mediocre selection (the undrinkable house red) and into a winner (a $17 bottle of the Greek white Kouras).

A yea-or-nay on taramasalata, however, is not required as the fish roe spread is served as a complimentary snack. The value of this gesture goes beyond the savings of $4.25. It frees up an appetizer slot for knife-surrendering grilled octopus ($9.50), lightly fried zucchini disks ($5.95), delectable saganaki (hot fried triangles of kefalotiri cheese; $6.25), and grilled halloumi (the salty Cypriot cheese; $5.95). A superb follow-up to mezze overload is decently grilled or broiled fish—whole red snapper ($21.95 for a 1-3/4 pounder) or fillet of sole ($14.95). Anything heavier would fill up valuable digestive capacity ordinarily reserved for desserts. Those with expandable storage space may relish the silky fillet of salmon with leeks and lemony cream sauce ($15.95), the grilled red mullet fillets with lightly creamed wine sauce ($15), and the juicy, lemon-scented roast piglet ($14.50). Steaks and chops ($14.95-19.95) reflect the Greek preference for oversizing and, to many tastes, overcooking.

For dessert, traditional ground walnut cake ($3) is so moist you can practically suck out the honey with a straw. That's meant as a compliment. Order too the creamy, sharp-flavored sheep's milk yogurt with honey ($3.75).

Kabab Café

🍴 Playing board games. Gossiping with and listening to the troubles of young diners. Smoking his long-tubed hookah (water pipe). These are a few of the things Ali El Sayed would rather do than cook. Ask the jolly Egyptian about Rita Abatzi and Rosa Ashkenazi, the two women (and old loves?) whose framed photos hang on the back wall and he will sit down and tell you about these star vocalists of 1930s rebetika music while your fellow diners (fifeen at most) are kept waiting for their kofta kebabs, vegetable

Cost	
	Lunch $8–30
	Dinner $15–40

Address 25-12 Steinway St, near Astoria Blvd

☎718/728-9858

Transportation N to Astoria Blvd; G,R to Steinway St

Open Tues–Sun 1–11pm

Accepts Cash only

Reservations Not accepted

EGYPTIAN

tarts, and hibiscus teas. No one complains. Such interludes are vital to a tiny, ragged, bric-a-brac dive with its own special rhythms. When the duets of Louis Armstrong and Ella Fitzgerald are playing on the hi-fi, the sizzling iron pans provide an accompaniment as sure and easy as a brush over a snare drum.

Despite its name, Kabab Café's true specialty is felafel. The reason is twofold. Firstly, it is prepared in the original Egyptian style with crushed and soaked green fava beans rather than the now common (at least in New York) chickpeas. Secondly, the balls are pan-fried in clean, shallow oil while most others are deep-fried in dubious oil. The result is hot, fresh, lightly spiced felafel cooked to a dark brown crisp. They're available as an appetizer ($5), in a pita sandwich ($5), on a platter ($8), or as part of the best option of all, a fabulous mezze with hummus, babaganoush, fava beans, and sliced fruit ($10 plus $4 for each additional person).

Ali also insists on being taken seriously for his more elaborate Egyptian cooking. He has a friendly rivalry with the chef at nearby Mombar (see p.368), who happens to be his brother. When you order a seafood special ($14–18), perhaps a pan-roasted whole red snapper buried under hacked vegetables, coarsely chopped garlic, cumin, and zatar (a Middle Eastern spice mix of sumac, thyme, and sesames), Ali brings the pan to the table. Holding the handle in one hand and tongs in the other, he fillets the whole fish on the spot. He's quite an act.

Karyatis

(icon) The neoclassical decor at Karyatis does not lie. The moderate prices do. In an argil-toned space thankfully devoid of glitz—and, for once, Aegean blue and white—Greek wall reliefs lifting scenes from the Parthenon are set in illuminated wall recesses. They, like the dried flowers, sculptured sconces, and shallow dishes of red peppercorn-dotted Peloponnese olive oil, indicate an establishment of good taste—surely *the* destination in Astoria for finer Greek cuisine. Conversely, the prices—entrees mostly in the mid-teens—offer no clue of how good and consistent this restaurant is when host Costa "Charlie" Tzivelekis is directing the show. Karyatis refers to the Karyatides, the six stone maidens who support the roof of the Erechtheum in ancient Athens. Here, the two replicas displayed on the rear wall uphold, albeit symbolically, chef Gregory Kargiakos' accomplishment.

Cost	$30–65

Address 35-03 Broadway,
between 35th & 36th Sts
☎718/204-0666
Transportation N to
Broadway; G,R to Steinway St
Open Daily 6pm–midnight
Accepts All major credit cards

The pikilia ($10.95 small/$14.95 large) assembles all the obligatory cold spreads on one exquisitely arranged platter. With its distinctively fluffy taramasalata (fish roe dip) and smoky melitzanosalata (eggplant dip), the ensemble is the highlight of the meal. Still, you shouldn't neglect the more uncommon hot appetizers: the northern Greek specialty spetsofai ($8.95), a gratin of peppers, sliced sausage, tomato, and thinly sliced eggplant baked under a salty lid of kasseri cheese; the grilled sepia (cuttlefish; $11.95), with twice the flavor of the usual frozen calamari; and crisp, golden croquettes of eggplant cooked with kefalograviera, the Greek version of Gruyère ($7.95).

Main courses also pose a quandary between trite but trusty items and less familiar fare. Select the moussaka ($13.95) or a grilled whole fish (about $15) and you won't go home in a funk. But why not experience the delectable moist shellfish in the seafood giouvetsi ($21.95), a Greek cross between paella and risotto with orzo in place of rice, or the armaki karyatis ($17.95), whose pristine lamb slices and veggies suggest a lamb pot au feu. The closing dinner dilemma is: should you stay or should you go? Stay for a pastry, say the kadaifi ($5), a nutty, shredded-wheat-like tuft. If you're after a honeyed dessert, go instead to a nearby cafe.

La Kasbah

🍽 Other than an intelligence briefing from trusted critics or friends, the follow-the-crowds formula is generally the most fruitful way to choose a restaurant. A preponderance of diners who share an eatery's ethnic heritage is especially promising. Still, the formula depends first on brave pioneers to try out an undiscovered and thus empty place and then some disciples to start filling its tables. La Kasbah has some pioneers, fewer disciples, and no followers. Consequently, a good Moroccan restaurant in a city with so few of them is strug-

Cost	$10–35

Address 25-70 Steinway St, between 25th & 28th Aves
☎718/726-2700
Transportation N,W to 30th Ave; R,V to Steinway St
Open Mon–Thurs noon–11pm, Fri & Sat noon–midnight, Sun noon–10pm
Accepts All major credit cards
Reservations Not accepted

MOROCCAN

gling, as are most other North African and Middle Eastern restaurants on Steinway Street. Sadly, La Kasbah won't have a crowd to be led until there is one to be joined.

The ambiance certainly isn't going to lure passers-by through the door. The glass tables, mirrors, and chandeliers represent chintzy glitz without even the appeal of reverse snobbery. However, such cold appetizers ($3.50) as zaalouk (stewed eggplant with tomatoes, garlic, and parsley) and charmela (its tomato and sweet pepper counterpart) soon warm you to the surroundings. And the cigares, crisp cigars of phyllo-rolled chicken, shrimp, or ground lamb confirm you're on to something.

Couscous comes in three varieties: the royal ($9.95), the tfaya ($8.95), and vegetables ($7.95). The tfaya—with its sweet-and-savory weave of sweetly golden (but not browned) stewed onions, golden raisins, chickpeas, and chicken or lamb (go with chicken)—has the edge. Of five tajeen (using La Kasbah's spelling for the conically lidded cooking pot) the nicest is the m'kali ($9.95), bursting with preserved lemon, tender lamb chunks, green olives, and french fries. What are fries doing in a tajeen? While no one can say, none will go untouched. On the minus side, don't even consider ordering the seafood bastilla instead of the traditional chicken one. That vermicelli-filled phyllo pie is simply dismal. The menu is rounded out by brochettes and kebab sandwiches. Two Moroccan pastries ($1.75) are great: the honey-crisp shebakia (Ramadan sesame cookies in a pretzel-like twist) and the horn-shaped kaab el ghazal made of almond paste.

367

Mombar

(icon) The eccentric design of this outwardly anonymous restaurant on Astoria's main Middle Eastern shopping strip is not, as you might imagine, the work of a starving artist paid in hummus and babaganoush by a bighearted restaurateur. The multiple collages of found fabric, furniture, and building materials were pieced together by Moustafa Rahman, the Gaudí of Egyptian cooking. His marble floor is a patterned mosaic of brick-sized fragments in pink, gray, tan, and black. A wooden pantry/curio case protrudes from the open-kitchen counter like mud-brick homes from the slopes of an Egyptian village. Colorful inlays turn each tabletop into a distinct work of art.

Cost	$25–65

Address 25-22 Steinway St,
between 25th Ave & Astoria
Blvd
☎718/726-2356
Transportation N,W to Astoria
Blvd; G, R to Steinway St
Open Tues–Sun 5pm–midnight
Accepts Cash only

EGYPTIAN

The restaurant is named for a mixed Egyptian sausage by a chef who has found religion in the artful mixing of disparate ingredients. The menu exhibits the same level of accomplishment as well as what outerborough residents call "Manhattan prices" to prove it. Too costly for many locals, Mombar is packed on weekends but still struggles for a school-night audience. All dinner roads lead from the Sahara mix ($8), a circular meze of first-rate hummus, foul (slow-cooked fava beans purée), intense babaganoush, and fresh fruit slices arranged around half-moon pita chips. An outstanding spread regrettably missing from that mix is besara ($7), a fava bean purée combined with molokhiya (an essential Egyptian leafy vegetable), cilantro, and a garnish of grilled onions.

An array of Middle Eastern and North African spices generously infuse main courses, some of which come with pyramids of rice. (You'll find more Ancient Egyptian imagery on the kitschy glassware.) Such permanent dishes as rabbit stew thickened with molokhiya greens ($18), molasses-glazed duck breast ($19), and sayadia (baked shrimp, mussels, and calamari; $18) are listed on the menu mostly to guide first-time and cautious diners. But a quick look around tells you the chef doesn't care much for convention. He prefers that you and he conjure up impromptu specials based on your tastes, his talents and moods, and what looked best to him during that day's forage through local markets. This close and varied collaboration between diners and chef produces Mombar's greatest collage of all.

Rizzo's

🍴 Sicilian pizza partisans generally prefer square slices to Neapolitan triangles because they're thicker and breadier. Some no doubt crave the hardened corners of these pan-baked pies. Still, the local version of sfincione, as the thick pizza of Palermo is known, is best appreciated as a platform for zesty tomato sauce. Even the cheese cognoscenti agree. Sicilian pizza, says Luigi Di Palo of Di Palo's cheese store in Little Italy, is "a thick piece of bread topped with sauce and maybe some cheese." And nowhere

Cost	$4–9

Address 30-13 Steinway St, between 30th & 31st Aves
☎718/721-9862
Transportation N,W to 30th Ave; R,V to Steinway St
Open Tues–Sat 11am–8pm, Sun noon–7pm
Accepts Cash only
Reservations Not accepted

PIZZA

are those squares better than at this tomato-lover's paradise. As long as the name "Rizzo's" burns in yellow neon with the green-lit "Fine Pizza" close behind there is hope for New York pizza-lovers who demand a good-quality tomato sauce to go with molten mozzarella, grated Romano, and a resilient crust.

Thinner and lighter than a typical Sicilian, Rizzo's amazing crust is the compact format for a thick layer of chunky sauce made from whole tomatoes. Joe Rizzo learned the classic recipe not in his native Sicily, but at Pizza Amore, a defunct chain of pizzerias. Rizzo's faux marble booths, fluorescent-blue wall menu, and $1.60 price for a pizza slice are obviously not as old as the small shop, which opened in 1959. But the family pride, personable service, and old-world quality are treasured relics from another time.

The most dramatic change in the pizzeria's history occurred during the mid-1990s when Dave Rizzo finally convinced his old man to let him develop a Neapolitan alternative. "When my father opened, pizza was still a relatively new ethnic food," explains Rizzo. "Everybody was willing to try whatever you had. Now young people know pizza and they expect it to be round." Dave's triangular slices accomplish for Neapolitan pizza what his father's squares did for Sicilian: the easy-chewing crust is thinner, lighter, and more of one delicate piece than its counterparts and, yep, there's more tomato sauce. The triangle has developed a loyal following, not all of them all that young. The cognoscenti, Dave Rizzo among them, request a quick reheat when ordering the Neapolitan slices to make their triangles crispier.

Taverna Kyclades

(Ⓘ) Contrary to stereotypes, Kyclades is not one of those folksy ethnic outposts where proud immigrants welcome you with open arms and old-country hospitality and show you faded snapshots of a family reunion held in a remote village. Rather, this is a cute little place where someone who hasn't smiled since 1997 throws a couple of menus your way and then comes back anywhere between one and twenty minutes later to take your order. Those who land an outdoor table either beside the watermelon stand or under the billboard advertising coopera-

Cost	$20–60

Address 33-07 Ditmars Blvd, between 33rd & 35th Sts
℡718/545-8666
Transportation N,W to Ditmars Blvd
Open Mon–Fri noon–11pm, Sat noon–midnight, Sun 4–11pm
Accepts All major credit cards
Reservations Not accepted

tive apartments hardly mind being ignored and left alone. Some even encourage it. Should they hang out all night draining one bottle of retsina after another, this disturbs only those waiting for their tables.

The Greek seafood dishes are dependably market-fresh, beginning with the appetizers—tender grilled octopus ($10.50), fried calamari ($7.95), fried smelt ($7.95), and grilled or fried sardines ($7.95). With those it's customary to pass around $4 plates of the traditional spreads—taramasalata (here the fish roe is extra fluffy and salty), skordalia (cold potato purée with almost enough garlic to choke you), and tzatziki (yogurt with cucumber). This onslaught of food could set you to wondering if orectika, the Greek word for appetizers, actually means appetite killers. Once they've been eaten up, the only thing preventing you from eighty-sixing the entrees is your inability to flag down a waiter.

Grilled whole fish, such as striped bass, red snapper, or porgy (market price from $14–20 per person) are what Kyclades does best. The prevailing and perhaps accurate condescension around these parts is that the grilled and likely overcooked salmon steak ($13.95), grilled swordfish ($17.50), and sizeable swordfish kebab ($15.95) are only requested by those terrified of fish bones. Faux pas or not, no one regrets ordering the fish steaks and, for that matter, those composed of lamb and beef. At $14.95 for succulent char-grilled lamb chops and $15.95 for a T-bone too large for its plate, each served with maybe two pounds of lemon potatoes, they're solid buys. But be careful: both come on the bone.

Tournesol

With its whitewashed tin ceiling, globe lights, pine-planked floor, red banquettes, and anaglypta-decorated walls, Tournesol bears a close resemblance to Manhattan's Impala Café (see p.94) and Brooklyn's Cafe LULUc (p.310). Is it possible the entrepreneurial Frenchmen behind these startups are using the same make-your-own-bistro kit? Owner Pascal Escriout, formerly the maitre d' at Artisanal (see p.237), at least distinguishes the first such bistro-on-a-shoestring in Queens by encouraging his chef to venture beyond the narrow steak-frites formula. Considering that Tournesol— "sunflower"—is a single subway stop from Grand Central, the incredibly low prices are attractive to Manhattanites, too.

| Cost | Lunch $12–40 |
| | Dinner $25–50 |

FRENCH

Address 50-12 Vernon Blvd, between 50th & 51st Aves
℡718/472-4355
Transportation 7 to Vernon Blvd-Jackson Ave
Open Mon–Thurs 11.30am–3pm & 5.30–11pm, Fri 11.30am–3pm & 5.30–11.30pm, Sat 11am–3pm & 5.30–11.30pm, Sun 11am–3pm & 5.30–11pm
Accepts Cash only
Reservations Not accepted

At eight bucks, the terrine of foie gras with Muscat wine is the most expensive *and* underpriced appetizer. Given the cost and quality, it's hard to make a convincing argument for any alternative. Still, the frisée salad with diced bacon lardons and poached egg ($6.50) is just fine for what it is. And the beef carpaccio with cep (like porcini) oil ($7) is fresh and elegant. Only the pan-seared sea scallops with a brunoise of vegetables ($7) disappoint. The halved scallops are not so much seared as they are quickly cooked on both sides without any color change. The problem might just be tasteless scallops.

To make his menu distinctive, chef Christophe Morvan is sometimes a tad too ambitious. But considering the prices, it would be churlish to quibble (although we're doing it anyway) about the excessive sweetness of the crisp-edged skate with red cabbage and mango sauce ($14) or a mound of saffron risotto overshadowed by the Parmesan disk that tops it and the mussels that encircle it ($16). These flaws are easily pardoned. Enjoying either dish requires little effort. As alternatives, there's the low-risk option of bacon-wrapped monkfish with eggplant and vegetables ($15) or the absolute certainty of crusty sliced hanger steak and golden frites ($13 lunch, $15 dinner). The molten-centered chocolate dome ($5) is the dessert you want.

ITALIAN

Trattoria L'Incontro

The pizza oven was not installed in the center of Trattoria L'Incontro's dining room to augment the central heating system. That may be the only way it has not been put to practical use. In addition to its pizza-baking, fish-roasting, and meat-roasting chores, the brick igloo accommodates the sauté pans, saucepans, and casseroles denied space in the kitchen's convection oven while serving as the ultimate restaurant come-on. Like a real estate agent who bakes a loaf of bread in a co-op just before prospective buyers arrive, chef-owner Rocco Sacramoni relies on the spellbinding, burning-wood fumes to ensnare unsuspecting passers-by. And once exposed to the charms of this spacious trattoria brightened by vineyard murals and hearty cooking, they invariably come back with their families or their dates.

Cost	$25–75

Address 21-76 31st St, between Ditmars Blvd & 21st Ave
☎718/721-3532
Transportation N,W to Ditmars Blvd
Open Sun & Tues–Thurs noon–10pm, Fri & Sat noon–11pm
Accepts All major credit cards
Reservations Suggested

Rocco and his mother/co-chef Tina are from Abruzzi, but you won't find much evidence of the abruzzese fondness for chile. Even the red sauce paired with the excellent fried calamari ($7.95) is tame unless you request otherwise. The pleasures of grilled sardines ($9.95) and grilled octopus ($9.95), the latter paired with a balsamic vinaigrette, as well as the grilled escarole with white beans, olive oil, and lemon ($7.95) are certainly not lost on Astoria's still sizeable Greek community. The addition of grated Asiago adds a hospitable, half-sweet/half-sharp bite to the San Marzano tomatoes, fresh basil, and mozzarella atop the golden, firm-crusted Margherita pizza ($5.95).

With several local places for simply grilled fish and meats already flourishing, the Sacramonis' impulse to do more than just lean on their centerpiece pizza oven is understandable. Fortunately, the excesses in pastas and main courses are minor. A splash of wine sauce does little harm to the oven-roasted whole orato seasoned with parsley, rosemary, and garlic ($24). And the veal chop stuffed with spinach, prosciutto, and Fontina ($25.95) is enticing, if not quite a convincing argument against the basic grilled veal chop. The notorious chocolate pizza ($8.95) is not truly a pizza and not purely chocolate. It's a crisp dessert panini of Nutella-filled pizza dough as well as a surefire temptation that real estate agents should know about.

Uncle George's

As resourceful and resilient as New Yorkers can be, the thought of living in a city without a 24/7 resource for fresh taramasalata, that fluffy and creamy fish roe spread, is too frightening to contemplate. That's why the Landmarks Preservation Commission should confer protection upon the cheap-eats champion Uncle George's. Spartan both in decor and by origin, the glass-enclosed cafe-restaurant may be architecturally indistin-

Cost	$8–35
Address 33-19 Broadway at 34th St	
☎718/626-0593	
Transportation N to Broadway	
Open Daily 24hr	
Accepts Cash only	
Reservations Not accepted	

guishable from most corner coffee shops. But surely some kind of official status is merited by so valuable an institution. While budget-minded students, couples, and families came by during the afternoon and early evening, the true beneficiaries of Uncle George's round-the-clock home cooking and hospitality are the hard-working men (restaurant workers, cabbies, etc) or hard-clubbing men and women of Astoria for whom 9-to-5 means only the short odds on a racehorse.

The Greek grub is not by anyone's estimation outstanding. But most dishes are pretty good, the portions are enormous, and the prices appear to predate the advent of color television. For starters, check out these rates: $2 for taramasalata, skordalia (garlic potato dip), or tzatziki (yogurt-cucumber dip). Or $5 for a large Greek salad with too much feta cheese (who's complaining?). And $6 for a plate of saganaki (salty, golden slices of fried kasseri cheese) that two can easily divvy up. Stuffed grape leaves big enough for three will set you back $7.

The best main courses come from the rotisserie, which is in the front of the restaurant: crisp-skinned roast half-chicken ($5), barbecued baby lamb ($11), or kokoretsi ($10). Whether you enjoy the succulent kokoretsi may depend on you not knowing about all the lamb organ meats with which it is prepared. If you've already read that sentence it's probably too late. The best fish alternatives are the grilled red snapper and fried red mullets (both $12). Or you can plod through the roast lamb with orzo ($8), the gloppy pastitsio ($7), and the ubiquitous side dish, lemon potatoes. For dessert, it's best to decamp to one of the nearby Greek pastry shops such as Omonia (32-20 Broadway) which, sadly, is closed between 3am and 8am.

Flushing

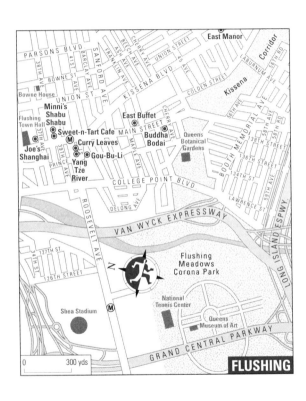

Buddha Bodai

In a strip mall beside the Queens Botanical Gardens, Flushing's resident Indian Hindus, observant Jews, vegetarian and lactose-intolerant Christians, Chinese, Korean, and Thai Buddhists and likely a fair number of atheists, agnostics, and secular humanists, too, are united in their adulation for chef Michael Wong. He's a culinary celebrity and master illusionist who puts only tofu, wheat gluten, mushrooms, and other vegetables into

| Cost | Lunch $6–30 |
| | Dinner $15–30 |

Address 42-96 Main St at Cherry Ave
☎718/939-1188
Transportation 7 to Main St
Open Daily 10.30am–11pm
Accepts MasterCard & Visa

his magic hat and pulls out sliced fish with Chinese vegetables ($9.95), General Tsao's chicken ($12.95), and lamb with mixed vegetables and garlic sauce ($12.95). So skilled is Wong's meatless trickery that rather than exhibit his delicious deceptions under artful lighting or muted spots, the carpeted dining room's floodlit glare is about 4000 watts too bright. Looking cool or hiding crow's feet would be the least of your reasons for wearing sunglasses throughout dinner.

Basically, this is a very good and inexpensive vegetarian, dairy-free Chinese family restaurant. Most start with the house special assorted appetizer ($12.95), a Shanghai-style, mostly cold sampler of vegetarian mock duck with shiitake mushrooms, crispy duck, bean curd chicken, and crunchy orange vegetables. These should be supplemented with a six-piece order of thin-skinned vegetable dumplings (steamed or pan-fried; $3.95). Kids love too the fold-your-own moo shu pancakes ($6.75).

It isn't only the absence of meats and dairy that puts Wong to the test. In his Buddhist cooking tradition, main courses must make do without the hits of garlic, onion, and scallions that might rouse sexual desire and disrupt meditation. He nevertheless produces such high-impact delights as ground vegetarian chicken wrapped in a crisp lettuce leaf ($9.95), meaty portobellos with an au poivre-like black pepper sauce ($10.95), chewy steak with Chinese broccoli ($12.95), and sautéed wide rice noodles with shreds of imitation beef ($7.95). You might imagine that the display of dry goods sold in the front of the restaurant would shed light on some of Wong's tricks. But it contains only organic radish seeds, abzuki beans, barley flakes, fenugreek, preserved black beans, and the like. You'll see few people buying.

MALAYSIAN

Curry Leaves

(ﾠ) The narrow restaurants on the north side of 40th Road in Flushing's Chinatown are folded into the streetscape like the pleated bellows of an accordion. To locate Curry Leaves you might have to resort to trying every door between numbers 129 and 141, crying out "roti canai" (the Indian-style crêpe) until someone answers back: "to stay or to go?" Beyond the recessed and pinched entranceway, the room widens

Cost	$9–35

Address 135-31 40th Rd, between Main & Prince Sts
☎718/762-9313
Transportation 7 to Main St
Open Daily 11am–11pm
Accepts Cash only
Reservations Not accepted

into a pleasant enough dining area with glass-topped, floral tablecloths and, for a tropical effect, balsa-wood siding. Of course no one is here to look at furniture. The draw is cheap, fresh, abundant, and spicy Malaysian chow.

The selections and prices are so similar to those at Manhattan Malaysian restaurants like Nyonya and Penang (see p.109 and p.136) that, when you place their takeout menus on top of one another and hold them up to the light, even the misspellings line up. Here the food is distinguished by the bold application of belachan, the dried, salty, fermented shrimp paste adored by Asian diners whose tolerance for its pungency is higher than a typical Westerner's. You first pick up its taste in rojak ($4.50), where it cuts into the sweetened soy sauce dressing a chunky salad of jicama, green mango, and cucumber. The belachan's influence is less apparent in achat ($2.95), a piquant pickled vegetable dish sprinkled with sesame seeds and chopped peanuts. The roti canai ($1.80) have large chunks of chicken in the curry dip.

Fish head curry ($13.95) rewards anyone with the courage to order it. It's a cross between a gumbo and a Thai seafood curry, with tomatoes, okra, eggplant, green beans, and fish pieces in a scintillating, golden, coconut fish broth. The fusion turns Chinese-Indian in mee goreng ($4.75), a stir-fried toss of smoky, wok-seared egg noodles with squid sauce, tofu, bean sprouts, and shrimp. Chile chicken ($14.95), which we know is Indian-style only because the menu says it is, comes as a whole, dark-and-crunchy-skinned bird atop a mild chile sauce. With dessert comes the refreshing discovery of chendal ($1.80), a shaved-ice confection with red beans, chewy jujubes, bean noodles, and coconut milk.

East Buffet

The mother of all New York City's Chinese buffets, East Buffet is the ideal family or big-group restaurant for those who don't know what they want until they see it, and maybe not even then. Seven head chefs are required to oversee the kitchens that supply and continually replenish the sprawling buffet with separate stations for sushi, dim sum, soups, noodles, Peking duck, raw oysters, American/Western hot foods, Asian barbecue (Korean short ribs) and satay (chicken, beef), along with dessert soups, pastries, and fruits. With clean, comfortably spaced dining areas that seat up to 400 people, the operation occupies the entire second floor of a glitzy shopping mall in a residential stretch near Flushing's Chinatown.

Cost	Lunch $12–30
	Dinner $25–40

Address 42-07 Main St, between Maple & Franklin Aves
☎718/353-6333
Transportation 7 to Main St
Open Sun–Thurs 11.30am–3pm & 5–10.30pm, Fri & Sat 11.30am–3pm & 5–11pm
Accepts MasterCard & Visa
Reservations Not accepted

CHINESE

   The college students are hardly alone in their determination to eat as much food for as little as possible. To that end, the best time to go is during weekend lunches when the buffet is just $8.99 ($5.99 for kids aged 3-10). But the selection expands and improves at night, especially on weekend evenings, when the dinner buffet goes up from $19.99 ($10.99 for kids) to $23.99 ($13.99 for kids). Value-motivated diners can stuff themselves on high-cost specialties like stir-fried lobster with ginger and scallions, Dungeness crabs, shark's fin soup, lacquered roast squab (very good!) and, from the carving board, Peking duck and beautiful prime rib. Should anyone be looking for us, we too can usually be found at the carving board (getting the duck and their steam buns while hot makes a big difference) or waiting for the next batches of lobster and crabs.
   Be sure to plan a stop at the dim sum bar, especially for the translucent casing and firm shrimp filling of the har gow. Other items to check out elsewhere include the winter melon seafood soup, the grilled cuttlefish, and such tong shi (sweet dessert soups) as white fungus with almonds and papaya, mung bean, coconut taro, and tapioca. Do not expend a single calorie of your total ingestion on anything Italian (lasagna, fettuccine alfredo).

Flushing

East Manor

If all-you-can-eat buffet restaurants rank in the Top Ten of outerborough dining no-nos, gaudy catering halls, especially wedding factories with the word "Manor" in their title, cannot be far behind. The latter are best kept for invitation-only affairs to which you have mercifully been snubbed. As such, the great danger of visiting East Manor, the glitzy and inordinately lavish offshoot of East Buffet (see p.379), is that the myriad pleasures of its Chinese buffet spreads can easily lead you to disregard the tenets so vital to successful New York restaurant navigation. To avoid a return to steam-table torment and reheat hell, remember that East Manor is the exception to those hard-and-fast rules.

Cost	$25–40

Address 46-45 Kissena Blvd
at Laburnum Ave
☎718/888-8998
Transportation 7 to Main St
Open Daily 4.30pm–2am
Accepts MasterCard & Visa
Reservations Not accepted

What makes East Manor so special is its incredible setup for the interactive dining experience known as Chinese hot pot or, in Japanese, shabu-shabu. At each table, a large, two-sided pot filled with a light chicken broth is set over a portable gas burner. Diners repeatedly visit the long buffet tables, choose from their extensive and continually replenished selection of raw seafood, raw meat, and raw vegetables and then cook it all themselves in the simmering broth. A variety of condiments and sauces is available for spicing and dipping. Rare is the opportunity when you can both cook and eat lobster, prawns, blue crabs, snow peas, spinach, watercress, black mushrooms, lamb, beef, chicken, pork, and even goose intestine at the same time and table. Kids love it—the concept that is, not the goose intestine.

The $23.95 weekend adult price (including tip) is remarkable in that it also includes full and free access to the sushi bar (not bad), the dumpling and dim sum bar (surprisingly good), the Peking duck carving station (excellent), the fruit and dessert bar (stick to the former), and a nightly selection of cooked entrees (of varying quality) that might include Mandarin-glazed salmon, grilled mushrooms, baked scallops, and Korean-style barbecued short ribs. The ninety-minute time limit on tables is rarely imposed. Besides, most groups are ready to throw in the white napkin after an hour of mad, blissful gorging.

Gou-Bu-Li

The legend of the little dog with the great buns flourishes at sixty Gou-Bu-Li restaurants in China and in one neon-lit eatery in Queens, New York. Gou-Zu, a master of bo zu (stuffed steamed buns), is said to have received the pivotal food review of his career more than 140 years ago from the Dowager, Mother of the Emperor. Her blurb—"eating them can extend one's life"—is inscribed next to a painting that hangs in the original Gou-Bu-Li shop in the northeastern Chinese city of Tianjin. Following that rave, the ambitious Gou-Zu had no time to socialize. People started to call him Gou-Bu-Li—"Gou-Zu not social." The name, and the buns, stuck.

Cost	$11–35

Address 135-28 40th Rd, between Main & Prince Sts
☎718/886-2121
Transportation 7 to Main St
Open Daily 11.30am–10.30pm
Accepts Cash only
Reservations Not accepted

The masters who skillfully shape the bo zu at this Flushing franchise were trained at company headquarters. Each bun is sealed with the uniform pleat that is a bo zu master's signature. The Dowager's enthusiasm for the buns is justified by the unusual texture of their bready skins. They manage to be chewy yet soft, resilient yet delicate. While some eighty varieties are prepared in China, only six are recreated in Flushing: minced mixed vegetables, pork (with scallion, ginger, soy sauce, and sesame oil), lamb, red bean, beef, and cabbage pork. A bamboo steamer filled with eight plump, teetering bo zu ($4.50–5.25) is accompanied by a small bowl of cilantro-scented beef both.

The fried noodles and noodle soups are unique to the Queens Gou-Bu-Li. Working from big blocks of paste, the noodle chefs adroitly shave strands of wheat noodles into giant woks of boiling water. The shaved noodles are used in soups with beef, pork, chicken, vegetables, or seafood (all $4.50). But you should go for the pan-fried noodles ($5.25 for pork; $5.95 for seafood) for a better appreciation of their remarkably chewy texture. Sized somewhere between linguine and fettuccine, these jagged-cut, chewy noodles expand the realm of pasta possibilities to untold heights. (It would have been interesting to know what the Dowager thought of them.) Unfortunately, Gou-Bu-Li has not been able to thrive on dumplings and noodles alone. And most attempts to extend the menu have fallen short.

Joe's Shanghai

(icon) No man is more responsible for the Shanghai uprising of the last decade than Joe Si, who opened this, the first of four Joe's Shanghais, in May 1995. Although his kitchen made a strong case for the sweet, bold-flavored cuisine of Jiangsu province as a timely alternative to the spicy sameness of Hunan and Szechuan or the subtlety of Cantonese, Joe's empire was effectively built on a single item: shao lung bao—steamed pork or crab-and-pork dumplings filled with scalding hot meat juices barely

Cost	$10–40

Address 136-21 37th Ave, between Main & Union Sts; plus other locations
☏718/539-3838
Transportation 7 to Main St
Open Sun–Thurs 11am–11pm, Fri & Sat 11am–midnight
Accepts Cash only
Reservations Not accepted

restrained by a flimsy casing. And although much of the cooking now seems as worn out as the carpeting, the shao lung bao remain unequalled.

The surest indicator of quality is the long wait for an order of eight dumplings (crab-and-pork $6.25; pork $4.25). That's because all table orders (as opposed to takeout) are prepared to order—a lofty claim supported by the composition of the soup dumplings, so called because the jellied fat stuffed inside them liquefies when steamed. Poke inside one of the crab-and-pork variety and you will find there is separation between the soft, moist crab and the harder, drier pork. Had they been refrigerated, the two would be congealed. The surge of fresh flavors is astonishing. Diner beware: attack the dumpling too quickly and your mouth will be burned by the hot juice. Start by putting the dumpling in a plastic spoon, top it with fresh soy sauce and shaved ginger, nibble a tiny hole in the wrapper, and then suck out a little of the liquid. The rest will spill into the spoon.

Other appetizers to ponder are the pan-fried, potsticker-like pork dumplings ($4.25) and such traditional cold dishes as smoked fish ($5.95), spicy pickled cabbage ($4.25), and mock vegetarian duck (in fact bean curd; $5.95). You could then go on to the likes of Shanghai pan-fried noodles (pork, beef, chicken, or vegetable; all $7.95); crispy yellowfish fingers battered in dry seaweed ($13.95); flabby pork shoulder braised in sweetened soy sauce ($13.50); the crusty and enormous pork meatballs known as Lion's Head ($12.50), and a braised whole fish ($13.95).

Minni's Shabu Shabu

Japanese by name and inspiration only, Minni's specializes in the one-pot, tabletop dining that's all the rage in Asian communities throughout the world. The Day-Glo soft drinks, cheery servers, and stylish young clientele spread over four bright, spanking clean, sleekly designed, taxi-yellow floors belong in a Far Eastern cartoon. At first glance, it's not immediately apparent where the puffs of steam rising from the tables are coming from. The stainless-steel pots are inserted through round openings in the laminate tabletops, where they come to rest atop hidden electrical heating elements. With the lip of the sunken pot at table level, diners have leverage when dropping and lifting foods from the clear chicken broth.

Cost	$11–25

Address 136-17 38th Ave, between Main & Union Sts
☎718/762-6277
Transportation 7 to Main St
Open Daily 11.30am–2am
Accepts All major credit cards
Reservations Not accepted

CHINESE

The illustrated placemat menu enumerates 25 dinner platters, ranging from a quartet of chicken and flawlessly curled pork, beef, and lamb ($9) to a fresh seafood combo ($12.95) of oysters, sliced fish, Manila clams, shrimp, squid, cuttlefish, and sea scallops. All such platters come with a plate of Chinese cabbage and greens, golden mushrooms, soft tofu, tofu skin, tempura, corn, vermicelli, fish balls, taro, and rice cake. Free access to the self-service sauce bar lets you flavor your broth and spice up your cooked ingredients with custom mixtures made from several sauces (soy, BBQ, peanut, fermented red bean, sweet-and-spicy, leek) as well as chopped cilantro, scallions, chiles, and garlic. Once back at the table, you may cook foods in any order you please, although starting with veggies will create a more flavorsome broth in which to prepare the best items—oysters, crabs ($2 apiece), and steamer-like clams. The broth is not merely a cooking liquid; it evolves into an interesting soup, depending on your cheffing skills. Remember that simmering times vary from about fifteen seconds for carpaccio-thin meat slices to the fifteen minutes it takes to hard-boil an egg.

Teriyaki-marinated squid and sliced Taiwanese sausage (both $2) are the best, if ultimately skippable, hibachi-style BBQ selections. Cold drinks include thick, non-dairy fruit smoothies (mango, star fruit, passionfruit), and Taiwanese iced tea with black, tapioca-like sago pearls.

There's another Minni's at 136-21 41st Ave, Flushing (☎718/886-9816).

CHINESE

Sweet-n-Tart Cafe

It's much too easy to overlook the savory dishes that turn this modern and lighthearted Chinese dessert cafe into a legitimate breakfast, lunch, and dinner destination. The rice dough for the juicy pan-fried dumplings ($4.35) achieves an elusive balance between delicacy and durability. The smooth congees (rice porridges; $2-7.95) are neither runny nor too thick. The noodle soup with shrimp and watercress dumpling makes a terrific little $4.25 meal. And you'd be hard-pressed to choose between the pleasures of rice steamed in a bamboo log with Chinese sausage and taro ($5.50) or rice steamed in lotus leaf with dried scallop and shrimp ($9.75). Turning towards the open kitchen which stretches across the back of the restaurant and giving a thumbs-up to the noodle cooks would at least let them know their efforts are appreciated.

Cost	$6–25

Address 136-11 38th Ave, near Main St; plus other locations
☎718/661-3380
Transportation 7 to Main St
Open Daily 9am–midnight
Accepts Cash only
Reservations Not accepted

Sweet-n-Tart's name and fame comes from its assortment of tong shui ("dessert soup"). Balancing the Yin and Yang of our bodies, these eighteen hot and fifteen cold dessert soups are believed to be extremely nourishing, and even curative. Yet it is the affordability and accessibility of the tong shui and not their medicinal qualities that draw the ABCs—American-born Chinese—to Sweet-n-Tart. For instance, although the black sesame paste soup ($2.50) is said to restore color to white hair, it would probably take several gallons of it to turn Steve Martin into a redhead. The quantity of silky, pudding-like milk with ginger juice ($3) required to greatly improve one's complexion might also make him obese. Rather, the fun in these little white bowls is in the variety of flavors, colors, and combinations, from the exotic (snow fungi, quail eggs, lotus seed) to the familiar (almond, walnut, tapioca). Even the deceptively ordinary pear with almond tong shui ($4.25) is a study in elegance, its dots of shaved almond floating over the clear soup like petals in a pond.

The post-dessert dessert menu is reason alone to drop by, maybe after dinner elsewhere. There are fabulous fruit shakes ($3.50), mango, watermelon, and kiwi among them; and mysterious ice creams ($2–4) mixed with fruit, red beans, Chinese Jell-o, and tapioca-like sago pearls.

Yang Tze River

When people have to wait for a table, it's usually best they be kept out of sight. The spectacle of restless and ravenous standees—as you surely would be if compelled to hang beside Yang Tze River's dumpling station without so much as a nibble—can make seated diners feel rushed and anxious. Yet here, the nightly line that pushes into the dining room animates it with a palpable energy that inspires diner, waiter, and chef Ping Zhu alike. Furthermore, the continuous supply of diners to refill the tables assures a steady supply of fresh foods to restock the kitchen. The Buffalo fish you're eating one night was probably still swimming the day before.

Cost	$8–40

Address 135-21 40th Rd, between Main & Prince Sts

☎718/353-8500

Transportation 7 to Main St

Open Daily 11am–midnight

Accepts Cash only

Reservations Not accepted

Groups are shuffled into cozy booths or seated around square tables that expand into larger round ones. Green murals portray the springtime splendor of the restaurant's namesake river. The Shanghai-style dinner begins with the customary cold appetizers (mostly $3.50), although there is nothing routine about Zhu's elegant assortment. Here you will find finely shredded bean curd bound to golden mushrooms and fresh cilantro; a nutty toss of bean curd and salty vegetables analogous to a Chinese tabouleh; and a mix of chicken, shrimp, and veggies in a gelatinous web of green bean sheets. From there it's on to—finally!—the dumplings, most assuredly the flavorful shao lung bao ($5.75) packed with dreamy quantities of crab meat, and the ethereal steamed vegetable dumplings ($5.25) filled with water chestnuts, carrots, black mushrooms, cabbage, bean curd, cellophane noodles, and various greens too microscopic to identify.

The good-value, $16.95 combination dinners, which include rice, soup, and a choice of three dishes, make it possible to eat family-style without dining as part of one. Still, it's better to round up a large group and share such chef's specialties as crispy duck ($8.95); Buffalo fish fillets immersed in a stupendous spicy red bean meat sauce ($6.95); and the brilliant if esoteric braised sea cucumber dotted with shrimp roe in a lush Shanghai "red" soy sauce reduced to the color and thickness of a Mexican mole ($19.95).

Woodside & Jackson Heights

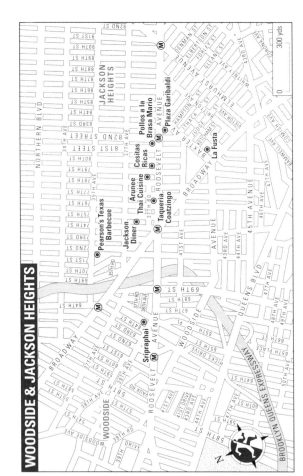

WOODSIDE & JACKSON HEIGHTS

JACKSON HEIGHTS

WOODSIDE

NORTHERN BLVD

BROADWAY

ROOSEVELT AVENUE

QUEENS BLVD

BROOKLYN QUEENS EXPRESSWAY

WOODSIDE AVE

Pearson's Texas Barbecue
Jackson Diner
Arunee Thai Cuisine
Taqueria Coatzingo
Cositas Ricas
Pollos a la Brasa Mario
Plaza Garibaldi
La Fusta
Sripraphai

0   300 yds

Arunee Thai Cuisine

The countrified Arunee is ideally suited to leisurely gatherings of families and friends. Beyond a vestibule sheathed in blond wood and strewn with plastic flowers to suggest a tropical hut is a proud but sober ethnic restaurant whose pale wainscoting, paintings of Bangkok's floating markets, faded photographs, and Thai artifacts give it a wonderfully dated quality. The tin-plated menu covers are engraved with an image of Buddha. Standing metal soup bowls shaped like springform pans are set over gas burners to keep their contents warm.

Cost	$7–45

Address 37-68 79th St, between 37th & Roosevelt Aves

☎718/205-5559

Transportation 7 to 82nd St

Open Mon–Fri 11am–10.30pm, Sat & Sun 11am–9.30pm

Accepts Cash only

Reservations Not accepted

And appetizers and entrees are presented in jade-green ceramic serving dishes by obliging waitresses.

Given that Thai diners are in the majority, you might think it a faux pas to order such generic standards as satay sticks (beef, pork, or chicken; $5.95), spicy beef salad ($8.95), or pad Thai ($6.95). They wouldn't agree. The beef is like candy, the pad Thai qualifies as a shrimp dish, and the marinade for the satay is so good you can easily do without the peanut goop. Venturing into less familiar territory, the chile-fired chicken soup ($4.75/$7.95) hits you on all sides with accents of lemongrass, coconut, and galangal. Crisp chicken wings with a stuffing (think egg roll) of pork, cellophane noodles, and onions ($5.95) served in a ceramic boat with sweet-sour chile dip are endlessly fascinating. If a French prodigy nailed down the stuffed wing thing he could create an international stir.

Anyone uneasy about ordering the whole steamed red snapper ($18.95 for a specimen that feeds three) ought to grow out of that fish-bone phobia here and now. Cooked with mixed veggies and a preserved plum sauce, each bite offers an exhilarating attack of sweet, salty, spicy, and pungent notes. Then allow yourself the untroubled amusement of guay tieow kie mao ($5.95)—essentially fettuccine and meat sauce. But be wary of all-in-one dishes like sizzling seafood ($9.95) with squid, shrimp, crab leg, mussels, and mixed vegetables, which end up being unfocused and messy. The dessert to see, and taste, is sangkhayo fakthong ($2.50), a coconut custard in a hollowed pumpkin shell.

COLOMBIAN

Cositas Ricas

Dario Franco built his first proto-type eatery by doing one thing well: rotisserie chicken (see Pollos a la Brasa Mario, p.395). For Cositas Ricos he could carry seven business cards, one for each activity: bakery, coffee shop, soda fountain, ice cream parlor, steakhouse, country kitchen, family restaurant. In other words, it's a Queens diner, an observation quickly confirmed by the vinyl booths, green neon lighting, and a glass-enclosed sidewalk cafe. The major distinction is that the language is Spanish, the accent is Colombian, and the waitresses are clad in knitted headscarves, cream-colored sports shorts, and leggings. Also, a close inspection of the croissants, donuts, and pastries displayed under the red neon sign *panaderia* ("bakery") reveals them to be about twice their usual size.

Cost	$8–35

Address 79-19 Roosevelt Ave at 80th St
☎718/478-1500
Transportation 7 to 82nd St
Open Daily 7am–2.30am
Accepts All major credit cards
Reservations Not accepted

You don't need to understand Spanish to hear what to order. The sizzling grill and whizzing blenders are in overdrive from early morning to even earlier morning, turning out succulent steaks and, to go with them, tropical fruit milkshakes. The extremely salty Romanian skirt steak comes swimming in fatty juices and is served with a country-style plate salad, rice, and fried yucca ($14.95). The equally sopping and nicely blackened palomilla (thin, top round steak) comes on a $9.50 platter with baby shrimp in salsa Diana (spicy meat sauce), rice, salad, and an arepa (corn cake). Despite the goofy appeal of these platters, you're better off with just a steak and a side of fried potato balls. The arepas rellenas (stuffed corn cakes), though, are sensational sandwiches: steaming hot, lightly gritty, and stuffed with spicy chorizo ($4.50), chopped beef ($4.50), and, best of all, chicken and tangy guacamole ($5.50).

The top-notch milkshakes ($3), among them mango, banana, and papaya, are poured from colorful plastic pitchers. The 33-percent-full pitcher is then left at the table so you can pour a refill, recalling the old New York soda fountains where steel canisters invariably contained enough for a glass and a half. Technicolor gelati are not especially good. But the pudding ($2.50), with its crunchy, crystalline topping, is a marvel of rich density. A three-inch wedge is enough for six.

La Fusta

The first thing that quadruple-bypass patients see upon their release from Elmhurst Hospital is the storefront of this great Argentine parrillada (grill). Nothing like a fat juicy steak after open-heart surgery, is there? To make matters worse, La Fusta caters to its sizeable lunch trade from the hospital it faces by cutting 20 percent off its already low prices. That brings down the cost of such cholesterol heavyweights as grilled sweetbreads to $8.50. If it's any consolation to those who succumb to temptation, La Fusta's beef is grass-fed, which means it's less fatty, and presumably lower in bad cholesterol, than its grain-fed counterparts. What's more, it's hard to imagine a less stressful venue for red-meat gorging. Opened in 1973, La Fusta—Spanish for "riding whip"—is a folksy place with jockey caps and photos of champion thoroughbreds hanging on the half-timbered walls.

Cost	$20–55

Address 80-32 Baxter Ave, between Broadway & Ketchum St
☎718/429-8222
Transportation 7 to 82nd St; R,V to Elmhurst Ave
Open Mon–Fri 11am–11pm, Sat 11am–11.45pm, Sun 2–11pm
Accepts All major credit cards
Reservations Suggested

ARGENTINIAN/STEAKHOUSE

No newfangled empanadas in these parts. The choice is limited to juicy ground beef ($2.50) and shredded chicken ($2.50), both fillings enriched with chopped egg and chopped green olives. These terrific half-moon pies look nothing alike. The hard, crisp, bubbly pastry of the beef empanada is the result of frying. The chicken empanada is baked and as a result has a much softer and lighter casing. Two other appetizers to consider are the "grilled" (actually it's baked) provolone sprinkled with dry oregano ($5), and the avocado and watercress salad for two ($9.50).

The front-running cut of beef is the juicy, two-inch-thick, extremely tasty grilled shell steak ($19.80 with potatoes). A medium-rare rendition cuts beautifully, its inside a vivid pink with some deep redness towards the center. It, like all steaks, can and should be slathered with superbly thin, garlic-concentrated chimichurri sauce, the condiment of chopped parsley, olive oil, and vinegar. Several meat alternatives may be compared in the mixed grill for two ($28.50), an inspired sampler containing rib steak, succulent skirt steak, beef tripe, sweetbreads, plump chorizo, and outstanding blood sausage. Unfortunately, both the fried and mashed potatoes are dreadful. Dolce de leche dessert crêpes ($4.80), torched for a caramelized effect, are sweeter than you could possibly imagine.

Jackson Diner

Cheap-eats champions who fondly recall the original Jackson Diner, probably the first 1950s Formica-and-chrome coffee shop to serve lamb vindaloo, approached its 1998 move with trepidation. The downside of a beloved eatery's success and subsequent expansion is too often higher prices and inferior food. Happily, the cartoonish, leaf-shaped fixtures suspended from the high ceiling of the whimsically designed, family-friendly new space have had little negative impact. Even before the appetizers arrive, the traditional trio of condiments attests to Jackson Diner's enduring reputation as one of the city's best inexpensive Indian restaurants and outer-borough dining adventures.

| Cost | Lunch $9–15 |
| | Dinner $18–35 |

Address 37-47 74th St, between 37th & Roosevelt Aves
☎718/672-1232
Transportation 7 to 74th St-Broadway; E,F,R,V to Roosevelt Ave-Jackson Heights
Open Sun–Thurs 11.30am–10.30pm, Fri & Sat 11.30am–11pm
Accepts Cash only
Reservations Not accepted

Most dinners start with golden pakora (fritters; $2.95–6.95), coconut-battered chicken malabar ($6.50), or the pea and potato turnovers that most people recognize as samosas ($2.95). Better to defy convention by sharing an entree as an appetizer. If, for example, you put the Kasmiri kebab ($10.95) next to any starter, it's guaranteed that the charred log of cheese-dipped, egg-washed chicken breast and its pile of grilled onions would vanish first. So why not build your entire dinner around entrees? The black lentils and red kidney beans in the ginger- and cilantro-spiced dal makhani ($8.50) are splendidly al dente. Compared to the soupy or gloppy renditions dished up elsewhere it's a godsend. The dosas (vegetable pancakes; $6.50–7.50) seem to stretch from 74th Street to Roosevelt Avenue. The eggplant purée baingan bhurta ($9.50) is rich in flavor and composition, while chicken, lamb, and goat dishes (all $10.95) cooked in the tandoor oven or the kadhai (Indian wok) are dependable.

Praise for the breads comes with one clarification or, rather, unclarification. Ask for them "dry." They will otherwise arrive slathered in ghee (clarified butter). This suggestion is not made only on nutritional grounds. The nan and paratha ($1.95–3.95) simply taste better without the grease. This review does not apply to the $5.95 lunch buffet, which is always a chancy proposition.

Pearson's Texas Barbecue

First-timers who hunt down Pearson's Texas Barbecue to a remote block of Dominican, Indian, and Middle Eastern shops in Jackson Heights are certain they've lost their way, very much like Robert Pearson himself. He is the Cockney hairdresser who moved from Texas to Connecticut to show the Yanks how to do barbecue. His first joint, Stick to Your Ribs, drew devotees from as far away as New York. Pearson eventually followed some of them home, opening a second, counter-service locale in Queens and then a restaurant on the Upper West Side that was doomed from

Cost	$10–30

Address 71-04 35th Ave, between 71st & 72nd Sts

☏718/779-7715

Transportation 7 to 74th St-Broadway; E,F,R,V to Roosevelt Ave-Jackson Heights

Open Wed 5.30–9pm, Thurs noon–9pm, Fri & Sat noon–10pm

Accepts Cash only

Reservations Not accepted

BARBECUE

the start. Later he sold out to his partner, Ellen Goldberg, who moved the business to the back of an Irish saloon, Legends Bar, and changed its name from Stick to Your Ribs to Pearson's Texas Barbecue.

As long as Goldberg was up for a name change, she might have instead called the barbecue joint Stick to Your Brisket, after the specialty that best rewards all those who've made it this far. That barbecued beef is carved to order from a hunk of point-cut brisket sitting on the cutting board, its luscious-looking meat dripping with fatty juices. The brisket is sold by the pound ($14) or as a sandwich ($6.45) on an almost crusty Portuguese roll that does a heck of a better job keeping the barbecue sauce and fatty juices off your fingers than the soft sandwich breads and buns you find down south. Pearson's also does right by tender, smoky, barbecued pork ribs ($14 per lb, figuring that to be four or five large ribs), pulled barbecue pork ($13 per lb; $5.95 as a sandwich), and pulled barbecued chicken ($13 per lb; $5.95 as a sandwich).

Sides—fries, onion rings, pork beans, coleslaw—are uniformly unremarkable. The tomato-based, lightly sour, thinner-than-ketchup barbecue sauce comes in four Texas-style grades: mild, medium, hot, and mean. Pearson himself used to describe the mean as being "far too hot for humans." Diners may prepare their own custom blends at the self-service sauce bar.

Woodside & Jackson Heights

Plaza Garibaldi

It was a quiet Sunday night, the jukebox was blaring, young women were swing-dancing between the tables, and the men were draining one Corona after another. What, you might wonder, would Plaza Garibaldi be like on a Saturday night? Returning six nights later, you'd find it filled with kids, teenagers, older couples, extended families—all Spanish-speaking. Early on, though the mariachi band starts setting up, the bar is half-empty. Things don't really pick up until other restaurants begin to close and their chefs and cooks finally clock off for the night. Plaza Garibaldi is the casual Jackson Heights eatery where many of the Mexicans who prepare American, Italian, and French food by day and night go to eat their native cooking. And once you've sampled the food, especially the garlicky steaks, and experienced the cheery, colorful atmosphere, it's easy to understand why.

Cost	$8–40

Address 82-12 Roosevelt Ave, between 82nd St & Baxter Ave
☎718/651-9722
Transportation 7 to 82nd St-Jackson Heights
Open Mon–Thurs 9am–2am, Fri–Sun 9am–3am
Accepts All major credit cards
Reservations Not accepted

Plaza Garibaldi prepares satisfying soft tacos at the going rate of $2 apiece. But with taco stands, trucks, and dives on every block of Roosevelt Avenue serving as good if not better versions, they seem pointless. Better to start with something oozy, either the enormous nachos plates ($4.25–9) or the wonderful pots of salty, spicy, queso fundido (cheese fondue) studded with diced chorizo ($4.50) and served with warm homemade tortilla chips. Then you want to address the steaks, shell or skirt, all blackened to a crisp yet dripping with juices—the most succulent piece of medium-well done beef you'll ever put fork and knife to. Steaks come unadorned or dressed to the max, but always with rice and beans. The bistec mixto puebla ($13.50) consists of skirt chunks sautéed on a hot griddle with pretty hot poblanos and onions, while bistec ranchero ($12) is smothered in tomato sauce and japapenos.

Along with the main ingredients (chicken $9.50, beef $10.50, shrimp $12), accessories kit, and stack of warm tortillas, the sizzling fajitas are loaded with more onions, mushrooms, and bell peppers than you can imagine. They can easily be shared; the heavenly flan ($2.50), never.

There's another Plaza Garibaldi at 102-16 Roosevelt Ave, Corona (☎718/478-3194).

Pollos a la Brasa Mario

Chickens are dancing in the windows of family-style Colombian restaurants throughout Jackson Heights and nobody's doing a thing to stop them. The sizzling hit that's making their bodies spin, pollo a la brasa ("chicken on the live coal"), is number one with a pullet. "It's typical for Columbia," noted Mike Fandino, a manager at Pollos a la Brasa Mario. "In Bogotá, you'll see five different chicken restaurants on one block, and they're all busy. Everyone has their favorite marinades." The best marinades for a dish that's popular throughout South America are rarely overpowered by individual spices or hot pepper. Though residual garlic and pronounced saltiness can be detected with every luscious bite, the remaining flavors—possibilities include rosemary, oregano, cinnamon, cumin, bay leaf, paprika, pepper, black pepper, cilantro, celery, onion, shallots, and olive oil—melt into the mushy, moist, and marvelous meat.

Cost	$7–25

Address 81-01 Roosevelt Ave
at 81st St; plus other locations
☎718/639-5555
Transportation 7 to 82nd St
Open Daily 24hr
Accepts Cash only
Reservations Not accepted

COLOMBIAN

The chickens at Mario, the neighborhood's best pollos, dissolve into succulent perfection by spinning and rotating in chorus-line precision over lava coals for about ninety minutes. The round-the-clock rotisserie positioned beside the window holds up to sixty glistening birds on six long spits. A half-chicken is $3.50; a whole, $6.95. The quarter chicken platter with rice, chicken consommé, a boring salad, and tedious fries ($7) is inconsequential beside the Mario's Special ($12). It includes a quarter-chicken, a grilled skirt steak, a grilled pork loin (not the whole loin), sliced avocado, an arepa (corn cake), white beans (yes, there's pork fat in there), and rice. But take away the chicken and the only other component of real interest is the beans, which can be ordered as a side dish. All the rest is done better at Mario's sister restaurant, Cositas Ricas (see p.390).

The red and white eatery, with its laminate tables and quick service, resembles a fast-food franchise decked out to evoke a Colombian chicken ranch. The daily menu extends beyond chicken to a number of typical dishes, among them fried or sautéed red snapper, shrimp, and rice, beef tripe stew, and beans with crackling pork skin. None of these dances like the pollos.

Woodside & Jackson Heights

Sripraphai

This great and cheap Thai place constitutes the ultimate test of restaurant radar—that is, one's ability to navigate alien territory and track down the best dining options. The small, modest eatery is hidden on a nondescript block of a lackluster side street with little pedestrian traffic. No Italian sports cars are parked in front. A peek through the doorway reveals only harsh fluorescent lighting, faux marble Formica tables, and a doorway television set—hardly surefire clues of excellence in the kitchen. There aren't even the requisite travel posters and folkloric wallhangings as indicators of ethnic pride.

Cost	$8–30

Address 64-13 39th Ave, between 64th & 65th Sts
☏718/899-9599
Transportation 7 to Woodside-61st St
Open Thurs–Tues 11am–10pm
Accepts Cash only
Reservations Not accepted

The first temptation of many critics is to praise a menu such as Sripraphai's for its authenticity. Although the food may in fact be true to its origins, that isn't actually its most notable characteristic. Rather, it is the brightness and clarity of the ingredients that stand out: the fiery yet focused kick of the red and green chile peppers tossed with ground meat and basil and served over perfumed rice ($6). The sweet crunch of Thai eggplants the size of figs in the green curry with chicken and coconut milk ($6.50). The gritty egg roll skin that encrusts the jumbo shrimp $6.50. The al dente stalks of the greenest imaginable Chinese broccoli set against the crispness of crackling fried pork nuggets and the silkiness of an oyster sauce ($7). If you try these specialties elsewhere after eating them here, you'll feel like you're dining while wearing sunglasses, nose-plugs, and a tongue guard.

The waitresses proudly wear baseball hats emblazoned with red chile peppers. Though friendly and helpful, they tend to bring all your dishes at once. It's thus wise to order in stages if that's the way you prefer to eat. And do bring your own wine or beer, especially when choosing dishes marked with a star for "hot and spicy." The iced longan drink will also put out periodic fires while stimulating your appetite. A large assortment of Thai snacks, including some rather unexotic Rice Crispy treats, are packaged in plastic containers and displayed in the back of the restaurant.

Taqueria Coatzingo

Cost	$7–30

Address 76-05 Roosevelt Ave,
between 76th & 77th Sts
☎718/424-1977
Transportation 7 to 74th St-
Broadway; F,E,R,V to Roosevelt
Ave-Jackson Heights
Open Daily 9am–6am
Accepts Cash only
Reservations Not accepted

MEXICAN

For three hours every morning, Christmas and Cinco de Mayo included, the tubes of multicolored neon that spell TACOS in the storefront window of Taqueria Coatzingo go dark. This is no cause for panic. By 9am the neon is back on, the griddle is hot, a syrupy ballad of Alejandro Fernandez is pumping from the jukebox, the TV is showing the previous night's soccer highlights, the blender is frothing the day's first maracuya (passion fruit) milkshake, and there's at least one warm corn tortilla with your name on it. Named after a town in Puebla, Mexico, this friendly if not English-fluent taqueria is the top sitdown eatery on Roosevelt Avenue for tacos, quesadillas, sopes (griddled corn-flour patties), enchiladas, chilaquiles (tortilla casseroles), tortas (Mexican sandwiches), and licuados de fruta (fresh tropical fruit shakes).

Among eleven taco varieties, the salty beef version is one of the most satisfying $2 bites anywhere. Its double layer of soft, warm corn tortillas stays at least two inches ajar, folded over too much steamy, shredded beef, creamy guacamole, roasted red chile sauce, and chopped cilantro for it to close any further. While the meat's saltiness hits you in the throat, the spicy chile buzzes your tongue, and the fresh lime and chopped cilantro cut through the grease. Elsewhere on the menu, quesadillas are trios of lightly crisped corn tortillas folded over cheese, chicken, and beef, topped with sour cream, and sprinkled with grated cheese ($6.95 with a decent salad). Enchiladas poblanas come five to an order ($7.95 with the same salad) with a choice of three sauces: green chile, red chile, or superbly rich mole.

Spicy chilaquiles ($7.95) consist of loosely layered tortillas, onions, hot sauce, and a choice of meats, including salty beef and broiled chicken. Surprisingly, the best chilaquile replaces meat with a fried egg, its broken yolk spilling into the tortillas. For sheer bulk go for the chicken milanese torta ($4.50), which, with its pounded breaded chicken thighs, beans, avocado, and jalapenos, is one solid sandwich. All that's required to make a meal of it are two hands and one mora (tropical blackberry) milkshake.

The Bronx

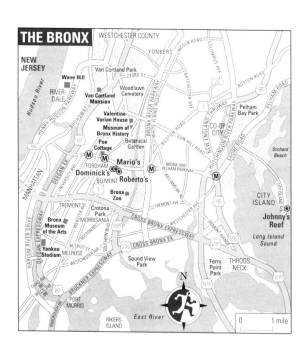

Dominick's

The Bronx's Belmont neighborhood is widely known by the name of its main drag, Arthur Avenue. And dining in the Bronx's Little Italy is often associated with the name of its most famous restaurant, Dominick's. The exalted reputation of this golden oldie from the doo-wop days is surely not justified by the quality of its food. On good days, the red-sauce cooking is no better than third-best in the neighborhood. Still, were you to suggest the possibility of a Bronx without Dominick's and its tacky wood paneling and suspended acoustic ceiling, the tears of even its arch competitors and loudest detractors would be among those shed over the Naugahyde tablecloths.

Cost	$25–45

Address 2335 Arthur Ave, between East 186th St & Convent Ave
☎718/733-2807
Transportation D to Fordham Rd; Bx 12 bus to Arthur Ave
Open Sun, Mon, Wed & Thurs noon–9pm, Fri & Sat noon–10pm
Accepts Cash only
Reservations Not accepted

ITALIAN

Though long adored by Bronxites, Yankees fans and players, and "tourists" from the other boroughs, Dominick's most devoted followers are suburban New Yorkers. For them, the joyful dinners are wistful, "coming home" reminders of what was lost when they, their parents, or grandparents moved away from this or any of the city's old ethnic enclaves to the burbs. Packed around communal tables with close friends and new acquaintances, they order the way they'd like to think their ancestors did. No menus, wine lists, prices, or desserts. Just a rushed recitation of "suggestions" from the waiter and then the essential question: red or white. The storied storefront is rendered on the label of the house red, an utterly drinkable Italian Merlot.

Most start with the cold antipasto, basically an unremarkable salad with roasted peppers, olives, thinly sliced salami, and provolone. Next up is a monstrous artichoke so overstuffed and so juicy that it ultimately collapses into its breadcrumbed spillage. To accompany good pastas like cavatelli and the stuffed shells, the chunky and peppery tomato sauce is far superior to the watery broccoli rabe. Top main courses include chicken scarpariello and the house steak (consume either Italian-American dish and you'll be sweating garlic for a week) and the standout veal Parmigiana, with its thick yet tender cutlets. There is little relation between how much you eat and how much you're charged, which will be about $25 to $35 per adult.

The Bronx

Johnny's Reef

What distinguishes City Island from any quaint, charming, run-of-the-mill New England fishing village is its Bronx accent. Boroughbreds don't go to City Island; they go to (say it in a millisecond) Ciddy-I-lin. And because the many moderate-to-expensive fish houses along City Island Avenue are generally disappointing, informed daytrippers distinguish themselves by bypassing them all for the tip-of-the-island pandemonium of this 55-year-old fried-fish cafeteria. Johnny's is clearly at the southern end of

Cost	$8-30

Address 2 City Island Ave, near Belden St
☎718/885-2090
Transportation 6 to Pelham Bay Park, then Bx 29 bus
Open Sun–Thurs 11am–11pm, Fri & Sat 11am–2am
Accepts Cash only
Reservations Not accepted

the island in location, price, and atmosphere. On weekends, the interior is as noisy, chaotic, and no-frills as a school cafeteria. In good weather, it's far nicer to sit at one of the blue picnic tables on the outdoor patio, beneath fishing lines suspended overhead in horizontal rows to ward off the seagulls. Nibble on some mushy corn on the cob, squint your eyes, and you can just about make out the edges of the Gatsby mansion F. Scott Fitzgerald imagined directly across Long Island Sound.

Generously portioned fried-fish platters (mostly $7–14) come with Idaho fries and a cup of coleslaw. The (usually fresh but sometimes frozen) fish is first dunked in an egg-and-butter batter, coated with cracker meal, and then deep-fried to order. The good-sized, firm, snappy shrimp used to be the best catch, but recent examples have lacked flavor. (This is true, sadly, not only at Johnny's but all over town.) Scallops, however, are moist and sweet, clams are plentiful, and for a good, strong-flavored fish you can't go wrong with the porgy.

The best time of year to visit Johnny's is also the busiest: June and July, peak softshell crab season. The fried crabs here are amazing, with a solid coating that keeps the meat crisp, sweet, and juicy. Careful, though, not to squirt crab juice in a companion's eye. An order of three small crabs is just $10. For dessert, the soft-serve ice cream is just fine, but the thick shakes made with it are too gloppy.

Mario's

🍴 One of the frustrations of dining at Mario's, a family-run fixture in the Bronx's Belmont section, is that insiders seated in the kitschy dining room are always eating something enticing that doesn't appear on the menu of mostly Neapolitan standards. The Migliuccis themselves can be spotted at the owners' table, heartily devouring something or other—maybe a garlicky mound of shimmering broccoli rabe tossed with chopped Italian sausage ($14.50)—that has not been listed on the menu since the restaurant opened in 1919. When the warmhearted Joseph Migliucci was asked

Cost	Lunch $20–65
	Dinner $30–65

Address 2342 Arthur Ave, between 184th & 186th St
☎718/584-1188
Transportation B,D to Fordham Rd
Open Sun & Tues–Thurs noon–10pm, Fri & Sat noon–11pm
Accepts All major credit cards
Reservations Not accepted

ITALIAN

why this was so, he simply chuckled and shrugged before noting that the broccoli rabe was even better with white beans and escarole. That dish too is unadvertised. Likewise, when a scene for a *Sopranos* episode was filmed at Mario's, Tony was served exclusively undocumented dishes, notably penne rustica ($14.95), with sausage, pancetta, butter, olive oil, and shallots; chicken royale ($17.95), with boneless breast propped over broccoli rabe and topped with prosciutto and melted mozzarella, and veal sorrentino ($17.95), layered with mozzarella, eggplant, and prosciutto.

This willingness to stray from the menu has a plus side. If you don't see something you want, osso buco ($18.50), say, or red snapper Livornese ($22), Joseph will gladly prepare it for you, providing he has the necessary ingredients. And if it's lunchtime and he lacks a key ingredient, he'll send someone out to get it. Being that this is Arthur Avenue, outstanding resources for meats, fish, cheeses, breads, pastries and all manner of imported Italian provisions are mere seconds away.

Whatever course of action you follow, be sure to fit the truly amazing, thin-crusted pizza into your plans. Many regulars order a large pie ($12.50 and up) as an hors d'oeuvre served even before the mixed cold antipasti, stuffed artichokes, clams oreganata, and octopus salad. Their anxiety is understandable. It's hard to relax, much less truly appreciate the balance of the meal, until you've cut into a pie. You could even regard pizza as a cheese course to be enjoyed immediately prior to—or in place of—the fresh-filled cannoli and homemade tiramisu.

ITALIAN

Roberto's

When one of Roberto's dispassionate waiters comes by to divvy up a pasta—say the magnificently simple farfalle with cauliflower, breadcrumbs, garlic, and oil—the first diner served does not wait until his companions get theirs before digging in. When someone wisely orders the broiled and grilled (but never dried-out) rabbit scented with rosemary and sided with spinach and roast potatoes, chef-owner Roberto Paciullo himself might stop by the table to ask if the recipient will be attacking the meat with his knife or his hands. Just two responses will put a smile on his face: "My hands," or "What's a knife?"

Cost	$30–65

Address 632 East 186th St at Belmont Ave
℡718/733-9503
Transportation B,D to Fordham Rd
Open Tues–Thurs noon–2.30pm & 5–11pm, Fri & Sat noon–2.30pm & 5pm–midnight, Sun 4pm–midnight
Accepts MasterCard & Visa
Reservations Not accepted

Despite recent renovations and the evocative photos of Paciullo's native Salerno hung on the walls, Roberto's is clearly not for genteel diners who care much about decor, service, presentation, etiquette, and desserts. (Habitués are actually relieved that Paciullo neglects desserts, as a sweetening of his tooth would only lengthen the wait for a table.) Protocol requires mostly that you follow his whims, choosing from the specials board or, better yet, asking him what you want to eat. At this writing the appetizers you'll have been "wanting" are grilled octopus ($12) and smoked mozzarella melted over grilled spinach, roasted peppers, and black olives ($12).

The most fascinating development in the chef's thinking is his insistence on small pasta shapes. He uses short-cut twists called strozzapretti ("strangled priest") with monkfish, shrimp, clams, and chicken and suggests that the dish be consumed with a spoon. His objection to long pasta and the fork is that fork-twirling leaves behind most of the juice and much of the flavor. And this loss would be considerable, as his incomparable pastas ($14–16) are steamed over the grill with the likes of cherry tomatoes and porcinis in a traditional method known as al cartoccio—"in the bag" (in this instance a pouch of aluminum foil). The objective, to trap the juice and flavor, is beautifully achieved. The one time you might defy the chef would be if he were to advise you against the veal affumicato ("smoked") layered with prosciutto, oozy smoked mozzarella, and sherry wine sauce.

Staten Island

STATEN ISLAND

NEW JERSEY

RCBK Ballpark
Ferry Terminal

Snug Harbour
Cultural Center

BAYONNE
BRIDGE

GOETHALS BRIDGE

RICHMOND TERRACE

ST. GEORGE

NEW
BRIGHTON

DR MARTIN LUTHER KING JR EX

●Deninos

FOREST AVE

The Narrows

FOREST AVENUE

Garibaldi-Merci
Museum

278

VICTORY BLVD

440

STATEN ISLAND EXPRESSWAY

278

VERRAZANO-
NARROWS
BRIDGE

BAY ST

VICTORY BLVD

Carol's Cafe ●

RICHMOND AVENUE

M

M

Trattoria
Romana

NEW
JERSEY

Jacques Marchais
Center of Tibetan Art

La Tourette
Park

RICHMOND ROAD

HYLAN BLVD

M

Nunzio's

RICHMOND AVENUE

Vorlezer's House

South Beach

ARTHUR KILL ROAD

Historic
Richmond
Town

Lower Bay

WEST SHORE EXPRESSWAY

RICHMOND PKY

Staten
Island
Lighthouse

Great
Kills
Harbor

ATLANTIC
OCEAN

ARTHUR KILL ROAD

440

AMBOY ROAD

DRUMGOOLE BLVD

HYLAN BLVD

N

Conference
House

Conference
House Park

0   2 miles

Carol's Café

Before naming any establishment after the chef, a restaurateur must consider the consequences should that chef ultimately walk out. A help-wanted ad listing the given name of Jean-Michel as a required qualification would draw a limited number of candidates. Luckily, although there are many Carols in New York, some of whom no doubt cook, there is little danger of that happening at Carol's Café. The enterprise is entirely unthinkable without sole proprietor Carol Frazzetti, an accomplished chef, cooking instructor, and Staten Island treasure who establishes a bond with her diners through the might of her personality as much as her food.

Cost	Lunch $12–25 Dinner $40–85

Address 1571 Richmond Rd at Seaview Ave
☎718/979-5600
Transportation Staten Island Railway to Dongan Hills
Open Wed–Fri 11am–3pm & 6–10pm, Sat 5–10pm
Accepts All major credit cards

Her civic pride is apparent the second you step into the historic space. The brick walls, wood floor, and ornate tin ceiling all date back to the gaslight-era depicted in old sepia photographs of Staten Island. And though there is nothing quaint about the dinner prices, which are ferociously expensive for so informal an outer-borough restaurant, there is an almost dated charm in coming across what used to be called a "Continental" menu delineated only by the passions of its author. For starters, you eat what Carol loves: crisp and golden crabcakes with a tangy sherry mayo ($11.95), say, or steamed mussels in a lyrical, spiced-to-order white wine broth ($9.95). Maple-roasted bacon rolls stuffed with chicken livers ($8.95) are a favorite.

Entrees vary wildly and wonderfully, from penne with shrimp, chopped broccoli rabe, roasted garlic cloves, and good extra virgin olive oil ($22.50) through herb-roasted whole sea bass submerged under breadcrumbs ($24.50) to a foie gras-intensified wild mushroom beef Wellington (37.95) as large and seldom seen as a man's derby. The owner's baking prowess is further evident in her reproductions from memory of cakes from Ebinger's, a dearly missed chain of New York bakeries. Your sweet tooth will be better spoiled, however, by such exclusives as an angel food cake ($7) so airy it nearly lifts off the table and a devilishly good peanut butter soufflé ($22 for two). The latter's mix of extravagance and whimsy is unmistakably Carol's.

407

Staten Island

Deninos

Opened by John and Mary Denino in 1937, the nondescript, red-brick tavern that is Deninos wasn't a pizza landmark then and it certainly doesn't look like one now, outside or in. The late Carlo Denino introduced pizza after he took over the family business from his parents in 1951 and slowly turned it into a Port Richmond institution. Well-concealed behind the bar and pool table up front is a utilitarian dining room where crispy-crust lovers leer at the kitchen door, waiting for the entrance of another classic pizza as rolled out by veteran baker John Comoletti.

Cost	$10–30

Address 524 Port Richmond Ave at Hooker Place
☎718/442-9401
Transportation 48 or 59 bus to Port Richmond Ave
Open Sun–Thurs 11.30am–11pm, Fri & Sat 11.30am–midnight
Accepts Cash only
Reservations Not accepted

When displaced Staten Islanders bemoan the hardships of a life away from their home borough, a large pizza ($8 and up) such as this invariably tops their list of laments. The crust slid out of the gas-heated brick oven is thin yet substantial, crisp yet not burned, flat yet slightly bubbly, firm yet not cardboard-like. This exceptional pizza platform lets Comoletti pile on the extra-fresh, first-rate toppings without fear of the pie turning soggy. While purists ordinarily prefer the oregano-dusted tomato and mozzarella standard, two less conventional pies also merit notice. The white pizza, with onion, garlic, and mozzarella, is spare and blissful, while the MOR (meatballs-onions-ricotta) pie is a wacky delight. A mammoth meatball the size of a softball is crumbled atop a pizza crust equipped to handle its weight. You should order that meatball on a hero sandwich if only to bear witness to its enormity. The only other food item you need to know about is the fried calamari ($6.75), a sensationally messy, crumb-and-scrap-filled pile of flour-dredged rings.

Carlo Denino never served desserts and his children Carla, Michael, and Michael (long story), thank goodness, have no intention of doing differently. Across the street from the tavern is Ralph's (501 Port Richmond Ave), a drive-in Italian ice stand opened by Ralph Silvestro in 1949 and run today by his grandsons. The true-flavored sweetness and perfectly smooth consistency of Ralph's homemade ices represent the perfect, post-pizza treat, and are a close second on that list of homesick Staten Islanders' laments.

Nunzio's

(icon) As the keeper of the crust, Bob Whiteaker had some explaining to do. It was spring 2002 and the heir to the Nunzio's pizza throne was proceeding with plans to tear down and rebuild the little pink stucco home of New York's best pizza-by-the slice without having the blueprints approved by his customers. As the head of a family business bought by his grandfather a year after its 1958 move from Staten Island's South Beach to Grant City, Whiteaker was certainly acting within his legal rights. But

Cost	$5–20

Address 2155 Hylan Blvd at Midland Ave

(phone)718/667-9647

Transportation Staten Island Railway to Grand City

Open Sun–Thurs 11am–9pm, Fri & Sat 11am–10pm

Accepts Cash only

Reservations Not accepted

what of the public trust? What about the tens of thousands of borough residents born after World War II who could barely fathom a world without Nunzio's? All he had to answer their concerns was a confusing sign posted outside the construction site: "Nothing's Changing." Excuse us, Mr. Whiteaker, but why would you be spending all that money on construction costs to change nothing?

Were people overreacting? Sure. Did everyone know what Whiteaker meant by "nothing's changing?" Of course. But the landmark specifications of the Nunzio's golden triangle need to be protected at all costs. That means a big yes to imported Italian tomatoes, whole-milk mozzarella, and grated Pecorino Romano cheese, and a loud no to oregano and canned, pre-seasoned tomato sauces that would hide the pure flavor of the elemental Nunzio's pizza ($1.50 and up for a slice; $10 and up for an eight-slice pie). Camouflage on these pies is left to optional toppings like sausage, peppers, onions, eggplant, mushrooms, and anchovies.

The slice's superiority cannot, however, be explained by ingredients alone. Baking is a craft. A select number of competitors use comparable recipes, but the results fall short. Some even have coal- or wood-burning brick ovens, whose intense heat imparts a smoky flavor to the crust. The gas heat Nunzio's employs lacks that advantage. One largely overlooked factor is the way the mozzarella is handled. Instead of shredding or slicing, Nunzio's cuts its cheese into cubes that melt more slowly as the pizza bakes. The thin crust comes out crisp and lightly browned, but the mozzarella maintains its pristine whiteness.

Staten Island

Trattoria Romana

It's one of the great imponderables of New York restaurant physics: whenever an outstanding-value but terribly congested eatery finally accedes to mob rule and expands, the enlarged space is invariably tougher on the knees, elbows, and eardrums than it was before. Co-owner/co-chef Anthony LoBianco insists he gave diners some extra breathing room when he doubled the capacity of Trattoria Romana from 60 to 120 in June 2001. But the upgrade, if there is indeed any, is comparable to moving from an anchovy can to a sardine can. To gain access to LeBianco and Vittorio Asoli's enormous homemade

| Cost | Lunch $15–40 |
| | Dinner $25–65 |

Address 1476 Hylan Blvd at Benton Ave
℡718/980-3113
Transportation Staten Island Railway to Old Town
Open Mon–Thurs noon–10.30pm, Fri & Sat noon–11pm, Sun 1am–9pm
Accepts All major credit cards
Reservations For large groups

pastas, wood-oven-baked pizzas, and wood-roasted meats and fish you must still allow yourself to become more intimately acquainted with the people sitting at the next table than you ever intended.

Between the menu-listed and unpublished dishes there are perhaps 500 things to order. That's not counting the delectable fried polenta cubes, which are served gratis and steaming hot. Most in-the-know diners start with the Sicilian-style, egg-brushed stuffed artichoke (seasonal price between $4.95 and $7.95) and then share a 12-inch pizza. These are not the hometown pizza triangles Staten Islanders fold in two and eat on the run but rather extremely thin, rigid pies that generally require a knife and a fork. The format suits both the standard Margherita ($6) and the standout boscaiola ("woodman's style") topped with sautéed broccoli rabe (yes, it's garlicky) and crumbled Italian sausage ($10.95).

That same broccoli rabe and sausage topping is periodically fitted into ravioli ($21). If it's a special during your visit, get it. Another pasta to look out for is pappardelle, which melts first into sautéed shiitakes, garlic, white wine, and olive oil, and then into your mouth ($12.95). Any meat or fish that's roasted or grilled in the wood oven is going to be good. The grilled rack of lamb ($24) would be delicious even without the Dijon mustard and oregano. Whole roasted striped bass ($23.95) is deboned tableside. Desserts include cannoli and a tiramisu that's neither too creamy or cakey. But some diners would happily settle for some more of those polenta cubes.

index

index of restaurants by name

A–Z note:
The Red Cat appears under R not T, La Paella under P, Il Buco under B, and Los Dos Molinos under D. But Cafe Luxembourg is a C, Bar Tabac is a B, and Les Halles an L. Well, you have to have rules.

11 Madison Park *see* **Eleven Madison Park**

71 Clinton Fresh Food   **117**

71 Clinton St,
near Rivington St
Lower East Side
℗212/614-6960
New American

92   **253**

45 East 92nd St
at Madison Ave
Upper East Side
℗212/828-5300
American

À Table   **329**

178 Lafayette Ave
at Adelphi St
Fort Greene
℗718/935-9121
French

L'Absinthe   **254**

227 East 67th St,
near 2nd Ave
Upper East Side
℗212/794-4950
French

aKa Café   **118**

49 Clinton St, between
Rivington & Stanton Sts
Lower East Side
℗212/979-6096
American

Al Di La   **335**

248 5th Ave at Carroll St
Park Slope
℗718/783-4565
Italian

Amarin Cafe   **353**

617 Manhattan Ave,
between Driggs &
Nassau Aves
Williamsburg & Greenpoint
℗718/349-2788
Thai

Amy Ruth's   **247**

113 West 116th St,
between Lenox
& 7th Aves
Harlem & Hamilton Heights
℗212/280-8779
Southern

Angelica Kitchen   **29**

300 East 12th St,
between 1st & 2nd Aves
East Village
℗212/228-2909
Vegetarian

Angelo & Maxie's   **63**

233 Park Ave South
at 19th St
Flatiron District, Gramercy
Park & Union Square
℗212/220-9200
Steakhouse

L'Annan   **64**

393 3rd Ave at 28th St
Flatiron District, Gramercy
Park & Union Square
℗212/686-5168
Vietnamese

Antonio   **158**

40 West 13th St,
between 6th & 7th Aves
West Village
℗212/645-4606
Italian

Aquagrill   **129**

210 Spring St at 6th Ave
SoHo
℗212/274-0505
Seafood

index

index

Cité Grill 213
120 West 51st St,
between 6th & 7th Aves
Midtown West
212/956-7262
American

City Bakery 69
3 West 18th St,
between 5th & 6th Aves
Flatiron District, Gramercy
Park & Union Square
212/366-1414
American

City Hall 141
131 Duane St,
between Church St &
West Broadway
TriBeCa
212/227-7777
American

Clay 105
202 Mott St,
near Spring St
Little Italy & Nolita
212/625-1105
Korean

Coco Roco 338
392 5th Ave,
between 6th & 7th Sts
Park Slope
718/965-3376
Peruvian

Col Legno 36
231 East 9th St,
between 2nd & 3rd Aves
East Village
212/777-4650
Italian

Comfort Diner 260
142 East 86th St,
between Lexington
& 3rd Aves
Upper East Side
212/426-8600
American

Congee Village 120
100 Allen St
at Delancey St
Lower East Side
212/941-1818
Chinese

Convivium Osteria 339
68 5th Ave,
between Bergen St
& St Mark's Ave
Park Slope
718/857-1833
Portuguese/Italian

Cooke's Corner 279
618 Amsterdam Ave
at 90th St
Upper West Side
212/712-2872
New American

Corner Bistro 159
331 West 4th St
at Jane St
West Village
212/242-9502
Hamburger

Cosi Sandwich Bar 214
1633 Broadway at 51st St
Midtown West
212/653-1600
American

Cositas Ricas 390
79-19 Roosevelt Ave
at 80th St
Woodside & Jackson
Heights
718/478-1500
Colombian

Craft Bar 70
43 East 19th St,
between Broadway
& Park Ave South
Flatiron District, Gramercy
Park & Union Square
212/780-0880
New American

Cub Room Cafe 132
183 Prince St,
near Sullivan St
SoHo
212/777-0030
American

Frank   **41**

88 2nd Ave,
between 5th & 6th Sts
East Village
☏212/420-0202
Italian

Funky Broome   **106**

176 Mott St at Broome St
Little Italy & Nolita
☏212/941-8628
Chinese

La Fusta   **391**

80-32 Baxter Ave,
between Broadway &
Ketchum St
Woodside & Jackson
Heights
☏718/429-8222
Argentinian/Steakhouse

Gage & Tollner   **301**

372 Fulton St at Red Hook
Lane & Smith St
Brooklyn Heights &
Downtown Brooklyn
☏718/875-5181
American

Gennaro   **281**

665 Amsterdam Ave,
between 92nd & 93rd Sts
Upper West Side
☏212/665-5348
Italian

Gino   **261**

780 Lexington Ave,
between 60th & 61st Sts
Upper East Side
☏212/758-4466
Italian

Good   **162**

89 Greenwich Ave,
between Bank & West
12th Sts
West Village
☏212/691-8080
New American

**Good Enough
to Eat**   **282**

483 Amsterdam Ave,
between 83rd & 84th Sts
Upper West Side
☏212/496-0163
American

Gou-Bu-Li   **381**

135-28 40th Rd, between
Main & Prince Sts
Flushing
☏718/886-2121
Chinese

**Grand Central
Oyster Bar**   **194**

Lower level, Grand
Central Terminal,
42nd St & Park Ave
Midtown East
☏212/490-6650
Seafood

Grilled Cheese NYC   **121**

168 Ludlow St, between
Houston & Stanton Sts
Lower East Side
☏212/982-6600
American

Grimaldi's   **302**

19 Old Fulton St, between
Front & Water Sts
Brooklyn Heights &
Downtown Brooklyn
☏718/858-4300
Pizza

Guastavino's   **262**

409 East 59th St,
between York & 1st Aves
Upper East Side
☏212/980-2455
American

**Hampton
Chutney Co.**   **133**

68 Prince St, between
Crosby & Lafayette Sts
SoHo
☏212/226-9996
Indian

Hangawi   **239**

12 East 32nd St, between
Madison & 5th Aves
Murray Hill & Kips Bay
☏212/213-0077
Korean/Vegetarian

index

The Tonic 13

108 West 18th St,
between 6th & 7th Aves
Chelsea
☎212/929-9755
New American

Tony's Burger 242

34 East 32nd St, between
Park & Madison Aves
Murray Hill & Kips Bay
☎212/779-7191
Hamburgers

**Totonno Pizzeria
Napolitano** 325

1524 Neptune Ave,
between 80th & 81st Sts
Coney Island, Brighton
Beach, Sheepshead Bay
& Homecrest
☎718/372-8606
Pizza

Tournesol 371

50-12 Vernon Blvd,
between 50th
& 51st Aves
Astoria & Long Island City
☎718/472-4355
French

Trata 271

1331 2nd Ave, between
70th & 71st Sts
Upper East Side
☎212/535-3800
Greek

**Trattoria
L'Incontro** 372

21-76 31st St, between
Ditmars Blvd & 21st Ave
Astoria & Long Island City
☎718/721-3532
Italian

Trattoria Romana 410

1476 Hylan Blvd at
Benton Ave
Staten Island
☎718/980-3113
Italian

Tuscan Square 231

16 West 51st St at
Rockefeller Plaza
Midtown West
☎212/977-7777
Italian

Tuscany Grill 297

8620 3rd Ave, between
86th & 87th Sts
Bay Ridge & Bensonhurst
☎718/921-5633
Italian

Uncle George's 373

33-19 Broadway
at 34th St
Astoria & Long Island City
☎718/626-0593
Greek

Union Square Cafe 83

21 East 16th St,
between Union Square
West & 5th Ave
Flatiron District, Gramercy
Park & Union Square
☎212/243-4020
New American

Veselka 60

144 2nd Ave at 9th St
East Village
☎212/228-9682
Ukrainian

Vice Versa 232

325 West 51st St,
between 8th & 9th Aves
Midtown West
☎212/399-9291
Italian

Village 100

62 West 9th St, between
5th & 6th Aves
Greenwich Village & NoHo
☎212/505-3355
French/American

**Virgil's Real
Barbecue** 233

152 West 44th St,
between Broadway & 6th
Ave
Midtown West
☎212/921-9494
Barbecue

index

index of restaurants by cuisine

American

See also:
Barbecue, Hamburgers,
New American, Southern,
Southwestern

Japanese

Jewish Deli

See also: Kosher

around the world

in twenty years

also look out for our maps,
phrasebooks, music guides
and reference books

ROUGH GUIDES TWENTY YEARS